UNITED KINGDOM

MINING LAWS AND REGULATIONS HANDBOOK

VOLUME 1

OIL AND GAS SECTOR: STRATEGIC INFORMATION AND REGULATIONS

International Business Publications, USA
Washington DC, USA - United Kingdom

UNITED KINGDOM
MINING LAWS AND REGULATIONS HANDBOOK
VOLUME 1 OIL AND GAS SECTOR: STRATEGIC INFORMATION AND REGULATIONS

UPDATED ANNUALLY

We express our sincere appreciation to all government agencies and international organizations which provided information and other materials for this handbook

Cover Design: **International Business Publications, USA**

2016 Edition Updated Reprint International Business Publications, USA
ISBN 1-4330-7842-2

For customer service and information, please contact:
in the USA: **International Business Publications, USA**
P.O.Box 15343, Washington, DC 20003
Phone: (202) 546-2103, Fax: (202) 546-3275.
E-mail: rusric@erols.com

Printed in the USA

UNITED KINGDOM

MINING LAWS AND REGULATIONS HANDBOOK

VOLUME 1

OIL AND GAS SECTOR: STRATEGIC INFORMATION AND REGULATIONS

TABLE OF CONTENTS

STRATEGIC AND BUSINESS PROFILES

STRATEGIC PROFILE

Capital and largest city	London 51°30′N 0°7′W51.500°N 0.117°W
Official language and national language	English
Recognised regional languages	Cornish, Irish, Scots, Scottish Gaelic, Ulster-Scots, Welsh
Ethnic groups (2011)	87.1% White 7.0% Asian 3.0% Black 2.0% Mixed 0.9% Other
Demonym	British, Briton
Government	Unitary parliamentary constitutional monarchy
- Monarch	Elizabeth II
- Prime Minister	David Cameron
Legislature	Parliament
- Upper house	House of Lords
- Lower house	House of Commons
	Formation
- Acts of Union 1707	1 May 1707
- Acts of Union 1800	1 January 1801
- Irish Free State Constitution Act	5 December 1922
	Area
- Total	243,610 km^2 (80th) 94,060 sq mi
- Water (%)	1.34
	Population
- 2013 estimate	64,100,000 (22nd)
- 2011 census	63,181,775 (22nd)
- Density	255.6/km^2 (51st) 661.9/sq mi
GDP (PPP)	2014 estimate
- Total	$2.435 trillion (10th)
- Per capita	$37,744 (27th)
GDP (nominal)	2014 estimate
- Total	$2.848 trillion (6th)
- Per capita	$44,141 (22nd)
Gini (2012)	▼32.8 medium · 33rd
HDI (2013)	▬0.892 very high · 14th
Currency	Pound sterling (GBP)
Time zone	GMT (UTC)
- Summer (DST)	BST (UTC+1)
Date format	dd/mm/yyyy (AD)

Drives on the	left
Calling code	+44
ISO 3166 code	GB
Internet TLD	.uk

The **United Kingdom of Great Britain and Northern Ireland** known as the **United Kingdom** (**UK**) or **Britain**, is a sovereign state in Europe. Lying off the north-western coast of the European mainland, the country includes the island of Great Britain (a term also applied loosely to refer to the whole country) , the north-eastern part of the island of Ireland, and many smaller islands. Northern Ireland is the only part of the UK that shares a land border with another state: the Republic of Ireland. Apart from this land border, the UK is surrounded by the Atlantic Ocean, with the North Sea in the east and the English Channel in the south. The Irish Sea lies between Great Britain and Ireland. The UK has an area of 243,610 square kilometres (94,060 sq mi) , making it the 78th-largest sovereign state in the world and the 11th-largest in Europe.

The United Kingdom is the 22nd-most populous country, with an estimated 64.1 million inhabitants. It is a constitutional monarchy with a parliamentary system of governance. Its capital city is London, an important global city and financial centre with the second-largest urban area in Europe, and its metropolitan area is the largest in European Union, with a population of about 14 million according Eurostat. The current monarch—since 6 February 1952—is Queen Elizabeth II. The UK consists of four countries: England, Scotland, Wales, and Northern Ireland. The latter three have devolved administrations, each with varying powers, based in their capitals, Edinburgh, Cardiff, and Belfast, respectively. Guernsey, Jersey, and the Isle of Man are not part of the United Kingdom, being Crown dependencies with the British Government responsible for defence and international representation. The UK has fourteen Overseas Territories, including the disputed Falkland Islands, Gibraltar, and Indian Ocean Territory.

The relationships among the countries of the United Kingdom have changed over time. Wales was annexed by the Kingdom of England under the Acts of Union of 1536 and 1543. A treaty between England and Scotland resulted in a unified Kingdom of Great Britain in 1707, which in 1801, merged with the Kingdom of Ireland to form the United Kingdom of Great Britain and Ireland. In 1922, five-sixths of Ireland seceded from the country, leaving the present formulation of the United Kingdom of Great Britain and Northern Ireland. British Overseas Territories, formerly colonies, are the remnants of the British Empire which, at its height in the late 19th and early 20th centuries, encompassed almost a quarter of the world's land mass and was the largest empire in history. British influence can be observed in the language, culture, and legal systems of many of its former colonies.

The United Kingdom is a developed country and has the world's sixth-largest economy by nominal GDP and tenth-largest by purchasing power parity. The country is considered to have a high-income economy and is categorised as very high in the Human Development Index, currently ranking 14th in the world. It was the world's first industrialised country and the world's foremost power during the 19th and early 20th centuries. The UK remains a great power with considerable economic, cultural, military, scientific, and political influence internationally. It is a recognised nuclear weapons state and its military expenditure ranks fifth or sixth in the world. The UK has been a permanent member of the United Nations Security Council since its first session in 1946. It has been a member state of the European Union (EU) and its predecessor, the European Economic Community (EEC) , since 1973; it is also a member of the Commonwealth of Nations, the Council of Europe, the G7, the G8, the G20, NATO, the Organisation for Economic Co-operation and Development (OECD) , and the World Trade Organization (WTO) .

Background: Great Britain, the dominant industrial and maritime power of the 19th century, played a leading role in developing parliamentary democracy and in advancing literature and science. At its zenith, the British Empire stretched over one-fourth of the earth's surface. The first half of the 20th century saw the UK's strength seriously depleted in two World Wars. The second half witnessed the dismantling of the Empire and the UK rebuilding itself into a modern and prosperous European nation. The UK currently is weighing the degree of its integration with continental Europe. A member of the EU, it chose to remain outside of the EMU for the time being. Constitutional reform is also a significant issue in the UK. Regional assemblies with varying degrees of power opened in Scotland, Wales, and Northern Ireland in 1999.

GEOGRAPHY

Location: Western Europe, islands including the northern one-sixth of the island of Ireland between the North Atlantic Ocean and the North Sea, northwest of France
Geographic coordinates: 54 00 N, 2 00 W

Map references: Europe

Area:
total: 244,820 sq km
land: 241,590 sq km
water: 3,230 sq km
note: includes Rockall and Shetland Islands
Area - comparative: slightly smaller than Oregon
Land boundaries:
total: 360 km
border countries: Ireland 360 km
Coastline: 12,429 km
Maritime claims:
continental shelf: as defined in continental shelf orders or in accordance with agreed upon boundaries
exclusive fishing zone: 200 nm
territorial sea: 12 nm
Climate: temperate; moderated by prevailing southwest winds over the North Atlantic Current; more than one-half of the days are overcast
Terrain: mostly rugged hills and low mountains; level to rolling plains in east and southeast

Elevation extremes:
lowest point: Fenland -4 m
highest point: Ben Nevis 1,343 m

Natural resources: coal, petroleum, natural gas, tin, limestone, iron ore, salt, clay, chalk, gypsum, lead, silica, arable land

Land use:
arable land: 25% *permanent crops:* 0%
permanent pastures: 46% *forests and woodland:* 10% *other:* 19%

Irrigated land: 1,080 sq km

Natural hazards: NA

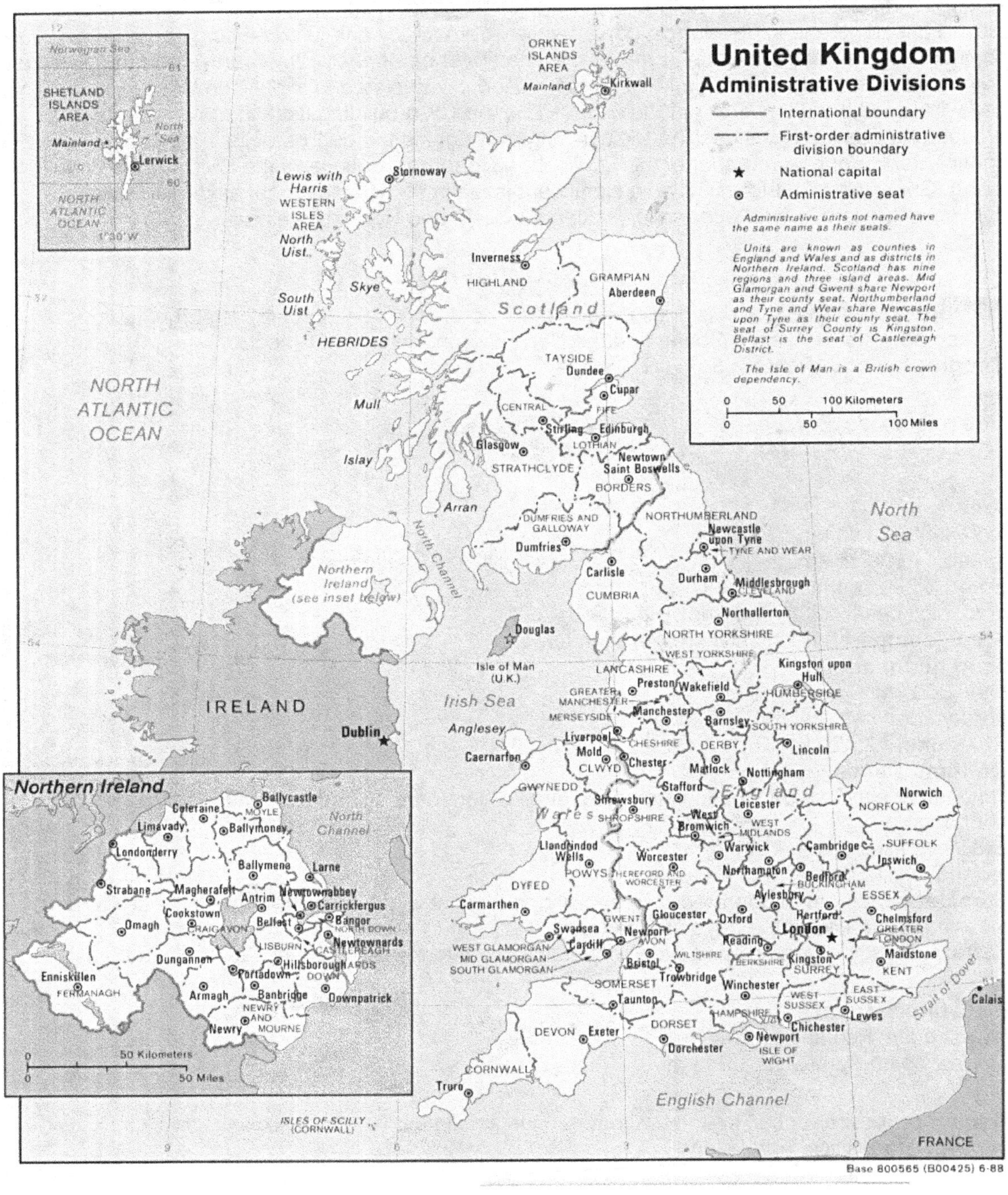

Environment - current issues: sulfur dioxide emissions from power plants contribute to air pollution; some rivers polluted by agricultural wastes; and coastal waters polluted because of large-scale disposal of sewage at sea

Environment - international agreements:
party to: Air Pollution, Air Pollution-Nitrogen Oxides, Air Pollution-Sulphur 94, Air Pollution-Volatile

Organic Compounds, Antarctic-Environmental Protocol, Antarctic Treaty, Biodiversity, Climate Change, Desertification, Endangered Species, Environmental Modification, Hazardous Wastes, Law of the Sea, Marine Dumping, Marine Life Conservation, Nuclear Test Ban, Ozone Layer Protection, Ship Pollution, Tropical Timber 83, Tropical Timber 94, Wetlands, Whaling
signed, but not ratified: Air Pollution-Persistent Organic Pollutants, Climate Change-Kyoto Protocol

Geography - note: lies near vital North Atlantic sea lanes; only 35 km from France and now linked by tunnel under the English Channel; because of heavily indented coastline, no location is more than 125 km from tidal waters

PEOPLE

Population: 59,511,464

Age structure:
0-14 years: 19% (male 5,816,313; female 5,519,479)
15-64 years: 65% (male 19,622,152; female 19,228,938)
65 years and over: 16% (male 3,864,612; female 5,459,970)
Population growth rate: 0.25%
Birth rate: 11.76 births/1,000 population
Death rate: 10.38 deaths/1,000 population
Net migration rate: 1.07 migrant(s) /1,000 population

Sex ratio:
at birth: 1.05 male(s) /female
under 15 years: 1.05 male(s) /female
15-64 years: 1.02 male(s) /female
65 years and over: 0.71 male(s) /female
total population: 0.97 male(s) /female

Infant mortality rate: 5.63 deaths/1,000 live births

Life expectancy at birth:
total population: 77.66 years
male: 74.97 years
female: 80.49 years

Total fertility rate: 1.74 children born/woman
Nationality:
noun: Briton(s) , British (collective plural)
adjective: British
Ethnic groups: English 81.5%, Scottish 9.6%, Irish 2.4%, Welsh 1.9%, Ulster 1.8%, West Indian, Indian, Pakistani, and other 2.8%
Religions: Anglican 27 million, Roman Catholic 9 million, Muslim 1 million, Presbyterian 800,000, Methodist 760,000, Sikh 400,000, Hindu 350,000, Jewish 300,000 (1991 est.)
Languages: English, Welsh (about 26% of the population of Wales) , Scottish form of Gaelic (about 60,000 in Scotland)

Literacy:
definition: age 15 and over has completed five or more years of schooling
total population: 99%

GOVERNMENT

Country name:

conventional long form: United Kingdom of Great Britain and Northern Ireland; note - Great Britain includes England, Scotland, and Wales
conventional short form: United Kingdom
abbreviation: UK

Government type:

constitutional monarchy and Commonwealth realm

Capital:

name: London
geographic coordinates: 51 30 N, 0 05 W
time difference: UTC 0 (5 hours ahead of Washington, DC, during Standard Time)
daylight saving time: +1hr, begins last Sunday in March; ends last Sunday in October
note: applies to the United Kingdom proper, not to its overseas dependencies or territories

Administrative divisions:

England: 27 two-tier counties, 32 London boroughs and 1 City of London or Greater London, 36 metropolitan districts, 56 unitary authorities (including 4 single-tier counties*)
two-tier counties: Buckinghamshire, Cambridgeshire, Cumbria, Derbyshire, Devon, Dorset, East Sussex, Essex, Gloucestershire, Hampshire, Hertfordshire, Kent, Lancashire, Leicestershire, Lincolnshire, Norfolk, North Yorkshire, Northamptonshire, Nottinghamshire, Oxfordshire, Somerset, Staffordshire, Suffolk, Surrey, Warwickshire, West Sussex, Worcestershire
London boroughs and City of London or Greater London: Barking and Dagenham, Barnet, Bexley, Brent, Bromley, Camden, Croydon, Ealing, Enfield, Greenwich, Hackney, Hammersmith and Fulham, Haringey, Harrow, Havering, Hillingdon, Hounslow, Islington, Kensington and Chelsea, Kingston upon Thames, Lambeth, Lewisham, City of London, Merton, Newham, Redbridge, Richmond upon Thames, Southwark, Sutton, Tower Hamlets, Waltham Forest, Wandsworth, Westminster
metropolitan districts: Barnsley, Birmingham, Bolton, Bradford, Bury, Calderdale, Coventry, Doncaster, Dudley, Gateshead, Kirklees, Knowlsey, Leeds, Liverpool, Manchester, Newcastle upon Tyne, North Tyneside, Oldham, Rochdale, Rotherham, Salford, Sandwell, Sefton, Sheffield, Solihull, South Tyneside, St. Helens, Stockport, Sunderland, Tameside, Trafford, Wakefield, Walsall, Wigan, Wirral, Wolverhampton
unitary authorities: Bath and North East Somerset, Blackburn with Darwen, Bedford, Blackpool, Bournemouth, Bracknell Forest, Brighton and Hove, City of Bristol, Central Bedfordshire, Cheshire East, Cheshire West and Chester, Cornwall, Darlington, Derby, Durham County*, East Riding of Yorkshire, Halton, Hartlepool, Herefordshire*, Isle of Wight*, Isles of Scilly, City of Kingston upon Hull, Leicester, Luton, Medway, Middlesbrough, Milton Keynes, North East Lincolnshire, North Lincolnshire, North Somerset, Northumberland*, Nottingham, Peterborough, Plymouth, Poole, Portsmouth, Reading, Redcar and Cleveland, Rutland, Shropshire, Slough, South Gloucestershire, Southampton, Southend-on-Sea, Stockton-on-Tees, Stoke-on-Trent, Swindon, Telford and Wrekin, Thurrock, Torbay, Warrington, West Berkshire, Wiltshire, Windsor and Maidenhead, Wokingham, York

Northern Ireland: 13 borough councils, 11 district council areas, 1 city and district council, 1 city council
borough councils: Antrim, Ards, Ballymena, Ballymoney, Carrickfergus, Castlereagh, Coleraine, Craigavon, Dungannon and South Tyrone, Larne, Limavady, Newtownabbey, North Down
city and district councils: Armagh
city councils: Lisburn
district council areas: Belfast, Banbridge, Cookstown, Derry, Down, Fermanagh, Magherafelt, Moyle, Newry and Mourne, Omagh, Strabane
Scotland: 32 council areas
council areas: Aberdeen City, Aberdeenshire, Angus, Argyll and Bute, Clackmannanshire, Dumfries and Galloway, Dundee City, East Ayrshire, East Dunbartonshire, East Lothian, East Renfrewshire, City of Edinburgh, Eilean Siar (Western Isles) , Falkirk, Fife, Glasgow City, Highland, Inverclyde, Midlothian, Moray, North Ayrshire, North Lanarkshire, Orkney Islands, Perth and Kinross, Renfrewshire, Shetland Islands, South Ayrshire, South Lanarkshire, Stirling, The Scottish Borders, West Dunbartonshire, West Lothian
Wales: 22 unitary authorities
unitary authorities: Blaenau Gwent, Bridgend, Caerphilly, Cardiff, Carmarthenshire, Ceredigion, Conwy, Denbighshire, Flintshire, Gwynedd, Isle of Anglesey, Merthyr Tydfil, Monmouthshire, Neath Port Talbot, Newport, Pembrokeshire, Powys, Rhondda Cynon Taff, Swansea, The Vale of Glamorgan, Torfaen, Wrexham

Dependent areas:

Anguilla, Bermuda, British Indian Ocean Territory, British Virgin Islands, Cayman Islands, Falkland Islands, Gibraltar, Montserrat, Pitcairn Islands, Saint Helena Ascension, and Tristan da Cunha, South Georgia and the South Sandwich Islands, Turks and Caicos Islands

Independence:

12 April 1927 (Royal and Parliamentary Titles Act establishes current name of the United Kingdom of Great Britain and Northern Ireland) ; notable earlier dates 927 (minor English kingdoms united) ; 3 March 1284 (enactment of the Statute of Rhuddlan uniting England and Wales) ; 1536 (Act of Union formally incorporates England and Wales) ; 1 May 1707 (Acts of Union formally unite England and Scotland as Great Britain) ; 1 January 1801 (Acts of Union formally unite Great Britain and Ireland as the United Kingdom of Great Britain and Ireland) ; 6 December 1921 (Anglo-Irish Treaty formalizes partition of Ireland; six counties remain part of the United Kingdom and Northern Ireland)

National holiday:

the UK does not celebrate one particular national holiday

Constitution:

unwritten; partly statutes, partly common law and practice; note - recent additions include the Human Rights Act of 1998, the Constitutional Reform and Governance Act 2010, the Parliamentary Voting System and Constituencies Act 2011, and the Fixed-term Parliaments Act 2011 (2011)

Legal system:

common law system; has nonbinding judicial review of Acts of Parliament under the Human Rights Act of 1998

International law organization participation:

accepts compulsory ICJ jurisdiction with reservations; accepts ICCt jurisdiction

Suffrage:

18 years of age; universal

Executive branch:

chief of state: Queen ELIZABETH II (since 6 February 1952) ; Heir Apparent Prince CHARLES (son of the queen, born 14 November 1948)
head of government: Prime Minister David CAMERON (since 11 May 2010)
cabinet: Cabinet of Ministers appointed by the prime minister
elections: the monarchy is hereditary; following legislative elections, the leader of the majority party or the leader of the majority coalition usually becomes the prime minister

Legislative branch:

description: bicameral Parliament consists of the House of Lords (760 seats - membership not fixed (there are 815 lords eligible for taking part in the work of the House of Lords consisting of 701 life peers, 88 hereditary peers, and 26 clergy - as of October 2015; members appointed by the monarch on the advice of the prime minister and non-party political members recommended by the House of Lords Appointments Commission) and the House of Commons (650 seats; members directly elected in single-seat constituencies by first-past-the-post vote to serve 5-year terms unless the House is dissolved earlier)
elections: House of Lords - no elections (note - in 1999, as provided by the House of Lords Act, elections were held in the House of Lords to determine the 92 hereditary peers who would remain there; elections are held only as vacancies in the hereditary peerage arise); House of Commons - last held on 8 May 2015 (next to be held by May 2020)
election results: House of Commons - percent of vote by party - Conservative 36.8%, Labor 30.5%, UKIP 12.7%, Lib Dems 7.9%, SNP 4.7%, Greens 3.8%, DUP 0.6%, Sinn Fein 0.6%, Plaid Cymru 0.6%, SDLP 0.3%, Ulster Unionist Party 0.4%, other 1.1%; seats by party - Conservative 330, Labor 232, SNP 56, Lib Dems 8, DUP 8, Sinn Fein 4, Plaid Cymru 3, SDLP 3, Ulster Unionist Party 2, UKIP 1, Greens 1, other 2

Judicial branch:

highest court(s) : Supreme Court (consists of 12 justices including the court president and deputy president)
note - the Supreme Court was established by the Constitutional Reform Act 2005 and implemented in October 2009, replacing the Appellate Committee of the House of Lords as the highest court in the United Kingdom
judge selection and term of office: judge candidates selected by an independent committee

of several judicial commissions, followed by their recommendations to the pr me minister, and appointed by Her Majesty The Queen; justices appointed during period of good behavior
subordinate courts: England and Wales - Court of Appeal (civil and criminal divisions) ; High Court; Crown Court; County Courts; Magistrates' Courts; Scotland - Court of Sessions; Sherrif Courts; High Court of Justiciary; tribunals; Northern Ireland - Court of Appeal in Northern Ireland; High Court; county courts; magistrates' courts; specialized tribunals

Political parties and leaders:

Conservative [David CAMERON]
Alliance Party (Northerm Ireland) [David FORD]
Democratic Unionist Party or DUP (Northern Ireland) [Peter ROBINSON]
Labor Party [Ed MILIBAND]
Liberal Democrats (Lib Dems) [Nick CLEGG]
Party of Wales (Plaid Cymru) [Leanne WOOD]
Scottish National Party or SNP [Alex SALMOND]
Sinn Fein (Northern Ireland) [Gerry ADAMS]
Social Democratic and Labor Party or SDLP (Northern Ireland) [Alasdair MCDONNELL]
Ulster Unionist Party (Northern Ireland) [Mike NESBITT]
United Kingdom Independent Party or UKIP [Nigel FARAGE]

Political pressure groups and leaders:

Campaign for Nuclear Disarmament
Confederation of British Industry
National Farmers' Union
Trades Union Congress

International organization participation:

ADB (nonregional member) , AfDB (nonregional member) , Arctic Council (observer) , Australia Group, BIS, C, CBSS (observer) , CD, CDB, CE, CERN, EAPC, EBRD, EIB, EITI (implementing country) , ESA, EU, FAO, FATF, G-20, G-5, G-7, G-8, G-10, IADB, IAEA, IBRD, ICAO, ICC (national committees) , ICRM, IDA, IEA, IFAD, IFC, IFRCS, IGAD (partners) , IHO, ILO, IMF, IMO, IMSO, Interpol, IOC, IOM, IPU, ISO, ITSO, ITU, ITUC (NGOs) , MIGA, MINUSMA, MONUSCO, NATO, NEA, NSG, OAS (observer) , OECD, OPCW, OSCE, Pacific Alliance (observer) , Paris Club, PCA, PIF (partner) , SELEC (observer) , UN, UNCTAD, UNESCO, UNFICYP, UNHCR, UNIDO, UNISFA, UNMISS, UNRWA, UNSC (permanent) , UPU, WCO, WHO, WIPO, WMO, WTO, ZC

Diplomatic representation in the US:

chief of mission: Ambassador Peter John WESTMACOTT (since 17 January 2012)
chancery: 3100 Massachusetts Avenue NW, Washington, DC 20008
telephone: (202) 588-6500
FAX: (202) 588-7850
consulate(s) general: Atlanta, Boston, Chicago, Denver, Houston, Los Angeles, Miami, New York, San Francisco
consulate(s) : Dallas, Orlando (FL)

Diplomatic representation from the US:

chief of mission: Ambassador Matthew W. BARZUN (since 15 August 2013)
embassy: 24 Grosvenor Square, London, W1K 6AH note - a new embassy is scheduled to open by the end of 2017 in the Nine Elms area of Wandsworth
mailing address: PSC 801, Box 40, FPO AE 09498-4040
telephone: [44] (0) 20 7499-9000
FAX: [44] (0) 20 7629-9124
consulate(s) general: Belfast, Edinburgh

Flag description:

blue field with the red cross of Saint George (patron saint of England) edged in white superimposed on the diagonal red cross of Saint Patrick (patron saint of Ireland) , which is superimposed on the diagonal white cross of Saint Andrew (patron saint of Scotland) ; properly known as the Union Flag, but commonly called the Union Jack; the design and colors (especially the Blue Ensign) have been the basis for a number of other flags including other Commonwealth countries and their constituent states or provinces, and British overseas territories

National symbol(s) :

lion (Britain in general) ; lion, Tudor rose (England) ; lion, unicorn, thistle (Scotland) ; dragon, daffodil, leek (Wales) ; harp, flax (Northern Ireland)

National anthem:

name: "God Save the Queen"

ECONOMY

Economy - overview:

The UK, a leading trading power and financial center, is the third largest economy in Europe after Germany and France. Over the past two decades, the government has greatly reduced public ownership. Agriculture is intensive, highly mechanized, and efficient by European standards, producing about 60% of food needs with less than 2% of the labor force. The UK has large coal, natural gas, and oil resources, but its oil and natural gas reserves are declining and the UK became a net importer of energy in 2005. Services, particularly banking, insurance, and business services, are key drivers of British GDP growth. Manufacturing, meanwhile, has declined in importance but still accounts for about 10% of economic output. After emerging from recession in 1992, Britain's economy enjoyed the longest period of expansion on record during which time growth outpaced most of Western Europe. In 2008, however, the global financial crisis hit the economy particularly hard, due to the importance of its financial sector.

Falling home prices, high consumer debt, and the global economic slowdown compounded Britain's economic problems, pushing the economy into recession in the latter half of 2008 and prompting the then BROWN (Labour) government to implement a number of measures to stimulate the economy and stabilize the financial markets; these included nationalizing parts of the banking system, temporarily cutting taxes, suspending public sector borrowing rules, and moving forward public spending on capital projects. Facing burgeoning public deficits and debt levels, in 2010 the CAMERON-led coalition government (between Conservatives and Liberal Democrats) initiated a five-year austerity program, which aimed to lower London's budget deficit from about 11% of GDP in 2010 to nearly 1% by 2015.

In November 2011, Chancellor of the Exchequer George OSBORNE announced additional austerity measures through 2017 largely due to the euro-zone debt crisis. The CAMERON government raised the value added tax from 17.5% to 20% in 2011. It has pledged to reduce the corporation tax rate to 21% by 2014. The Bank of England (BoE) implemented an asset purchase program of £375 billion (approximately $605 billion) as of December 2013. During times of economic crisis, the BoE coordinates interest rate moves with the European Central Bank, but Britain remains outside the European Economic and Monetary Union (EMU) . In 2012, weak consumer spending and subdued business investment weighed on the economy, however, in 2013 GDP grew 1.4%, accelerating unexpectedly in the second half of the year because of greater consumer spending and a recovering housing market. The budget deficit is falling but remains high at nearly 7% and public debt has continued to increase.

GDP (purchasing power parity) :

$2.387 trillion
country comparison to the world: 9
$2.343 trillion (2012 est.)
$2.341 trillion (2011 est.)
note: data are in 2013 US dollars

GDP (official exchange rate) :

$2.49 trillion

GDP - real growth rate:

1.8%
country comparison to the world: 152
0.1% (2012 est.)
0.9% (2011 est.)

GDP - per capita (PPP) :

$37,300
country comparison to the world: 34
$37,100 (2012 est.)
$37,300 (2011 est.)
note: data are in 2013 US dollars

Gross national saving:

10.5% of GDP
country comparison to the world: 132
11% of GDP (2012 est.)
13.7% of GDP (2011 est.)

GDP - composition, by end use:

household consumption: 66.5%
government consumption: 21.4%
investment in fixed capital: 13.8%
investment in inventories: 0.4%
exports of goods and services: 31.1%
imports of goods and services: -33.2%

GDP - composition, by sector of origin:

agriculture: 0.7%
industry: 20.5%
services: 78.9%

Agriculture - products:

cereals, oilseed, potatoes, vegetables; cattle, sheep, poultry; fish

Industries:

machine tools, electric power equipment, automation equipment, railroad equipment, shipbuilding, aircraft, motor vehicles and parts, electronics and communications equipment, metals, chemicals, coal, petroleum, paper and paper products, food processing, textiles, clothing, other consumer goods

Industrial production growth rate:

-0.3%
country comparison to the world: 169

Labor force:

30.15 million
country comparison to the world: 20

Labor force - by occupation:

agriculture: 1.4%
industry: 18.2%
services: 80.4% (2006 est.)

Unemployment rate:

7.2%
country comparison to the world: 76
7.8% (2012 est.)

Population below poverty line:

16.2% (2011 est.)

Household income or consumption by percentage share:

lowest 10%: 1.7%
highest 10%: 31.1% (2012)

Distribution of family income - Gini index:

32.3 (2012)
country comparison to the world: 104
34 (2005)

Budget:

revenues: $1.023 trillion
expenditures: $1.112 trillion

Taxes and other revenues:

41.1% of GDP
country comparison to the world: 33

Budget surplus (+) or deficit (-) :

-3.6% of GDP
country comparison to the world: 138

Public debt:

91.1% of GDP
country comparison to the world: 20
88.7% of GDP (2012 est.)
note: data cover general government debt, and include debt instruments issued (or owned) by government entities other than the treasury; the data include treasury debt held by foreign entities; the data include debt issued by subnational entities, as well as intra-governmental debt; intra-governmental debt consists of treasury borrowings from surpluses in the social funds, such as for retirement, medical care, and unemployment; debt instruments for the social funds are not sold at public auctions

Fiscal year:

6 April - 5 April

Inflation rate (consumer prices) :

2%

country comparison to the world: 71
2.7% (2012 est.)

Central bank discount rate:

0.5% (31 December 2013 est.)
country comparison to the world: 134
0.5% (2012 est.)

Commercial bank prime lending rate:

4.4% (31 December 2013 est.)
country comparison to the world: 157
4.22% (31 December 2012 est.)

Stock of narrow money:

$111.6 billion (28 February 2014 est.)
country comparison to the world: 33
$101.8 billion (31 December 2012 est.)

Stock of broad money:

$2.881 trillion (28 February 2014 est.)
country comparison to the world: 6
$3.401 trillion (31 December 2012 est.)

Stock of domestic credit:

$3.636 trillion (31 December 2013 est.)
country comparison to the world: 7
$3.756 trillion (31 December 2012 est.)

Market value of publicly traded shares:

$3.019 trillion
country comparison to the world: 4
$2.903 trillion (31 December 2011)
$3.107 trillion (31 December 2010 est.)

Current account balance:

-$93.6 billion
country comparison to the world: 192
-$93.6 billion (2012 est.)

Exports:

$813.2 billion
country comparison to the world: 5

$801.7 billion (2012 est.)

Exports - commodities:

manufactured goods, fuels, chemicals; food, beverages, tobacco

Exports - partners:

Germany 11.3%, US 10.5%, Netherlands 8.8%, France 7.4%, Ireland 6.2%, Belgium 5.1% (2012)

Imports:

$782.5 billion
country comparison to the world: 5
$777.6 billion (2012 est.)

Imports - commodities:

manufactured goods, machinery, fuels; foodstuffs

Imports - partners:

Germany 12.6%, China 8%, Netherlands 7.5%, US 6.7%, France 5.4%, Belgium 4.4%, Norway 4% (2012)

Reserves of foreign exchange and gold:

$87.48 billion (31 December 2013 est.)
country comparison to the world: 25
$105.1 billion (31 December 2012 est.)

Debt - external:

$9.577 trillion (31 December 2013 est.)
country comparison to the world: 3
$9.457 trillion (31 December 2012 est.)

Stock of direct foreign investment - at home:

$1.557 trillion (31 December 2013 est.)
country comparison to the world: 2
$1.321 trillion (31 December 2012 est.)

Stock of direct foreign investment - abroad:

$1.884 trillion (31 December 2013 est.)
country comparison to the world: 2
$1.81 trillion (31 December 2012 est.)

Exchange rates:

British pounds (GBP) per US dollar -
0.6391
0.6307 (2012 est.)
0.6472 (2010 est.)
0.6175 (2009)
0.5302 (2008)

ENERGY

Electricity - production:

365.7 billion kWh
country comparison to the world: 12

Electricity - consumption:

323.3 billion kWh
country comparison to the world: 12

Electricity - exports:

3.103 billion kWh
country comparison to the world: 34

Electricity - imports:

17.53 billion kWh
country comparison to the world: 10

Electricity - installed generating capacity:

89.24 million kW (31 December 2012)
country comparison to the world: 13

Electricity - from fossil fuels:

76% of total installed capacity (2012 est.)
country comparison to the world: 99

Electricity - from nuclear fuels:

11.2% of total installed capacity (2012 est.)
country comparison to the world: 15

Electricity - from hydroelectric plants:

4.8% of total installed capacity (2012 est.)

country comparison to the world: 126

Electricity - from other renewable sources:

8% of total installed capacity (2012 est.)
country comparison to the world: 31

Crude oil - production:

771,800 bbl/day
country comparison to the world: 26

Crude oil - exports:

637,800 bbl/day
country comparison to the world: 20

Crude oil - imports:

1.053 million bbl/day
country comparison to the world: 12

Crude oil - proved reserves:

3.122 billion bbl (1 January 2013 est.)
country comparison to the world: 30

Refined petroleum products - production:

1.343 million bbl/day
country comparison to the world: 16

Refined petroleum products - consumption:

1.217 million bbl/day
country comparison to the world: 19

Refined petroleum products - exports:

526,400 bbl/day
country comparison to the world: 13

Refined petroleum products - imports:

566,700 bbl/day
country comparison to the world: 11

Natural gas - production:

38.48 billion cu m
country comparison to the world: 25

Natural gas - consumption:

51.63 billion cu m
country comparison to the world: 15

Natural gas - exports:

8.949 billion cu m
country comparison to the world: 27

Natural gas - imports:

48.26 billion cu m
country comparison to the world: 8

Natural gas - proved reserves:

244 billion cu m (1 January 2013 est.)
country comparison to the world: 44

Carbon dioxide emissions from consumption of energy:

178.5 million Mt

COMMUNICATIONS

Telephones - main lines in use:

33.01 million
country comparison to the world: 9

Telephones - mobile cellular:

82.109 million
country comparison to the world: 18

Telephone system:

general assessment: technologically advanced domestic and international system
domestic: equal mix of buried cables, microwave radio relay, and fiber-optic systems
international: country code - 44; numerous submarine cables provide links throughout Europe, Asia, Australia, the Middle East, and US; satellite earth stations - 10 Intelsat (7 Atlantic Ocean and 3 Indian Ocean) , 1 Inmarsat (Atlantic Ocean region) , and 1 Eutelsat; at least 8 large international switching centers

Broadcast media:

public service broadcaster, British Broadcasting Corporation (BBC) , s the largest broadcasting corporation in the world; BBC operates multiple TV networks with regional and local TV service; a mixed system of public and commercial TV broadcasters along with satellite and cable systems provide access to hundreds of TV stations throughout the world; BBC operates multiple national, regional, and local radio networks with multiple transmission sites; a large number of commercial radio stations as well as satellite radio services are available

Internet country code:

.uk

Internet hosts:

8.107 million
country comparison to the world: 15

Internet users:

51.444 million (2009)
country comparison to the world: 7

TRANSPORTATION

Airports:

460
country comparison to the world: 18

Airports - with paved runways:

total: 271
over 3,047 m: 7
2,438 to 3,047 m: 29
1,524 to 2,437 m: 89
914 to 1,523 m: 80
under 914 m: 66

Airports - with unpaved runways:

total: 189
1,524 to 2,437 m: 3
914 to 1,523 m: 26
under 914 m:
160

Heliports:

9

Pipelines:

condensate 502 km; condensate/gas 9 km; gas 28,603 km; liquid petroleum gas 59 km; oil 5,256 km; oil/gas/water 175 km; refined products 4,919 km; water 255 km

Railways:

total: 16,454 km
country comparison to the world: 17
broad gauge: 303 km 1.600-m gauge (in Northern Ireland)
standard gauge: 16,151 km 1.435-m gauge (5,248 km electrified)

Roadways:

total: 394,428 km
country comparison to the world: 16
paved: 394,428 km (includes 3,519 km of expressways)

Waterways:

3,200 km (620 km used for commerce)
country comparison to the world: 32

Merchant marine:

total: 504
country comparison to the world: 22
by type: bulk carrier 33, cargo 76, carrier 4, chemical tanker 58, container 178, liquefied gas 6, passenger 7, passenger/cargo 66, petroleum tanker 18, refrigerated cargo 2, roll on/roll off 31, vehicle carrier 25
foreign-owned: 271 (Australia 1, Bermuda 6, China 7, Denmark 43, France 39, Germany 59, Hong Kong 12, Ireland 1, Italy 3, Japan 5, Netherlands 1, Norway 32, Sweden 28, Taiwan 11, Tanzania 1, UAE 8, US 14)
registered in other countries: 308 (Algeria 15, Antigua and Barbuda 1, Argentina 2, Australia 5, Bahamas 18, Barbados 6, Belgium 2, Belize 4, Bermuda 14, Bolivia 1, Brunei 2, Cabo Verde 1, Cambodia 1, Cayman Islands 2, Comoros 1, Cook Islands 2, Cyprus 7, Georgia 5, Gibraltar 6, Greece 6, Honduras 1, Hong Kong 33, Indonesia 2, Italy 2, Liberia 22, Liberia 32, Luxembourg 5, Malta 21, Marshall Islands 12, Marshall Islands 3, Moldova 3, Nigeria 2, NZ 1, Panama 37, Panama 5, Saint Kitts and Nevis 1, Saint Vincent and the Grenadines 6, Sierra Leone 1, Singapore 6, Thailand 6, Tonga 1, US 4, unknown 1)

Ports and terminals:

major seaport(s) : Dover, Felixstowe, Immingham, Liverpool, London, Southampton, Teesport (England) ; Forth Ports (Scotland) ; Milford Haven (Wales)
oil terminals: Fawley Marine terminal, Liverpool Bay terminal (England) ; Braefoot Bay terminal, Finnart oil terminal, Hound Point terminal (Scotland)
container port(s) (TEUs) : Felixstowe (3,248,592) , London (1,932,000) , Southampton (1,324,581)

MILITARY

Military branches:

Army, Royal Navy (includes Royal Marines) , Royal Air Force

Military service age and obligation:

16-33 years of age (officers 17-28) for voluntary military service (with parental consent under 18) ; no conscription; women serve in military services, but are excluded from ground combat positions and some naval postings; as of October 2009, women comprised 12.1% of officers and 9% of enlisted personnel in the regular forces; must be citizen of the UK, Commonwealth, or Republic of Ireland; reservists serve a minimum of 3 years, to age 45 or 55; 17 years 6 months of age for voluntary military service by Nepalese citizens in the Brigade of Gurkhas; 16-34 years of age for voluntary military service by Papua New Guinean citizens

Manpower available for military service:

males age 16-49: 14,856,917
females age 16-49: 14,307,316

Manpower fit for military service:

males age 16-49: 12,255,452
females age 16-49: 11,779,679

Manpower reaching militarily significant age annually:

male: 383,989
female: 365,491

Military expenditures:

2.49% of GDP
country comparison to the world: 28
2.48% of GDP (2011)
2.49% of GDP (2010)

TRANSNATIONAL ISSUES

Disputes - international:

in 2002, Gibraltar residents voted overwhelmingly by referendum to reject any "shared sovereignty" arrangement between the UK and Spain; the Government of Gibraltar insisted on equal participation in talks between the two countries; Spain disapproved of UK plans to grant Gibraltar greater autonomy; Mauritius and Seychelles claim the Chagos Archipelago (British Indian Ocean Territory) ; in 2001, the former inhabitants of the archipelago, evicted 1967 - 1973, were granted U.K. citizenship and the right of return, followed by Orders in Council in 2004 that banned rehabitation, a High Court ruling reversed the ban, a Court of Appeal refusal to hear the case, and a Law Lords' decision in 2008 denied the right of return; in addition, the United Kingdom created the world's largest marine protection area around the Chagos islands prohibiting the extraction of any natural resources therein; UK rejects sovereignty talks requested by Argentina, which still claims the Falkland Islands (Islas Malvinas) and South Georgia and the South Sandwich Islands; territorial claim in Antarctica (British Antarctic Territory) overlaps Argentine claim and partially overlaps Chilean claim; Iceland, the UK, and Ireland dispute Denmark's claim that the Faroe Islands' continental shelf extends beyond 200 nm

Refugees and internally displaced persons:

refugees (country of origin) : 11,249 (Somalia) ; 10,302 (Zimbabwe) ; 11,368 (Iran) ; 10,010 (Eritrea) ; 9,166 (Afghanistan) (2013)
stateless persons: 205 (2012)

Illicit drugs:

producer of limited amounts of synthetic drugs and synthetic precursor chemicals; major consumer of Southwest Asian heroin, Latin American cocaine, and synthetic drugs; money-laundering center

IMPORTANT INFORMATION FOR UNDERSTANDING UK

Official Name: The United Kingdom of Great Britain and Northern Ireland

BASIC PROFILE

GEOGRAPHY

Area: 244,820 sq. km. (94,525 sq. mi.) ; slightly smaller than Oregon.
Cities: *Capital*--London (metropolitan pop. about 7.1 million) . *Other cities*--Birmingham, Glasgow, Leeds, Sheffield, Liverpool, Bradford, Manchester, Edinburgh, Bristol, Belfast.
Terrain: 30% arable, 50% meadow and pasture, 12% waste or urban, 7% forested, 1% inland water. *Land use*--25% arable, 46% meadows and pastures, 10% forests and woodland, 19% other.
Climate: Generally mild and temperate; weather is subject to frequent changes but to few extremes of temperature.

PEOPLE

Nationality: *Noun*--Briton(s) . *Adjective*--British.
Population: 59.1 million.
Annual population growth rate : 0.24%.
Major ethnic groups: British, Irish, West Indian, South Asian.
Major religions: Church of England (Anglican) , Roman Catholic, Church of Scotland (Presbyterian) , Muslim.
Major languages: English, Welsh, Irish Gaelic, Scottish Gaelic.
Education: *Years compulsory*--12. *Attendance*--nearly 100%. *Literacy*--99%.
Health: *Infant mortality rate* --5.78/1,000. *Life expectancy* --males 75 yrs.; females 80 yrs.
Work force (28 million) : *Services*--75.2%; *manufacturing*--15.6%; construction-- 6.5%; *agriculture and fishing*--1.9%; *energy and water*--0.8%.

GOVERNMENT

Type: Constitutional monarchy.
Constitution: Unwritten; partly statutes, partly common law and practice.
Branches: *Executive*--monarch (head of state) , prime minister (head of government) , cabinet. *Legislative*--bicameral parliament: House of Commons, House of Lords; Scottish Parliament, Welsh Assembly, and Northern Ireland Assembly. *Judicial*--magistrates' courts, county courts, high courts, appellate courts, House of Lords.
Subdivisions: Municipalities, counties, parliamentary constituencies, province of Northern Ireland, and Scottish regions.
Political parties: In Great Britain: Conservative; Labour; Liberal Democrats; also, in Scotland: Scottish National Party; in Wales: Plaid Cymru (Party of Wales) . In Northern Ireland: Ulster Unionist Party, Social Democratic and Labour Party, Democratic Unionist Party, Sinn Fein, Alliance Party and other smaller parties.
Suffrage: British subjects and citizens of other Commonwealth countries and the Irish Republic resident in the U.K., at 18.

ECONOMY

Natural resources: Coal, oil, natural gas, tin, limestone, iron ore, salt, clay, chalk, gypsum, lead, silica.
Agriculture (1.8% of GDP) : *Products*--cereals, oilseed, potatoes, vegetables, cattle, sheep, poultry, fish.
Industry (31.5% of GDP) : *Types*--steel, heavy engineering and metal manufacturing, textiles, motor vehicles and aircraft, construction, electronics, chemicals.
Trade : *Exports*--$267.6 billion: manufactured goods, fuels, chemicals; food, beverages, tobacco. *Major markets*--U.S., Germany, France, the Netherlands, Ireland. *Imports*--$311 billion: manufactured goods, machinery, fuels, foodstuffs. *Major suppliers*--Germany, U.S., France, the Netherlands, Japan.

PEOPLE

A group of islands close to continental Europe, the British Isles have been subject to many invasions and migrations, especially from Scandinavia and the continent, including Roman occupation for several centuries. Contemporary Britons are descended mainly from the varied ethnic stocks that settled there before the 11th century. The pre-Celtic, Celtic, Roman, Anglo-Saxon, and Norse influences were blended in Britain under the Normans, Scandinavian Vikings who had lived in Northern France. Although Celtic languages persist in Wales, Scotland and Northern Ireland, the predominant language is English, which is primarily a blend of Anglo-Saxon and Norman French.

A census is taken simultaneously in all parts of the UK every ten years.[313] The Office for National Statistics is responsible for collecting data for England and Wales, the General Register Office for Scotland and the Northern Ireland Statistics and Research Agency each being responsible for censuses in their respective countries. In the 2011 census the total population of the United Kingdom was 63,181,775. It is the third-largest in the European Union, the fifth-largest in the Commonwealth and the 21st-largest in the world. In mid-2014 net long-term international migration contributed more to population growth, for the first time since mid-2011. In mid-2012 and mid-2013 natural change contributed the most to population growth.

Between 2001 and 2011 the population increased by an average annual rate of approximately 0.7%.This compares to 0.3% per year in the period 1991 to 2001 and 0.2% in the decade 1981 to

1991. The 2011 census also confirmed that the proportion of the population aged 0–14 has nearly halved (31% in 1911 compared to 18 in 2011) and the proportion of older people aged 65 and over has more than tripled (from 5 to 16%).It has been estimated that the number of people aged 100 or over will rise steeply to reach over 626,000 by 2080.

England's population in 2011 was found to be 53 million. It is one of the most densely populated countries in the world, with 417 people resident per square kilometre in mid-2014.[320] with a particular concentration in London and the south-east. The 2011 census put Scotland's population at 5.3 million, Wales at 3.06 million and Northern Ireland at 1.81 million.[319] In percentage terms England has had the fastest growing population of any country of the UK in the period from 2001 to 2011, with an increase of 7.9%.

In 2012 the average total fertility rate (TFR) across the UK was 1.92 children per woman.[323] While a rising birth rate is contributing to current population growth, it remains considerably below the 'baby boom' peak of 2.95 children per woman in 1964, below the replacement rate of 2.1, but higher than the 2001 record low of 1.63.[323] In 2012, Scotland had the lowest TFR at only 1.67, followed by Wales at 1.88, England at 1.94, and Northern Ireland at 2.03. In 2011, 47.3% of births in the UK were to unmarried women.[325] A government figure estimated that there are 3.6 million homosexual people in Britain comprising 6% of the population

HISTORY

The Roman invasion of Britain in 55 BC and most of Britain's subsequent incorporation into the Roman Empire stimulated development and brought more active contacts with the rest of Europe. As Rome's strength declined, the country again was exposed to invasion, including the pivotal incursions of the Angles, Saxons, and Jutes in the fifth and sixth centuries AD up to the Norman conquest in 1066. Norman rule effectively ensured Britain's safety from further intrusions; certain institutions, which remain characteristic of Britain, could develop. Among these are a political, administrative, cultural, and economic center in London; a separate but established church; a system of common law; distinctive and distinguished university education; and representative government.

UNION

Both Wales and Scotland were independent kingdoms that resisted English rule. The English conquest of Wales succeeded in 1282 under Edward I, and the Statute of Rhuddlan established English rule 2 years later. To appease the Welsh, Edward's son (later Edward II) , who had been born in Wales, was made Prince of Wales in 1301. The tradition of bestowing this title on the eldest son of the British Monarch continues today. An act of 1536 completed the political and administrative union of England and Wales.

While maintaining separate parliaments, England and Scotland were ruled under one crown beginning in 1603, when James VI of Scotland succeeded his cousin Elizabeth I as James I of England. In the ensuing 100 years, strong religious and political differences divided the kingdoms. Finally, in 1707, England and Scotland were unified as Great Britain, sharing a single parliament at Westminster.

Ireland's invasion by the Anglo-Normans in 1170 led to centuries of strife. Successive English kings sought to conquer Ireland. In the early 17th century, largescale settlement of the north from Scotland and England began. After its defeat, Ireland was subjected, with varying degrees of success, to control and regulation by Britain.

The legislative union of Great Britain and Ireland was completed on January 1, 1801, under the name of the United Kingdom. However, armed struggle for independence continued sporadically into the 20th century. The Anglo-Irish Treaty of 1921 established the Irish Free State, which subsequently left the Commonwealth and became a republic after World War II. Six northern, predominantly Protestant, Irish counties have remained part of the United Kingdom.

BRITISH EXPANSION AND EMPIRE

Begun initially to support William the Conqueror's (c. 1029-1087) holdings in France, Britain's policy of active involvement in continental European affairs endured for several hundred years. By the end of the 14th century, foreign trade, originally based on wool exports to Europe, had emerged as a cornerstone of national policy.

The foundations of sea power were gradually laid to protect English trade and open up new routes. Defeat of the Spanish Armada in 1588 firmly established England as a major sea power. Thereafter, its interests outside Europe grew steadily. Attracted by the spice trade, English mercantile interests spread first to the Far East. In search of an alternate route to the Spice Islands, John Cabot reached the North American continent in 1498. Sir Walter Raleigh organized the first, short-lived colony in Virginia in 1584, and permanent English settlement began in 1607 at Jamestown, Virginia. During the next two centuries, Britain extended its influence abroad and consolidated its political development at home.

Great Britain's industrial revolution greatly strengthened its ability to oppose Napoleonic France. By the end of the Napoleonic Wars in 1815, the United Kingdom was the foremost European power, and its navy ruled the seas. Peace in Europe allowed the British to focus their interests on more remote parts of the world, and, during this period, the British Empire reached its zenith. British colonial expansion reached its height largely during the reign of Queen Victoria (1837-1901) . Queen Victoria's reign witnessed the spread of British technology, commerce, language, and government throughout the British Empire, which at its greatest extent encompassed roughly one-fifth to one-quarter of the world's area and population. British colonies contributed to the United Kingdom's extraordinary economic growth and strengthened its voice in world affairs. Even as the United Kingdom extended its imperial reach overseas, it continued to develop and broaden its democratic institutions at home.

20TH CENTURY

By the time of Queen Victoria's death in 1901, other nations, including the United States and Germany, had developed their own industries; the United Kingdom's comparative economic advantage had lessened, and the ambitions of its rivals had grown. The losses and destruction of World War I, the depression of the 1930s, and decades of relatively slow growth eroded the United Kingdom's preeminent international position of the previous century.

Britain's control over its empire loosened during the interwar period. Ireland, with the exception of six northern counties, gained independence from the United Kingdom in 1921. Nationalism became stronger in other parts of the Empire, particularly in India and Egypt.

In 1926, the U.K., completing a process begun a century earlier, granted Australia, Canada, and New Zealand complete autonomy within the Empire. They became charter members of the British Commonwealth of Nations (now known as the Commonwealth) , an informal but closely knit association that succeeded the Empire. Beginning with the independence of India and Pakistan in 1947, the remainder of the British Empire was almost completely dismantled. Today, most of Britain's former colonies belong to the Commonwealth, almost all of them as independent members. There are, however, 13 former British colonies--including Bermuda, Gibraltar, the Falkland Islands, and others--which have elected to continue their political links with London and are known as United Kingdom Overseas Territories.

Although often marked by economic and political nationalism, the Commonwealth offers the United Kingdom a voice in matters concerning many developing countries. In addition, the Commonwealth helps preserve many institutions deriving from British experience and models, such as parliamentary democracy, in those countries.

GOVERNMENT

The United Kingdom does not have a written constitution. The equivalent body of law is based on statute, common law, and "traditional rights." Changes may come about formally through new acts of parliament, informally through the acceptance of new practices and usage, or by judicial precedents. Although parliament has the theoretical power to make or repeal any law, in actual practice the weight of 700 years of tradition restrains arbitrary actions.

Executive government rests nominally with the Monarch but actually is exercised by a Committee of Ministers (cabinet) traditionally selected from among the members of the House of Commons and, to a lesser extent, the House of Lords. The prime minister is normally the leader of the largest party in the Commons, and the government is dependent on its support.

Parliament represents the entire country and can legislate for the whole or for any constituent part or combination of parts. The maximum parliamentary term is 5 years, but the prime minister may ask the Monarch to dissolve parliament and call a general election at any time. The focus of legislative power is the 650-member House of Commons, which has sole jurisdiction over finance. The House of Lords, although shorn of most of its powers, can still review, amend, or delay temporarily any bills except those relating to the budget. The House of Lords has more time than the House of Commons to pursue one of its more important functions--debating public issues. In 1999, the government removed the automatic right of hereditary peers to hold seats in the House of Lords. The current house consists of appointed life peers who hold their seats for life and 92 hereditary peers who will hold their seats only until final reforms have been agreed upon and implemented. The judiciary is independent of the legislative and executive branches but cannot review the constitutionality of legislation.

The separate identities of each of the U.K.'s constituent parts also is reflected in their respective governmental structures. Up until the recent devolution of power to Scotland and Wales, a cabinet minister (the Secretary of State for Wales) handled Welsh affairs at the national level with the advice of a broadly representative council for Wales. Scotland maintains, as it did before union with England, different systems of law (Roman-French) , education, local government, judiciary, and national church (the Church of Scotland instead of the Church of England) . In addition, separate departments grouped under a Secretary of State for Scotland, who also is a cabinet member, handled most domestic matters. In late 1997, however, following approval of referenda by Scottish and Welsh voters (though only narrowly in Wales) , the British Government introduced legislation to establish a Scottish parliament and a Welsh Assembly. Elections for the two bodies were held May 6, 1999. The Welsh Assembly opened on May 26, and the Scottish parliament opened on July 1, 1999. The devolved legislatures have largely taken over most of the functions previously performed by the Scottish and Welsh offices.

Devolved government was reestablished in Northern Ireland in December 1999 under the terms of the Good Friday Agreement, which established the basis for ending the political divisions and violence that had plagued Northern Ireland for decades. The Good Friday Agreement provides for a 108-member elected Assembly, overseen by a 12-minister Executive Committee (cabinet) in which unionists and nationalists share leadership responsibility. While Northern Ireland elects 18 representatives to the Westminster parliament in London, the two Sinn Fein MPs who won seats in the last election have refused to claim their seats.

Northern Ireland had its own parliament and prime minister from 1921 to 1973, when the British Government imposed direct rule in order to deal with the deteriorating political and security situation. From 1973, the Secretary of State for Northern Ireland, based in London, was responsible for the region, including efforts to resolve the issues that lay behind the "the Troubles."

By the mid-1990s, gestures toward peace encouraged by successive British Governments and by President Clinton began to open the door for restored local government in Northern Ireland. An IRA cease-fire and nearly 2 years of multiparty negotiations, led by former U.S. Senator George Mitchell, resulted in the Good Friday Agreement of April 10, 1998, which was subsequently approved by majorities in both Northern Ireland and the Republic of Ireland. Key elements of the Agreement include devolved government, a commitment of the parties to work toward "total disarmament of all paramilitary organizations," police reform, and enhanced mechanisms to guarantee human rights and equal opportunity. The Good Friday Agreement also called for formal cooperation between the Northern Ireland institutions and the Government of the Republic of Ireland, and it established the British-Irish Council, which includes representatives of the British and Irish Governments as well as the devolved Governments of Northern Ireland, Scotland and Wales.

The parties disagree over the implementation of key elements of the Good Friday Agreement, and sporadic violence by paramilitary organizations continues to threaten the normalization process. The key parties, nevertheless, remain committed to the peace process and continue to work for full implementation of the agreement. While Unionists insist that actual decommissioning of paramilitary weapons should precede normalization of political and security arrangements, they have acknowledged the significance of intermediate steps, including the inspection of IRA arms dumps in June 2000 by independent international inspectors. Movement on decommissioning has been mirrored by progress on political and security normalization.

The United States remains firmly committed to the peace process in Northern Ireland and continues to support normalization of institutions as the best means to ensure that all parties' commitment to relying solely on peaceful and democratic means to resolve issues. U.S. Government policy on Northern Ireland condemns all acts of terrorism and violence, perpetrated by any party on either side. It also cautions all Americans to question closely any appeal for financial or other aid from groups involved in the Northern Ireland conflict to ensure that contributions do not end up in the hands of those who support violence, either directly or indirectly.

The U.S. also is committed to Northern Ireland's economic development and to date has given or pledged contributions of more than $300 million to the International Fund for Ireland. The fund provides grants and loans to businesses to improve the economy, redress inequalities of employment opportunity, and improve crossborder business and community ties.

PRINCIPAL GOVERNMENT OFFICIALS

Head of State--Her Majesty Queen Elizabeth II

Portfolio	Minister
Cabinet ministers	
Prime Minister First Lord of the Treasury Minister for the Civil Service	The Rt Hon. David Cameron MP
Deputy Prime Minister Lord President of the Council	The Rt Hon. Nick Clegg MP
First Secretary of State Leader of the House of Commons	The Rt Hon. William Hague MP
Chancellor of the Exchequer	The Rt Hon. George Osborne MP
Secretary of State for the Home Department	The Rt Hon. Theresa May MP
Secretary of State for Foreign and Commonwealth Affairs	The Rt Hon. Philip Hammond MP
Lord Chancellor Secretary of State for Justice	The Rt Hon. Chris Grayling MP
Secretary of State for Defence	The Rt Hon. Michael Fallon MP
Secretary of State for Business, Innovation and Skills President of the Board of Trade	The Rt Hon. Vince Cable MP
Secretary of State for Work and Pensions	The Rt Hon. Iain Duncan Smith MP
Secretary of State for Health	The Rt Hon. Jeremy Hunt MP
Secretary of State for Communities and Local Government Minister for Faith	The Rt Hon. Eric Pickles MP
Secretary of State for Education Minister for Women and Equalities	The Rt Hon. Nicky Morgan MP
Secretary of State for International Development	The Rt Hon. Justine Greening MP
Secretary of State for Energy and Climate Change	The Rt Hon. Ed Davey MP
Secretary of State for Transport	The Rt Hon. Patrick McLoughlin MP
Secretary of State for Scotland	The Rt Hon. Alistair Carmichael MP
Secretary of State for Northern Ireland	The Rt Hon. Theresa Villiers MP
Secretary of State for Wales	The Rt Hon. Stephen Crabb MP
Secretary of State for Culture, Media and Sport	The Rt Hon. Sajid Javid MP
Secretary of State for Environment, Food and Rural Affairs	The Rt Hon. Elizabeth Truss MP
Chief Secretary to the Treasury	The Rt Hon. Danny Alexander MP
Also attending Cabinet meetings	
Leader of the House of Lords Lord Privy Seal	The Rt Hon. The Baroness Stowell of Beeston MBE (PC)

Chief Whip in the House of Commons Parliamentary Secretary to the Treasury	The Rt Hon. Michael Gove MP
Minister for the Cabinet Office Paymaster General	The Rt Hon. Francis Maude MP
Minister of State for Government Policy Chancellor of the Duchy of Lancaster	The Rt Hon. Oliver Letwin MP
Minister of State for the Cabinet Office Minister of State for Schools	The Rt Hon. David Laws MP
Minister of State for Universities, Science and Cities	The Rt Hon. Greg Clark MP
Attorney General	The Rt Hon. Jeremy Wright MP
Minister without Portfolio Co-Chairman of the Conservative Party	The Rt Hon. Grant Shapps MP
Minister of State for Business and Enterprise Minister of State for Energy Minister for Portsmouth	The Rt Hon. Matthew Hancock MP
Minister of State for Employment	The Rt Hon. Esther McVey MP
Minister of State for Foreign and Commonwealth Affairs	The Rt Hon. The Baroness Anelay of St Johns DBE (PC)

The United Kingdom maintains an embassy in the United States at 3100 Massachusetts Ave. NW, Washington, DC 20008 (tel. 202-588-6500; fax 202-588-7870) .

POLITICAL CONDITIONS

Current Labour Prime Minister Tony Blair was elected on May 1, 1997, with a massive 176-seat majority in the House of Commons. Labour's victory ended an 18-year run of Conservative (Tory) Party rule in the U.K.. Blair worked hard to reorganize and reenergize the Labour Party, moving it steadily to the center of the political spectrum. Both main British parties support a strong transatlantic link but have become increasingly absorbed by European issues as Britain's economic and political ties to the continent grow in the post-Cold War world. Prime Minister Blair has promised that the U.K. will play a leading role in Europe. Britain's relationship with Europe, in particular its potential participation in the single European currency, the euro, is a subject of considerable political discussion in the U.K. Whether Britain will adopt the euro is likely to be a defining issue in the next U.K. national elections, which could take place as early as spring 2001.

U.S.-U.K. RELATIONS

The United Kingdom is one of the United States' closest allies, and British foreign policy emphasizes close coordination with the United States. Bilateral cooperation reflects the common language, ideals, and democratic practices of the two nations. Relations were strengthened by the U.K.'s alliance with the United States during both World Wars and its role as a founding member of NATO, in the Korean conflict, and the Persian Gulf War. The United Kingdom and the United States continually consult on foreign policy issues and global problems and share major foreign and security policy objectives. In the United Nations, the U.K. is a permanent member of the Security Council.

The U.K. is a founding member of the North Atlantic Treaty Organization (NATO) and has been a member of the European Community (now European Union) since 1973. The U.K. is one of NATO's major European maritime powers and ranked third in 1996 among NATO countries in total defense expenditure.

The British armed forces are charged with protecting the United Kingdom and its overseas territories, promoting Britain's wider security interests, and supporting international peacekeeping efforts. The 44,000-member Royal Navy is in charge of the U.K.'s independent strategic nuclear arm, which consists of four Trident missile submarines. The Royal Marines provide commando units for amphibious assault and for specialist reinforcement forces in and beyond the NATO area. The British Army, with a reported strength of 110,000 in 1999, including 7,600 women, and the Royal Air Force with a strength of 55,000, along with the Royal Navy and Royal Marines, are active and regular participants in NATO and other coalition operations.

TRADE AND INVESTMENT

The United Kingdom has the fourth-largest economy in the world, has one of the largest economies in the European Union, and is a major international trading power. London ranks with New York as a leading international financial center.

The U.K. is the fourth-largest U.S. market after Canada, Japan, and Mexico; U.S. exports to the U.K. in 1999 were $38.3 billion. For the first time in 5 years, the U.S. ran a deficit with the U.K., importing $39.2 billion in 1999. The U.K. is a large source of foreign tourists in the U.S.

The U.S. and the U.K. share the world's largest investment partnership. U.S. investment in the U.K. reached $213.1 billion in 1999, while U.K. investment is valued at $183.0 billion. This investment sustains over one million American jobs.

Since 1979, the British Government has privatized most state-owned companies, including British Steel, British Airways, British Telecom, British Coal, British Aerospace, and British Gas, although in some cases the government retains a "golden share" in these companies. The Labour government has continued the privatization policy of its predecessor, including by encouraging "public-private partnerships" (partial privatization) in such areas as the National Air Traffic Control System.

The United Kingdom is an energy-rich nation with significant reserves of oil and gas in the North Sea and the Irish Sea and large coal resources. A total of 150 million tons of oil were produced in the U.K. in 1999. U.K. offshore areas should be an important source of continued production and new discoveries for some years. U.S. oil and oil-service companies participate actively in the North Sea oil industry and consider the United Kingdom an attractive environment for future investment.

PRINCIPAL U.S. OFFICIALS

Ambassador--Matthew W. Barzun
Matthew W. Barzun [BARZ'n] - Ambassador of the United States of America to the United Kingdom of Great Britain and Northern Ireland
Matthew W. Barzun has been America's ambassador to the UK since 2013. Previously he served as U.S. Ambassador to Sweden from 2009-2011.

Deputy Chief of Mission--David T. Johnson
Minister-Counselor for Political Affairs--Maura Connelly

Minister-Counselor for Commercial Affairs--Stephan Wasylko
Minister-Counselor for Economic Affairs--Mark Tokola
Minister-Counselor for Public Affairs--Rick Roberts
Minister-Counselor for Management Affairs--Richard Jaworski
Minister-Counselor for Consular Affairs--John Caulfield
Regional Security Officer--Robert G. Reed
U.S. Consul General in Belfast--Dean Pittman
Principal Officer in Edinburgh--Cecile Shea

The U.S. Embassy in the United Kingdom is located at: 24 Grosvenor Sq., W1A 'AE, London (tel. [44] (207) 499-9000; fax [44] (207) 409-1637) . Internet website: http://www.usembassy.org.U.K.

ECONOMY

Currency	Pound sterling (GBP)
Fiscal year	1 April – 31 March
Trade organisations	European Union, OECD and World Trade Organization Statistics
GDP	$2,848 trillion (Nominal, 2014) , $2.435 trillion (PPP, 2014)
GDP rank	5th (nominal) / 8th (PPP)
GDP growth	▲+0.7% Q3 2014 (3.0% year/year, 2.8% annualised) .
GDP per capita	$45,208 (19th, PPP, 2013)
GDP by sector	Agriculture: 0.6% Construction: 6.4% Production: 14.6% Services: 78.4%
Inflation (CPI)	▼1.0% RPI: ▼2.0% (November 2014) . This is the lowest since 2002.
Base Borrowing Rate	0.5%
Population below poverty line	16.2%
Gini coefficient	▬0.34
Labour force	30.8 million (November 2014) (Employment rate 73.2% which is a record high)
Labour force by occupation	Agriculture: 1.5% Industry: 18.8% Services: 79.7%
Unemployment	6.0%, 1.96 million (September 2014) ,
Average gross salary	£2,308 / €2,756 / $3,729 monthly (9th highest)
Average net salary	£1,730 / €2,064 / $2,793 monthly (6th highest in the world)
Main industries	List
Ease-of-doing-business rank	▲8th
	External
Exports	▲$813.2 billion (4th; 2013 est.)
Export goods	List Manufactured goods Chemicals Food Beverages

	Tobacco Automotive vehicles and components Computer programming Finance Entertainment Clothes Fuel oil and petroleum products Industrial supplies and materials Military arms and equipment pharmaceuticals Other.
Main export partners	Germany 11.3%, United States 10.5%, Netherlands 8.8%, France 7.4%, Republic of Ireland 6.2%, Belgium 5.1% (2012)
Imports	▲$782.5 billion (4th; 2013 est.)
Import goods	
Main import partners	Germany 12.6%, China 8%, Netherlands 7.5%, United States 6.7%, France 5.4%, Belgium 4.4% (2012)
FDI stock	Inward: ▲$1.321 trillion(3rd) Outward: ▲$1.884 trillion(2nd)
Current account	▼-£59.2 billion
Gross external debt	▲$2,327,361,000,000 (2nd)
Net international investment position	▼-£182 billion / 9.1% GDP (2012)
	Public finances
Public debt	▲£1,457.20 billion (November 2014) (79.5% GDP)
Budget deficit	▼+£107.4 billion (2013–2014 FY)
Revenues	£648 billion (2014–2015 FY) $1.06 trillion (2014 est. CIA-WFB)
Expenses	£732 billion (2014–2015 FY) $1.21 trillion (2014 est. CIA-WFB)
Economic aid	$10 billion (2012) (donor)
Credit rating	Standard & Poor's: AAA (Domestic) AAA (Foreign) AAA (T&C Assessment) Outlook: Stable Moody's: Aa1 Outlook: Stable Fitch: AA+

	Outlook: STABLE
Foreign reserves	▲$95.54 billion (31 December 2012, CIA-WFB)

The **United Kingdom** has the 6th-largest national economy in the world (and 3rd largest in Europe) measured by nominal GDP and 8th-largest in the world (and 2nd-largest in Europe) measured by purchasing power parity (PPP) . The UK economy comprises (in descending order of size) the economies of England, Scotland, Wales and Northern Ireland In 2013 the UK was the 4th-largest exporter in the world and the 4th-largest importer, and had the 2nd-largest stock of inward foreign direct investment and the 2nd-largest stock of outward foreign direct investment. The UK is one of the world's most globalised economies.

The service sector dominates the UK economy, contributing around 78% of GDP; the financial services industry is particularly important and London is one of the world's largest financial centres. The British aerospace industry is the second- or third-largest national aerospace industry depending on the method of measurement. The pharmaceutical industry plays an important role in the economy and the UK has the third-highest share of global pharmaceutical R&D. The automotive industry is also a major employer and exporter. The British economy is boosted by North Sea oil and gas production; its reserves were valued at an estimated £250 billion in 2007. There are significant regional variations in prosperity, with the South East of England and southern Scotland the richest areas per capita. London has the largest city GDP in Europe.

In the 18th century the UK was the first country to industrialise and during the 19th century had a dominant role in the global economy. From the late 19th century the Second Industrial Revolution in the United States and Germany presented an increasing economic challenge, and the costs of fighting World War I and World War II further weakened the UK's relative position. However it still maintains a significant role in the world economy, particularly in financial services and the knowledge economy.

More recently, the UK entered a recession during the Financial crisis of 2007–08, its first for nearly two decades, and initially experienced a deeper downturn than all of the G7 except Japan. However, since 2013 the UK has been in a nascent economic recovery and is firmly in expansion territory. As of Q3 2014, the UK economy is 3.4% above its pre-crisis peak in Q1 2008 and growth in 2014 is forecast to be 3.2% which is the fastest of any major developed economy, and the fastest for the UK since 2003. Consequently, the UK is currently creating more jobs than the entirety of all countries in the European Union combined and unemployment is currently falling at record levels. The UK became the 5th largest economy in 2014, overtaking France. The UK is predicted to become the largest economy in Europe by 2030.

Government involvement in the British economy is primarily exercised by HM Treasury, headed by the Chancellor of the Exchequer, and the Department for Business, Innovation and Skills. Since 1979 management of the UK economy has followed a broadly laissez-faire approach. The Bank of England is the UK's central bank and its Monetary Policy Committee is responsible for setting interest rates. The currency of the UK is the pound sterling, which is also the world's third-largest reserve currency after the US dollar and the euro, and also the fourth most valued currency in the world, behind the Kuwaiti Dinar, Bahraini Dinar, and Omani Rial, and the most valued currency outside the Middle East. The UK is a member of the Commonwealth of Nations, the European Union, the G7, the G8, the G20, the International Monetary Fund, the Organisation for Economic Co-operation and Development, the World Bank, the World Trade Organisation and the United Nations.

NORTH SEA OIL EXPLORATION

In the oil industry, the term "North Sea" often includes areas such as the Norwegian Sea and the area known as "West of Shetland", "the Atlantic Frontier" or "the Atlantic Margin" that is not geographically part of the North Sea. Brent crude is still used today as a standard benchmark for pricing oil, although the contract now refers to a blend of oils from fields in the northern North Sea.

The UK Continental Shelf Act came into force in May 1964. Seismic exploration and the first well followed later that year. It and a second well on the Mid North Sea High were dry, as the Rotliegendes was absent, but BP's *Sea Gem* rig struck gas in the **West Sole Field** in September 1965. The celebrations were short-lived because the Sea Gem sank with the loss of 13 lives after part of the rig collapsed as it was moved away from the discovery well. The **Viking Gas Field** was discovered in December 1965 with the Conoco/National Coal Board well 49/17-1, finding the gas-bearing Permian Rotliegend Sandstone at a depth of 2,756 m subsea. Larger gas finds followed in 1966—**Leman Bank**, **Indefatigable** and **Hewett**, but by 1968 companies had lost interest in further exploration of the British sector, a result of a ban on gas exports and low prices offered by the only buyer, British Gas. West Sole came onstream in May 1967. Licensing regulations for Dutch waters were not finalised until 1967.

The situation was transformed in December 1969, when Phillips Petroleum discovered oil in Chalk of Danian age at Ekofisk, in Norwegian waters in the central North Sea. The same month, Amoco discovered the **Montrose Field** about 217 km (135 mi) east of Aberdeen. BP had been awarded several licences in the area in the second licensing round late in 1965, but had been reluctant to work on them. The discovery of Ekofisk prompted them to drill what turned out to be a dry hole in May 1970, followed by the discovery of the giant Forties Oil Field in October 1970. The following year, Shell Expro discovered the giant Brent oilfield in the northern North Sea east of Shetland in Scotland and the Petronord Group discovered the Frigg gas field. The Piper oilfield was discovered in 1973 and the Statfjord Field and the **Ninian Field** in 1974, with the Ninian reservoir consisting of Middle Jurassic sandstones at a depth of 3000 m subsea in a "westward tilted horst block".

Oil production started from the **Argyll & Duncan Oilfields** (now **Ardmore**) in June 1975 followed by Forties Oil Field in November of that year. The inner Moray Firth **Beatrice Field**, a Jurassic sandstone/shale reservoir 1829 m deep in a "fault-bounded anticlinal trap", was discovered in 1976 with well 11/30-1, drilled by the Mesa Petroleum Group (named after T. Boone Pickens' wife Bea, "the only oil field in the North Sea named for a woman") in 49 m of water.

After the 1973 oil crisis, the oil price had quadrupled. The 1979 oil crisis ("second") caused another tripling.

Volatile weather conditions in Europe's North Sea have made drilling particularly hazardous, claiming many lives (see Oil platform) . The conditions also make extraction a costly process; by the 1980s, costs for developing new methods and technologies to make the process both efficient and safe, far exceeded NASA's budget to land a man on the moon. The exploration of the North Sea has been a story of continually pushing the edges of the technology of exploitation (in terms of what can be produced) and later the technologies of discovery and evaluation (2-D seismic, followed by 3-D and 4-D seismic; sub-salt seismic; immersive display and analysis suites and supercomputing to handle the flood of computation required) .

The Gullfaks oil field was discovered in 1978. The **Snorre Field** was discovered in 1979, producing from the Triassic Lunde Formation and the Triassic-Jurassic Statfjord Formation, both fluvial sandstones in a mudstone matrix. The Oseberg oil field and Troll gas field were also discovered in 1979. The Miller oilfield was discovered in 1983. The **Alba Field** produces from sandstones in the middle Eocene Alba Formation at 1860 m subsea and was discovered in 1984 in UKCS Block 16/26. The **Smorbukk Field** was discovered in 1984 in 250–300 m of water that produces from Lower to Middle Jurassic sandstone formations within a fault block. The Snohvit Gas Field and the Draugen oil field were discovered in 1984. The Heidrun oil field was discovered in 1985.

The largest field discovered in the past 25 years is **Buzzard** also located off Scotland, found in June 2001 with producible reserves of almost 64×10^6 m^3 (400m bbl) and an average output of 28 600 m^3 to 30 200 m^3 (180,000-190,000 bbl) per day.

The largest field found in the past five years on the Norwegian part of the North Sea, is the Johan Sverdrup oil field which was discovered in 2010, with further oil of the same field was discovered the next year. Total reserves of the field are estimated at 1.7 to 3.3 billion barrels of gross recoverable oil and Johan Sverdrup is expected to produce 120,000 to 200,000 barrels of oil per day. Production start is planned to happen in 2018. It is one of the largest discoveries made in the Norwegian Continental Shelf

RESERVES AND PRODUCTION

North Sea Oil and Gas Fields

The British and Norwegian sections hold most of the remainder of the large oil reserves. It is estimated that the Norwegian section alone contains 54% of the sea's oil reserves and 45% of its gas reserves. More than half of the North Sea oil reserves have been extracted, according to official sources in both Norway and the UK. For Norway, the Norwegian Petroleum Directorate gives a figure of 4,601 million cubic metres of oil (corresponding to 29 billion barrels) for the Norwegian North Sea alone (excluding smaller reserves in Norwegian Sea and Barents Sea) of which 2,778 million cubic metres (60%) has already been produced prior to January 2007. UK sources give a range of estimates of reserves, but even using the most optimistic "maximum" estimate of ultimate recovery, 76% had been recovered at end 2010. Note the UK figure includes fields which are not in the North Sea (onshore, West of Shetland) .

United Kingdom Continental Shelf production was 137 million tonnes of oil and 105 billion m^3 of gas in 1999. (1 tonne of crude oil converts to 7.5 barrels) . The Danish explorations of Cenozoic stratigraphy, undertaken in the 1990s, showed petroleum rich reserves in the northern

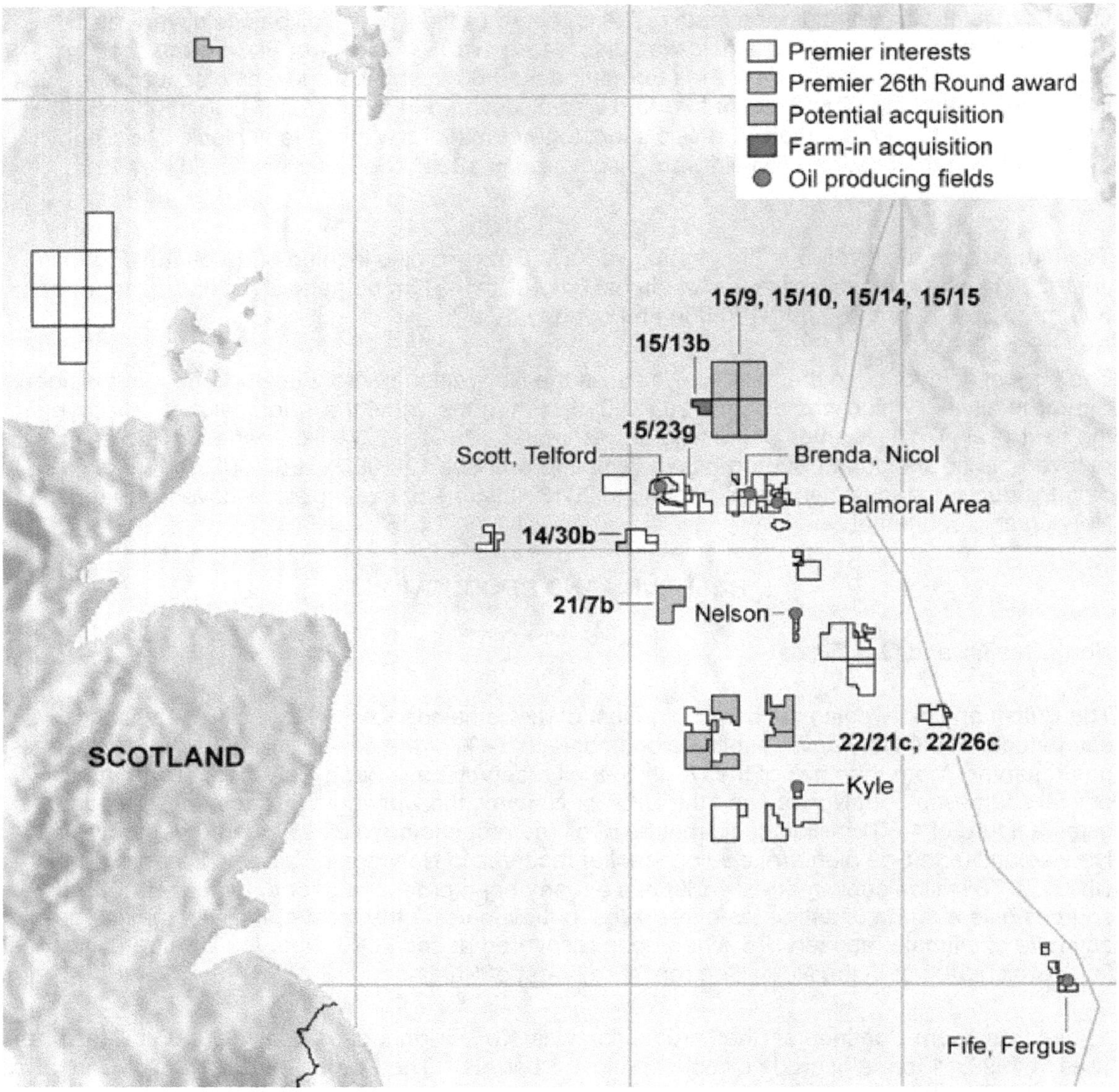

Danish sector, especially the Central Graben area. The Dutch area of the North Sea followed through with onshore and offshore gas exploration, and well creation.

Exact figures are debatable, because methods of estimating reserves vary and it is often difficult to forecast future discoveries.

Peaking in 1999, production of North Sea oil was nearly 950,000 m³ (6 million barrels) per day. Natural gas production was nearly 280×10^9 m³ (10 trillion cubic feet) in 2001 and continues to increase, although British gas production is in sharp decline.

UK oil production has seen two peaks, in the mid 1980s and late 1990s, with a decline to around 300×10^3 m³ (1.9 million barrels) per day in the early 1990s. Monthly oil production peaked at 13.5×10^6 m³ (84.9 million barrels) in January 1985 although the highest annual production was seen in 1999, with offshore oil production in that year of 407×10^6 m³ (398 million barrels) and had declined to 231×10^6 m³ (220 million barrels) in 2007. This was the largest decrease of any other oil exporting nation in the world, and has led to Britain becoming a net importer of crude for the first time in decades, as recognized by the energy policy of the United Kingdom. The production is expected to fall to one-third of its peak by 2020. Norwegian crude oil production as of 2013 is 1.4 mbpd. This is a more than 50% decline since the peak in 2001 of 3.2 mbpd.

LICENSING

Following the 1958 Continental shelf convention and after some disputes on the rights to natural resource exploitation the national limits of the exclusive economic zones were ratified. Five countries are involved in oil production in North Sea. All operate a tax and royalty licensing regime. The respective sectors are divided by median lines agreed in the late 1960s

- **United Kingdom** – The Department of Energy and Climate Change (DECC – formerly the Department of Trade and Industry) grants licences. The UKCS (United Kingdom Continental Shelf) is divided into quadrants of 1 degree latitude and one degree longitude. Each quadrant is divided into 30 blocks measuring 10 minutes of latitude and 12 minutes of longitude. Some blocks are divided further into part blocks where some areas are relinquished by previous licensees. For example, block 13/24a is located in quad 13 and is the 24th block and is the 'a' part block. The UK government has traditionally issued licences via periodic (now annual) licensing rounds. Blocks are awarded on the basis of the work programme bid by the participants. The UK government has actively solicited new entrants to the UKCS via "promote" licensing rounds with less demanding terms and the fallow acreage initiative, where non-active licences have to be relinquished.
- **Norway** – The Norwegian Petroleum Directorate (NPD Website in English) grants licences. The NCS is also divided into quads of 1 degree by 1 degree. Norwegian licence blocks are larger than British blocks, being 15 minutes of latitude by 20 minutes of longitude (12 blocks in a quad) . Like in Britain, there are numerous part blocks formed by re-licensing relinquished areas.
- **Denmark** – The Danish Energy Authority (website in English) administers the Danish sector. The Danes also divide their sector of the North Sea into 1 degree by 1 degree quadrants. Their blocks, however, are 10 minutes latitude by 15 minutes longitude. Part blocks exist where partial relinquishments have taken place.
- **Germany** – Germany and the Netherlands share a quadrant and block grid—quadrants are given letters rather than numbers. The blocks are 10 minutes latitude by 20 minutes longitude. Germany has the smallest sector in the North Sea.
- **Netherlands** – The Dutch sector is located in the Southern Gas Basin and shares a grid pattern with Germany

CARBON DIOXIDE SEQUESTRATION

In the North Sea, Norway's Statoil natural-gas platform Sleipner strips carbon dioxide out of the natural gas with amine solvents and disposes of this carbon dioxide by geological sequestration ("Carbon sequestration") . Sleipner reduces emissions of carbon dioxide by approximately one million tonnes a year. The cost of geological sequestration is minor relative to the overall running costs. As of April 2005, BP is considering a trial of large-scale sequestration of carbon dioxide stripped from power plant emissions in the Miller oilfield as its reserves are depleted.

UK ENERGY SECTOR: STRATEGIC INFORMATION

ENERGY SECTOR PROFILE

COUNTRY OVERVIEW

Location	Western Europe, islands including the northern one-sixth of the island of Ireland between the North Atlantic Ocean and the North Sea, northwest of France
Population	60,441,457
Languages	English, Welsh (about 26% of the population of Wales), Scottish form of Gaelic (about 60,000 in Scotland)
Religion	Christian (Anglican, Roman Catholic, Presbyterian, Methodist) 71.6%, Muslim 2.7%, Hindu 1%, other 1.6%, unspecified or none 23.1% (2001 census)
Ethnic Group(s)	white 92.1%, black 2%, Indian 1.8%, Pakistani 1.3%, mixed 1.2%, other 1.6% (2001 census)

ECONOMIC OVERVIEW

Gross Domestic Product	$2.2 trillion
Real GDP Growth Rate (2004E, 2005E, 2006F)	3.2%, 1.8%, 2.2%
Unemployment Rate	4.7%
External Debt	$7.1 trillion
Exports	$380 million
Exports - Commodities	manufactured goods, fuels, chemicals; food, beverages, tobacco
Exports - Partners	US 15%, Germany 10.7%, France 9.2%, Ireland 6.8%, Netherlands 6.1%, Belgium 5.2%, Spain 4.5%, Italy 4.2%
Imports	$461 million
Imports - Commodities	manufactured goods, machinery, fuels; foodstuffs
Imports - Partners	Germany 13%, US 9.2%, France 7.5%, Netherlands 6.6%, Belgium 5%, Italy 4.3%, China 4.2%
Current Account Balance	-$48 million

ENERGY OVERVIEW

Proven Oil Reserves	4 billion barrels
Oil Production	1.9 million barrels per day, of which 85% was crude oil.
Oil Consumption	1,8 million barrels per day
Crude Oil Distillation Capacity	1.9 million barrels per day
Proven Natural Gas Reserves	18.8 trillion cubic feet
Natural Gas Production	3.6 trillion cubic feet
Natural Gas Consumption	3,360.2 billion cubic feet
Recoverable Coal Reserves	242.5 million short tons
Coal Production	30.6 million short tons
Coal Consumption	68.8 million short tons
Electricity Installed Capacity	74 gigawatts
Electricity Production	369.9 billion kilowatt hours
Electricity Consumption	346.1 billion kilowatt hours
Total Energy	9.8 quadrillion Btus*, of which Oil (35%), Natural Gas (34%), Coal (16%),

Consumption	Nuclear (11%), Other Renewables (1%), Hydroelectricity (0%)
Total Per Capita Energy Consumption	166 million Btus
Energy Intensity	6,147 Btu per $2000-PPP**

ENVIRONMENTAL OVERVIEW

Energy-Related Carbon Dioxide Emissions	564.6 million metric tons, of which Oil (41%), Natural Gas (34%), Coal (25%)
Per-Capita, Energy-Related Carbon Dioxide Emissions	9.5 metric tons
Carbon Dioxide Intensity	0.4 Metric tons per thousand $2000-PPP**
Environmental Issues	by 2005 the government aims to reduce the amount of industrial and commercial waste disposed of in landfill sites to 85% of 1998 levels and to recycle or compost at least 25% of household waste, increasing to 33% by 2015; between 1998-99 and 1999-2000, household recycling increased from 8.8% to 10.3%
Major Environmental Agreements	party to: Air Pollution, Air Pollution-Nitrogen Oxides, Air Pollution-Sulfur 94, Air Pollution-Volatile Organic Compounds, Antarctic-Environmental Protocol, Antarctic-Marine Living Resources, Antarctic Seals, Antarctic Treaty, Biodiversity, Climate Change, Climate Change-Kyoto Protocol, Desertification, Endangered Species, Environmental Modification, Hazardous Wastes, Law of the Sea, Marine Dumping, Marine Life Conservation, Ozone Layer Protection, Ship Pollution, Tropical Timber 83, Tropical Timber 94, Wetlands, Whaling signed, but not ratified: Air Pollution-Persistent Organic Pollutants
Oil and Gas Industry	
Organization	Private sector active in all aspects of industry.
Major Oil/Gas Ports	Bacton, St. Fergus, Teeside, Easington, Isle of Grain, Cruden Bay, Sullom Voe, Flotta, Nigg Bay, Southampton
Foreign Company Involvement	Extensive, including many European and U.S. firms. The largest include Total, Chevron, BHP, Amerada Hess.
Major Oil Fields (production, bbl/d)	Schiehallion (98,900), Foinaven (72,600), Alba (67,100), Captain (66,000), Forties (55,300)
Major Natural Gas Fields	Elgin, Franklin, Halley, Scoter, Shearwater
Major Pipelines (length)	Forties-Cruden Bay (110 miles), Ninnan-Sullom Voe (110 miles), Piper-Flotta (130 miles), Cormorant-Sullom Voe (93 miles), Norpipe (220 miles), Shearwater-Elgin (SEAL), Scottish Area Gas Evacuation (SAGE, 200 miles), Central Area Transmission System (CATS, 250 miles), Far North Liquids and Gas System (FLAGS), Interconnector, Frigg.
Major Refineries (capacity, bbl/d)	Fawley (326,000), Stanlow (296,400), Killingholme South Humberside (221,300), South Killingholme (221,000), Coryton Essex (163,400),

* The total energy consumption statistic includes petroleum, dry natural gas, coal, net hydro, nuclear, geothermal, solar, wind, wood and waste electric power. The renewable energy consumption statistic is based on International Energy Agency (IEA) data and includes hydropower, solar, wind, tide, geothermal, solid biomass and animal products, biomass gas and liquids, industrial and municipal wastes. Sectoral shares of energy consumption and carbon emissions are also based on IEA data.

**GDP figures from OECD estimates based on purchasing power parity (PPP) exchange rates.

Background

With its significant North Sea reserves, the United Kingdom is a major European oil and natural gas producer.

The United Kingdom (UK) is an important political and economic power in Europe and the world. It has the second-largest economy in the European Union (EU) with a nominal 2005 gross domestic product (GDP) of $2.2 trillion. The UK economy grew by 1.8 percent in 2005, with growth of 2.2 percent forecasted for 2006. While the UK has been a member of the EU since 1973, it does not participate in the European single currency, the Euro.

The UK is the largest producer of oil and natural gas in the EU. However, after years of being a net exporter of both fuels, the UK became a net importer of natural gas in 2004. Government estimates also predict that the country will become a net importer of oil by the end of the decade. Production from UK oil and natural gas fields peaked in the late 1990s and has declined steadily over the past several years, as the discovery of new reserves has not kept pace with the maturation of existing fields. In response, the government has begun a three-pronged approach to address the predicted domestic shortfalls: 1) increasing domestic production through efficiency gains and the exploitation of marginal fields; 2) establishing necessary import infrastructure, such as liquefied natural gas (LNG) receiving terminals and transnational pipelines; and 3) investing in energy conservation and renewables.

OIL

The UK is the largest oil producer in the EU, but production has declined since peaking in 1999. According to *Oil and Gas Journal (OGJ),* the UK had 4.0 billion barrels of proven crude oil reserves in 2006, the most of any EU member country. The UK consumed 1.8 million barrels per day (bbl/d) of oil in 2005, mostly flat from the previous year. The importance of oil to the UK economy has declined slightly over the past two decades, with oil's contribution to total energy consumption falling from in 37 percent in 1983 to 35 percent in 2003.

Exploration and Production

The UK Continental Shelf (UKCS), located in the North Sea off the eastern coast of the UK, contains the bulk of the country's oil reserves. There are also sizable reserves in the North Sea north of the Shetland Islands, with smaller amounts in the North Atlantic. Besides these offshore assets, the UK also has the Wytch Farm field, the largest onshore oil field in Europe.

Total oil production (including condensates, natural gas liquids, and refinery gain) in the UK was 1.87 million bbl/d in 2005, a 10 percent decline from 2004 and 37 percent below the peak of production in 1999. The UK government expects oil production in the country to continue to decline, reaching 1.38 million bbl/d by 2009. Reasons for this decline include 1) the overall maturity of the country's oil fields 2) the application of new crude oil extraction technologies that lead to field exhausted at a quicker rate, and 3) increasing costs as production shifts to more remote and inhospitable regions.

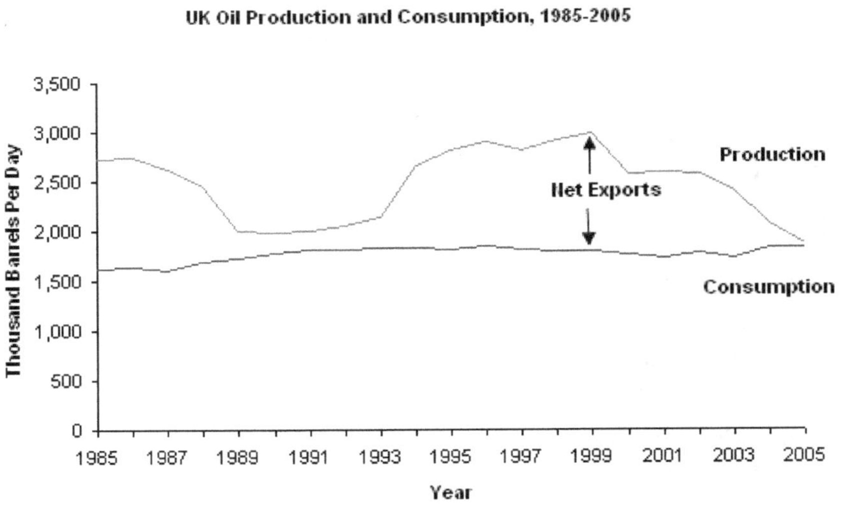

Source: *International Energy Annual 2003*; internal EIA estimates

Most of the UK crude oil grades are light and sweet (30° to 40° API), which generally makes them attractive to foreign buyers. The UK has been a net exporter of crude oil since 1981. According to the British Department of Trade and Industry (DTI), the largest destinations of crude oil exports in 2004 were the United States (28 percent), the Netherlands (21 percent), Germany (17 percent), and France (14 percent). Much of the crude oil exported to the Netherlands is not actually consumed there, but rather sold at the Rotterdam spot market. In 2005, the UK exported 219,000 bbl/d of crude oil and 167,000 bbl/d of petroleum products to the U.S., contributing 2.2 percent and 4.8 percent to total U.S. crude oil and petroleum product imports, respectively.

SECTOR ORGANIZATION

BP is the largest oil producer in the UK, with 26 fields producing a total of 471,600 bbl/d in 2004, according to *OGJ*. BP also operates the single-largest oil field in the UK, Schiehallion, with 2004 production of 98,900 bbl/d. Other large oil producers in the UK include Shell, ChevronTexaco, and Total.

As UK oil fields mature, the industry has shifted focus from discovering new reserves to increasing the productivity of existing fields and developing smaller, previously avoided ones. This trend has prompted oil major such as BP and Shell to begin selling their UK assets in order to focus on high growth, international opportunities. The result has been the entry into the UK oil sector of many smaller operators. In 2003, U.S.-based Apache purchased BP's Forties field for $630 million, and other smaller operators, such as Talisman, Perenco, and Paladin Resources, have acquired significant production assets in the country. In late 2004, EnCana announced that it would sell its North Sea assets to Canada-based Nexen for $2 billion. In 2005, Denmark's Maersk Oil and Gas and UK natural gas company Centrica purchased the North Sea assets of U.S.-based Kerr McGee for $3 billion. These companies find smaller and maturing fields more economically viable than do the oil majors, because they have lower overhead costs, are more flexible, and often employ newer production and recovery technologies.

PIPELINES

There is an extensive network of pipelines in the UK to carry oil extracted from North Sea platforms to coastal terminals in Scotland and northern England. BP operates the 110-mile, 36-inch Forties-Cruden Bay pipeline, linking fields in the Forties system to the oil terminal at Cruden Bay, Scotland. The company also operates a 110-mile, 36-inch pipeline connecting the Ninnian system to the Sullom Voe oil terminal on Shetland Island. Total operates a 150-mile, 24-inch pipeline linking the Bruce and Forties fields to Cruden Bay and a 130-mile, 30-inch pipeline connecting the Piper system with Flotta on Orkney Island. Shell and Esso jointly operate a 93-mile, 36-inch connection between the Cormorant oil field and Sullom Voe. Talisman Energy owns a 37-mile, 16-inch pipeline connection between its Beatrice field and the Nigg Bay oil terminal. There are also numerous, small pipelines that connect each North Sea oil platform to these major backbones. Finally, the UK does have a few onshore crude oil pipelines, including a 90-mile, underground pipeline operated by BP that links the Wytch Farm field to the refinery at Fawley and the nearby oil export terminal at Southampton.

UK Crude Oil Imports and Exports, by Trading Partner, 2004

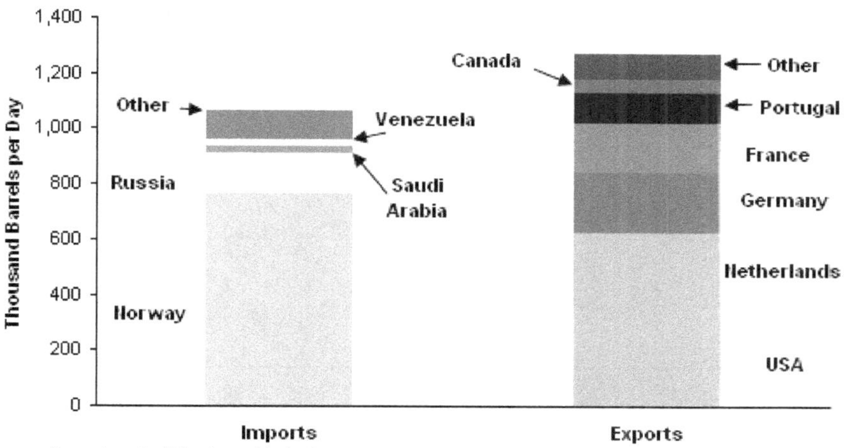

Source: Department of Trade and Industry

The UK has a single international crude oil pipeline, the 220-mile, 34-inch Norpipe operated by ConocoPhillips. With a capacity of 900,000 bbl/d, Norpipe connects Norwegian oil fields in the Ekofisk system to the oil terminal and refinery at Teesside.

DOWNSTREAM

The UK had 1.9 million bbl/d of refining capacity in 2006, according to *OGJ*. ExxonMobil operates the single-largest refinery in the country, the 326,000-bbl/d Fawley facility in southern England. However, BP controls the largest total amount of refining capacity, with facilities in Grangemouth, Scotland (196,000 bbl/d) and Coryton, England (163,000 bbl/d). Other companies with significant refining capacity in the UK include Total (325,000 bbl/d), Shell (296,000 bbl/d), ConocoPhillips (221,000 bbl/d), and ChevronTexaco (210,000 bbl/d). According to DTI, refinery utilization in the UK was near 90 percent in 2004. The UK maintains an active international trade in refined petroleum products, exporting 36.1 million metric tons (mt) and importing 26.4 million mt in 2004.

NATURAL GAS

The UK is one of the largest natural gas producers in the world.

According to *OGJ*, the UK held an estimated 18.8 trillion cubic feet (Tcf) of proven natural gas reserves in 2006, a 10 percent decline from the previous year. Most of these reserves occur in three distinct areas: 1) associated fields in the UKCS; 2) non-associated fields in the Southern Gas Basin, located adjacent to the Dutch sector of the North Sea; and 3) non-associated fields in the Irish Sea. In order to take advantage of its domestic reserves, the UK government has encouraged the use of natural gas, including its substitution for coal and oil in industrial consumption and electricity production. As a result, natural gas consumption in the UK reached 3.4 Tcf in 2003. Further, the percentage of total energy consumption sourced from natural gas in the UK has increased from 20 percent in 1980 to 34 percent in 2003. In 2004, the UK was a net importer of natural gas for the first time since 1996.

EXPLORATION AND PRODUCTION

The UK produced 3.6 Tcf of natural gas in 2003, about the same as the previous year, but a decrease from the peak of 3.8 Tcf in 2000. The country is the fourth-largest producer of natural gas in the world, behind Russia, the United States, and Canada. The largest concentration of natural gas production in the UK is the Shearwater-Elgin area of the Southern Gas Basin. The area contains five gas fields, Elgin (Total), Franklin (Total), Halley (Talisman), Scoter (Shell), and Shearwater (Shell). Most of the leading oil companies in the UK are also the leading natural gas producers, including BP, Shell, and Total. The major gas distribution companies in the UK, such as Centrica and BG Group, also have a presence in this production sector. Like the oil industry, smaller independents have been able to acquire some maturing assets from larger operators, who find it difficult to profitably operate these older, declining fields.

UK Natural Gas Production and Consumption, 1983-2003

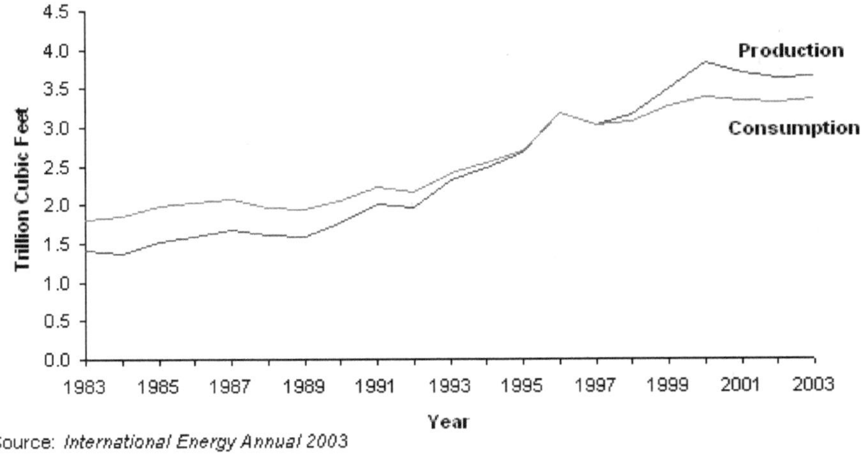

Source: *International Energy Annual 2003*

SECTOR ORGANIZATION

Private companies control the UK natural gas sector, including production, distribution, and transmission. The largest gas distributor in the UK is now Centrica, a spin-off of the distribution assets of formally state-owned British Gas. National Grid Transeco (NGT), formed in 2002 through the merger of Lattice and former parastatal National Grid, controls the domestic gas transmission system.

PIPELINES

Domestic System

There are four main pipeline systems in the UK that carry natural gas from offshore platforms to coastal landing terminals. First, the Shearwater-Elgin Line (SEAL), operated by Total, transports gas from the Shearwater-Elgin area to the landing terminal at Bacton, England. Second, ExxonMobil operates the 200-mile, 30-inch Scottish Area Gas Evacuation (SAGE), which transports associated natural gas from UKGS fields to the landing terminal at St. Fergus, Scotland. Third, the 250-mile, 36-inch Central Area Transmission System (CATS), operated by BP, links fields in the Graben area of the UKCS to Teeside. Finally, Shell operates the Far North Liquids and Gas System (FLAGS) linking associated gas deposits in the Brent oil system with St. Fergus. Once brought onshore, the responsibility for transporting natural gas throughout the country belongs to NGT. The company operates over 4,200 miles of transmission lines in the UK.

International Pipelines

A consortium of companies, led by BG, Ruhrgas, and Distrigas, operates the Interconnector pipeline between Bacton, England and Zeebrugge, Belgium. The Interconnector, inaugurated in 1998, is capable of bi-direction operation, meaning either it can export natural gas from the UK to continental Europe ("Forward Mode"), or it can import natural gas into the UK ("Reverse Mode"). For most of its career, the Interconnector operated in Forward Mode, with a capacity of 1.9 Bcf/d. However, since mid-2005, the system has operated mostly in Reverse Mode, with a recent expansion increasing this capacity to 1.6 Bcf/d. The operators of the Interconnector plan to expand the system's Reverse Mode capacity to 2.3 Bcf/d by the end of 2006.

The UK also imports natural gas through the Frigg pipeline system, operated by Total. Frigg connects the St. Fergus gas terminal with the Frigg gas field in the Norwegian sector of the North Sea. Finally, the UK-Eire Interconnector connects the UK with the Republic of Ireland, running from Moffat, Scotland to Dublin.

In 2003, the UK and Norway finalized the necessary political conditions for construction of the Langeled pipeline system linking Norway's Ormen Lange natural gas field to Easington, England. The 750-mile Langeled would be the longest sub sea pipeline in the world, with an initial capacity of 1.9 Bcf/d and planned maximum capacity of 2.9 Bcf/d. Construction on the project has begun, with completion expected by 2007.

Gasunie plans to build a 146-mile gas pipeline linking Balgzand, the Netherlands to Bacton, England. Initial construction on the Balgzand-Bacton Line (BBL) began in October 2004, with completion of the project expected by the end of 2006. According to Gasunie, the BBL will have an initial capacity of 1.1 Bcf/d, with a maximum capacity of 1.7 Bcf/d.

World's Largest Natural Gas Producers, 1993-2003

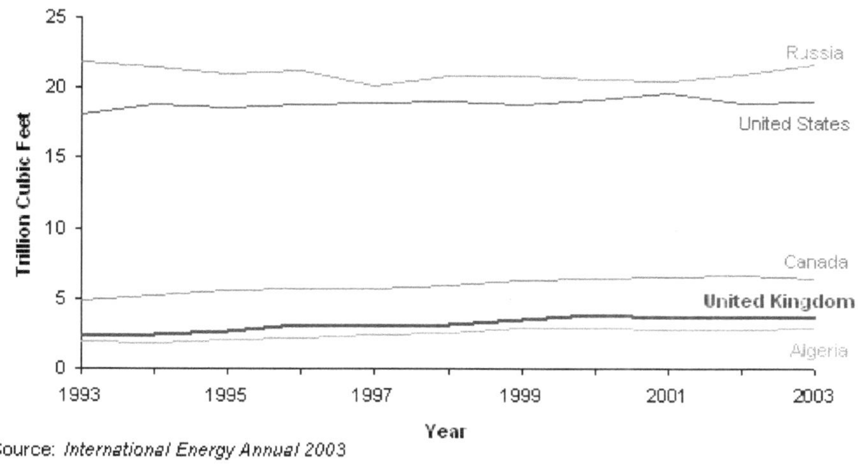

Source: *International Energy Annual 2003*

LIQUEFIED NATURAL GAS (LNG)

Currently, the UK has a single LNG import terminal, the NGT's Grain LNG on the Isle of Grain. The facility has a sendout capacity of 420 Bcf/d, which NGT plans to expand to 1.3 Bcf/d by the end of 2007. Algeria's Sonatrach and BP are the principle importers using the terminal.

ExxonMobil and Qatar Petroleum have received regulatory approval for the South Hook LNG receiving terminal in Milton Haven, Wales. The terminal will receive its LNG from the Qatargas II liquefaction project in Ras Laffin, Qatar, which is also a joint project between the two companies. The South Hook LNG project should come online by 2007, with an initial capacity of 1.0 Bcf/d and a maximum capacity of 2.1 Bcf/d by 2009.

Finally, BG has collaborated with Netherlands-based Petroplus and Malaysia-based Petronas to also build an LNG receiving terminal in Milton Haven, on the site of an existing natural gas storage facility owned by Petroplus. Dragon received regulatory approval from Ofgem in early 2005, and the project should start receiving cargos by the end of 2008 at an initial sendout capacity of 580 Mmcf/d.

COAL

Most UK coal consumption is for power generation.

The UK had an estimated 243 million short tons (Mmst) of recoverable coal reserves in 2003. The country produced 30.6 Mmst in 2003, the fifth-most in the EU. Coal production in the UK has declined steadily and dramatically over the past several decades. Decreasing domestic consumption and a surge of low-cost imports have been the principle causes of the production decline. According to DTI, the UK now imports more coal than it produces domestically, with South Africa and Australian representing the principle source of these imports.

In order to meet its obligations under the Kyoto Protocol, the UK likely will continue to phase out coal consumption and production. Nevertheless, the UK government continues to provide financial support to the industry. In June 2003, the UK government launched the Coal Investment Aid program, with a budget of up to $111 million. The goal of the project is to create or safeguard jobs in the UK coal industry by encouraging coal producers to enter into investment projects that maintain access to reserves.

ELECTRICITY

Natural gas-fired power stations are replacing coal as the principle source of the UK power supply. The UK had installed electricity generation capacity of 74.0 gigawatts (GW) in 2003. Also in 2003, the UK generated 369.9 billion kilowatthours (Bkwh) of electricity while consuming 346.1 Bkwh. Most electricity generation comes from conventional thermal sources (74 percent), followed by nuclear (23 percent), other renewables (2 percent), and hydroelectricity (1 percent).

SECTOR ORGANIZATION

The UK has a privatized electricity sector, where generators and distributors trade electricity on a wholesale market. The largest power producer in the country is British Energy (BE), which controls most of the nuclear power capacity and generates about 20 percent of the total electricity supply. Other important generating companies include E.ON UK, RWE npower, Scottish and Southern Energy (SSE), and ScottishPower (SP). Twelve regional monopolies control electricity distribution in the UK, most of which are owned by the leading generation companies. NGT owns and operates the national transmission system in England and Wales, whereas SSE and SP operate the grid in Scotland, and Northern Ireland Electricity (NIE), a subsidiary of the Viridian Group, operates the grid in Northern Ireland.

UK Electricity Generation, by Source, 1983-2003

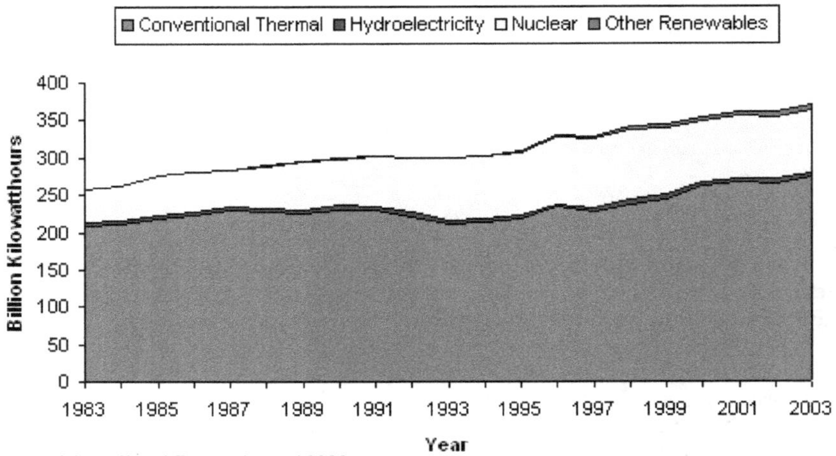

Source: *International Energy Annual 2003*

The UK has slowly integrated the formally-separate electricity markets of its component parts (England, Northern Ireland, Scotland, and Wales). The British government formed the New Electricity Trading Arrangements (NETA) in 2001 to integrate the electricity markets of England and Wales. In 2005, the British government extended NETA to Scotland as the British Energy Transmission and Trading Arrangements (BETTA). There are plans to eventual incorporate Northern Ireland in to the BETTA. In addition, SP and SSE have increased the transmission capacity between England and Scotland to allow them to sell more electricity to English and Welsh customers.

CONVENTIONAL THERMAL

As mentioned above, conventional thermal plants provide the bulk of the electricity supply in the UK. According to DTI, conventional thermal generation in 2004 consisted of natural gas (53 percent), coal (44 percent), oil (2 percent), and other (1 percent). One of the largest power plants in the UK is the Drax facility in North Yorkshire, which consists of six coal-fired units with total capacity of 4,000 megawatts (MW). The long-term trend in UK power generation has been a move from coal-fired plants to combined-cycle, gas-fired turbines (CCGFT). As a result, according to DTI, electricity generation from CCGFTs increased from zero in 1989 to 137.7 Bkwh in 2004.

Nuclear

BE operates eight nuclear power stations in the UK, including seven stations using advanced, gas-cooled reactors (AGR) and one (Sizewell B) using a pressurized-water reactor (PWR). All of the AGR reactors will reach the end of their designed lifetime by 2023. British Nuclear Fuels Limited (BNFL), owned by the UK government, operates four nuclear plants containing first generation, magnesium-oxide (Magnox) reactors. The UK originally built 11 of these plants in the 1950s, and BNFL will close the remaining four by 2010. BNFL plans to convert one closed plant, Chapelcross, into a co-firing plant burning a combination of coal and locally grown willow trees.

UK Electricity Generation from Thermal Sources, 1989-2004

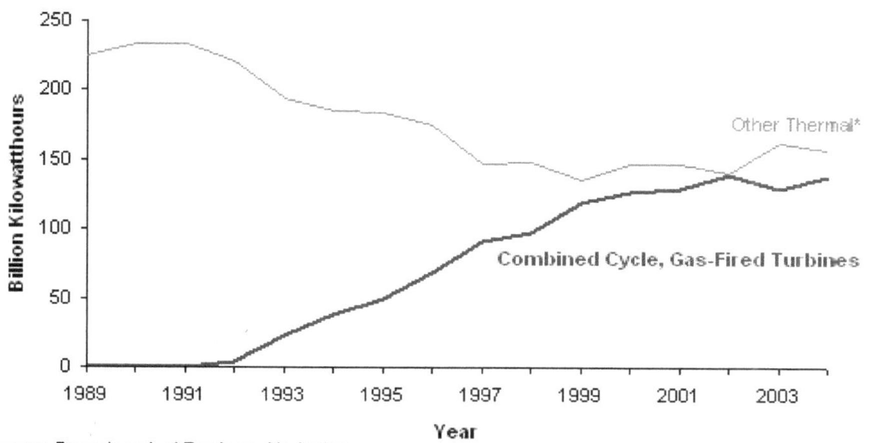

Source: Department of Trade and Industry

*Oil plants, traditional gas turbines, and thermal

RENEWABLES

The UK government has introduced regulations that require electricity distributors to source a portion of their electricity supply from renewables (including hydroelectricity), currently 3 percent but set to rise to 10 percent by 2010. Investments in wind power have increased substantially, aiming to take advantage of the natural geographic advantage that the UK has in this regard. Another area of increased interest has been wave power. In 2004, the Pelamis project off the coast of Orkney delivered the first ever supply of electricity from wave energy to the UK national grid. Finally, hydroelectricity has regained attention, especially in Scotland, including the potential construction of the 100-MW Glendoe project.

ENVIRONMENT

The UK is an Annex I country under the Kyoto Protocol.

The UK emitted 564.6 million metric tons (Mmt) of energy-related carbon dioxide in 2003. The country is one of only four Western European countries to achieve a drop in carbon dioxide emissions since 1990. While carbon dioxide emissions have declined, total energy consumption has increased over the same period by 11.2 percent, reaching 9.8 quadrillion British thermal units (Btu) in 2003.

The UK has ratified the Kyoto Protocol; however, the EU has decided to meet its requirements under the Protocol as a whole, rather than as individual signatories, with each member state given a different emissions target by the EU Commission. Under the EU plan, the UK must reduce its carbon dioxide emissions by 12.5 percent below the 1990 level during the 2008-2012 commitment period; the country was 8 percent above this target during 2003.

The UK has seen dramatic improvements in air quality in recent decades, especially reductions in sulfur dioxide emissions: The principle driving force behind these reductions has been the transition away from coal-fired power plants, the drastic reduction in the use of coal for residential heating, and general economic shift from an industry-focused to service-based economy. In 2001, the UK government introduced the Climate Change Levy, a surcharge on energy produced from carbon dioxide-emitting sources charged to commercial and industrial energy users. By exempting renewable energy sources and co-generation facilities, the Levy has encouraged large energy consumers to increase conservation measures.

UK OIL AND GAS EXPLORATION: IMPORTANT INFORMATION AND REGULATIONS

LICENSING OVERVIEW

The Petroleum Act 1998 vests all rights to the nation's petroleum resources in the Crown. But the Secretary of State (for Trade and Industry - i.e. the Government) can grant licences that confer exclusive rights to "search and bore for and get" petroleum. Each of these licences confers such rights over a limited area and for a limited period.

Most Licences follow a standard format, but BERR is flexible in this and ready to consider adapting new licences to suit special scenarios. The Secretary of State has discretion in the granting of licences, which he exercises to ensure maximum exploitation of this valuable national resource, but there are other considerations that he must also take into account - protection of the environment and the interests of other users of the sea, for instance.

Licences can be held by a single company or by several working together, but in legal terms there is only ever a single Licensee, however many companies it may include. All the companies on a Licence share joint and several liability for operations conducted under it. Each Licence actually takes the form of a Deed, which binds the Licensee to obey the licence conditions regardless of whether or not s/he is using the Licence at any given moment.

BERR expects companies to work their licences. In recent years, the amount of acreage that has been left untouched, and those exclusive rights unexploited, has become a matter of concern and has led PILOT (formerly the Oil & Gas Industry Task Force) to instigate the Fallow Initiative.

HISTORY

The UK's onshore petroleum licensing regime was set up under the impetus of the fuel demands of the First World War, although the first licences weren't issued until 1935.
Offshore licensing began with the North Sea boom of the sixties. The Ministry of Power issued the first offshore licence, P001, in 1964, and its successor the Department of Trade & Industry issued the one-thousandth licence in 1999.

GEOGRAPHY

BERR's Licensing system covers oil and gas within Great Britain, its territorial sea and on the UK Continental Shelf (UKCS). Northern Ireland's offshore waters are subject to the same licensing system as the rest of the United Kingdom Continental Shelf. Northern Ireland receives a biennial payment from overall royalty and rental payments calculated in proportion to Northern Ireland's population. Northern Ireland issues its own Licences to cover its onshore area, independently of BERR (contact: the Department of Enterprise, Trade and Investment's Energy Division; tel: 028 9052 9900).

The Isle of Man issues Licences for its own onshore area and territorial waters (contact: the Economic Development Group of the Isle of Man's Department of Trade & Industry; tel: 01624 687175).

The designated area of the UKCS has been refined over the years by a series of designations under the Continental Shelf Act 1964 following the conclusion of boundary agreements with neighbouring states. The most recent is the Scottish Adjacent Waters Boundaries Order 1999 (No. 1126) implementing an agreement reached with the Faeroe Islands.

RENTALS

Each licence carries an annual charge, called a rental. Rentals fall due each year on the licence anniversary (except that for pre-20th Round Seaward Production Licences in their Initial Terms, rentals only fell due in Year 1). They are charged at an escalating rate on each square kilometre that the Licence covers at that date.

Rentals have two purposes: they encourage Licensees to surrender acreage they don't want to exploit, so as to free it up for others who do; and they concentrate their minds on the acreage they actually decide to keep.

Usually the companies on a licence make agreements among themselves (e.g. Joint Operating Agreements) that regulate how to apportion costs, including rentals payments. However, the licence simply provides that each company is jointly-and-severally liable to the Secretary of State for all liabilities and obligations arising thereunder, and it is not for BERR to determine how the rentals should be apportioned. BERR will therefore invoice a single company (known as the Licence Administrator and nominated by the licence group) for a single rental payment for each licence each year; and will not collect separate rental payments within a single licence.

TERMS (PERIODS)

Seaward Production Licences and Petroleum Exploration and Development Licences are valid for a sequence of periods, called Terms. These Terms are designed to follow the typical lifecycle of a field: exploration, appraisal, production. Each Licence expires automatically at the end of each Term, unless the Licensee has made enough progress to earn the chance to move into the next Term.

The Initial Term is usually an exploration period. For Seaward Production Licences it's normally set at four years, although it can be longer for 'frontier' Licences. For Petroleum Exploration and Development Licences it's set at six years. The Initial Term carries a Work Programme of exploration activity that BERR and the Licensee will have agreed as part of the application process. The Licence expires at the end of the Initial Term unless the Licensee has completed the Work Programme by then. At that time the Licensee must also relinquish a fixed amount of acreage (usually 50%), which is another attempt to ensure that the Licensee has explored the whole acreage by then.

The Second Term is intended for appraisal and development. It lasts for four years for Seaward Production Licences and five for Petroleum Exploration and Development Licences. The Licence expires at the end of the Second Term unless the Secretary of State has approved a Development Plan by then.

The Third Term is intended for production. It lasts for 18 years for Seaward Production Licences and 20 for Petroleum Exploration and Development Licences. The Secretary of State has the discretion to extend it if production is continuing, but BERR reserves the right to reconsider the provisions of the Licence before doing so, especially the acreage and rentals.

The qualifying criteria to continue into the next Term are of course minima. BERR sets no maximum rate of progress, and all other things being equal would be more than happy to see a Licensee progress through exploration and appraisal to production before the end of the Initial Term, if it were possible. It would not shorten the Licence's overall life.

RELINQUISHMENTS/SURRENDERS

Licensees are entitled to 'determine' (i.e. surrender) a Licence, or part of the acreage covered by it, at any time (unless the licence is still in its Initial Term and the Work Programme has not been completed). In fact, BERR positively encourages the surrender of acreage unless the Licensee

actually intends to work it, and a minimum relinquishment of acreage at the end of the Initial Term is actually a condition of most Licences.
Partial surrenders are subject to restrictions on the complexity of the area relinquished, because we do not wish to create unlicensed areas so irregular in shape that they would be unattractive to other companies.

MULTIBLOCK LICENCES

Many licences cover more than one block. The term "multiblock licences" has come to refer to offshore licences where the blocks have widely-divergent licence groups of companies. The reason is generally that the blocks are scattered geographically.
We recognise the problems that can arise and we have undertaken not to issue any more licences covering scattered areas. In principle we would also be happy to split existing multiblock licences, and are currently working with industry to work out a way to do so.

ONSHORE LICENCES AND LANDOWNERS

The Secretary of State issues landward production licences (Petroleum Exploration and Development Licences) under powers granted by the Petroleum Act 1998. They confer the right to search for, bore for and get hydrocarbons under that legislation, but they do not confer any exemption from other legal/regulatory requirements, such as any need to gain access rights from landowners, health and safety regulations, or planning permission from relevant local authorities. In particular, nothing in Part I of the Act confers, or enables the Secretary of State to confer, any right to enter on or interfere with land (see section 9(2) of the Act). However, it should also be noted that section 7(1) of the Act applies the Mines (Working Facilities and Support) Act 1966 in England, Wales and Scotland for the purpose of enabling a Licensee to acquire such ancillary rights as may be required for the exercise of the rights granted by the Licence.
To see whether any particular site is covered by a Licence (e.g. during house conveyancing), consult the relevant map elsewhere on this site. Anyone requiring further advice should email us at approvals@berr.gsi.gov.uk, or write to Licensing & Consents Unit (Oil & Gas Licensing Administration), Bay 2130, Dept of Trade & Industry, 1 Victoria Street, London SW1H 0ET, including the Ordnance Survey coordinates of the site in question (note that we do not record or use postal addresses or postcodes).

COAL-RELATED HYDROCARBONS

The UK's coal reserves are managed by the Coal Authority, and access to coal formations for any purpose requires their agreement.

Certain processes capture native hydrocarbons whose immediate origin lies in coal seams. They require permission not only from the Coal Authority (to access the coal) but also a licence from DECC (to capture the hydrocarbons). These processes include coalbed methane (CBM, which entails the liberation of native methane from virgin coal seams) and vent gas (also called mines gas, which entails the capture of methane from working or disused mines). However, underground coal gasification (UCG, which generates a mixture of gases including non-native methane) does not require a Petroleum Act licence; just a licence from the Coal Authority, who classify it as a coal-mining operation.

LEGISLATIVE BACKGROUND

PETROLEUM ACT 1998

Part I of the Petroleum Act 1998 (and before it, the 1934 Act) vests all rights to petroleum in the Crown, including the rights to search for, bore for and get it. It then goes on to empower the

Secretary of State to grant Licences to search for and bore for and get petroleum to such persons as he thinks fit. Part III of the Act deals with Submarine pipelines and Part IV deals with Abandonment of Offshore Installations.

MODEL CLAUSES

As with any licensing system, many of the detailed regulatory provisions are laid down in conditions attached to the licences. The Petroleum Act is rather unusual in that it requires these conditions ("Model Clauses") to be published first in secondary legislation. Up to the 19th Round, the model clauses were incorporated into licences by means of a single short paragraph, but from the 20th round onwards they have been set out in full in the licence itself, for the sake of clarity. It is the Licensee's responsibility to understand these conditions and ensure they are observed. The Model Clauses currently in use for Seaward Production Licences can be inspected on the OPSI website at the Petroleum Licensing (Production) (Seaward Areas) Regulations 2008 (2008/225). Those used for Landward Production Licences and for Seaward Exploration Licences are at the

TYPES OF LICENCE

OFFSHORE

Production Licences The main type of offshore Licence is the Seaward Production Licence, of which DECC and its predecessors have now granted more than a thousand. In spite of their name they don't cover just production - they cover the full life of a field from exploration to decommissioning. They cover relatively small areas - typically a couple of hundred square kilometres.

DECC recognises that a single kind of Licence won't suit all circumstances. In recent years, we have issued Licences in three variations of the 'Traditional' Production Licence: the 'Promote' Licence, the 'Frontier' Licence and Licences specially drafted to cover the redevelopment of a decommissioned field (cf. Argyll/Ardmore).

Exploration Licences Some companies carry out exploratory surveys over wide areas of the offshore sector, and don't need exclusive rights to do it. Production Licences would be impractical and prohibitively expensive for such activities; hence DECC also issues Exploration Licences. Exploration Licences run for three years at a time, and allow exploration anywhere on the United Kingdom Continental Shelf except on any area that is covered at the time by a Production Licence. (If the holder of an Exploration Licence wants to explore acreage covered by a Petroleum Licence, it will need the agreement of the holder of the Production Licence.)

ONSHORE

Petroleum Exploration and Development Licences Onshore production licences are called Petroleum Exploration and Development Licences (PEDLs), but they're similar in form to the offshore production licences, with Model Clauses and a three-Term lifetime.

Completion of the agreed exploration Work Programme in the six-year Initial Term is a precondition for entry into the Second, and approval of a Development Plan in the five-year Second Term is a precondition for entry into the Third.

Before 1996, DTI issued a sequence of separate licences for each stage of an onshore field's life: an Exploration Licence, an Appraisal Licence, a Development Licence and a Production Licence. We introduced PEDLs at the Eighth Licensing Round to reduce the bureaucratic burden of issuing a series of Licences.

Supplementary Seismic Survey Licences If the Operator of a landward Production Licence (PEDL, AL, DL, etc) wants to shoot a seismic survey right up to the boundary of his licensed area, he actually has to operate his survey equipment a little way outside it. If that means working in unlicensed acreage, he can seek a Supplementary Seismic Survey Licence (SSSL), which lasts for one year and covers a kilometre-wide strip adjacent to the existing Production Licence.
A SSSL will only be issued to the Operator of the Production Licence, not to its partners. DECC needs to be told the coordinates of the additional area. As a double-check we also require an A4 map of the area.

Any new Production Licence that is subsequently issued over the same acreage will automatically terminate the SSSL. If there's only a partial overlap, the SSSL will cease to operate on that overlap .

OLDER TYPES OF ONSHORE LICENCE

There are several other types of onshore licence. DECC no longer issues any of them, but a number of them are still in force. These are: Mining Licences, Exploration Licences, Development Licences, Appraisal Licences and Production Licences.
Mining Licences [Text to follow]

Exploration Licences (XL or EXL), Production Licences (PL), Appraisal Licences (AL) and Development Licences (DL) The Petroleum (Production) (Landward Areas) Regulations 1984 replaced the previous system of two types of licence (Exploration Licences (XL) and Production Licences (PL)), with three: a new type of Exploration Licence (EXL), Appraisal Licences (AL) and Development Licences (DL).

The Department of Energy issued EXLs from the First Onshore Licensing Round (1986) until the Sixth (1992).

Each Exploration Licence (EXL) ran for six years and carried an agreed Work Programme (just like the six-year Initial Term of a modern PEDL). The five-year Appraisal Licence gave the Licensee time to prepare a Development Programme and get long-term planning permission. Only if both of those were in place would the Department consider issuing a 20-year Development Licence.

Today, if one of the few surviving EXLs reaches its expiry date (and if the Work Programme has been completed, of course) it can be converted to PEDL terms. That means that from then on it has effect as though it had been issued as a PEDL in the first place and is now entering its "second" term, (although its name doesn't change, so it is still called - for instance - EXL141).

Methane Drainage Licences Many coalmines vent methane to the atmosphere, or else accumulate methane that must be dealt with by the mine-owner. Either way, the methane can create a health & safety issue, and as a very powerful greenhouse gas (up to 22 times more potent than CO_2), it presents an environmental problem as well.

Technically, capturing the drained methane requires a Licence under the Petroleum Act 1998, but safety is the Government's first priority and to regularise methane drainage we are generally prepared to issue a Methane Drainage Licence (MDL) for a nominal fee.

An MDL grants permission to get natural gas "*in the course of operations for making and keeping safe mines whether or not disused*". It grants no exclusive rights, so it can overlap geographically with one or more PEDLs. MDLs generally cover much smaller areas than PEDLs - typically each covers one mine, although the Coal Authority holds a licence that covers the whole country.

Note: Under the Energy Act 1976, as amended by the Gas Act 1986, the Secretary of State's consent is required to dispose of natural gas (whether at source or elsewhere) by flaring or by releasing it unignited into the atmosphere. There are a number of exemptions, including flaring that is already covered by one of the Licences listed here and gas supplied by a public gas supplier. For further details, contact: Ivor Newman; tel: 020 7215 5163; fax: 020 7215 5292.

AWARD OF LICENCES

LICENSING ROUNDS

DECC issues licences through competitive Licensing Rounds. We believe that this method yields better-quality bids than other methods. Unlike auctions, for instance, it does not divert significant sums of money away from exploration work, and it gives a much better expectation that a Licence will be awarded to the bid that promises to optimise the exploitation of the UK's petroleum resources. We are committed to a regular timetable of one onshore and one offshore Licensing Round each year.

OUT-OF-ROUND APPLICATIONS

The vast majority of Seaward Production Licences or Petroleum Exploration and Development Licences are issued in Licensing Rounds, but particular cases may present compelling reasons to issue a Licence outside a Round. It rests with the company seeking an Out-of-Round Licence to make a case to DECC that we should invite Out-Of-Round Applications. Even if we do so, though, in most cases the Hydrocarbons Licensing Directive, as implemented by the Hydrocarbons Licensing Directive Regulations, still require us to follow the usual procedures, including an invitation for applications in the European Journal at least 90 days in advance.
In the past, we have accepted clear grounds of urgency (for example, temporary availability of a drilling rig). We will also consider cases where there is no prospect of competition anyway (generally because the acreage can only be of interest to a company whose existing licence covers adjoining acreage). Any request to invite Out-Of-Round applications must show why the case is so unusual that an exception is justified - we would not consider simple impatience, or expectations of oil price movements, for instance.

HOW TO APPLY FOR A SEAWARD PRODUCTION LICENCE OR A PETROLEUM EXPLORATION AND DEVELOPMENT LICENCE

Once DECC has invited applications, whether in a Licensing Round or out-of-round, they must be made on the correct Application Form. There is guidance about applying for Licences during a Licensing Round. Anyone seeking a Licence out-of-round must first convince DECC to invite applications. Such an approach should be made in writing to John Arnott in our Policy Unit. If we decide to invite applications, use the same Application Form. For most purposes the Guidance also applies to out-of-round applications.

HOW TO APPLY FOR AN EXPLORATION LICENCE

You can apply at any time for a new Seaward Exploration Licence (or for an extension to an existing Seaward Exploration Licence), using this Exploration Licence Application Form which should be emailed to approvals@decc.gsi.gov.uk. Seismic surveys are subject to a consent procedure. Consent for any particular survey may be subject to the need for an environmental impact assessment. For further guidance, contact the Environmental Management Team at DECC (email: emt@berr.gsi.gov.uk).

HOW TO APPLY FOR A SUPPLEMENTARY SEISMIC SURVEY LICENCE

The Operator of an onshore Production Licence (PEDL, EXL, AL, DL, etc) can apply for an adjoining Supplementary Seismic Survey Licence at any time, using the attached Application Form. The completed Application Form must be accompanied by an A4 map of the area to be licensed.
Queries and requests to:
Ricki Kiff
Tel: 020 7215 5032
Email: ricki.kiff@decc.gsi.gov.uk
Fax: 020 7215 5070

LICENCE ASSIGNMENTS (TRANSFERS)

A company that is party to a Licence may wish to sell an interest to another. Such a transfer is referred to here as a Licence Assignment.

Licence Assignments are prohibited except with the consent of the Secretary of State. An assignment made without prior consent would be viewed very seriously by DECC. It constitutes grounds for immediate revocation of the licence under the terms of the Model Clauses attached to very licence. This restriction applies just as much to assignments between sister companies within a single company group as to assignments between unrelated companies. It also applies to the withdrawal of a company from a Licence, which entails the assignment of its rights to the remaining companies.

There is a type of transaction in which two or more companies already on a licence adjust the proportions of their shares of the licence interests/liabilities, and nobody enters or leaves the licence. These transactions are made by adjusting a Joint Operating Agreement (or similar agreement among the companies), and do not qualify for these purposes as Licence Assignments. They are discussed elsewhere.

OVERVIEW OF PROCEDURES

DECC operates a simple email-based procedure, based on a short checklist of relevant information, and our requirements are encapsulated in an Application Form. If we receive a fully-completed Form, we usually won't need any further information (though we do reserve the right to call for additional information if we think it necessary).

This is a marked reduction in regulation over earlier systems, under which applicants had to submit pre-execution drafts of all the relevant legal documentation, including Deeds of Assignment and novations of relevant agreements, all of which had to be examined by DECC lawyers.

We have also suspended our former requirement to be supplied with executed copies of all the documentation after completion. However, we do still require notification of completion, and have added a facility to make this easy (each consent carries a simple notification slip to be completed and returned to us by the assignee(s) as soon as possible after completion).

Before applications are submitted to us, we expect them to have been agreed, at least in principle, by all other parties whose consent will be required; in particular the other parties to the Licence. There is a box on the Form (S8) in which you can give confirmation of this.

When we receive an application we routinely seek advice about it from the Licensing and Consents Unit's Asset Teams, Exploration Team, Decommissioning Unit, DECC's financial advisers and others. We also circulate details of each application to Inland Revenue's Oil Taxation Office (OTO).

POLICY

DECC believes that, on the whole, a good volume of licence assignments is a good thing, to the extent that it means that companies are improving their alignment on each licence. But that is not to say that we regard licences as merely tradable assets, and we expect companies to buy licence interests with a view to exploiting them, not merely to sell them on.

That said, there are a number of issues that can cause concern about any particular assignment. **Technical and financial capacity of the Licensee** DECC will need to be satisfied that the proposed new company is suitable to be on the licence. That means checking its capacity to participate fully in licence operations and to discharge its licence obligations (see also Suitability of licensees).

Decommissioning costs Financial capacity will be an even greater concern if significant decommissioning costs are likely to be incurred by Licensees in the near future. There is a dedicated Decommissioning Unit based in Aberdeen with the task of ensuring that future decommissioning liabilities are covered.

New entrants to the UK DECC will always take a company's track record into account. If the company is new to the UK, we will try to take account of a track record gained overseas. Where the proposed licensee is a subsidiary of a foreign parent, DECC will generally require an undertaking from the parent to support the licensee in its licence operations (see also Suitability of licensees).

Effect on operatorship arrangements DECC will not approve any assignment if it would result in a licence having no approved operator. So when an operator seeks to leave a licence, it will need to ensure that its remaining partners have agreed a replacement operator and that DECC is ready to approve their choice. This is especially important where production operatorship is concerned. Approving an operator can take time, especially a production operator with no previous track record of operating on the UKCS.

Licence alignment This is not usually a concern for DECC, but we might feel the need to look carefully at a case where one company gains a completely dominant position on a Licence, or a case where one company has such a small interest that it is not motivated to participate fully in the exploitation of a Licence and yet is in a position to block it. In general, this is more likely to be a concern where a field or a prospect near to development is affected.

Intragroup assignments DECC has no objection in principle to assignments to a sister company, but if they are made specifically for the purpose of a subsequent disposal of the Licence interests via a corporate sale, then DECC will generally want to know who the buyer is before we approve it. Where the reason for the assignment is tax-related, we recommend discussing it with the Oil Taxation Office first.

Fragmentation of Licence interests In some circumstances, the creation of very small Licence interests may be of questionable advantage to the UKCS. It may, for instance, prejudice the Licence group's attempts to agree on new work by introducing new voices. On the other hand, any such drawbacks may be outweighed by a new Licensee's expertise or experience. As a general rule, we suggest that any Licensee seeking to create small Licence interests (under 5%) should justify the transaction in "Extra information" on the application form.

Infrastructure Again, this is a conceivable rather than a routine issue, but DECC might be concerned if, for instance, it seemed that an infrastructure owner was seeking to enter a licence group to influence tariffing negotiations.

OPOL DECC expects all operators to be members of the Offshore Pollution Liability Association Ltd and to register each off its separate operatorships. Prospective new operators, to be approved as part of a Licence assignment, can satisfy DECC that they are members by including their OPOL numbers at the appropriate place on the form.

PROCEDURES

It's the current holder of the licence interest who requires permission to transfer it. So it is the current licence holder that must make the formal application to DECC, even though in many cases much of the information that DECC needs will have to come from the acquiring company. We have created an Application Form with space for all the information that we need in most cases. We reserve the right to call for additional information in specific cases. Use of the Form is recommended but not obligatory, though of course we will not grant consent unless we have all the information that we need.

Downloading the form The Application Form is available in an MS Word2000 format. As an illustration there is also a sample application form, filled in for a fictional application. You can apply for consent to any number of assignments on the same form - just create extra rows as necessary by copying and pasting.

Completing the form The form must be completed in full, in accordance with the Guidance Note. Please avoid excessive precision in specifying the size of a licence interest (e.g. "23.26716589%"). As important as it may seem to companies, DECC does not generally record such figures beyond two decimal places..

Submitting the form The completed form needs to be submitted to Licensing Administration. Email applications are quickest and best - submit to approvals@decc.gsi.gov.uk. If you prefer you can post or fax the application to: , :

Oil & Gas Licensing Administration (ERDU),
1 Victoria Street,
London,
SW1H 0ET
(Fax: 020 7215 5070)

We strongly advise you not to send applications to named individuals, who may be absent when it arrives. We advise companies seeking to enter a Licence to have ready the information indicated elsewhere so as to reduce delay.

APPROVAL

If DECC is content that the transfer should proceed, we will send the Secretary of State's consent to the applicant, copying it to the assignee. At the same time we will approve the amendment/novation of related agreements other than Operating Agreements, which are dealt with separately (see Open Approval (Operating Agreements)).

The Secretary of State's assignment consent(s) and operator approval(s) will be valid for three months after the predicted Execution/Handover Date(s) inserted in the Application Form. If any completions are delayed longer than that, you will require an extension, which we will generally be able to consider on receipt of a revised Completion Date, and confirmation that the information contained in the original application is still valid.

Use of the consent to execute the assignment is conditional on the assignee's notification to us within two weeks. There is a confirmation slip on each consent email to enable this.

EXECUTION

Any consent granted by the Secretary of State will be made conditional on the Deed of Assignment conforming substantially to a draft approved by the Secretary of State. There are currently two such approved drafts. The first is contained in the PILOT Master Deed, which sets out agreed assignment procedures and forms agreed by PILOT. LOGIC has provided guidance to the use of the Master Deed separately. DECC recommends use of the Master Deed procedures.The alternative is the Approved Model Deed of Assignment. The second approved draft is attached. If you choose to use the Approved Model Deed of Assignment, you may only depart from it in such ways as do not materially alter its effect (for instance, by moving company names to a Schedule). It does not, however, include execution or attestation clauses, which should be added as required. For instance you can disapply the Contracts (Rights of Third Parties) Act 1999 in relation to the Deed, and/or (b) provide for the execution of the Deed in counterpart.

The Approved Model Deed of Assignment leaves it to you to decide whether jurisdiction should lie with the English or Scottish Courts (it is traditional to apply Scottish law to Licences covering Scottish land and waters, and English law to others).

The Approved Model Deed of Assignment is applicable to all licence assignments, whether Offshore or Onshore.

Use of either of the approved drafts is not compulsory; but if you want to use a different draft, you will have to submit a copy in advance, bearing in mind that it will have to be considered by DECC lawyers, and that will considerably increase the processing time.

"NO OBJECTION IN PRINCIPLE"

Sometimes, licensees ask DECC to confirm that we have "no objection in principle" to a proposed transfer, particularly in the case of an Earn-In agreement, in which the assignee's expenditure necessarily comes before the assignment. If DECC receives enough of the information listed in that we would need to consider the actual assignment, we may be able to issue such an opinion. Almost by definition, this will be before all details are available so we won t be able to offer any binding undertaking, and it will not replace the formal consent described above.
If you want such an opinion, make an application as if for the actual assignment, filling in as much of the Application Form as possible, and making clear that you are only seeking a "no objection in principle" response.

In general this option should be avoided unless there's a good reason for it, because it doubles the amount of time that DECC has to devote to each transfer and so causes delay for all.

PROCESSING TIME

The time to process any particular application will depend on such factors as its complexity, the quality of the information initially provided to us, the number of other applications we are processing at the same time, etc. In general, we will aim to process a straightforward case in 10 working days (although we cannot guarantee that response time in any particular case). Production Operatorship and financial checks in particular can take longer – the overall processing time will increase to 25-30 days where (straightforward) financial checks are involved.

PIPELINES

If any proposed assignment would affect either the Holder of a Pipeline Works Authorisation (PWA) or the Operator, User or Owner information for any offshore pipeline, the Holder of the PWA must seek a variation to the relevant Pipeline Works Authorisation (PWA). DECC strongly advises that the variation should be sought as soon as possible, and at least 28 days before the proposed completion of the assignment, so as not to delay it. The contact for such an approach is Christopher Duguid (email: Chris.Duguid@decc.gsi.gov.uk; tel: 01224 254056).

LICENCE RELINQUISHMENTS

There are two ways in which a licensee can give up acreage. He can give up (or "surrender") part of the Licensed Area while the licence continues over the remainder, or he can give up (or "determine") the entire licence. The licensee can do either one at any time, subject to a few conditions.

To surrender acreage or determine a licence, complete the licence determination form and email it to licence.relinquishments@decc.gsi.gov.uk. It can only be used for one licence at a time.

RESTRICTIONS

There are two restrictions to the licensee's right to surrender or determine:
"Non-Standard" surrenders are surrenders of irregular shapes defined by very short lines, or which leave a very small licensed area. The exact definition is in the Clause headed "Areas surrendered" on each licence (see for example the 2004 Model Clauses Regulations). Non-Standard determinations require DECC assent.

A licensee may not make a surrender or determination if it would prevent fulfilment of a licence obligation. For example, where a Licence carries a Work Programme with a Firm Well Commitment, the Licensee cannot determine the licence without drilling the well (nor surrender acreage if it includes a location specified in the Commitment as the place where the well is to be drilled).

NOTICE PERIODS

Recent Seaward Production Licences (P1155 and later) require one month's notice to DECC before determination/surrender. This can be achieved by submitting the form in good time and specifying an effective date at least one month away.
Earlier Seaward Production Licences specify six months' notice. In practice, DECC will often accept just one month's notice, but we reserve the right to insist on the full six months especially where there is a need to issue directions to plug and seal wells. Note that this may affect the licensee's liability for rentals at the next licence anniversary. Therefore DECC strongly recommends that licensees should ensure there are no producing or suspended wells on any acreage before they seek to surrender/relinquish it.
Companies losing their licence involvement Occasionally, a surrender may leave a company with no beneficial interest under the Licence. Nevertheless, the surrender does not have the effect of removing that company from the licence; it will remain a party to the licence unless and until it withdraws by assigning its rights under the licence to the remaining companies. Usually the assignment would be made effective on the same date as the surrender, though it does not need to be. Note that all assignments need the Secretary of State's prior permission. Application can be made simply by entering the name of the departing company at Q9 of the form.

RELINQUISHMENT REPORTS

For Seaward licences from P1064 upwards, DECC requires a Relinquishment Report at the time of determination. This is done using powers conferred by the Model Clauses that were invoked in a paragraph in the covering letter that accompanied each new licence issued in the 21st and later Rounds. It has also been agreed within PILOT that DECC would request Relinquishment reports for older Licences where a whole licence relinquishment or relinquishment of non-contiguous blocks in multiblock licences are submitted.
Such reports should comply with the attached guidelines and be submitted within three months of the request. All queries about these reports should be to addressed to Jen Brzozowska (tel: 020 7215 5138).

DATA RETENTION OBLIGATIONS AND THE NHDA

DECC takes seriously the obligation, borne jointly and severally by all licensees in the licence group at the time of determination, to hold licence data in perpetuity. In future DECC will take steps to scrutinise **long** term data management strategies at licence determination and would remind all licensees that the only way of gaining relief from this obligation is to place licence data in the National Hydrocarbons Data Archive (NHDA), the option strongly preferred by DECC. For more information on the NHDA please contact Phil Harrison (phil.harrison@decc.gsi.gov.uk) at DECC, or Colin Graham (ccg@bgs.ac.uk) at BGS or go to the NHDA website (www.bgs.ac.uk/nhda/home.html).

FILLING THE FORM IN

We will assume that the form has been submitted in accordance with the wishes of the entire Licence group under the terms of the Joint Operating Agreement or similar agreement. DECC cannot accept responsibility for ensuring that the terms of a JOA have been complied with. But we would like to know if any dissenting party has been outvoted (see Q8).
We encourage the use of email, but it is not compulsory. If you want to carry out the process by post, you can send the completed form (entering your postal address for our reply at Box 4) to:

Licensing Exploration and Developments (Licence determinations)
Department of Trade & Industry
1 Victoria Street
London
SW1H 0ET.

PART 1: CONTACT DETAILS

Include details of the person we should approach for further information, and to whom we will reply. If you want us to reply on paper, enter the postal address at Box 4.

PART 2: NATURE OF DETERMINATION/SURRENDER

Enter the subject Licence and the Block(s). Attach (or enclose) a map showing the acreage before the determination/surrender, indicating the position and status of any approved fields and wells within the licensed area.
For a surrender, indicate clearly which acreage is to be retained and which surrendered.
At 6), indicate whether you are determining the whole licence: if you are, you can skip Part 3 and go straight to Part 4.

PART 3: AREA TO BE SURRENDERED

There's no need to complete this part if you are determining a whole licence.
Coordinates Enter the grid coordinates that define the area to be surrendered (not the area to be retained). For offshore Licences use ED50 datum, and for onshore Licences use the National

Grid datum (these are the systems used to define the coordinates in the Licence itself). Show the location within the currently-licensed area of any wells or fields.
Subareas Specify any subarea that lies wholly within the area to be surrendered, and so will disappear as a result of this surrender.
Departing companies Enter the names of any companies left with no beneficial interest in the licence who seek the Secretary of State's approval of an assignment to withdraw from the licence.

PART 4: QUESTIONS

Licence group agreement As already noted DECC cannot take responsibility for ensuring that an application is made in accordance with the terms of whatever agreements exist between different companies. We would nevertheless like to know if any party to the Licence objects to the determination/surrender, even if it is not able to block it. In such cases enter the name of the dissenting party here.

Work Programme Note any element of the Initial Term Work Programme that remains to be completed. Obviously this should only apply to a Licence in its Initial Term.
Wells List all wells on acreage that will become unlicensed, together with the status of each one (producing, suspended, abandoned, etc.).

Fallow acreage Specify any fallow acreage to be surrendered/determined.
Effective date Enter the effective date of the surrender/determination, bearing in mind the strictures on Notice periods above.

CHANGE OF CONTROL OF LICENSEE

The Model Clauses do not impose any requirement for the Secretary of State's approval of a change of control of a Licensee (e.g. at a corporate takeover), but they do specify it as grounds for revocation (if the Licensee has failed to comply with an instruction from DECC to make a further change of control).

This can result in a request (for instance, by a bank that is financing the takeover) for comfort that the Secretary of State will not exercise that power. DECC is generally willing to accept such requests, but they are not a part of DECC's statutory responsibilities and we cannot undertake to accord them the same priority as those jobs that are. Nor will we be able to offer any cast-iron promises - any comfort we give will be based on the information available at the time, and limited accordingly.

Details of the change of control should be sent by email to Approvals@decc.gsi.gov.uk The following information must be included in this email:

- The new corporate parent's name, place of incorporation and company registration number
- Post-change of control pro-forma balance sheet for the licensee and a consolidated post-change of control pro-forma balance sheet for the new corporate parent
- A list from the new corporate parent of its prospective subsidiary's UKCS licence holdings and commitments (especially those arising from Work Programmes, from the Fallow Initiative or the Stewardship Process) and a statement that it will support the licensee in meeting these commitments.

Additionally, DECC may seek further information including, but not limited to, evidence of adequate ongoing funding arrangements and assurances from the new corporate parent of continuing technical and financial support for its subsidiary

LICENCE EXTENSIONS

FIRST-ROUND LICENCES; PRODUCTION-LINKED EXTENSIONS IN 2010

The remaining First-Round Licences, as well as the segregation licences P291, P292 and P323, are set to expire in 2010. All cover at least one currently-producing field; so they will have to be extended if production is not to be terminated early. The number of licences, and especially the number of fields, mean that this will be a considerable task.

This is a new task for everyone, and DECC's plans have been evolving as we consult with the licensees affected and as we start to consider individual cases. The intended approach is described in more detail in the following series of documents, which are based on letters sent to licensees as part of the consultation process:

1. Letter dated 27 November 2007
2. Letter dated 15 May 2008
3. Letter dated 11 July 2008
4. Letter dated 20 April 2009

For additional info, please contact

Mike Hawkins
Tel: 0300 068 6038
Fax: 0300 068 5003
Email: mike.hawkins@decc.gsi.gov.uk

SUITABILITY OF LICENSEES

DECC works to maximise the exploitation of the nation's petroleum resources by Licensees. We believe that we can best achieve this with a mix of companies, from the multinational super-giants to small niche players. But Production Licences confer exclusive rights, so we must be satisfied that no Licensee will block that exploitation because of a lack of technical or financial capacity. In addition, the Government has essential requirements, such as the establishment of a tax base.

NEW ENTRANTS

Companies who wish to acquire or join a licence and who are new to the UK will have to provide the financial information described elsewhere, plus the following additional information:< acceptable. be to likely is what us with explore stage early an at them discuss welcome are etc plans, financial models, business new radically present planning companies and requirements, its explain happy DECC but themselves, ?introduce? visit entrants prospective for requirement no There procedure. pre-registration have we so merits, own on case each looks>

FINANCIAL CAPACITY OF LICENSEES

The financial capacity of companies on the UKCS is becoming more of an issue for BERR as large companies contract to core areas, and are replaced elsewhere by smaller companies - sometimes very small companies.

This is an evolving policy area, but at all times our considerations will be informed by BERR's objective (Obj 4) to ensure the continuity and security of energy supply at affordable prices through competitive markets, whilst minimising environmental impacts and delivering social objectives.

It is an integral part of our work towards this objective to promote worthwhile activity (seismic, drilling and development). It is also essential that we protect the taxpayer from uncovered liabilities.

In this light, a company's financial capacity can be relevant to our work in several ways:

- where BERR expects or desires work to be carried out on a licence, a company's presence may stop that work if it can't afford to pay its share of the bills in good time; and
- in an extreme case, a company could become insolvent and leave liabilities and obligations unpaid.

BERR will not award a licence, nor consent to an assignment of a licence, to a company that cannot demonstrate the financial capacity to meet its expected commitments, liabilities and obligations; or to one that is insolvent or appears to be in danger of becoming so.

Need for financial capacity

Financial capacity becomes especially relevant where there is a clear programme of new work that needs to be funded, such as exploration drilling. In some cases, the work may constitute a commitment to the Secretary of State (e.g. an Initial Term Work Programme, or work designed to end a licence's fallow status). Such work is very important to the achievement of BERR's objectives, and we will want to be satisfied that any new company on a licence can provide its share of the necessary funding in good time, so as not to delay or prevent the work.

In any particular case there may not be any high-priority work of this sort, in which case it's much less likely that the company need demonstrate anything more than its viability.

All other things being equal, BERR would not seek to impose commercial choices on anybody. For example, if a company wanted to join two licences and its capacity was equal to one or the other but not both, we would hope to be able to let the company make up its own mind which licence to join.
BERR's Exploration Unit will be able to discuss Initial Term Work Programmes and Fallow Acreage. The relevant Field Team will be able to discuss its expectation of new work on existing fields.

Level of financial capacity
The capacity that must be demonstrated is the ability to meet in timely fashion the actual costs that may reasonably be expected to arise.

Decommissioning
The obligation to pay decommissioning costs is a very important issue, but BERR handles it separately and it is not part of any of the procedures described here.

We expect the company to provide reasonable and realistic estimates of those costs, including contingencies (for example, including the cost of a sidetrack when drilling a well). Where an estimate looks unrealistically low, we may want to see evidence that it can be achieved (for example, a signed agreement with a drilling company).

Ultimately, we will use our own estimates and assumptions if we are unconvinced by those provided by the company.

Acceptable financial arrangements
It's understandable that companies want to know which financial arrangements will be acceptable to BERR. But BERR prefers to be flexible and open to ideas than to be prescriptive. Therefore we do not propose to dictate a range of acceptable options and close the door to any others, and can only give general guidance about the approach we will take.

In general, the capacity that we need to see demonstrated is the ability to continue in business for the foreseeable future, and to fund the anticipated work. The way in which a company can demonstrate this will vary from one case to the next, depending especially on the company's size:

- Many oil companies are so big that their net worth alone is enough to assure us that they will be able to raise funding where necessary, or can even fund the work from their own internal resources. So BERR will generally be satisfied by evidence that the company's net worth is greater than the estimated cost by a significant margin, and will not need to consider specific funding arrangements.
- A company whose net worth is not significantly larger than the estimated cost of its proposed commitments will have to prove its capacity by reference to specific funding arrangements. In such a case, BERR will require that the funding be already in place (e.g. by means of an existing loan from a bank). BERR may exceptionally consider firm commitments of funding if they come from a very reliable source, like a recognised bank, that is genuinely independent of the company (commitments from directors to answer cash calls from their own company are not acceptable). The prospect of a future share issue is not likely to be acceptable, unless a recognised financial institution has bindingly underwritten (in the British sense, i.e. guaranteed) it.

Naturally, when it comes to processing times, radically new and unfamiliar arrangements will detain us longer than simple and familiar ones.

Documentation
The evidence that we will need to see depends on the case, but usually all we need is: audited annual accounts plus five-year balance sheet, profit and loss and cashflow forecasts. If these are provided upfront, then we will be able to process a case that much faster than if we have to chase them.

Where financial capacity is not currently available to the licensee but is committed from some third party such as a bank, we will want to see a signed copy of the agreement effecting that commitment. Other parts of a company's case may also need to be supported by documentation (for example, a drilling contract if the cost appears to be very low).

Parent companies

BERR requires a Parent Company Guarantee whenever there is a Parent with significant financial capacity. The only exception would be the case where the parent has no significant assets of its own, so that a Parent Company Guarantee would be redundant. BERR has produced two standard forms of words, which should be printed under the company letterhead and signed on the company's behalf.

TECHNICAL EXPERTISE

Non-operators don't need to demonstrate as high a level of technical expertise, but we do expect the Operating Committee to be able to exercise responsible oversight. That means that we wouldn't allow a significant vote to be exercised by a company without the technical expertise.

NEW ENTRANTS

Companies who wish to acquire or join a licence and who are new to the UK will have to provide the financial information described elsewhere, plus the following additional information:

- Full name, number and address as on the Certificate of Incorporation.
- Place of incorporation and/or principal place of business.
- Location from which activities related to the licence will be managed/controlled.

RESIDENCE REQUIREMENTS

There are different levels of residence requirement, depending on what a company proposes to do.

To be a **Licensee** a company must have a place of business within the UK. That means either (a) a staffed presence in the UK, (b) registration of a UK company at Companies House, or (c) registration of a UK branch of a foreign company at Companies House. This requirement exists both for any company applying for a new licence and for any company seeking to join an existing licence by assignment. It applies to all licences and to all companies, whether operator or not. To be a party to a Licence that covers a **producing field**, a company must either (a) be registered at Companies House as a UK company, or (b) carry on its business through a fixed place of business in the UK (which normally requires a staffed presence). This is a tax requirement. For more information on the meaning of 'fixed place', refer to section 148 Finance Act 2003. Article 5 of the OECD Guidelines also contains more information on the meaning of 'fixed place'.

To be an **operator** there may be additional practical requirements. DECC will generally consider proximity and ease of communications as factors in an operator's ability to manage operations properly. {For example, DECC may consider that a particular field in the Southern North Sea might be operated equally satisfactorily from either side of the North Sea, but not from the other end either of Britain or of Europe.} Such issues will be considered on a case-by-case basis.

PARTNERSHIPS

Partnerships of various types have been common in the UK for many years. Limited Liability Partnerships (LLPs), however, are new to the UK having been introduced by the Limited Liability Partnership Act 2000.

DECC has no objection in principle to the appearance of partnerships on Petroleum Act Licences. At present, though, there are none, and before allowing a partnership of any sort to join a licence, DECC would want to be satisfied about several possible concerns:

- The Secretary of State must be assured that decommissioning costs remain satisfactorily covered by the decommissioning provisions of Part IV of the Petroleum Act 1998;

- With a 1907 partnership, it is not clear that the Secretary of State would have any control over the withdrawal of the General Partner from the partnership and/or from the UK;
- 1907 partnerships are not subject to the same controls as companies, in that they are less secure in the assets they purportedly hold;
- The Secretary of State's powers of revocation, implemented in the Model Clauses, can be triggered by a change of control of a company that is party to a licence, but they would not readily apply to a partnership where the idea of a change of control is less well defined.

DECC would also wish to discuss with HMRC the tax position of partnerships. Further information can be found on HMRC's website at www.hmrc.gov.uk.

Of these concerns, DECC is preparing to address the decommissioning position of LLPs in forthcoming legislation. We are always ready to consider suggestions of ways to address the other concerns.

To discuss LLPs in the context of decommissioning provisions, contact Keith Mayo. To discuss them in the context of adherence to a licence contact Mike Hawkins. For the taxation angle, go to http://www.hmrc.gov.uk/oto/new_entrants.htm.
All other queries about the suitability of licensees should be addressed to

Tracy Selby   Tel: 020 7215 5096   Email: tracy.selby@decc.gsi.gov.uk
Fax: 020 7215 5070
DECC Licensing Administration (Energy Development Unit)

JOINT OPERATING AGREEMENTS

When several companies are party to a Licence, they usually make an agreement among themselves governing future operations. Such an agreement is commonly called a Joint Operating Agreement (JOA). Creating or amending a JOA commonly entails the apportionment of at least some of the rights granted by a Petroleum Act licence. As such, it requires the consent of the Secretary of State(see, for example, Model Clause 41(5) in the most recent seaward Production Licences). Some Operating Agreements are created as the result of the unitisation of a field across several different Licences - they are usually called Unit Operating Agreements.

DECC issued the Open Permission (Operating Agreements), which grants prior approval to most instances of the creation, amendment or novation of Operating Agreements. (In brief the conditions and exclusions relate to Pre-Emption clauses, registration with OPOL, the creation of controlling interests and the assignment of rights to parties outside the Licence.)

- In this context, an Open Permission is a type of approval that the Secretary of State issues once and for all, covering a whole class of regulated acts. It is not issued to any particular person or company, and so can be relied upon by anyone at any time If a company is satisfied that the Open Permission describes the act that it is proposing, complying with any conditions and restrictions on its use, then it can go ahead and perform the act under the Open Permission, and doesn't need any further individual permission. Nor can the company be given a copy of the Open Permission in its own name - an individual person or company cannot apply for an Open Permission.
- It is the responsibility of any person proposing to use an Open Permission to satisfy him- or herself of all its provisions, and that they are all complied with.
- Where an act is already permitted under the terms of an Open Permission, the Secretary of State will not further approve it by an additional individual approval. On the other hand,

where an act is excluded from the Open Permission by its conditions or restrictions, the Secretary of State is not prevented from granting individual approval in response to an individual application.

Anyone wishing to create, amend or novate an Operating Agreement should first examine the text of the Open Permission (Operating Agreements) to decide whether the act has already been granted prior approval. If so, no further permission from the Secretary of State is needed, and in the case of this Open Permission there is no need to notify DECC of intention to use it. Note, however, that there is a requirement to provide certain information to DECC about the new Operating Agreement within two weeks after execution. Such notification may be made by email to approvals@decc.gsi.gov.uk, or by post to Licensing & Consents Unit, Department of Trade & Industry, 1 Victoria Street, London SW1H 0ET.

If you consider that your proposed creation/novation/amendment of an Operating Agreement is excluded from the cover of the Open Permission (Operating Agreements), you may still apply for individual approval. Exclusion of an act from the most relevant Open Permission is not necessarily an indication that the Secretary of State is opposed in principle to the act and will never be prepared to approve it. In some cases (such as the exclusion of Operating Agreements that non-Licensees are party to) it simply reflects DECC's need for individual scrutiny in certain circumstances. However, other exclusions clearly reflect DECC policy - this applies to the requirement for compliance with PILOT/PPWG on Pre-Emption. Even there the Secretary of State is not prevented from issuing an individual approval, but in general any company seeking it should expect to have to make a special case for an exception to be made.

The Open Permission only covers the apportionment of rights granted by the Licence and relating to petroleum won and saved, and any proceeds of its sale. Any particular agreement may be subject to other regulatory provisions (including other controls imposed by the Model Clauses), and if so it remains the responsibility of the licensee to comply with those provisions. In particular, nothing in this Approval has any effect on controls on licence assignments, operator approvals or the Petroleum Act's decommissioning provisions.
Any queries should be addressed to:

Tracy Selby Tel: 020 7215 5069 Email: tracy.selby@decc.gsi.gov.uk
Fax: 020 7215 5070

CHARGES ON LICENCES

It is common practice for banks lending money to companies to demand a charge on the company's assets, as a form of collateral. Creation of a charge on a Petroleum Act Licence is controlled under the Model Clauses attached to each Licence (under "Restrictions on assignment, etc").

THE OPEN PERMISSION (CREATION OF SECURITY RIGHTS OVER LICENCES)

Any Licensee wishing to create such a charge should first consider the terms of the Open Permission (Creation of Security Rights over Licences), looking carefully at the Conditions of Use. Where the Open Permission has already granted consent to the creation of the Charge, the Licensee can go ahead and do it without seeking any further individual approval from DECC. In fact, in such cases DECC will not grant an individual approval, even if asked.

The Open Permission carries as a condition of use an obligation to notify DECC of certain details of the charge within 10 days of its creation (the size of the loan secured thereby, the Licences affected, and the identity of the chargee). Notification should be made by email to approvals@decc.gsi.gov.uk or to our postal address. There is no form to fill in, nor any prescribed format.

In the event of a subsequent default on a loan by the borrower, the lender may w sh to seek enforcement of the charge so as to get a Licence interest transferred to itself (possibly after appointing a receiver). This would constitute a Licence assignment, which is controlled in its own right under the Model Clauses. If faced with a request for consent to such an assignment, DECC will take into account all relevant factors, one of which will be the reasonable expectations of the lender. However, the Secretary of State must exercise his discretion in each specific case, which cannot be fettered by earlier promises to take, or not to take, any particular course of action; and DECC will not make any such promises.

The Open Permission covers charges made to trustees on behalf of other financial institutions, and it also covers the crystallisation of a floating charge into a fixed charge.

INDIVIDUAL APPROVALS

Exclusion of a charge from the Open Permission should not necessarily be interpreted as a final refusal. It may be that DECC will be content to grant an individual approval after careful scrutiny. We will consider requests for individual approval on receipt of a written application (to approvals@decc.gsi.gov.uk or to our postal address) that includes: (a) the reason why the charge is excluded from the Open Permission; and (b) all the information called for in the Open Permission's notification requirement (of course, in any particular case we reserve the right to call for such other information as we see fit).
Any queries should be addressed to:

Mike Hawkins Tel: 020 7215 5098 Email: michael.hawkins@decc.gsi.gov.uk

PROGRESSING PARTNERSHIP - STREAMLINED TRANSFER AND PRE-EMPTION ARANGEMENTS "MASTER DEED"

THE UKOOA/PPWG 'MASTER DEED'

The "Master Deed" was developed by UKOOA's Progressing Partnership Working Group (PPWG), DECC, and a number of other interested organisations. It will greatly expedite the transfer of offshore licence interests and other agreements relating to associated assets and infrastructure; and it introduces a standard pre-emption regime to give confidence to incoming companies. The offshore oil industry has given the Master Deed broad support, with 178 companies,holding 99% of licence interests, having signed up already.

New Transfer Arrangements

Under former practice, a deal could be significantly delayed by the need to get a range of signatures applied to many documents, even when all parties are content with it. Under the Master Deed, Licensees have appointed an Administrator to act as their attorney for the execution of proforma documents. The Administrator is a specially-created subsidiary of UKOOA called 'UKCS Administrator Limited'. The service will actually be provided by LOGIC (the 'Service Provider') on behalf of the Administrator under a separate 'Services Agreement'. The disposing company will pay a small fee for the service (currently £350 for up to 5 transfers).

Use of the New Transfer Arrangements is voluntary for the party disposing of its interest. If it does not wish to use them, it is free to stay with the traditional arrangements. The New Transfer Arrangements do not affect any existing rights of objection to an assignment or provisions for the granting or withholding of consents.

The New Transfer Arrangements represent a clear improvement on current practice. This is a big step forward in terms of clarity and efficiency, encouraging new entrants and generally making for a more efficient commercial environment.

New Pre-emption Arrangements

A number of new entrants have expressed concerns to DECC about the risk of being pre-empted even after extensive (and expensive) negotiation to conclude a deal. The standard new arrangements replace the range of provisions that existed previously (though they do not take effect where there had been none before), giving buyers confidence and clarity.

When informed of a proposed Licence Assignment, companies on a Licence will have an initial seven-day period in which to waive or reserve their rights to pre-emption; and then, if they have reserved their rights, a 30-day period in which to decide whether or not actually to pre-empt.

Any queries should be addressed to:
The LOGIC Master Deed dedicated website at: www.masterdeed.com
Or the dedicated contact at LOGIC for enquiries on the Master Deed is:
Pia Mandler
E-Business Adviser
Tel: 01224 853452
Fax: 01224 853429

A number of licence-related activities require individual approval, often (but not always) from DTI. In considering applications for such approval, we routinely seek advice from other Government Departments and statutory nature conservation agencies such as the Joint Nature Conservation Committee. These other bodies have administrative requirements of their own. For instance, they may have defined minimum processing times; they may wish to warn applicants of other regulatory controls; or they may have concerns about certain kinds of activity at certain times of the year. To the extent that we are aware of such requirements we have set them out in this document, but it does not purport to be an exhaustive list of all such issues. Against each requirement we have indicated the originating organisation(s)[1], and any queries are best addressed to them.

It is the responsibility of anyone planning oil and gas activity on the UKCS to familiarise themselves with and comply with all the regulatory requirements that relate to it, and we strongly advise early consultation with all interested organisations. Failure to do so may result in the activity being delayed, or even prevented altogether.

Section 1 – UKCS-wide issues

The notes in this Section apply to all acreage on the United Kingdom Continental Shelf.

[1] The acronyms used in this Note indicate authorship: "DTI" means the Department of Trade & Industry's Oil & Gas Environmental & Decommissioning Branch, based in Aberdeen; "JNCC" is the Joint Nature Conservation Committee; "SEERAD" is the Scottish Executive Environment and Rural Affairs Department; "MoD" is the Ministry of Defence; "DEFRA" is the Department for Environment, Food and Rural Affairs; and "DT" is the Department of Transport.

A – EU ENVIRONMENTAL ASSESSMENT, HABITATS AND BIRDS DIRECTIVES

A1 In 1999, the Government applied the EU Environmental Assessment Directive to certain categories of offshore oil and gas activities, by means of the **Offshore Petroleum Production and Pipelines (Assessment of Environmental Effects) Regulations 1999 (SI 1999/360)**. The Regulations require DTI to make an assessment of the environmental impact before deciding whether to authorise various offshore activities, including the drilling of wells, the installation of pipelines and most categories of field development. If a significant environmental impact is likely a full Environmental Impact assessment must be carried out, including the submission of an Environmental Statement. Guidance is available on the Oil and Gas website at www.og.dti.gov.uk. [DTI]

A2 In 2001, the Government applied the EU Habitats and Birds Directives to all oil and gas activities on the UKCS by means of the **Offshore Petroleum Activities (Conservation of Habitats) Regulations 2001 (SI 2001/1754)**. The Regulations make provision for the protection of a range of specific habitats and species that are considered to be important in the European context. Under the Regulations, DTI is required to take account of the potential impact of offshore oil and gas activities on those habitats and species, which may be protected by “relevant sites” or given more general protection in UKCS waters. DTI takes a precautionary approach when asked to approve activities that could have a significant effect on such habitats and species or on areas that are or may become candidate or designated "relevant sites". Further guidance is available on the Oil and Gas website at www.og.dti.gov.uk. [DTI]

A3 Under the 2001 Regulations, some survey consents, well consents, pipeline and development consents, must be supported by an environmental case (a stand-alone environmental narrative or a section in a formal Environmental Statement) to demonstrate that the proposed operations are unlikely to have a significant adverse effect on, important habitats or species, or the conservation objectives of any potential or existing "relevant site".

A4 The Regulations do not seek to prohibit offshore activities; just to ensure that they are undertaken in an environmentally-responsible way. Nevertheless, it is possible that DTI's consultees will recommend that certain activities should not be approved (e.g. siting a drilling rig or permanent structure at a "relevant site"), or that the approval should be subject to certain conditions (e.g. that all drilling muds must be taken ashore for disposal) or that an Appropriate Assessment might be required. We advise applicants to contact DTI as early as possible, so that we can put them in touch with the consultees to discuss potential environmental sensitivities. [DTI/JNCC/DEFRA/SEERAD]

B - SEISMIC SURVEYS, SHALLOW BOREHOLES AND DRILLING OPERATIONS

B1 You may not prospect or carry out geological surveys, or drill for the purpose of obtaining geological information, except with prior consent granted under the Offshore Petroleum Activities (Conservation of Habitats) Regulations 2001 (SI 2001/1754). Such consent is applied for using a PON14A form, and in some cases it will be necessary to submit an environmental assessment to support the application. For seismic surveys and high-resolution seismic site surveys an additional “survey close-out form” needs to be completed at the end of the survey. Guidance is available on the Oil and Gas website at www.og.dti.gov.uk.

B2 Any seismic survey consent will require that the survey be conducted in accordance with the most recently published guidelines for minimising acoustic disturbance to marine mammals. The Joint Nature Conservation Committee (JNCC) has published guidelines that can be found at www.jncc.gov.uk. Further advice can be obtained directly from JNCC. [JNCC].

B3 You may not drill a well without considering the Offshore Petroleum Production and Pipelines (Assessment of Environmental Effects) Regulations 1999. This consideration would be either submission of a PON15B to obtain a direction that EIA need not be carried out, or by submitting an Environmental Statement. Guidance is available from the Oil and Gas website at www.og.dti.gov.uk.

B4 Some blocks and part-blocks are particularly environmentally sensitive at certain times of year – for instance, because of seabird vulnerability, cetacean abundance or fish spawning. A list summarising the seasonal sensitivities that have been notified to DTI is attached at **Section 2**. We also advise applicants to consult the Seabird Vulnerability and Cetacean Abundance Maps on UK-DMAP (BODC Bidston), and the Fisheries Sensitivities Maps on the UKOOA website (www.ukooa.co.uk) at an early stage; and to seek advice directly from JNCC, DEFRA and SEERAD if in any doubt. [JNCC/DEFRA/SEERAD]

B5 As part of the application for consent to undertake a geological survey, or to drill a borehole or well, the applicant must confirm which organisations have been consulted. DTI may require evidence both of the consultations and the outcome. For example, DTI may require information relating to prior consultation with:

- the Department for Environment, Food and Rural Affairs (for operations to be carried out in English or Welsh waters);
- the Scottish Executive Environment and Rural Affairs Department (for operations to be carried out in Scottish waters);
- the Environment and Heritage Service (for operations in Northern Irish waters);
- the Joint Nature Conservation Committee, or coastal conservation bodies such as English Nature and Scottish Natural Heritage;
- any organisation which the fisheries liaison officer consults in accordance with Clause F1 to the Licence;
- those local authorities with responsibility for the coastline adjacent to the location of the proposed activity.

We strongly advise applicants to undertake prior consultation with all organisations that might have an interest in the proposed activity, and to allow at least 30 days for those prior consultations. [JNCC]. Further guidance can be obtained from DTI.

B6 DTI will aim to process applications for consents well environmental approvals within 28 days, or 90 days in cases where a full Environmental Statement is needed. Any applicant needing a faster turnaround time should discuss with DTI and relevant consultees as early as possible. [DTI]

CHEMICALS, MUDS, CUTTINGS, ETC

B7 Under the **Offshore Chemicals Regulations 2002 (SI 2002/1355) all use and discharge** of offshore chemicals (including drilling fluids) require a permit. The licensee must therefore submit an application for such a permit, which will provide details of the quantities of all chemicals to be used and discharged during the course of offshore activities, and to provide permit returns confirming the quantities used and discharged. DTI may include conditions in the chemical permit restricting the use and/or discharge of particular chemicals. DTI's consultees may recommend special conditions (e.g. that all spent or unused muds and cuttings must be transferred ashore for disposal). Licensees should therefore contact DTI as early as possible, to discuss the chemical permitting requirements. [DTI/JNCC]

C - OIL SPILLS

C1 The **Merchant Shipping (Oil Pollution, Preparedness, Response and Co-operation Convention) Regulations 1998 (SI 1998/1056)** require there to be in place an approved oil spill contingency plan before any drilling or development activity can begin. Such a plan, or associated Environmental Statement, must contain detailed reference to the measures being taken to minimise risk of spillage during operations. Any oil spill contingency plan or Environmental Statement must include an assessment of the cumulative oil spill risk. DTI will consider such an assessment in determining whether to grant approval of field development [JNCC].

F - FISHERIES AND OTHER USERS OF THE SEA

Note that **Clause F1** on the Licence requires the appointment of a Fisheries Liaison Officer, and **Clause F2** requires the removal of debris resulting from activities carried out under the Licence. Licensees are advised to consult DEFRA, SEERAD and UKOOA about the very important question of relations with the fishing industry. UKOOA has published Guidelines for Fisheries Liaison and administers the UKOOA Fisherman's Compensation Fund. [SEERAD/DEFRA]

F5 There are a number of important shipping routes in the UKCS. The need to safeguard navigation may restrict oil and gas activity in or near these routes. Licensees are advised to consult DTLR before undertaking any activity that could interfere with safe navigation, allowing at least 90 days for this prior consultation as it could result in a requirement for a shipping intensity survey. Following completion of the consultation, licensees should submit the resulting assessment to DTI at least 30 days before submitting the request for approval of the proposed activity. On the basis of the assessment results, DTI may refuse consent, impose extra conditions on any consent, or require the activity to be relocated. [DT]

UKCS OFFSHORE LICENSING

The licensing system in the UK Continental Shelf (UKCS) has been active for over 40 years. The area of the UKCS has been defined over the years under the Continental Shelf Act, 1964. The Petroleum Act, 1998 states that all rights to UK petroleum sources belong to the Crown, however BERR (formerly DTI) have permission to grant licences to 'search and bore for and get' petroleum.

Licences are granted in the form of a deed. In legal terms there is only one licensee, however this may be represented by several companies who share the benefits and liabilities from the operations conducted under the licence. Licences carry a rental (or annual fee) which are due on the anniversary of the licence award and are in place to encourage companies only to hold onto acreage which they will actually exploit.

The terms or phases of a licence tend to represent the stages of **exploration**, **appraisal development** and **production**. 'Multiblock licences' refer to offshore blocks which are geographically scattered as opposed to adjacent. However, BERR have decided to cease issue of these. Mandatory relinquishments at the end of the Initial Term create part blocks, the open parts of which are available for re-licensing. For commercial and operational reasons the Licensees may have defined sub-areas (not related to the Licensing process) which may create complications where further partial relinquishments are requested.

There are two broad categories of licence: **Exploration** and **Production**.

- **Exploration** licences are sought by companies who wish to explore large areas of the seabed for seismic survey opportunities. Licences are non-exclusive and valid for three years (extendable for a further three years) and enable access for surveying and shallow drilling over areas which are not currently covered by a Production licence. (Although, with permission, surveys can extend into these licensed areas).

- **Production** Licences are required by anyone who wishes to exploit UKCS oil and gas resources and are categorised into: Traditional, Promote and Frontier licences. Production licences span the entire process from exploration to decommissioning. These licences give exclusive rights to the licensee. Licensees must supply regular updates to BERR and separate consents are required for significant activity and developments.

LICENSING ROUNDS: PREPARATION

Offshore licences were first granted in 1964 and BERR (formerly DTI) currently aim to hold one offshore licensing round per year. The 25th Round, awards were announced in Q4 2007 and the information regarding licences awarded in this round can be accessed from BERR here.

All areas of the UKCS that have undergone a Strategic Environmental Assessment (DEAL) are offered up for licence every year, including all blocks recently relinquished. Ahead of each licensing round, BERR conducts a review of fallow licences with a view to completing relinquishments and including these areas within the forthcoming round.

LICENSING ROUNDS: APPLICATIONS

Round information is published annually in the EU Official Journal and on the BERR website (click here). Applications must be received within 90 days after publishing and should include information about the company's: background; technical capacity; geological case; finances and environmental competence.

Whilst the vast majority of seaward production and exploration licences are awarded in rounds, BERR are willing to accept out of round licence applications in extenuating circumstances. Further information can be found here on the BERR website.

Click here to find out more about **how to apply** for a production or exploration licence from BERR.

LICENSING ROUNDS: ASSESSMENT CRITERIA

BERR ask the following questions in their review of Traditional and Frontier licence applications:

- Are financial requirements of the project satisfied by the operator and/or its partners?
- Is there evidence to suggest that environmental policies on paper are achievable and realistic?
- Is the operator technically competent? For all applications (including those for Promote Licences) a mark scheme is used which analyses the extent of geological evaluation of the block and operators are invited to give a technical presentation encompassing this information together with their aims

LICENSING ROUNDS: AWARDS

BERR make a recommendation to the Minister on which licences to award which, if accepted, are announced in a statement to Parliament, in letters to applicants and via a press release.

LICENCE ASSIGNMENTS

In cases where a company wishes to divest their licensed asset to another, they must request permission from the Secretary of State and the successful transfer is called a Licence

Assignment. The majority of transfers on the UKCS are conducted under MasterDeed. Click here to visit the standard industry agreement for UKCS licence transactions.

Companies on a licence share their interests and liabilities through a Joint Operating Agreement (JOA

IMPORTANT STATISTICAL INFORMATION

DRILLING ACTIVITY

(A) Offshore exploration drilling (1) : exploration wells started in each geographical area

	1998	1999	2000	2001	2002	2003	2004	2005	2006	2007	2008	Q1 - 2009
Southern N Sea	12	3	3	7(2)	5(2)	8(1)	8	7(1)	7	10	5	1
Central N Sea (4)	16(1)	11(1)	12(3)	8	7	11(1)	14(1)	25(6)	14(1)	18(2)	22(2)	1
Northern N Sea	9(2)	2(1)	6(1)	5(1)	1	4	4(1)	6	6	4	14(1)	1
West of England/ Wales	2	-	-	-	-	1	-	3(1)	-	-	-	-
West of Shetland(3)	6	2	6	3	3	2	3(1)	-	2	2	3	-
Channel/ SW Approaches	-	-	-	-	1	-	-	-	-	-	-	-
Total all areas (2)	45(3)	18(2)	27(4)	24(3)	16(2)	26(2)	29(3)	41(8)	29(1)	34(2)	44(3)	3

(B) Offshore appraisal drilling (1) : appraisal wells started in each geographical area

	1998	1999	2000	2001	2002	2003	2004	2005	2006	2007	2008	Q1 - 2009
Southern N Sea	2(1)	5(2)	3	2(2)	4	3	2(1)	3	9	5(2)	14(2)	2
Central N Sea (4)	13(5)	10	11(1)	22(9)	16(8)	12(6)	8(1)	16(8)	22(14)	56(36)	26(15)	9(7)
Northern N Sea	17(10)	2(1)	17(10)	11(8)	7(3)	1	22(9)	14(7)	5(1)	12(2)	18(7)	1(1)
West of England/ Wales	-	-	-	1	-	1	-	-	3	-	-	-
West of Shetland(3)	-	-	2(1)	-	1	3(3)	2(1)	1	5(2)	4(1)	3(2)	-

Channel/ SW Approaches	-	-	-	-	-	-	-	-	-	-	-	-
Total all areas (2)												
32(16)	17(3)	34(12)	35(19)	29(11)	19(9)	34(12)	37(15)	41(17)	77(41)	61(26)	12(8)	

(C) Offshore development drilling (1) : development wells started in each geographical area

	2000	2001	2002	2003	2004	2005	2006	2007	2008	Q1 - 2009
Southern N Sea	29(12)	14(7)	33(16)	33(21)	12(6)	28(11)	27(14)	31(15)	21(12)	5(2)
Central N Sea (4)	70(27)	124(54)	97(56)	78(38)	96(44)	120(59)	93(37)	101(54)	83(48)	15(3)
Northern N Sea	107(36)	121(43)	116(52)	74(16)	52(16)	59(20)	69(26)	27(13)	55(34)	7(3)
West of England/ Wales	8(2)	16(10)	6(3)	10(4)	1	6(3)	-	-	-	-
West of Shetland(3)	10(7)	11(3)	11(3)	12(4)	6(3)	17(7)	12(6)	6	11(5)	4(4)
Total all areas (2)	224(84)	286(117)	263(130)	207(83)	167(69)	230(100)	201(83)	165(82)	170(99)	31(12)

(D) Onshore drilling (1) : numbers of wells drilled

	1998	1999	2000	2001	2002	2003	2004	2005	2006	2007	2008	Q1 - 2009
Exploration	5	6	8	5	14(1)	3(1)	3	6(1)	8(1)	14(1)	9	4
Appraisal	9(4)	2(1)	6	1	-	1	-	2	7(4)	1	11(4)	-
Development	21(13)	11(5)	11(6)	20(17)	18(13)	17(11)	14(7)	21(14)	12(6)	14(3)	20(11)	4
Total (2)	35(17)	19(6)	25(6)	26(17)	32(14)	21(12)	17(7)	29(15)	27(11)	29(5)	40(15)	8

PETROLEUM ACT 1998

PART I PETROLEUM

1 MEANING OF "PETROLEUM"

In this Part of this Act "petroleum"—
(a) includes any mineral oil or relative hydrocarbon and natural gas existing in its natural condition in strata; but
(b) does not include coal or bituminous shales or other stratified deposits from which oil can be extracted by destructive distillation.

2 RIGHTS TO PETROLEUM VESTED IN HER MAJESTY

(1) Her Majesty has the exclusive right of searching and boring for and getting petroleum to which this section applies.
(2) This section applies to petroleum (including petroleum in Crown land) which for the time being exists in its natural condition in strata in Great Britain or beneath the territorial sea adjacent to the United Kingdom.
(3) For the purposes of subsection (2), "Crown land" means land which—
(a) belongs to Her Majesty or the Duchy of Cornwall;
(b) belongs to a government department; or
(c) is held in trust for Her Majesty for the purposes of a government department.
(4) Subsection (1) is subject to paragraph 4 of Schedule 3 and subsection (2) is subject to paragraph 5(3) of that Schedule.

3 LICENCES TO SEARCH AND BORE FOR AND GET PETROLEUM

(1) The Secretary of State, on behalf of Her Majesty, may grant to such persons as he thinks fit licences to search and bore for and get petroleum to which this section applies.
(2) This section applies to—
(a) petroleum to which section 2 applies; and
(b) petroleum with respect to which rights vested in Her Majesty by section 1(1) of the [1964 c. 29.] Continental Shelf Act 1964 (exploration and exploitation of continental shelf) are exercisable.
(3) Any such licence shall be granted for such consideration (whether by way of royalty or otherwise) as the Secretary of State with the consent of the Treasury may determine, and upon such other terms and conditions as the Secretary of State thinks fit.
(4) Subsection (1) is subject to paragraph 4 of Schedule 3.

4 LICENCES: FURTHER PROVISIONS

(1) The Secretary of State shall make regulations prescribing—
(a) the manner in which and the persons by whom applications for licences under this Part of this Act may be made;
(b) the information to be included in or provided in connection with any such application;
(c) the fees to be paid on any such application;
(d) the conditions as to the size and shape of areas in respect of which licences may be granted;
(e) model clauses which shall, unless he thinks fit to modify or exclude them in any particular case, be incorporated in any such licence.
(2) Different regulations may be made for different kinds of licence.
(3) Any such regulations shall be made by statutory instrument which shall be subject to annulment in pursuance of a resolution of either House of Parliament.

(4) As soon as practicable after granting a licence under section 3, the Secretary of State shall publish notice of the fact in the London Gazette stating—
(a) the name of the licensee; and
(b) the situation of the area in respect of which the licence has been granted,
and, if that area or any part of it is in Scotland, the Secretary of State shall also publish the notice in the Edinburgh Gazette.
(5) Any information which the Commissioners of Inland Revenue possess in connection with petroleum won by virtue of a licence granted under section 3—
(a) may be disclosed by the Commissioners to the Secretary of State, or to an officer of his who is authorised by him to receive such information, in connection with provisions of the licence relating to royalty payments; but
(b) shall not be disclosed by a person to whom it is disclosed under paragraph (a) except—
(i) as authorised by the licence;
(ii) to a person to whom it could have been disclosed under paragraph (a); or
(iii) for the purposes of proceedings (which may be arbitration proceedings) in connection with the licence.

5 EXISTING LICENCES

(1) In this section, the "current model clauses" means, in relation to any paragraph of Schedule 1, the model clauses which, immediately before the commencement of this Act, would be incorporated in a licence granted under section 2 of the [1934 c. 36.] Petroleum (Production) Act 1934 if the licence, when granted, had incorporated the model clauses mentioned in that paragraph.
(2) The reference in subsection (1) to the model clauses which, immediately before the commencement of this Act, would be incorporated in a licence is a reference to those model clauses as they would then have effect but as if any reference (however expressed) in a model clause to an enactment repealed and re-enacted by this Act were, or (where the context requires) included, a reference to the corresponding provision of this Act.
(3) For the purposes of subsection (2), any provision of a model clause which would have effect (or would have a particular effect) only in relation to a licence of a description of which none is in force immediately before the commencement of this Act shall be treated as not then having effect (or as not then having that effect).
(4) The Secretary of State shall, in an order made before the commencement of this Act, reproduce the current model clauses in relation to each paragraph of Schedule 1.
(5) Subject to subsections (7) and (8), any licence granted under section 2 of the Petroleum (Production) Act 1934 which—
(a) is in force immediately before the commencement of this Act; and
(b) when granted, incorporated any of the model clauses mentioned in any paragraph of Schedule 1,
shall on the commencement of this Act have effect as if it incorporated, in place of the relevant model clauses, the current model clauses reproduced in relation to that paragraph in the order under subsection (4).
(6) For the purposes of subsection (5), the relevant model clauses, in relation to any licence, are the model clauses which the licence incorporates immediately before the commencement of this Act other than any model clause which—
(a) was incorporated into the licence when it was granted; and
(b) is not within any paragraph of Schedule 1.
(7) Where immediately before the commencement of this Act any such licence incorporates model clauses subject to any amendment or modification, or with the omission of any model clause, the current model clauses reproduced under subsection (4) shall have effect in relation to that licence—
(a) subject to the same amendment or modification; or

(b) as the case may be, with the omission of the model clause corresponding to the model clause omitted from the licence.
(8) Where before the commencement of this Act model clauses (the "substitute model clauses") set out in any regulations made under section 6 of the [1934 c. 36.] Petroleum (Production) Act 1934 have been substituted for the model clauses originally incorporated in any licence granted under section 2 of that Act, the licence shall be treated for the purposes of this section as if, when granted, it had incorporated the substitute model clauses.
(9) It is hereby declared that any provision incorporated in a licence by virtue of subsection (5) may be altered or deleted by an instrument under seal executed by the Secretary of State and the licensee or, as respects Scotland, by an instrument subscribed by the Secretary of State and the licensee in accordance with the [1995 c. 7.] Requirements of Writing (Scotland) Act 1995.
(10) Where any provision is replaced by virtue of subsection (5)—
(a) a reference in any document to that provision (or which immediately before the commencement of this Act is to be construed as a reference to that provision) shall, except so far as the nature of the document or context otherwise requires, be construed as a reference to the replacement; and
(b) anything done under or for the purposes of that provision shall, except where the context otherwise requires, be treated as having been done under or for the purposes of the replacement.
(11) The order to be made under subsection (4) shall be made by statutory instrument, shall be laid before Parliament after being made and shall come into force on the commencement of this Act.

6 REPAYMENTS FOR DEVELOPMENT

(1) Where any person has paid to the Secretary of State a sum by way of royalty under the terms of a licence granted under section 3, the Secretary of State may with the approval of the Treasury repay to him the whole or a part of that sum if the Secretary of State considers it expedient to do so for the purpose of facilitating or maintaining the development of the petroleum resources of the United Kingdom.
(2) Where for any chargeable period for the purpose of a licence granted under section 3 any person has been required to deliver petroleum to the Secretary of State under the terms of that licence, subsection (1) shall have effect as if for that period that person had paid to the Secretary of State by way of royalty such sum, or (where he has been required to deliver some but not all of the petroleum which he could have been required to deliver) such additional sum as he would have been required to pay under the terms of the licence if he had not been required to deliver the petroleum.
(3) Any repayment and right to a repayment under this section shall be disregarded for the purposes of income tax, corporation tax and petroleum revenue tax.

7 ANCILLARY RIGHTS

(1) Subject to the provisions of this section, the [1966 c. 4.] Mines (Working Facilities and Support) Act 1966 shall apply (in England and Wales and Scotland) for the purpose of enabling a person holding a licence under this Part of this Act to acquire such ancillary rights as may be required for the exercise of the rights granted by the licence.
(2) In its application for the purposes of this section, the Mines (Working Facilities and Support) Act 1966 shall have effect as if—
(a) references to a person having a right to work minerals included references to a person holding a licence under this Part of this Act;
(b) references to minerals included references to petroleum; and
(c) references to the working of minerals included references to the getting, carrying away, storing, treating and converting of petroleum.

(3) Without prejudice to the generality of subsection (1) of section 2 of the [1966 c. 4.] Mines (Working Facilities and Support) Act 1966, that Act shall have effect for the purposes of this section as if the ancillary rights mentioned in that subsection included—
(a) a right to enter upon land and to sink boreholes in the land for the purpose of searching for and getting petroleum; and
(b) a right to use and occupy land for—
(i) the erection of such buildings;
(ii) the laying and maintenance of such pipes; and
(iii) the construction of such other works,
as may be required for the purpose of searching and boring for and getting, carrying away, storing, treating and converting petroleum.
(4) Where an application is made to the court under the Mines (Working Facilities and Support) Act 1966 by virtue of this section—
(a) in deciding—
(i) whether to grant any right applied for; or
(ii) what terms and conditions, if any, should be imposed upon the grant of such a right, the court shall have regard, among other considerations, to the effect on the amenities of the locality of the proposed use and occupation of the land in respect of which the right is applied for;
(b) in determining the amount of any compensation to be paid in respect of the grant of any right, an additional allowance of not less than 10 per cent. shall be made on account of the acquisition of the right being compulsory;
(c) the costs in connection with the application incurred by the applicant shall not be ordered to be paid by any person from whom a right is sought to be obtained; and
(d) the costs in connection with the application incurred by each person from whom a right is sought to be obtained shall be ordered to be paid by the applicant unless the court is satisfied that an unconditional offer in writing was made by the applicant to that person of a sum as compensation equal to or greater than the amount of any compensation awarded to him by the court.

8 POWER TO INSPECT PLANS OF MINES

(1) For the purpose of ascertaining on behalf of the Secretary of State the position of the workings, actual and prospective, of any mines or abandoned mines through or near which it is proposed to sink any borehole for the purpose of searching for or getting petroleum, any officer appointed by the Secretary of State shall have the same powers with respect to the production and inspection and the taking of copies of relevant documents as may under section 20 of the [1974 c. 37.] Health and Safety at Work etc. Act 1974 be exercised by an inspector acting for the purpose mentioned in subsection (1) of that section.
(2) For the purposes of subsection (1)—
(a) "relevant documents" means plans, sections, drawings or other similar documents which, by virtue of paragraph 16 of Schedule 3 to that Act of 1974, are required to be kept;
(b) "an inspector" means an inspector appointed under section 19 of that Act; and
(c) subsections (2) and (3) of section 19 of that Act shall be disregarded.

9 SUPPLEMENTARY

(1) Nothing in this Part of this Act shall be construed as imposing any liability on any person where in the course of mining or other lawful operations petroleum is set free.
(2) Nothing in this Part of this Act shall be construed as conferring, or as enabling the Secretary of State to confer, on any person, whether acting on behalf of Her Majesty or not, any right which he does not enjoy apart from this Part of this Act to enter on or interfere with land.
(3) The issue of an authorisation within the meaning of Part III of this Act shall be deemed not to derogate from a licence granted under section 3 which is for the time being in force.

PART II OFFSHORE ACTIVITIES

10 APPLICATION OF CRIMINAL LAW ETC

(1) Her Majesty may by Order in Council provide that, in such cases and subject to such exceptions as may be prescribed by the Order, any act or omission which—
(a) takes place on, under or above an installation in waters to which this section applies or any waters within 500 metres of any such installation; and
(b) would, if taking place in any part of the United Kingdom, constitute an offence under the law in force in that part,
shall be treated for the purposes of that law as taking place in that part.
(2) Her Majesty may by Order in Council provide that, in such cases and subject to such exceptions as may be prescribed by the Order, a constable shall on, under or above any installation in waters to which this section applies or any waters within 500 metres of such an installation have all the powers, protection and privileges which he has in the area for which he acts as constable.
(3) Subsection (2) is without prejudice to any other enactment or rule of law affording any power, protection or privilege to constables.
(4) Where a body corporate is guilty of an offence by virtue of an Order in Council under this section and that offence is proved to have been committed with the consent or connivance of, or to be attributable to any neglect on the part of, any director, manager, secretary or other similar officer of the body corporate or any person who was purporting to act in any such capacity, he as well as the body corporate shall be guilty of that offence and shall be liable to be proceeded against and punished accordingly.
(5) Where the affairs of a body corporate are managed by its members, subsection (4) shall apply in relation to acts and defaults of a member in connection with his functions of management as if he were a director of the body corporate.
(6) Proceedings for anything that is an offence by virtue of an Order in Council under this section may be taken, and the offence may for all incidental purposes be treated as having been committed, in any place in the United Kingdom.
(7) The waters to which this section applies are—
(a) the territorial sea adjacent to the United Kingdom;
(b) waters in an area designated under section 1(7) of the [1964 c. 29.] Continental Shelf Act 1964; or
(c) waters in an area specified under subsection (8).
(8) Her Majesty may from time to time by Order in Council specify any area which—
(a) is in a foreign sector of the continental shelf; and
(b) comprises any part of a cross-boundary field,
as an area as respects which the powers conferred by this section and section 11 are exercisable.
(9) In this section—

- "cross-boundary field" means a field that extends across the boundary between waters falling within paragraph (a) or (b) of subsection (7) and a foreign sector of the continental shelf;
- "field" means a geological structure identified as such by Order in Council under subsection (8).

(10) This section applies to installations notwithstanding that they are for the time being in transit.
(11) A statutory instrument containing an Order in Council under this section shall be subject to annulment in pursuance of a resolution of either House of Parliament.

11 APPLICATION OF CIVIL LAW

(1) Her Majesty may by Order in Council—
(a) provide that, in such cases and subject to such exceptions as may be prescribed by the Order, questions arising out of acts or omissions taking place on, under or above waters to which this section applies in connection with any activity mentioned in subsection (2) shall be determined in accordance with the law in force in such part of the United Kingdom as may be specified in the Order; and
(b) make provision for conferring jurisdiction with respect to such questions on courts in any part of the United Kingdom so specified.
(2) The activities referred to in subsection (1) are—
(a) activities connected with the exploration of, or the exploitation of the natural resources of, the shore or bed of waters to which this section applies or the subsoil beneath it; and
(b) without prejudice to the generality of paragraph (a), activities carried on from, by means of or on, or for purposes connected with, installations to which subsection (3) applies.
(3) This subsection applies to any installation which is or has been maintained, or is intended to be established, for the carrying on of any of the following activities, namely—
(a) the exploitation or exploration of mineral resources in or under the shore or bed of waters to which this section applies;
(b) the storage of gas in or under the shore or bed of such waters or the recovery of gas so stored;
(c) the conveyance of things by means of a pipe, or system of pipes, constructed or placed on, in or under the shore or bed of such waters; and
(d) the provision of accommodation for persons who work on or from an installation which is or has been maintained, or is intended to be established, for the carrying on of an activity within paragraph (a), (b) or (c) or this paragraph.
(4) The fact that an installation has been maintained for the carrying on of an activity within subsection (3) shall be disregarded for the purposes of that subsection if, since it was so maintained, it has been outside waters to which this section applies or has been maintained for the carrying on of an activity not falling within that subsection.
(5) Any jurisdiction conferred on a court under this section shall be without prejudice to any jurisdiction exercisable apart from this section by that or any other court.
(6) This section applies to installations notwithstanding that they are for the time being in transit.
(7) A statutory instrument containing an Order in Council under this section shall be subject to annulment in pursuance of a resolution of either House of Parliament.
(8) The waters to which this section applies are—
(a) tidal waters and parts of the sea in or adjacent to the United Kingdom up to the seaward limits of the territorial sea;
(b) waters in an area designated under section 1(7) of the [1964 c. 29.] Continental Shelf Act 1964;
(c) waters in an area specified under section 10(8); and
(d) in relation to installations which are or have been maintained, or are intended to be established, in waters within paragraph (a), (b) or (c), waters in a foreign sector of the continental shelf which are adjacent to such waters.

12 PROSECUTIONS

(1) Subject to subsection (2), this subsection applies to—
(a) any offence alleged to have been committed on, under or above an installation in waters to which section 10 applies or any waters within 500 metres of such an installation; and
(b) any offence committed on or as respects an aircraft which is not registered in the United Kingdom which is an offence created by virtue of paragraph 6(5) of Part III of Schedule 13 to the [1982 c. 16.] Civil Aviation Act 1982.
(2) Subsection (1) does not apply to any offence to which subsection (5) applies nor to any offence under, or under any provision which has effect under—

(a) the Customs and Excise Acts 1979, or any enactment to be construed as one with those Acts or any of them;
(b) except where it is created by virtue of paragraph 6(5) of Part III of Schedule 13 to the Civil Aviation Act 1982, that Act or any enactment to be construed as one with that Act;
(c) the [1987 c. 21.] Pilotage Act 1987;
(d) the [1994 c. 23.] Value Added Tax Act 1994 or any enactment to be construed as one with that Act;
(e) the [1995 c. 21.] Merchant Shipping Act 1995; or
(f) Part III or IV of this Act.
(3) No proceedings for an offence to which subsection (1) applies shall be instituted—
(a) in England and Wales, except by or with the consent of the Director of Public Prosecutions unless prosecution of the offence there requires the consent of the Attorney General;
(b) in Northern Ireland, except by or with the consent of the Director of Public Prosecutions for Northern Ireland unless prosecution of the offence there requires the consent of the Attorney General for Northern Ireland.
(4) Section 3 of the [1878 c. 73.] Territorial Waters Jurisdiction Act 1878 (restriction on prosecutions) shall not apply to any proceedings for an offence to which subsection (1) or (5) applies.
(5) This subsection applies to—
(a) any offence under section 23 of the [1987 c. 12.] Petroleum Act 1987 (safety zones); and
(b) any offence under any provision made under the [1971 c. 61.] Mineral Workings (Offshore Installations) Act 1971 which has effect by virtue of—
(i) paragraph (1) of regulation 6 (savings) of the [S.I. 1993/1823.] Offshore Safety (Repeals and Modifications) Regulations 1993; or
(ii) paragraph (1) of regulation 6 (savings) of the [S.R. (N.I.) 1993 No. 384.] Offshore Safety (Repeals and Modifications) Regulations (Northern Ireland) 1993.

13 INTERPRETATION OF PART II

In this Part of this Act—

- "foreign sector of the continental shelf" has the meaning given by section 48(1); and
- "installation" includes any floating structure or device maintained on a station by whatever means.

PART III SUBMARINE PIPELINES

14 CONSTRUCTION AND USE OF PIPELINES

(1) No person shall—
(a) execute in, under or over any controlled waters any works for the construction of a pipeline; or
(b) use a controlled pipeline of which the construction was begun on or after 1st January 1976, except in accordance with an authorisation given in writing by the Secretary of State.
(2) In this Part of this Act—

- "controlled pipeline" means so much of any pipeline as is in, under or over controlled waters; and
- "controlled waters" means the territorial sea adjacent to the United Kingdom and the sea in any area designated under section 1(7) of the [1964 c. 29.] Continental Shelf Act 1964.

15 AUTHORISATIONS

(1) Schedule 2 (applications for and issue of authorisations) shall have effect.

(2) The Secretary of State shall not issue an authorisation to a person other than a body corporate.
(3) Any authorisation in respect of a controlled pipeline may contain such terms as the Secretary of State thinks appropriate including in particular terms as to—
(a) the duration of the authorisation, including the method of ascertaining its duration;
(b) the persons or kinds of persons who are authorised to execute the works in question or to use the pipeline or are so authorised if the Secretary of State consents to the execution of the works or the use of the pipeline by them;
(c) in the case of a works authorisation—
(i) the route of the pipeline;
(ii) the boundaries within which any works may be executed in pursuance of the authorisation;
(iii) the design and capacity of the pipeline or of part of it; and
(iv) the steps to be taken to avoid or reduce interference by the pipeline with fishing or with other activities connected with the sea or the sea bed or subsoil;
(d) the things authorised to be conveyed by the pipeline;
(e) the steps to be taken to ensure that funds are available to discharge any liability for damage attributable to the release or escape of any thing from the pipeline;
(f) the transactions relating to the pipeline which are not to be entered into, and the other things relating to the pipeline which are not to be done, without the consent of the Secretary of State;
(g) the persons who may be permitted to acquire an interest in the pipeline and who may not be permitted to retain such an interest;
(h) the operation of the pipeline, including the methods by which it is to be operated and the persons by whom it may be operated;
(i) the information to be provided in respect of the pipeline; and
(j) the giving by the Secretary of State, with respect to matters specified in the authorisation, of directions which shall have effect as terms of the authorisation.
(4) Unless the Secretary of State considers that there are special circumstances by reason of which the duration of an authorisation should be limited, an authorisation shall provide for its duration to be unlimited subject to the following provisions of this Part of this Act.
(5) Subsection (6) applies where a works authorisation contains a term (the "variation term") requiring that—
(a) the capacity of the controlled pipeline to which it relates or of any part of the pipeline shall be greater than that proposed in the application for the authorisation; or
(b) any of the route of the pipeline shall be different from that so proposed.
(6) Where this subsection applies, the Secretary of State may, subject to section 17(7), serve a notice in accordance with subsection (7) on—
(a) the holder of the authorisation; and
(b) any other person who made representations to the Secretary of State that the capacity should be greater than that proposed as mentioned in subsection (5) or that any of the route should be different from that so proposed.
(7) A notice under subsection (6) shall—
(a) specify the sums or the method of determining the sums which the Secretary of State considers should be paid to the holder by the other person for the purpose of defraying so much of the cost of constructing the pipeline as is attributable to the variation term;
(b) require the other person to make, within a specified period, arrangements which the Secretary of State considers are appropriate to ensure that those sums will be paid to the holder if he constructs the pipeline or a relevant part of it in accordance with the variation term or satisfies the Secretary of State that he will so construct it;
(c) provide that the holder may, if those arrangements are not made by the other person within the specified period, elect in the specified manner that—
(i) the variation term shall have effect with such modifications as are specified with a view to eliminating the consequences of the representations of the other person; and
(ii) the provisions included in the notice by virtue of paragraph (d) shall cease to have effect; and

(d) authorise the holder, if he satisfies the Secretary of State that the pipeline or a relevant part of it has been or will be constructed in accordance with the variation term, to recover those sums from the other person.
(8) In subsection (7), "specified" means specified in the notice.

16 COMPULSORY MODIFICATIONS OF PIPELINES

(1) If in the case of a controlled pipeline it appears to the Secretary of State, on the application of a person other than the owner of the pipeline—
(a) that the capacity of the pipeline can and should be increased by modifying apparatus and works associated with the pipeline; or
(b) that the pipeline can and should be modified by installing in it a junction through which another pipeline may be connected to the pipeline,
then, subject to section 17(8), the Secretary of State may, after giving the owner of the pipeline an opportunity of being heard about the matter, serve on the owner and the applicant a notice in accordance with subsection (2).
(2) A notice under subsection (1) shall—
(a) specify the modifications which the Secretary of State considers should be made in consequence of the application;
(b) specify the sums or the method of determining the sums which the Secretary of State considers should be paid to the owner by the applicant for the purpose of defraying the cost of the modifications;
(c) require the applicant to make, within the period specified for the purpose in the notice, arrangements which the Secretary of State considers appropriate to secure that those sums will be paid to the owner if he carries out the modifications or satisfies the Secretary of State that he will carry them out;
(d) require the owner, if the applicant makes those arrangements within that period, to carry out the modifications within a period specified for the purpose in the notice; and
(e) authorise the owner, if he satisfies the Secretary of State that he has carried out or will carry out the modifications, to recover those sums from the applicant.
(3) References in subsections (1) and (2) to modifications include, in the case of modifications of any apparatus and works, references to changes in, substitutions for and additions to the apparatus and works.
(4) For the purposes of section 14(1) a notice under subsection (1) of this section requiring a person to carry out modifications authorises him to carry out the modifications; but nothing in Schedule 2 shall apply to such a notice.

17 ACQUISITION OF RIGHTS TO USE PIPELINES

(1) Subsections (2) and (3) apply where a person applies to the Secretary of State for a notice under this section securing to the applicant a right to have conveyed, by a controlled pipeline of which he is not the owner, quantities specified in the application of things which are of a kind so specified and which the pipeline is designed to convey.
(2) The Secretary of State shall—
(a) give notice to the owner of the pipeline and the applicant that he proposes to consider the application; and
(b) after the expiry of 21 days beginning with the date on which notice under paragraph (a) was served, but before considering the application, give them an opportunity of being heard with respect to the application.
(3) Where the Secretary of State is satisfied that, if he served a notice under this section the pipeline in question could be operated in accordance with the notice without prejudicing its efficient operation for the purpose of conveying, on behalf of its owner, the quantities of permitted substances which the owner requires or may reasonably be expected to require, the Secretary of State may serve such a notice on the owner and the applicant.

(4) In subsection (3), "permitted substances" means the things which may be conveyed by the pipeline in accordance with an authorisation (or, if no authorisation for the use of the pipeline is required by section 14(1), means the things which the pipeline is designed to convey).
(5) A notice under this section may contain such provisions as the Secretary of State considers appropriate for any of the following purposes—
(a) to secure to the applicant, without prejudicing the efficient operation of the pipeline for the purpose mentioned in subsection (3), the right to have conveyed by the pipeline the quantities specified in the application of the things so specified;
(b) to secure that the exercise of the right is not prevented or impeded;
(c) to regulate the charges which may be made for the conveyance of things by virtue of the right; and
(d) to secure to the applicant the right to have a pipeline of his connected to the pipeline by the applicant or owner.
(6) Such a notice may also authorise the owner to recover from the applicant payments by way of consideration for any right mentioned in subsection (5)(a) or (d) of amounts specified in the notice or determined in accordance with the notice.
(7) Before serving a notice under section 15(6) on a person other than the holder of the relevant authorisation, the Secretary of State shall give that person an opportunity to make an application under subsection (1) in respect of the proposed pipeline to which the authorisation relates; and subsections (1) to (6) shall have effect for this purpose as if references to a pipeline and the owner of it were references to the proposed pipeline and the proposed owner of it.
(8) Before serving a notice under section 16(1) on a person other than the owner of the relevant pipeline, the Secretary of State shall give that person particulars of the modifications which he proposes to specify in the notice and an opportunity to make an application under subsection (1) in respect of the pipeline; and subsections (1) to (6) shall have effect for this purpose as if references to a pipeline were references to the pipeline as it would be with those modifications.
(9) The use of a pipeline by any person in accordance with a right secured to him by virtue of this section is not a contravention of section 14(1); but a person to whom a right is so secured may not assign the right to any other person.

18 TERMINATION OF AUTHORISATIONS

(1) An authorisation shall cease to be in force at the earliest of the following—
(a) where the duration of the authorisation is not expressed to be unlimited, the time at which that duration expires as specified by or ascertained under the terms of the authorisation;
(b) the time (if any) agreed in writing by the holder and the Secretary of State as the time at which the authorisation is to cease to be in force; and
(c) the time specified in a notice under subsection (2) or (6).
(2) If it appears to the Secretary of State that the execution of works authorised by a works authorisation has not been begun at the expiry of the period specified in subsection (3), he shall serve on the holder a notice stating that the authorisation is to cease to be in force at a time specified in the notice.
(3) The period referred to in subsection (2) is—
(a) the period of three years beginning with the date when the authorisation is expressed to come into force; or
(b) such longer period beginning with that date as the Secretary of State has, on the application of the holder, specified in a notice served under this paragraph on the holder during the period mentioned in paragraph (a).
(4) For the purpose of subsection (2), the Secretary of State shall disregard the execution of any of the works which he considers should be disregarded for that purpose.
(5) The Secretary of State shall not serve a notice under subsection (3)(b) unless—
(a) he is satisfied that notice of the application under that provision has been served on—

(i) the persons on whom, in accordance with Schedule 2, notice of the application for the authorisation was served or such of them as the Secretary of State considers appropriate in the circumstances; and
(ii) such other persons, if any, as he considers appropriate in the circumstances; and
(b) he has considered any written representations about the application under subsection (3)(b) made during such a period as he considers reasonable by any of the persons on whom notice of the application was served in accordance with paragraph (a).
(6) Subject to subsections (7) and (8), if the Secretary of State considers that the holder of an authorisation—
(a) has contravened a term of the authorisation; or
(b) has contravened any provision of a notice which, under section 16 or 17, was served on him in his capacity as the owner of the pipeline (or the proposed owner of the proposed pipeline) to which the authorisation relates,
the Secretary of State may serve on the holder a notice stating that the authorisation is to cease to be in force at a time specified in the notice.
(7) The Secretary of State shall not serve a notice under subsection (6) without first giving the holder of the authorisation an opportunity to make written representations to him.
(8) The Secretary of State shall not serve a notice under subsection (6) in consequence of a contravention if the Secretary of State considers that—
(a) having regard to the nature and consequences of the contravention and to any previous contravention, it would be unreasonable to terminate the authorisation in consequence of the contravention; and
(b) the holder has taken adequate steps to prevent similar contraventions in future.
(9) When an authorisation ceases to be in force the Secretary of State shall publish in the London and Edinburgh and Belfast Gazettes, or in such of them as he considers appropriate, a notice stating that it has ceased to be in force.

19 VESTING OF PIPELINES ON TERMINATION OR SUBSEQUENT ISSUE OF AUTHORISATIONS

(1) When an authorisation ceases to be in force the controlled pipeline to which it relates shall, by virtue of this subsection, be transferred to and vest in the Secretary of State free from encumbrances, except that nothing in this subsection prejudices—
(a) any interest belonging to the Crown Estate or to Her Majesty in right of the Duchy of Lancaster or to the Duchy of Cornwall; or
(b) any right conferred by a notice relating to the pipeline under section 17.
(2) Where the Secretary of State proposes to issue an authorisation to any person in respect of a pipeline vested in the Secretary of State by virtue of subsection (1) he may agree with that person, on terms which may include provision for that person to make payments to the Secretary of State, that the authorisation is to include a statement that subsection (3) applies to the authorisation.
(3) Where an authorisation includes such a statement the pipeline to which the authorisation relates shall, by virtue of this subsection and at the time specified in the authorisation, be transferred to and vest in the holder of the authorisation subject to any interest or right then subsisting in respect of the pipeline by virtue of paragraph (a) or (b) of subsection (1).

20 INSPECTORS ETC

(1) The Secretary of State may appoint, as inspectors to assist him in the execution of this Part of this Act, such number of persons appearing to him to be qualified for the purpose as he considers appropriate from time to time; and the Secretary of State may make, to or in respect of any person so appointed, such payments by way of remuneration or otherwise as the Secretary of State determines with the approval of the Minister for the Civil Service.
(2) The Secretary of State may by regulations make provision with respect to—

(a) the powers and duties of—
(i) inspectors appointed under subsection (1); and
(ii) any other persons acting on the directions of the Secretary of State in connection with the execution of this Part of this Act; and
(b) the facilities to be accorded to such inspectors and other persons.
(3) For the purpose of enforcing regulations made under subsection (2), an inspector appointed under subsection (1) shall have the same powers under section 38 of the [1974 c. 37.] Health and Safety at Work etc. Act 1974 (institution of proceedings in England and Wales) as he would have if he were an inspector appointed by the Health and Safety Executive under section 19 of that Act who is authorised to act for the purposes of the regulations.
(4) In the application of this section to Northern Ireland, subsection (3) shall have effect as if—
(a) the references to sections 19 and 38 of the Health and Safety at Work etc. Act 1974 were references to Articles 21 and 35, respectively, of the [S.I. 1978/1039 (N.I. 9).] Health and Safety at Work (Northern Ireland) Order 1978; and
(b) the reference to the Health and Safety Executive were a reference to the Department of Economic Development.
(5) A statutory instrument containing regulations under subsection (2) shall be subject to annulment in pursuance of a resolution of either House of Parliament.

21 ENFORCEMENT

(1) Any person who—
(a) contravenes any provision of section 14(1); or
(b) contravenes any provision of a notice under section 16 or 17 served on him in his capacity as the owner of the pipeline to which the notice relates in a case where no authorisation for the use of the pipeline is required by section 14(1); or
(c) makes a statement which he knows is false in a material particular, or recklessly makes a statement which is false in a material particular, for the purpose of inducing the Secretary of State—
(i) to issue any authorisation; or
(ii) to agree under section 18(1)(b) that an authorisation is to cease to be in force; or
(iii) to specify a period under section 18(3)(b); or
(iv) not to serve a notice under section 18(6),
shall be guilty of an offence and liable on summary conviction to a fine not exceeding the statutory maximum or on conviction on indictment to a fine.
(2) If a person executes any works in contravention of section 14(1) the Secretary of State may at any time serve on him a notice requiring him to remove such of the works as are specified in the notice as works to be removed.
(3) The recipient of a notice under subsection (2) shall comply with the notice within the period specified in the notice; and if he fails to do so the Secretary of State may comply with the notice on his behalf and recover from him any expenses reasonably incurred in doing so.
(4) If a person executes any works in contravention of section 14(1) and the Secretary of State considers that it is urgently necessary to do such things in relation to the works as he could have required that person to do by a notice under subsection (2), the Secretary of State may do those things and recover from that person any expenses reasonably incurred in doing so.
(5) The fact that any thing is done or omitted—
(a) by the recipient of a notice under subsection (2) for the purpose of complying with the notice; or
(b) by the Secretary of State under subsection (3) or (4),
shall not relieve him from liability for any damage which is attributable to the act or omission and for which he would have been liable had the act or omission not been authorised by this section; but the Secretary of State shall be entitled to recover from the person who executed the works in question the amount of any damages which, in consequence of the works, are paid by the Secretary of State by virtue of this subsection.

22 CRIMINAL PROCEEDINGS

(1) Proceedings for an offence under section 21(1) or created by regulations made under this Part of this Act (a "relevant offence") may be taken, and the offence may for all incidental purposes be treated as having been committed, in any place in the United Kingdom.
(2) Proceedings for a relevant offence alleged to have been committed in, under or over controlled waters shall not be instituted in England and Wales except—
(a) by the Secretary of State or by a person authorised in that behalf by the Secretary of State; or
(b) by or with the consent of the Director of Public Prosecutions.
(3) Proceedings for a relevant offence alleged to have been committed in, under or over controlled waters shall not be instituted in Northern Ireland except—
(a) by the Secretary of State or by a person authorised in that behalf by the Secretary of State; or
(b) by or with the consent of the Director of Public Prosecutions for Northern Ireland.
(4) Subsections (2) and (3) do not apply to proceedings for an offence created by regulations made under section 20.
(5) In proceedings for a relevant offence an averment in the information, complaint or indictment that anything was done or situated in, under or over controlled waters shall, unless the contrary is proved, be sufficient evidence of the matter stated in the averment.
(6) Where a relevant offence committed by a body corporate is proved to have been committed with the consent or connivance of, or to be attributable to any neglect on the part of, any director, manager, secretary or other similar officer of the body corporate or any person who was purporting to act in any such capacity, he as well as the body corporate shall be guilty of that offence and shall be liable to be proceeded against and punished accordingly.
(7) In subsection (6), in relation to a body corporate which—
(a) is established by or under any enactment for the purpose of carrying on under public ownership any industry or part of an industry or undertaking; and
(b) is a body whose affairs are managed by its members,

- "director" means a member of the body corporate.

(8) In any proceedings for—
(a) an offence under paragraph (a) of subsection (1) of section 21 of executing works or using a pipeline otherwise than in accordance with the terms of the relevant authorisation; or
(b) an offence under paragraph (b) of that subsection of contravening any provision of a notice,
it shall be a defence to prove that the accused used all due diligence to comply with those terms or, as the case may be, with that provision.
(9) Section 3 of the [1878 c. 73.] Territorial Waters Jurisdiction Act 1878 (restriction on prosecutions) shall not apply to any proceedings for a relevant offence.

23 CIVIL LIABILITY FOR BREACH OF STATUTORY DUTY

(1) Breach of a duty imposed on any person by regulations made under this Part of this Act which state that this subsection applies to such a breach shall be actionable so far, and only so far, as the breach causes personal injury.
(2) References in—
(a) the [1976 c. 30.] Fatal Accidents Act 1976; and
(b) Article 3(1) of the [S.I. 1977/1251 (N.I. 18).] Fatal Accidents (Northern Ireland) Order 1977,
to a wrongful act, neglect or default shall include references to any such breach which is so actionable.
(3) Nothing in subsections (1) and (2) prejudices any action which lies apart from the provisions of those subsections.
(4) A defence to a charge which is available by virtue of section 25(3)(c) shall not be a defence in any civil proceedings whether they are brought by virtue of this section or otherwise.

(5) For the purposes of subsection (1) any such regulations as are mentioned in that subsection shall bind the Crown, and references in those regulations to employees shall for those purposes include persons in the service of the Crown; but nothing in this subsection—
(a) confers any right of action on a person as a member of the armed forces of the Crown; or
(b) authorises proceedings against Her Majesty in her private capacity or in right of the Duchy of Lancaster or against the Duke of Cornwall.
(6) In subsection (1) "personal injury" includes any disease, any impairment of a person's physical or mental condition and any fatal injury.

24 APPLICATION OF PART III

(1) Where no initial or terminal point of a pipeline is situated in the United Kingdom or controlled waters, the pipeline shall be disregarded for the purposes of this Part of this Act except this subsection and subsection (2).
(2) The Secretary of State may by order provide that specified provisions of this Part of this Act shall apply, subject to such modifications (if any) as are specified, to the whole or any part of a pipeline of a kind mentioned in subsection (1); but an order under this subsection shall contain only such provisions as the Secretary of State considers are consistent with the jurisdiction which belongs to the United Kingdom under international law.
(3) The Secretary of State may in regulations provide that specified provisions of this Part of this Act shall not apply to a pipeline of a specified kind or shall not apply to such a pipeline while any specified condition is satisfied.
(4) In this section "specified", in relation to an order or regulations, means specified in the order or, as the case may be, the regulations.
(5) A statutory instrument containing an order under subsection (2) or regulations under subsection (3) shall be subject to annulment in pursuance of a resolution of either House of Parliament.

25 ORDERS AND REGULATIONS

(1) Before making any regulations under this Part of this Act, the Secretary of State shall consult such organisations in the United Kingdom as he considers are representative of persons who will be affected by the regulations.
(2) In making regulations under section 20, the Secretary of State shall have regard to the extent of the jurisdiction which belongs to the United Kingdom under international law.
(3) Any regulations under this Part of this Act may provide—
(a) for the creation of offences which, subject to paragraph (b), are punishable on summary conviction by a fine not exceeding the statutory maximum and on conviction on indictment by imprisonment for a term not exceeding two years and a fine;
(b) for the maximum punishment for an offence created by the regulations to be less than that authorised by paragraph (a) and for such an offence to be punishable only on summary conviction; and
(c) for the matters which are to be a defence to a charge of an offence created by the regulations.
(4) Regulations under this Part of this Act—
(a) may be limited so as to apply only in prescribed cases or may exclude prescribed cases from the application of the regulations;
(b) may provide for a case to be excluded from the application of the regulations only so long as conditions specified in the regulations are satisfied.
(5) The Health and Safety Executive may, by directions given to such persons as it considers appropriate, provide for any such regulations not to apply in a case specified in the directions so long as conditions so specified are satisfied.
(6) In its application to Northern Ireland, subsection (5) shall have effect as if the reference to the Health and Safety Executive were a reference to the Department of Economic Development for Northern Ireland.

(7) Any order or regulations under this Part of this Act—
(a) may make different provision for different circumstances; and
(b) may include such incidental, supplemental and transitional provision as the Secretary of State considers appropriate in connection with the order or regulations.
(8) Without prejudice to the generality of paragraph (b) of subsection (7), provision that may be included in regulations by virtue of that paragraph includes provision for the payment of fees in respect of consents and certificates required by the regulations.
(9) Section 14 of the [1978 c. 30.] Interpretation Act 1978 (implied power to amend) shall not apply in relation to the power conferred by section 24(2).
(10) Any power conferred by this Part of this Act to make an order or regulations shall be exercisable by statutory instrument.

26 MEANING OF "PIPELINE"

(1) Except where the context otherwise requires, in this Part of this Act "pipeline" means a pipe or system of pipes (excluding a drain or sewer) for the conveyance of any thing, together with any apparatus and works associated with such a pipe or system.
(2) For the purposes of this Part of this Act the apparatus and works associated with such a pipe or system are—
(a) any apparatus for inducing or facilitating the flow of any thing through, or through a part of, the pipe or system;
(b) any apparatus for treating or cooling any thing which is to flow through, or through part of, the pipe or system;
(c) valves, valve chambers and similar works which are annexed to, or incorporated in the course of, the pipe or system;
(d) apparatus for supplying energy for the operation of any apparatus or works mentioned in paragraphs (a) to (c);
(e) apparatus for the transmission of information for the operation of the pipe or system;
(f) apparatus for the cathodic protection of the pipe or system; and
(g) any structure used or to be used solely for the support of a part of the pipe or system.
(3) The Secretary of State may by order provide that a part of a pipeline specified in the order shall be treated for the purposes of this Part of this Act, except this subsection, as a pipeline.

27 MEANING OF "OWNER"

(1) For the purposes of this Part of this Act "owner" in relation to a pipeline, and "proposed owner" in relation to a proposed pipeline, mean the person for the time being designated as the owner of the pipeline, or as the case may be as the proposed owner of the proposed pipeline, by an order made by the Secretary of State.
(2) An order designating a person as the proposed owner of a proposed pipeline may also provide for him to be designated as the owner of the pipeline in question at a time determined by or under the order.
(3) Before designating a person under subsection (1) or (2), the Secretary of State shall give the person an opportunity of being heard with respect to the matter.
(4) Where a person for the time being designated under subsection (1) or (2) requests the Secretary of State in writing to cancel the designation, the Secretary of State shall—
(a) consider the request; and
(b) if he considers it appropriate to do so, give the person an opportunity of being heard in connection with the request.

28 INTERPRETATION OF PART III

(1) Except where the context otherwise requires, in this Part of this Act the following expressions have the following meanings—

- "authorisation" means an authorisation required by section 14;
- "construction", in relation to a pipeline, includes placing, and cognate expressions shall be construed accordingly;
- "controlled pipeline" and "controlled waters" have the meanings given to them by section 14;
- "enactment" includes an enactment of the Parliament of Northern Ireland or of the Northern Ireland Assembly;
- "heard" means heard on behalf of the Secretary of State by a person appointed by him for the purpose;
- "holder", in relation to an authorisation, means the person to whom the authorisation was issued;
- "notice" means notice in writing;
- "pipeline", in relation to an application for a works authorisation, means the proposed pipeline in respect of which the application is made;
- "prescribed" means prescribed by regulations; and
- "works authorisation" means an authorisation—

  (a)

  for works for the construction of a pipeline; or

  (b)

  for such works and for the use of the pipeline.

(2) For the purposes of this Part of this Act, works at any place in, under or over controlled waters for the purpose of determining whether the place is suitable as part of the site of a proposed pipeline and the carrying out of surveying operations for the purpose of settling the route of a proposed pipeline are not works for the construction of a pipeline.

(3) Any reference in this Part of this Act to a contravention of a provision of this Part or regulations made or directions given under this Part includes a reference to a failure to comply with that provision.

(4) Subsections (1) to (3) of section 49 of the [1962 c. 58.] Pipe-lines Act 1962 (service of documents) have effect as if—

(a) references to that Act included references to this Part of this Act; and

(b) in subsection (3), after "arrangements agreed" there were inserted "or in accordance with regulations under Part III of the Petroleum Act 1998".

(5) In the application of subsection (4) to Northern Ireland, section 49(1) to (3) of the Pipe-lines Act 1962 shall have effect as if it extended to Northern Ireland.

(6) Except so far as this Part of this Act otherwise expressly provides, nothing in this Part of this Act—

(a) confers a right of action in any civil proceedings (other than proceedings for recovery of a fine) in respect of any contravention of this Part of this Act or an order or regulations made under it;

(b) affects any restriction imposed by or under any other enactment, whether public. local or private; or

(c) derogates from any right of action or other remedy (whether civil or criminal) in proceedings instituted otherwise than under this Act.

(7) Subsection (6) is subject to section 18 of the [1978 c. 30.] Interpretation Act 1978 (duplicated offences).

PART IV ABANDONMENT OF OFFSHORE INSTALLATIONS

29 PREPARATION OF PROGRAMMES

(1) The Secretary of State may by written notice require—
(a) the person to whom the notice is given; or
(b) where notices are given to more than one person, those persons jointly,
to submit to the Secretary of State a programme setting out the measures proposed to be taken in connection with the abandonment of an offshore installation or submarine pipeline (an "abandonment programme").
(2) A notice under subsection (1) shall either specify the date by which the abandonment programme is to be submitted or provide for it to be submitted on or before such date as the Secretary of State may direct.
(3) A notice under subsection (1) may require the person to whom it is given to carry out such consultations as may be specified in the notice before submitting an abandonment programme.
(4) An abandonment programme—
(a) shall contain an estimate of the cost of the measures proposed in it;
(b) shall either specify the times at or within which the measures proposed in it are to be taken or make provision as to how those times are to be determined;
(c) if it proposes that an installation or pipeline be left in position or not wholly removed, shall include provision as to any continuing maintenance that may be necessary.
(5) A person who submits an abandonment programme to the Secretary of State under this section shall at the same time pay to him such fee in respect of his expenditure under this Part of this Act as may be determined in accordance with regulations under section 39.
(6) The Secretary of State may exercise his powers under this section notwithstanding that an abandonment programme has previously been submitted for the installation or pipeline in question, but only if he rejected that programme under section 32 or has withdrawn his approval of it under section 35.

30 PERSONS WHO MAY BE REQUIRED TO SUBMIT PROGRAMMES

(1) A notice under section 29(1) shall not be given to a person in relation to the abandonment of an offshore installation unless at the time when the notice is given he is within any of the following paragraphs—
(a) the person having the management of the installation or of its main structure;
(b) a person to whom subsection (5) applies in relation to the installation
(c) a person outside paragraphs (a) and (b) who is a party to a joint operating agreement or similar agreement relating to rights by virtue of which a person is within paragraph (b);
(d) a person outside paragraphs (a) to (c) who owns any interest in the installation otherwise than as security for a loan;
(e) a company which is outside paragraphs (a) to (d) but is associated with a company within any of those paragraphs.
(2) A notice under section 29(1) shall not be given to a person in relation to the abandonment of a submarine pipeline unless at the time when the notice is given he is within any of the following paragraphs—

(a) a person designated as the owner of the pipeline by an order made by the Secretary of State under section 27;
(b) a person outside paragraph (a) who owns any interest in the whole or substantially the whole of the pipeline, otherwise than as security for a loan;
(c) a company which is outside paragraphs (a) and (b) but is associated with a company within one of those paragraphs.
(3) The Secretary of State may by written notice require a person appearing to the Secretary of State to be within any of the paragraphs of subsection (1) or (2) to give him, within such time as may be specified in the notice, the name and address of every other person whom the recipient of the notice believes to be within any of those paragraphs in relation to the installation or pipeline concerned.
(4) A person who without reasonable excuse fails to comply with a notice under subsection (3) shall be guilty of an offence.
(5) This subsection applies to a person in relation to an offshore installation if—
(a) he has the right to exploit or explore mineral resources in any area, or to store gas in any area and to recover gas so stored; and
(b) any activity mentioned in subsection (6) is carried on from, by means of or on the installation, or if he had such a right when any such activity was last so carried on.
(6) The activities referred to in subsection (5) are—
(a) the exploitation or exploration of mineral resources, or the storage or recovery of gas, in the exercise of the right mentioned in subsection (5)(a);
(b) the conveyance in the area so mentioned, by means of a pipe or system of pipes, of minerals got, or gas being stored or recovered, in the exercise of that right; and
(c) the provision of accommodation for persons who work on or from an installation which is or has been maintained, or is intended to be established, for the carrying on of an activity falling within paragraph (a) or (b) or this paragraph.
(7) The fact that an installation has been maintained for the carrying on of an activity within subsection (6) shall be disregarded for the purposes of paragraph (c) of that subsection if, since it was so maintained, the installation—
(a) has been outside relevant waters or, where it was so maintained in a part of a foreign sector of the continental shelf adjacent to those waters, the area consisting of those waters and that part; or
(b) has been maintained for the carrying on of an activity which is not within that subsection.
(8) For the purposes of this section, one company is associated with another if one of them controls the other or a third company controls both of them; and one company controls another if it possesses or is entitled to acquire—
(a) one half or more of the issued share capital of the company;
(b) such rights as would entitle it to exercise one half or more of the votes exercisable in general meetings of the company;
(c) such part of the issued share capital of the company as would entitle it to one half or more of the amount distributed if the whole of the income of the company were in fact distributed among the shareholders; or
(d) such rights as would, in the event of the winding up of the company or in any other circumstances, entitle it to receive one half or more of the assets of the company which would then be available for distribution among the shareholders,
or if it has the power, directly or indirectly, to secure that the affairs of the company are conducted in accordance with its wishes.
(9) In determining whether, by virtue of subsection (8), one company controls another, the first-mentioned company shall be taken to possess—
(a) any rights and powers possessed by a person as nominee for it; and
(b) any rights and powers possessed by a company which it controls (including rights and powers which such a company would be taken to possess by virtue of this paragraph).

31 SECTION 29 NOTICES: SUPPLEMENTARY PROVISIONS

(1) Subject to subsection (3), the Secretary of State shall not give a notice under section 29(1) in relation to an offshore installation to a person within paragraph (d) or (e) of section 30(1) if the Secretary of State has been and continues to be satisfied that adequate arrangements (including financial arrangements) have been made by a person or persons within paragraph (a), (b) or (c) to ensure that a satisfactory abandonment programme will be carried out.
(2) Subject to subsection (3), the Secretary of State shall not give a notice under section 29(1) in relation to a submarine pipeline to a person within paragraph (b) or (c) of section 30(2) if the Secretary of State has been and continues to be satisfied that adequate arrangements (including financial arrangements) have been made by a person or persons within paragraph (a) to ensure that a satisfactory abandonment programme will be carried out.
(3) Subsections (1) and (2) shall not apply if there has been a failure to comply with a notice under section 29(1) or if the Secretary of State has rejected a programme submitted in compliance with such a notice.
(4) The Secretary of State shall not give a notice to a person under section 29(1) without first giving him an opportunity to make written representations as to whether the notice should be given.
(5) Where the Secretary of State has given a notice under section 29(1) in relation to an installation or a pipeline, he may at any time before the programme required by it is submitted withdraw the notice or give (subject to the preceding provisions of this section) a further notice under section 29(1) (whether in substitution for or in addition to any notice already given); and if he does so he shall inform the recipients of any other notices which have been given in relation to that installation or pipeline and not withdrawn.
(6) Neither the withdrawal of a notice given under section 29(1) nor the giving of a further notice shall relieve the recipient of any other notice of his duty to submit a programme (jointly, in a case where more than one notice is given and not withdrawn, with the recipients of the other notices).

32 APPROVAL OF PROGRAMMES

(1) The Secretary of State may either approve or reject a programme submitted to him under section 29.
(2) If he approves a programme, the Secretary of State may approve it with or without modifications and either subject to conditions or unconditionally.
(3) Before approving a programme with modifications or subject to conditions, the Secretary of State shall give the persons who submitted the programme an opportunity to make written representations about the proposed modifications or conditions.
(4) If he rejects a programme, the Secretary of State shall inform the persons who submitted it of his reasons for doing so.
(5) The Secretary of State shall act without unreasonable delay in reaching a decision as to whether to approve or reject a programme.

33 FAILURE TO SUBMIT PROGRAMMES

(1) If a notice under section 29(1) is not complied with, or if the Secretary of State rejects a programme submitted in compliance with such a notice, the Secretary of State may himself prepare an abandonment programme for the installation or pipeline concerned.
(2) With a view to exercising his powers under subsection (1) of this section, the Secretary of State may by written notice require any of the persons to whom notice was given under section 29(1) to provide him, within such time as may be specified in the notice, with such records and drawings and such other information as may be so specified.
(3) A person who without reasonable excuse fails to comply with a notice under subsection (2) shall be guilty of an offence.
(4) The Secretary of State may recover from any of the persons to whom a notice was given under section 29(1) any expenditure incurred by the Secretary of State in preparing an

abandonment programme under this section, and any fee that would have been payable on the submission of a programme by those persons.
(5) A person liable to pay any sum to the Secretary of State by virtue of subsection (4) shall also pay interest on that sum for the period beginning with the day on which the Secretary of State notified him of the sum payable and ending with the date of payment.
(6) The rate of interest payable in accordance with subsection (5) shall be a rate determined by the Secretary of State as comparable with commercial rates.
(7) Where the Secretary of State prepares an abandonment programme under this section, he shall inform the persons to whom notice was given under section 29(1) of its terms; and when he has done so, the following provisions of this Part of this Act shall have effect as if the programme had been submitted by those persons and approved by the Secretary of State.

34 REVISION OF PROGRAMMES

(1) Where the Secretary of State has approved a programme submitted to him under section 29—
(a) either he or the persons who submitted it acting together may propose an alteration to the programme or to any condition to which it is subject; and
(b) either he or any of those persons may propose that any person who by virtue of section 36 has a duty to secure that the programme is carried out shall cease to have that duty, or that a person who does not already have that duty shall have it (either in addition to or in substitution for another person).
(2) In the case of a proposal of the kind mentioned in subsection (1)(b), any person who would if the proposed change were made have a duty to secure that the programme is carried out must be a person who—
(a) if the programme relates to an offshore installation, is within paragraph (a), (b), (c), (d) or (e) of section 30(1) when the proposal is made, or has been within one of those paragraphs at some time since the giving of the first notice under section 29(1) in relation to the installation; and
(b) if the programme relates to a submarine pipeline, is within paragraph (a), (b) or (c) of section 30(2) when the proposal is made, or has been within one of those paragraphs at some time since the giving of the first notice under section 29(1) in relation to the pipeline.
(3) The Secretary of State shall not propose that a person who is or has been within paragraph (d) or (e) (but no other paragraph) of section 30(1) or paragraph (b) or (c) (but not paragraph (a)) of section 30(2) shall have a duty to secure that a programme is carried out unless it appears to the Secretary of State that a person already under that duty has failed or may fail to discharge it.
(4) A proposal under subsection (1) shall be made by written notice given—
(a) if the proposal is the Secretary of State's, to each of the persons by whom the programme was submitted; and
(b) in any other case, to the Secretary of State;
and a person giving notice to the Secretary of State shall at the same time pay to him such fee in respect of his expenditure under this Part of this Act as may be determined in accordance with regulations under section 39.
(5) Where the Secretary of State has made a proposal under subsection (1)(a), he shall give an opportunity to make written representations about it to each of the persons who submitted the programme.
(6) Where a proposal has been made under subsection (1)(b), the Secretary of State shall give an opportunity to make written representations about it to every person (other than one who made the proposal) who will if the proposed change is made—
(a) have a duty to secure that the programme is carried out; or
(b) cease to have that duty.
(7) The Secretary of State shall determine whether a change proposed under subsection (1) is to be made and shall then give notice of his determination, and of his reasons for it, to—
(a) every person who, before the determination was made, had a duty to secure the carrying out of the programme; and

(b) any person who has that duty as a result of the determination.
(8) Where the Secretary of State determines that a change proposed in accordance with this section shall be made, this Part of this Act shall thereafter have effect as if the programme had been approved by the Secretary of State after being submitted under section 29 with the alterations, or as the case may be by the persons, specified in the determination.

35 WITHDRAWAL OF APPROVAL

(1) The Secretary of State may at the request of one or more of the persons who submitted an abandonment programme withdraw his approval of the programme.
(2) If a request under subsection (1) is made by some but not all of the persons who submitted the programme, the Secretary of State shall give the others an opportunity to make written representations as to whether his approval should be withdrawn.
(3) The Secretary of State shall after determining whether to withdraw his approval of an abandonment programme give notice of his determination to each of the persons who submitted the programme.

36 DUTY TO CARRY OUT PROGRAMMES

Where an abandonment programme is approved by the Secretary of State, it shall be the duty of each of the persons who submitted it to secure that it is carried out and that any conditions to which the approval is subject are complied with.

37 DEFAULT IN CARRYING OUT PROGRAMMES

(1) If an abandonment programme approved by the Secretary of State is not carried out or a condition to which the approval is subject is not complied with, the Secretary of State may by written notice require any of the persons who submitted the programme to take such remedial action as may be specified in the notice within such time as may be so specified.
(2) A person who fails to comply with a notice given to him under subsection (1) shall be guilty of an offence unless he proves that he exercised due diligence to avoid the failure.
(3) If a notice under subsection (1) is not complied with, the Secretary of State may carry out the remedial action required by the notice, and may recover any expenditure incurred by him in doing so from the person to whom the notice was given.
(4) A person liable to pay any sum to the Secretary of State by virtue of subsection (3) shall also pay interest on that sum for the period beginning with the day on which the Secretary of State notified him of the sum payable and ending with the date of payment.
(5) The rate of interest payable in accordance with subsection (4) shall be a rate determined by the Secretary of State as comparable with commercial rates.

38 FINANCIAL RESOURCES

(1) At any time after the Secretary of State has given a notice under section 29(1) to any person and before he has approved an abandonment programme for the installation or pipeline concerned, he may by written notice require that person within such time as may be specified in the notice—
(a) to provide such information relating to the financial affairs of that person; and
(b) to supply copies of such documents relating to those affairs,
as may be so specified.
(2) In order to satisfy himself that a person who has a duty to secure that an abandonment programme is carried out will be capable of discharging that duty, the Secretary of State may at any time by written notice require that person, within such time as may be specified in the notice—
(a) to provide such information; and
(b) to supply copies of such documents,

as may be so specified.
(3) A person who—
(a) without reasonable excuse fails to comply with a notice under subsection (1) or (2); or
(b) in purported compliance with such a notice provides information which he knows to be false in a material particular or recklessly provides information which is false in a material particular, shall be guilty of an offence.
(4) If the Secretary of State is not satisfied that a person will be capable of discharging the duty imposed on him by section 36, he may by written notice, after consulting the Treasury, require that person to take such action as may be specified in the notice within such time as may be so specified.
(5) The Secretary of State shall not give notice to a person under subsection (4) without first giving him an opportunity to make written representations as to whether the notice should be given.
(6) A person who fails to comply with a notice under subsection (4) shall be guilty of an offence unless he proves that he exercised due diligence to avoid the failure.

39 REGULATIONS

(1) The Secretary of State may make regulations relating to the abandonment of offshore installations and submarine pipelines.
(2) Without prejudice to the generality of subsection (1), regulations under this section may—
(a) prescribe standards in respect of the dismantling, removal and disposal of installations and pipelines;
(b) prescribe standards and safety requirements in respect of anything left in the water in cases where an installation or pipeline is not wholly removed;
(c) make provision for the prevention of pollution;
(d) make provision for inspection, including provision as to the payment of the costs of inspection;
(e) make provision as to the determination of the amount of any fees that are payable to the Secretary of State under this Part of this Act.
(3) Regulations under this section may include provision making it an offence, in such cases as may be prescribed in the regulations, to contravene the regulations.
(4) Where regulations under this section create an offence, they shall make provision as to the mode of trial and punishment of offenders; but—
(a) any provision as to punishment on summary conviction shall not authorise a fine exceeding the statutory maximum or imprisonment; and
(b) any provision as to punishment on conviction on indictment shall not authorise imprisonment for a term exceeding two years.
(5) Before making regulations under this section the Secretary of State shall consult organisations in the United Kingdom appearing to him to be representative of those persons who will be affected by the regulations; and he shall not make regulations relating to the amount of any fees without the consent of the Treasury.
(6) Regulations under this section shall be made by statutory instrument, which shall be subject to annulment in pursuance of a resolution of either House of Parliament.

40 OFFENCES: PENALTIES

A person guilty of an offence under section 30, 33, 37 or 38 shall be liable—
(a) on summary conviction, to a fine not exceeding the statutory maximum;
(b) on conviction on indictment, to imprisonment for a term not exceeding two years, or to a fine, or to both.

41 OFFENCES: GENERAL

(1) Proceedings for an offence under section 30, 33, 37 or 38 or under regulations made under section 39 shall not be instituted in England and Wales except—

(a) by the Secretary of State or by a person authorised in that behalf by the Secretary of State; or
(b) by or with the consent of the Director of Public Prosecutions.
(2) Proceedings for an offence under section 30, 33, 37 or 38 or under regulations made under section 39 shall not be instituted in Northern Ireland except—
(a) by the Secretary of State or by a person authorised in that behalf by the Secretary of State; or
(b) by or with the consent of the Director of Public Prosecutions for Northern Ireland.
(3) Where an offence committed by a body corporate under section 30, 33, 37 or 38 or under regulations made under section 39 is proved to have been committed with the consent or connivance of, or to be attributable to any neglect on the part of, any director, manager, secretary or other similar officer of the body corporate or any person who was purporting to act in any such capacity, he as well as the body corporate shall be guilty of that offence and shall be liable to be proceeded against and punished accordingly.
(4) Where the affairs of a body corporate are managed by its members, subsection (3) shall apply in relation to acts and defaults of a member in connection with his functions of management as if he were a director of the body corporate.
(5) If an offence under section 37 or under regulations made under section 39 is committed outside the United Kingdom, proceedings for the offence may be taken, and the offence may for all incidental purposes be treated as having been committed, in any place in the United Kingdom.
(6) Section 3 of the [1878 c. 73.] Territorial Waters Jurisdiction Act 1878 (restriction on prosecutions) shall not apply to proceedings for an offence to which subsection (1) of this section applies.

42 VALIDITY OF SECRETARY OF STATE'S ACTS

(1) If any person is aggrieved by any of the acts of the Secretary of State mentioned in subsection (2) and desires to question its validity on the ground that it was not within the powers of the Secretary of State or that the relevant procedural requirements had not been complied with, he may within 42 days of the day on which the act was done make an application to the court under this section.
(2) The acts referred to in subsection (1) are—
(a) the giving of a notice under section 29(1);
(b) the approval of a programme under section 32;
(c) the rejection of a programme under section 32;
(d) a determination under section 34;
(e) a determination under section 35;
(f) the giving of a notice under section 38(4).
(3) If on an application under this section the court is satisfied that the act in question was not within the powers of the Secretary of State or that the applicant has been substantially prejudiced by a failure to comply with the relevant procedural requirements, the court may quash the act.
(4) Except as provided by this section, the validity of any of the acts of the Secretary of State referred to in subsection (1) shall not be questioned in any legal proceedings whatever.
(5) In this section "the relevant procedural requirements"—
(a) in relation to the giving of a notice under section 29(1), means the requirements of section 31(4);
(b) in relation to the approval of a programme under section 32, means the requirements of section 32(3);
(c) in relation to the rejection of a programme under section 32, means the requirements of section 32(4);
(d) in relation to a determination under section 34, means the requirements of section 34(5), (6) and (7);
(e) in relation to a determination under section 35, means the requirements of section 35(2);
(f) in relation to the giving of a notice under section 38(4), means the requirements of section 38(5).
(6) In this section, "the court" means—

(a) in relation to England and Wales, the High Court;
(b) in relation to Scotland, the Court of Session;
(c) in relation to Northern Ireland, the High Court.

43 NOTICES

Any notice or other communication authorised or required to be given by this Part of this Act may be sent by post (but this is without prejudice to any other method of transmission).

44 MEANING OF "OFFSHORE INSTALLATION"

(1) In this Part of this Act, "offshore installation" means any installation which is or has been maintained, or is intended to be established, for the carrying on of any activity to which subsection (2) applies.
(2) This subsection applies to any activity mentioned in subsection (3) which is carried on from, by means of or on an installation which is maintained in the water, or on the foreshore or other land intermittently covered with water, and is not connected with dry land by a permanent structure providing access at all times and for all purposes.
(3) The activities referred to in subsection (2) are—
(a) the exploitation, or the exploration with a view to exploitation, of mineral resources in or under the shore or bed of relevant waters;
(b) the storage of gas in or under the shore or bed of relevant waters or the recovery of gas so stored;
(c) the conveyance of things by means of a pipe, or system of pipes, constructed or placed on, in or under the shore or bed of relevant waters; and
(d) the provision of accommodation for persons who work on or from an installation which is or has been maintained, or is intended to be established, for the carrying on of an activity falling within paragraph (a), (b) or (c) or this paragraph.
(4) In this Part of this Act, "relevant waters" means—
(a) tidal waters and parts of the sea in or adjacent to the United Kingdom up to the seaward limits of the territorial sea;
(b) waters in an area designated under section 1(7) of the [1964 c. 29.] Continental Shelf Act 1964; and
(c) such inland waters as may for the time being be specified for the purposes of this paragraph by Order in Council;
but Her Majesty may by Order in Council provide that, in such cases and subject to such exceptions and modifications as may be prescribed by the Order, this Part of this Act shall have effect as if—
(i) any reference in this Part of this Act to relevant waters included a reference to waters in any area specified under section 10(8); and
(ii) in relation to an installation which is or has been maintained, or is intended to be established, in relevant waters, any reference in subsection (3) to relevant waters included a reference to waters in a foreign sector of the continental shelf which are adjacent to such waters.
(5) For the purposes of this section—

- "inland waters" means waters within the United Kingdom other than tidal waters and parts of the sea;
- "installation" includes—

  (a)

  any floating structure or device maintained on a station by whatever means; and

(b)

in such cases and subject to such exceptions as may be prescribed by Order in Council, any apparatus or works which are by virtue of section 26 to be treated as associated with a pipe or system of pipes for the purposes of Part III of this Act,

but, subject to paragraph (b), does not include any part of a pipeline within the meaning of that section;

- "modifications" includes additions, omissions and alterations.

(6) The fact that an installation has been maintained for the carrying on of an activity falling within subsection (3) shall be disregarded for the purposes of this section if, since it was so maintained, the installation—
(a) has been outside relevant waters or, where it was so maintained in a part of a foreign sector of the continental shelf adjacent to those waters, the area consisting of those waters and that part; or
(b) has been maintained for the carrying on of an activity not falling within that subsection.
(7) Any statutory instrument containing an Order under subsection (4) shall be subject to annulment in pursuance of a resolution of either House of Parliament.

45 INTERPRETATION OF PART IV

In this Part of this Act—

- "abandonment programme" has the meaning given by section 29;
- "foreign sector of the continental shelf" has the meaning given by section 48(1);
- "offshore installation" has the meaning given by section 44;
- "relevant waters" has the meaning given by section 44(4);
- "submarine pipeline" means a pipeline within the meaning of section 26 which is in, under or over waters in—

(a)

the territorial sea adjacent to the United Kingdom; or

(b)

an area designated under section 1(7) of the [1964 c. 29.] Continental Shelf Act 1964.

PART V MISCELLANEOUS AND GENERAL

46 NORTHERN IRELAND AND ISLE OF MAN SHARES OF PETROLEUM REVENUE

(1) Where petroleum is delivered to the Secretary of State under the terms of a licence granted under section 3 by virtue of subsection (2)(b) of that section, then, for the purposes of section 2 of the [1968 c. 75.] Miscellaneous Financial Provisions Act 1968 (Northern Ireland and Isle of Man shares of revenue from the continental shelf), the proceeds from the licence shall be taken to include the proceeds of the sale of the petroleum less—
(a) any sums paid by the Secretary of State in respect of the petroleum or the delivery or treatment of the petroleum; and
(b) any expenses incurred by the Secretary of State in connection with the sale.

(2) In this section "petroleum" has the same meaning as in Part I of this Act.

47 LOANS FOR DEVELOPMENT

(1) Where it appears to the Secretary of State expedient to do so for the purpose of facilitating or maintaining the development of the petroleum resources of the United Kingdom, he may with the approval of the Treasury—
(a) make loans to an oil company on terms determined by him; or
(b) guarantee on such terms the repayment of the principal of and the payment of interest on loans made to an oil company by another person.
(2) The aggregate amount for the time being outstanding in respect of the principal of loans made under subsection (1)(a) shall not exceed £50,000,000.
(3) The aggregate amount of—
(a) the principal sums in respect of which guarantees under subsection (1)(b) are for the time being in force; and
(b) the payments on account of principal sums which have been made by the Secretary of State under such guarantees and not recovered by him,
shall not exceed £600,000,000.
(4) Immediately after making a loan or giving a guarantee under subsection (1), the Secretary of State shall lay a statement relating to it before each House of Parliament.
(5) Where any sum is issued for fulfilling a guarantee given under subsection (1) the Secretary of State shall, as soon as possible after the end of each financial year (beginning with that in which the sum is issued and ending with that in which all liability in respect of the principal of the sum and in respect of interest thereon is finally discharged), lay before each House of Parliament a statement relating to that sum.
(6) In subsection (1) "oil company" means a body corporate which in the opinion of the Secretary of State has as its principal object—
(a) the production of petroleum;
(b) the refining of petroleum;
(c) the production and refining of petroleum; or
(d) the supplying of petroleum in a case where any of its other objects is one of those mentioned in paragraphs (a) to (c).

48 INTERPRETATION

(1) In this Act "foreign sector of the continental shelf" means an area within which rights are exercisable with respect to the sea bed and subsoil and their natural resources by a country or territory outside the United Kingdom.
(2) Any reference in this Act to the commencement of this Act shall be construed as a reference to the commencement of this Act in accordance with section 52(4).
(3) Each of Parts II, III and IV of this Act—
(a) so far as it applies to individuals, applies to them whether or not they are British citizens; and
(b) so far as it applies to bodies corporate, applies to them whether or not they are incorporated under the law of any part of the United Kingdom.

49 TRANSITIONAL PROVISIONS AND SAVINGS

Schedule 3 (transitional provisions and savings) shall have effect.

50 CONSEQUENTIAL AMENDMENTS

Schedule 4 (consequential amendments) shall have effect.

51 REPEALS AND REVOCATIONS

(1) The enactments mentioned in Part I of Schedule 5 (which include certain enactments which are spent) shall be repealed to the extent specified in the third column of that Part of that Schedule.
(2) The instruments mentioned in Part II of that Schedule (which include certain provisions which are spent) shall be revoked to the extent specified in the third column of that Part of that Schedule.

52 COMMENCEMENT

(1) Section 5(1) to (4) and (11) and this section shall come into force on the passing of this Act.
(2) The provisions mentioned in subsection (3) shall come into force on such day as the Secretary of State may by order appoint, and different days may be appointed for different provisions or different purposes.
(3) The provisions referred to in subsection (2) are—

- in Schedule 4, paragraphs 8, 10, 11, 13, 34 and 40; and
- in Schedule 5, the repeals of—
- the [1978 c. 46.] Employment (Continental Shelf) Act 1978;
- section 287(5) of the [1992 c. 52.] Trade Union and Labour Relations (Consolidation) Act 1992; and
- section 201(5) of the [1996 c. 18.] Employment Rights Act 1996.

(4) Subject to subsections (1) and (2), this Act shall come into force on such day as the Secretary of State may by order appoint.
(5) Orders under this section shall be made by statutory instrument.

53 SHORT TITLE AND EXTENT

(1) This Act may be cited as the Petroleum Act 1998.
(2) This Act, except for sections 7 and 8, extends to Northern Ireland.

SCHEDULES

Section 5.

SCHEDULE 1 MODEL CLAUSES INCORPORATED IN LICENCES WHEN GRANTED

1 The model clauses (other than the model clause entitled "Right to search and bore for and get petroleum") set out in Parts I and III of Schedule 2 to the [S.R.& O. 1935/426.] Petroleum (Production) Regulations 1935 as amended by the [S.I. 1954/1378.] Petroleum (Production) (Amendment) Regulations 1954 and the [S.I. 1957/1697.] Petroleum (Production) (Amendment) Regulations 1957 (mining licences).
2 The model clauses (other than model clause 2) set out in Schedule 2 to the [S.I. 1964/708.] Petroleum (Production) (Continental Shelf and Territorial Sea) Regulations 1964 (production licences for areas in controlled waters).
3 The model clauses (other than model clause 2) set out in Schedule 3 to the [S.I. 1966/898.] Petroleum (Production) Regulations 1966 (production licences for landward areas).
4 The model clauses (other than model clause 2) set out in Schedule 4 to the Petroleum (Production) Regulations 1966 (production licences for seaward areas).
5 The model clauses (other than model clause 2) set out in Schedule 4 to the Petroleum (Production) Regulations 1966 as amended by the [S.I. 1971/814.] Petroleum (Production) (Amendment) Regulations 1971 (production licences for seaward areas).

6 The model clauses (other than model clause 2) set out in Part II of Schedule 2 to the [1975 c. 74.] Petroleum and Submarine Pipe-lines Act 1975 (production licences for seaward areas).
7 The model clauses (other than model clause 2) set out in Schedule 4 to the [S.I. 1976/1129.] Petroleum (Production) Regulations 1976 (production licences for landward areas).
8 The model clauses (other than model clause 2) set out in Schedule 4 to the [1982 c. 23.] Petroleum (Production) Regulations 1976 as amended by the Oil and Gas (Enterprise) Act 1982 (production licences for landward areas).
9 The model clauses (other than model clause 2) set out in Schedule 5 to the Petroleum (Production) Regulations 1976 (production licences for seaward areas).
10 The model clauses (other than model clause 2) set out in Schedule 5 to the Petroleum (Production) Regulations 1976 as amended by the [S.I. 1978/929.] Petroleum (Production) (Amendment) Regulations 1978 (production licences for seaward areas).
11 The model clauses (other than model clause 2) set out in Schedule 5 to the Petroleum (Production) Regulations 1976 as amended by the Petroleum (Production) (Amendment) Regulations 1978 and the [S.I. 1980/721.] Petroleum (Production) (Amendment) Regulations 1980 (production licences for seaward areas).
12 The model clauses (other than model clause 2) set out in Schedule 5 to the Petroleum (Production) Regulations 1976 as amended by the Petroleum (Production) (Amendment) Regulations 1978, the [S.I. 1980/721.] Petroleum (Production) (Amendment) Regulations 1980 and the [1982 c. 23.] Oil and Gas (Enterprise) Act 1982 (production licences for seaward areas).
13 The model clauses (other than model clause 2) set out in Schedule 4 to the [S.I. 1982/1000.] Petroleum (Production) Regulations 1982 (production licences for landward areas).
14 The model clauses (other than model clause 2) set out in Schedule 5 to the Petroleum (Production) Regulations 1982 (production licences for seaward areas).
15 The model clauses (other than model clause 2) set out in Schedule 5 to the Petroleum (Production) Regulations 1982 as amended by the [1987 c. 12.] Petroleum Act 1987 (production licences for seaward areas).
16 The model clauses (other than model clause 2) set out in Schedule 8 to the Petroleum (Production) Regulations 1982 (methane drainage licences).
17 The model clauses (other than model clause 2) set out in Schedule 5 to the [S.I. 1984/1832.] Petroleum (Production) (Landward Areas) Regulations 1984 as amended by the Petroleum Act 1987 (development licences).
18 The model clauses (other than model clause 2) set out in Schedule 4 to the [S.I. 1988/1213.] Petroleum (Production) (Seaward Areas) Regulations 1988 (production licences for seaward areas).
19 The model clauses (other than model clause 2) set out in Schedule 4 to the Petroleum (Production) (Seaward Areas) Regulations 1988 as amended by the [1992 c. 15.] Offshore Safety Act 1992 (production licences for seaward areas).
20 The model clauses (other than model clause 2) set out in Schedule 4 to the Petroleum (Production) (Seaward Areas) Regulations 1988 as amended by the Offshore Safety Act 1992 and the [S.I. 1995/1435.] Petroleum (Production) (Seaward Areas) (Amendment) Regulations 1995 (production licences for seaward areas).
21 The model clauses (other than model clause 2) set out in Schedule 4 to the Petroleum (Production) (Seaward Areas) Regulations 1988 as amended by the Offshore Safety Act 1992, the Petroleum (Production) (Seaward Areas) (Amendment) Regulations 1995 and the [S.I. 1996/2964.] Petroleum (Production) (Seaward Areas) (Amendment) Regulations 1996 (production licences for seaward areas).
22 The model clauses (other than model clause 2) set out in Schedule 5 to the Petroleum (Production) (Seaward Areas) Regulations 1988 (exploration licences for seaward areas and landward areas below the low water line).
23 The model clauses (other than model clause 2) set out in Schedule 5 to the Petroleum (Production) (Seaward Areas) Regulations 1988 as amended by the Offshore Safety Act 1992 (exploration licences for seaward areas and landward areas below the low water line).

24 The model clauses (other than model clause 2) set out in Schedule 5 to the Petroleum (Production) (Seaward Areas) Regulations 1988 as amended by the Offshore Safety Act 1992 and the Petroleum (Production) (Seaward Areas) (Amendment) Regulations 1995 (exploration licences for seaward areas and landward areas below the low water line).
25 The model clauses (other than model clause 2) set out in Schedule 3 to the [S.I. 1991/981.] Petroleum (Production) (Landward Areas) Regulations 1991 (exploration licences for landward areas).
26 The model clauses (other than model clause 2) set out in Schedule 5 to the Petroleum (Production) (Landward Areas) Regulations 1991 (appraisal licences for landward areas).
27 The model clauses (other than model clause 2) set out in Schedule 6 to the Petroleum (Production) (Landward Areas) Regulations 1991 (development licences for landward areas).

SCHEDULE 2 AUTHORISATIONS UNDER SECTION 14

PART I WORKS AUTHORISATIONS

1 (1) The Secretary of State may by regulations make provision as to—
(a) the manner in which an application for a works authorisation is to be made; and
(b) the information to be included in or provided in connection with an application.
(2) Without prejudice to the generality of sub-paragraph (1), regulations under this paragraph may require the payment of fees in connection with an application.
(3) A statutory instrument containing regulations under this paragraph shall be subject to annulment in pursuance of a resolution of either House of Parliament.
2 The Secretary of State shall, on receiving an application for a works authorisation—
(a) decide whether the application is to be considered further or rejected; and
(b) serve notice of his decision on the applicant and—
(i) in the case of a decision that the application is to be considered further, shall give the applicant such directions with respect to the application as the Secretary of State considers appropriate for the purposes of paragraph 3; and
(ii) in the case of a decision to reject the application, shall include in the notice a statement of the reasons for the decision except any reason which in the opinion of the Secretary of State it would be against the national interest to state.
3 Where the Secretary of State serves on an applicant notice under paragraph 2 that the application is to be considered further, the applicant shall—
(a) publish, in such manner as the Secretary of State directs, a notice which—
(i) contains such particulars of the application as the Secretary of State directs; and
(ii) states that representations with respect to the application may be made in writing to the Secretary of State within the period of 28 days beginning with the date on which the notice is first published in accordance with this paragraph or within such longer period beginning with that date as is specified in the notice in accordance with a direction of the Secretary of State; and
(iii) states where the map mentioned in sub-paragraph (b) may be inspected during the period specified in the notice under paragraph (ii);
(b) secure that a map of such scale and containing such particulars as the Secretary of State directs is available for inspection by the public free of charge from 10 a.m. to 4 p.m. on each weekday during the period so specified; and
(c) serve a copy of the notice on such persons as the Secretary of State directs;
and the Secretary of State shall defer his further consideration of the application until he is satisfied that the applicant has complied with this paragraph.
4 (1) This paragraph applies where the Secretary of State decides that an application for a works authorisation is to be considered further and is of the opinion, either on his own initiative (except in relation to the purpose mentioned in paragraph 6(b)) or in consequence of representations made to him by the applicant or any other person,—
(a) that the route proposed for the pipeline or part of it in the application ought to be altered in a particular manner for any of the purposes mentioned in paragraph 6; or

(b) that the capacity proposed for the pipeline or part of it in the application ought to be increased for any of the purposes mentioned in paragraph 6(b) or (d).
(2) Where this paragraph applies, the Secretary of State shall, before deciding whether to issue an authorisation in consequence of the application, serve notice of his opinion—
(a) on the applicant; and
(b) where the opinion relates to an alteration of the route proposed for the pipeline or part of it on—
(i) any persons whom the Secretary of State considers are likely to be affected by the alteration; or
(ii) any person appearing to the Secretary of State to represent such persons.
(3) In any notice of his opinion served under this paragraph the Secretary of State shall state the reasons for his opinion except any reason which he considers that it would be against the national interest to state.
5 (1) Where under paragraph 4 the Secretary of State serves on the applicant notice of his opinion he shall give him an opportunity of being heard with respect to the opinion; and where the applicant is heard the Secretary of State may give such other persons, if any, as he thinks fit an opportunity to be heard at the hearing.
(2) Where under paragraph 4 the Secretary of State serves on any person other than the applicant notice of his opinion, he shall state in the notice that representations in writing with respect to the opinion may be made to the Secretary of State within a period specified in the notice.
6 The purposes referred to in paragraph 4(1) are—
(a) the purpose of avoiding or reducing danger to navigation, to persons engaged in and vessels and equipment used for fishing, to some structure or apparatus (which may be the pipeline) or to marine flora or fauna;
(b) the purpose of facilitating the use of the pipeline by persons other than the applicant where it appears to the Secretary of State that such persons desire to use the pipeline;
(c) the purpose of avoiding or reducing interference with fishing or the exploitation of mineral resources;
(d) any other purpose which the Secretary of State considers proper.
7 Where the Secretary of State—
(a) is satisfied that an applicant for a works authorisation has complied with paragraph 3; and
(b) has considered any representations relating to the application which were made to the Secretary of State—
(i) within the period specified in the notice published in respect of the application under paragraph 3(a);
(ii) at a hearing held under paragraph 5(1); and
(iii) in accordance with a notice served by the Secretary of State in respect of the application under paragraph 5(2),
he shall decide whether to issue an authorisation in consequence of the application.
8 (1) Where the Secretary of State decides not to issue a works authorisation in consequence of an application he shall serve on—
(a) the applicant; and
(b) each person on whom a copy of notice of the application was required to be served under paragraph 3(c),
a notice stating the decision and, in the case of the notice served on the applicant, stating also the reasons for the decision except any reason which the Secretary of State considers that it would be against the national interest to state.
(2) Where the Secretary of State decides to issue a works authorisation in consequence of an application he shall—
(a) serve notice of the decision on—
(i) the applicant;
(ii) each person mentioned in sub-paragraph (1)(b); and

(iii) any other person who made representations as mentioned in paragraph 7(b)(ii) or (iii); and
(b) publish a copy of the notice in the London and Edinburgh and Belfast Gazettes, or in such of them as he considers appropriate, and in any other publication which he considers appropriate.
9 (1) Sub-paragraphs (2) and (3) apply where the Secretary of State issues a works authorisation.
(2) The Secretary of State shall serve on the persons on whom notice in respect of the authorisation was required to be served by paragraph 8(2)(a)(ii) and (iii) a notice stating that the authorisation has been issued and containing—
(a) the name and address of the person to whom it was issued;
(b) such particulars as the Secretary of State considers appropriate of—
(i) the route of the pipeline;
(ii) its authorised capacity;
(iii) the things authorised to be conveyed by it; and
(iv) the persons authorised to use it; and
(c) such other information (if any) about the pipeline as the Secretary of State considers appropriate.
(3) The Secretary of State shall publish a copy of the notice in the London and Edinburgh and Belfast Gazettes, or in such of them as he considers appropriate, and in any other publication which he considers appropriate.

PART II OTHER AUTHORISATIONS

10 Where the Secretary of State issues an authorisation other than a works authorisation, he shall publish in the London and Edinburgh and Belfast Gazettes or in such of them as he considers appropriate, and in any other publication which he considers appropriate, a notice stating that the authorisation has been issued and containing—
(a) the name and address of the person to whom it was issued;
(b) such particulars as the Secretary of State considers appropriate of—
(i) the route and capacity of the relevant pipeline;
(ii) the things authorised to be conveyed by it; and
(iii) the persons authorised to use it; and
(c) such other information (if any) about the pipeline as the Secretary of State considers appropriate.

SCHEDULE 3 TRANSITIONAL PROVISIONS AND SAVINGS

PART I GENERAL

1 (1) The repeal (or revocation) and re-enactment of provisions in this Act does not affect the continuity of the law.
(2) Any subordinate legislation made or other thing done, or having effect as if made or done, under or for the purposes of any provision repealed, or revoked, and re-enacted by this Act shall, if in force or effective immediately before the commencement of the corresponding provision of this Act, have effect thereafter as if made or done under or for the purposes of that corresponding provision.
(3) Any reference (express or implied) in this Act or any other enactment or in any instrument or document—
(a) to any provision of this Act, or
(b) to things done or falling to be done under or for the purposes of any provision of this Act,
shall (so far as the context permits) be construed as including, in relation to times, circumstances or purposes in relation to which the corresponding provision repealed, or revoked, by this Act had effect, a reference—
(i) to that corresponding provision, or
(ii) to things done or falling to be done under or for the purposes of that corresponding provision, as the case may be.

(4) Any reference (express or implied) in any enactment or in any instrument or document—
(a) to any provision repealed, or revoked, and re-enacted by this Act, or
(b) to things done or falling to be done under or for the purposes of any such provision,
shall (so far as the context permits) be construed as including, in relation to times, circumstances or purposes in relation to which the corresponding provision of this Act has effect, a reference—
(i) to that corresponding provision, or
(ii) to things done or falling to be done under or for the purposes of that corresponding provision, as the case may be.
(5) Without prejudice to the generality of sub-paragraph (4), where a power conferred by an Act is expressed to be exercisable in relation to enactments contained in Acts passed before or in the same Session as the Act conferring the power, the power is also exercisable in relation to provisions of this Act which reproduce such enactments.
(6) Sub-paragraphs (1) to (5) have effect instead of section 17(2) of the [1978 c. 30.] Interpretation Act 1978 (but are without prejudice to any other provision of that Act).
2 The repeal by this Act of an enactment previously repealed subject to savings does not affect the continued operation of those savings.

PART II SPECIFIC PROVISIONS

PROPERTY IN PETROLEUM

3 The repeal by this Act of section 1(1) of the [1934 c. 36.] Petroleum (Production) Act 1934 does not affect the vesting in Her Majesty of property in petroleum which is so vested immediately before the commencement of this Act.

EXISTING LICENCES

4 Nothing in section 2 or 3 shall be taken to prejudice any right conferred by any licence granted under section 2 of the Petroleum (Production) Act 1934 which is in force immediately before the commencement of this Act so long as the licence remains in force.
5 (1) Nothing in this Act affects the validity of the licence granted on 26th March 1923 under the [1918 c. 52.] Petroleum (Production) Act 1918 to the Duke of Devonshire relating to an area near Hardstoft in the county of Derbyshire.
(2) Without prejudice to the generality of paragraph 1(2), that licence shall, if in force immediately before the commencement of this Act, have effect as if granted under this Act.
(3) So long as that licence remains in force, section 2 shall not apply to petroleum which at the commencement of the Petroleum (Production) Act 1934 might lawfully be got under that licence.
6 (1) Where, immediately before the commencement of this Act—
(a) a person is exercising a function of a kind mentioned in clause 22 of the clauses set out in Part II of Schedule 2, or Part II of Schedule 3, to the [1975 c. 74.] Petroleum and Submarine Pipe-lines Act 1975 in connection with a licence granted under section 2 of the Petroleum (Production) Act 1934; and
(b) by virtue of section 19(6) of the [1975 c. 74.] Petroleum and Submarine Pipe-lines Act 1975, he is deemed to be approved by the Secretary of State as respects that function in connection with that licence,
he shall continue to be deemed to be so approved.
(2) Any act or omission which occurred at a time before a licence was altered by virtue of section 18 of the Petroleum and Submarine Pipe-lines Act 1975 shall not be treated as contravening the provisions of the licence as so altered or as authorising the revocation of the licence if at that time it did not contravene the provisions of the licence or authorise the revocation of it.
7 Without prejudice to paragraph 1, any reference in any enactment to a licence under the [1934 c. 36.] Petroleum (Production) Act 1934 (or under section 2 of that Act) shall (except where the context otherwise requires) include a reference to a licence granted, or treated as granted, under section 3 of this Act.

8 (1) In relation to any time after the commencement of this Act, section 1 of the [1983 c. 59.] Petroleum Royalties (Relief) Act 1983 and sections 1 and 2 of the [1989 c. 1.] Petroleum Royalties (Relief) and Continental Shelf Act 1989 shall have effect as if each reference (whether direct or indirect) in any of those provisions to model clauses set out in—
(a) the Petroleum and Submarine Pipe-lines Act 1975; or
(b) regulations made under section 6 of the Petroleum (Production) Act 1934,
were a reference to the corresponding model clauses set out in the order under section 5.
(2) This paragraph is without prejudice to the generality of section 5(10).

Submarine pipelines: safety regulations etc.

9 Any reference in—
(a) section 20 to Part III of this Act; or
(b) section 22 or 23 to regulations made under Part III of this Act,
includes a reference to regulations made under section 26 of the Petroleum and Submarine Pipe-lines Act 1975 which are in force immediately before the commencement of this Act.
10 Without prejudice to the generality of paragraph 2, the repeal of Part III of the Petroleum and Submarine Pipe-lines Act 1975 shall not affect any instrument to the extent that, immediately before the commencement of this Act, it applies section 26 of the Petroleum and Submarine Pipe-lines Act 1975.
11 (1) The substitution by this Act of paragraph (b) of section 1(3) of the Offshore Safety Act 1992 and the repeal by this Act of the reference in paragraph (c) of that provision to section 11(2)(a) of the Petroleum Act 1987 so far as relating to safety requirements shall not affect the power conferred by section 1(2)(b) of that Act of 1992.
(2) The substitution by this Act of paragraph (b) of Article 3(3) of the Offshore, and Pipelines, Safety (Northern Ireland) Order 1992 and the repeal by this Act of the reference in paragraph (c) of that provision to section 11(2)(a) of the Petroleum Act 1987 so far as relating to safety requirements shall not affect the power conferred by Article 3(2)(b) of that Order.

Submarine pipelines: authorisations granted before 1st October 1982

12 Where, immediately before the commencement of this Act, an authorisation granted before 1st October 1982 under Part III of the [1975 c. 74.] Petroleum and Submarine Pipe-lines Act 1975 is in force in relation to any pipeline, that pipeline shall not be regarded for the purposes of section 18(6) to (8) or 19(1) as comprising any such associated apparatus as is mentioned in section 26(1)(b).

Fatal Accidents Act 1976: deaths before 1st September 1976

13 The reference in section 23(2)(a) to the [1976 c. 30.] Fatal Accidents Act 1976 includes a reference to the [1846 c. 93.] Fatal Accidents Act 1846.

SCHEDULE 4 CONSEQUENTIAL AMENDMENTS

The Mining Industry Act 1926 (c. 28)

1 At the end of section 23 of the Mining Industry Act 1926 (facilities to be given to National Environment Research Council) there shall be added—
"(6) In subsection (1) above, the expression "minerals" includes petroleum within the meaning of Part I of the Petroleum Act 1998.".

The Continental Shelf Act 1964 (c. 29)

2 (1) The Continental Shelf Act 1964 shall be amended as follows.
(2) In section 1 (exploration and exploitation of continental shelf), subsection (3) and, in subsection (8), the words from "and "petroleum"" to the end shall be omitted.

(3) In section 6 (wireless telegraphy) and section 7 (radioactive substances) for "section 23 of the Oil and Gas (Enterprise) Act 1982" there shall be substituted "section 11 of the Petroleum Act 1998".
(4) At the end of section 8 (submarine cables and pipe-lines) there shall be added—
"(1A) It is hereby declared that the reference in subsection (1) of this section to pipe-lines under the high seas includes pipe-lines under the territorial sea adjacent to the United Kingdom.".

THE MISCELLANEOUS FINANCIAL PROVISIONS ACT 1968 (C. 75)

3 In section 2 of the Miscellaneous Financial Provisions Act 1968 (Northern Ireland and Isle of Man shares of revenue from continental shelf), in subsection (5) for the words following "under" there shall be substituted "section 3 of the Petroleum Act 1998 by virtue of subsection (2)(b) of that section".

THE PREVENTION OF OIL POLLUTION ACT 1971 (C. 60)

4 For section 23 of the Prevention of Oil Pollution Act 1971 there shall be substituted—

"23 POWER OF SECRETARY OF STATE TO GRANT EXEMPTIONS.

The Secretary of State may exempt any discharge of, or of a mixture containing, oil from any of the provisions of this Act or of any regulations made thereunder, either absolutely or subject to such conditions as he thinks fit.".

THE FINANCE ACT 1973 (C. 51)

5 In Schedule 15 to the Finance Act 1973 (territorial extension of charge to tax: supplementary provisions), in paragraphs 2, 4(1)(a) and 4A(1)(a) for "the Petroleum (Production) Act 1934" there shall be substituted "Part I of the Petroleum Act 1998".

THE OFFSHORE PETROLEUM DEVELOPMENT (SCOTLAND) ACT 1975 (C. 8)

6 In section 20 of the Offshore Petroleum Development (Scotland) Act 1975 (short title, interpretation and extent), in the definition of "petroleum" in subsection (2), for "the Petroleum (Production) Act 1934" there shall be substituted "Part I of the Petroleum Act 1998".

THE OIL TAXATION ACT 1975 (C. 22)

7 (1) The Oil Taxation Act 1975 shall be amended as follows.
(2) In section 1 (petroleum revenue tax), in subsection (1) for "the Petroleum (Production) Act 1934" there shall be substituted "Part I of the Petroleum Act 1998".
(3) In section 12 (interpretation of Part I), in the definition of "licence" in subsection (1), for "the Petroleum (Production) Act 1934" there shall be substituted "Part I of the Petroleum Act 1998".
(4) In section 21 (citation, interpretation and construction), subsection (5) shall cease to have effect.
(5) In Schedule 1 (determination of oil fields), in paragraph 1(2)(a) for "the Petroleum (Production) Act 1934" there shall be substituted "Part I of the Petroleum Act 1998".
(6) In Schedule 2 (management and collection of petroleum revenue tax), in paragraph 2(2)(c) for "the Petroleum (Production) Act 1934" there shall be substituted "Part I of the Petroleum Act 1998".
(7) In Schedule 3 (petroleum revenue tax: miscellaneous provisions), in paragraph 4 for "the Petroleum (Production) Act 1934" there shall be substituted "Part I of the Petroleum Act 1998".

THE SEX DISCRIMINATION ACT 1975 (C. 65)

8 In section 10 of the Sex Discrimination Act 1975 (employment at establishment in Great Britain), in subsection (5)—

(a) for the words from "exploration" to "natural resources" there shall be substituted "any activity within section 11(2) of the Petroleum Act 1998"; and
(b) after "1964" there shall be inserted "or specified under section 10(8) of the Petroleum Act 1998".

THE FATAL ACCIDENTS AND SUDDEN DEATHS INQUIRY (SCOTLAND) ACT 1976 (C. 14)

9 In section 9 of the Fatal Accidents and Sudden Deaths Inquiry (Scotland) Act 1976 (application to continental shelf), for "section 23 of the Oil and Gas (Enterprise) Act 1982" there shall be substituted "section 11 of the Petroleum Act 1998".

THE FAIR EMPLOYMENT (NORTHERN IRELAND) ACT 1976 (C. 25)

10 In section 49(3) of the Fair Employment (Northern Ireland) Act 1976 (employment at establishment in Northern Ireland)—
(a) for the words from "the exploration" to "natural resources" there shall be substituted "any activity within section 11(2) of the Petroleum Act 1998"; and
(b) after "1964" there shall be inserted "or specified under section 10(8) of the Petroleum Act 1998".

THE RACE RELATIONS ACT 1976 (C. 74)

11 In the Race Relations Act 1976, in sections 8(5) (employment at establishment in Great Britain) and 9(3) (exception for seamen recruited abroad)—
(a) for the words from "exploration" to "natural resources" there shall be substituted "any activity within section 11(2) of the Petroleum Act 1998"; and
(b) after "1964" there shall be inserted "or specified under section 10(8) of the Petroleum Act 1998".

THE ENERGY ACT 1976 (C. 76)

12 In section 9 of the Energy Act 1976 (liquefaction of offshore natural gas), in subsection (6) for the words from "licences" to "1964" there shall be substituted "licences granted under Part I of the Petroleum Act 1998 by virtue of section 3(2)(b) of that Act".

THE SEX DISCRIMINATION (NORTHERN IRELAND) ORDER 1976 (S.I. 1976/1042 (N.I. 15))

13 In Article 13(5) of the Sex Discrimination (Northern Ireland) Order 1976 (employment at establishment in Northern Ireland)—
(a) for the words from "exploration" to "natural resources" there shall be substituted "any activity within section 11(2) of the Petroleum Act 1998"; and
(b) after "1964" there shall be inserted "or specified under section 10(8) of the Petroleum Act 1998".

THE PATENTS ACT 1977 (C. 37)

14 In section 132 of the Patents Act 1977 (application of Act), in subsection (4)—
(a) for "section 22(5) of the Oil and Gas (Enterprise) Act 1982" there shall be substituted "section 10(8) of the Petroleum Act 1998"; and
(b) for "section 23(2)" there shall be substituted "section 11(2)".

THE GAS LEVY ACT 1981 (C. 3)

15 In section 1 of the Gas Levy Act 1981 (gas levy), in subsection (3) for the definition of "petroleum production licence" there shall be substituted—
""petroleum production licence" means a licence granted under section 3 of the Petroleum Act 1998;".

THE FINANCE ACT 1981 (C. 35)

16 In section 118 of the Finance Act 1981 (licence payments other than royalties), in subsection (2)(c) for "section 41(3) of the Petroleum and Submarine Pipe-lines Act 1975" there shall be substituted "section 6(1) of the Petroleum Act 1998".

THE CIVIL JURISDICTION AND JUDGMENTS ACT 1982 (C. 29)

17 In the Civil Jurisdiction and Judgments Act 1982, in—
(a) paragraph 9 of Schedule 5 (proceedings excluded from Schedule 4); and
(b) paragraph 10 of Schedule 9 (proceedings excluded from Schedule 8),
for "section 23 of the Oil and Gas (Enterprise) Act 1982" there shall be substituted "section 11 of the Petroleum Act 1998".

THE PETROLEUM ROYALTIES (RELIEF) ACT 1983 (C. 59)

18 In section 1 of the Petroleum Royalties (Relief) Act 1983 (royalty exemption for petroleum from certain new offshore fields), in the definition of "petroleum" in subsection (3), for "the said Act of 1934" there shall be substituted "Part I of the Petroleum Act 1998".

THE TELECOMMUNICATIONS ACT 1984 (C. 12)

19 In section 107 of the Telecommunications Act 1984 (application to territorial waters and the continental shelf etc.)—
(a) in subsection (1) for "section 23 of the Oil and Gas (Enterprise) Act 1982" there shall be substituted "section 11 of the Petroleum Act 1998"; and
(b) subsection (3) shall be omitted.

THE FOOD AND ENVIRONMENT PROTECTION ACT 1985 (C. 48)

20 After section 7 of the Food and Environment Protection Act 1985 there shall be inserted—

"7A APPLICATION OF PART II: FURTHER PROVISIONS.

Nothing in this Part of this Act shall apply to anything done—
(a) for the purpose of constructing or maintaining a pipeline as respects any part of which an authorisation (within the meaning of Part III of the Petroleum Act 1998) is in force; or
(b) for the purpose of establishing or maintaining an offshore installation within the meaning of Part IV of that Act.".

THE OIL AND PIPELINES ACT 1985 (C. 62)

21 In section 6 of the Oil and Pipelines Act 1985 (interpretation), for the definition of "petroleum" there shall be substituted—
""petroleum" has the same meaning as in Part I of the Petroleum Act 1998;".

THE GAS ACT 1986 (C. 44)

22 In section 62 of the Gas Act 1986 (exclusion of certain agreements from the Restrictive Trade Practices Act 1976), in the definition of "petroleum production licence" in subsection (6), after "the Petroleum (Production) Act 1934" there shall be inserted ", Part I of the Petroleum Act 1998".

THE PETROLEUM ACT 1987 (C. 12)

23 In section 24 of the Petroleum Act 1987 (safety zones: supplementary), in subsection (1)(b) for "section 33 of the Petroleum and Submarine Pipe-lines Act 1975" there shall be substituted "section 26 of the Petroleum Act 1998".

THE TERRITORIAL SEA ACT 1987 (C. 49)

24 In section 2 of the Territorial Sea Act 1987 (enactments and instruments not affected), in subsection (4)—
(a) in paragraph (a), after "1934" there shall be inserted "or section 4 of the Petroleum Act 1998"; and
(b) in paragraph (b), after "1934" there shall be inserted "or Part I of the said Act of 1998" and for "that section" there shall be substituted "either of those sections".

THE INCOME AND CORPORATION TAXES ACT 1988 (C. 1)

25 In section 502 of the Income and Corporation Taxes Act 1988 (interpretation of Chapter V of Part XII), in the definition of "oil" in subsection (1), for "the Petroleum (Production) Act 1934" there shall be substituted "Part I of the Petroleum Act 1998".

THE PETROLEUM ROYALTIES (RELIEF) AND CONTINENTAL SHELF ACT 1989 (C. 1)

26 In section 1 of the Petroleum Royalties (Relief) and Continental Shelf Act 1989 (royalty exemption: Southern Basin and landward areas), in the definition of "petroleum" in subsection (3), for "the said Act of 1934" there shall be substituted "Part I of the Petroleum Act 1998".

THE CAPITAL ALLOWANCES ACT 1990 (C. 1)

27 (1) The Capital Allowances Act 1990 shall be amended as follows.
(2) In section 62A (special allowance for demolition costs related to offshore machinery or plant), in subsection (3)(a) for "Part I of the Petroleum Act 1987" there shall be substituted "Part IV of the Petroleum Act 1998".
(3) In section 116 (oil licences etc.), in subsection (2) for "the Petroleum (Production) Act 1934" there shall be substituted "Part I of the Petroleum Act 1998".
(4) In section 138A (disposal of oil licences etc.), in the definitions of "overseas petroleum" and "petroleum" in subsection (4), for "the Petroleum (Production) Act 1934" there shall be substituted "Part I of the Petroleum Act 1998".

THE FOOD SAFETY ACT 1990 (C. 16)

28 In section 58 of the Food Safety Act 1990 (territorial waters and the continental shelf)—
(a) in subsection (2) for "section 23 of the Oil and Gas (Enterprise) Act 1982" there shall be substituted "section 11 of the Petroleum Act 1998";
(b) in the definition of "installation" in subsection (4), for "section 23" there shall be substituted "section 11".

THE AVIATION AND MARITIME SECURITY ACT 1990 (C. 31)

29 In section 14 of the Aviation and Maritime Security Act 1990 (ancillary offences), in subsection (3) for "section 22 of the Oil and Gas (Enterprise) Act 1982" there shall be substituted "section 10 of the Petroleum Act 1998".

THE SOCIAL SECURITY CONTRIBUTIONS AND BENEFITS ACT 1992 (C. 4)

30 In section 120 of the Social Security Contributions and Benefits Act 1992 (employment at sea: continental shelf operations), in subsection (2) for "subsection (6) of section 23 of the Oil and Gas (Enterprise) Act 1982" there shall be substituted "subsection (8) of section 11 of the Petroleum Act 1998".

THE SOCIAL SECURITY CONTRIBUTIONS AND BENEFITS (NORTHERN IRELAND) ACT 1992 (C. 7)

31 In section 166 of the Social Security Contributions and Benefits (Northern Ireland) Act 1992 (special classes of persons), in subsection (3) for "section 23 of the Oil and Gas (Enterprise) Act 1982" there shall be substituted "section 11 of the Petroleum Act 1998".

THE TAXATION OF CHARGEABLE GAINS ACT 1992 (C. 12)

32 (1) The Taxation of Chargeable Gains Act 1992 shall be amended as follows.
(2) In section 193 (roll-over relief not available for gains on oil licences), in subsection (1) for "the Petroleum (Production) Act 1934" there shall be substituted "Part I of the Petroleum Act 1998".
(3) In section 196 (interpretation of sections 194 and 195), in the definitions of "oil" and "overseas petroleum" in subsection (5), for "the Petroleum (Production) Act 1934" there shall be substituted "Part I of the Petroleum Act 1998".
(4) In Schedule 3 (assets held on 31st March 1982), in paragraph 7(2)(c) for "the Petroleum (Production) Act 1934" there shall be substituted "Part I of the Petroleum Act 1998".

THE OFFSHORE SAFETY ACT 1992 (C. 15)

33 (1) The Offshore Safety Act 1992 shall be amended as follows.
(2) In section 1 (application of Part I of Health and Safety at Work etc. Act 1974 for offshore purposes)—
(a) in subsection (3), for paragraph (b) there shall be substituted—
"(b) sections 20 and 25 of the Petroleum Act 1998;",and in paragraph (c) the words from "section" to "requirements and" shall be omitted;
(b) in subsection (4), for the definitions of "pipe-line" and "pipe-line works" there shall be substituted—
""pipe-line" means, subject to subsection (4A), a controlled pipeline within the meaning of Part III of the Petroleum Act 1998; and
"pipe-line works" means works of any of the following kinds, namely—
(a) assembling or placing a pipe-line or length of pipe-line;
(b) inspecting, testing, maintaining, adjusting, repairing, altering or renewing a pipe-line or length of pipe-line;
(c) changing the position of or dismantling or removing a pipe-line or length of pipe-line;
(d) opening the bed of the sea for the purposes of works mentioned in paragraphs (a) to (c), tunnelling or boring for those purposes and other works needed for or incidental to those purposes;
(e) works for the purpose of determining whether a place is suitable as part of the site of a proposed pipe-line and the carrying out of surveying operations for the purpose of settling the route of a proposed pipe-line.";
(c) after subsection (4) there shall be inserted—
"(4A) In this section "pipe-line" does not include—
(a) any pipe-line so far as it forms part of the equipment of a vessel or vehicle; or
(b) any apparatus and works associated with a pipe or system of pipes and prescribed for the purpose of this paragraph by regulations made by the Secretary of State.
(4B) A statutory instrument containing regulations made by virtue of subsection (4A) shall be subject to annulment in pursuance of a resolution of either House of Parliament; and section 25 of the Petroleum Act 1998 shall apply in relation to any such regulations as it applies in relation to regulations under section 20 of that Act."; and
(d) in subsection (5), paragraph (b) and, in paragraph (c), the words "16(1) or" shall be omitted and at the end of paragraph (c) there shall be inserted— "; or
(d) section 14(2) or 45 of the Petroleum Act 1998,".
(3) In section 3 (consequential provisions), in subsections (2)(b) and (4) for "section 2 of the Petroleum (Production) Act 1934" there shall be substituted "section 3 of the Petroleum Act 1998".

(4) In section 5 (directions for preserving security of petroleum and petroleum products), in the definition of "petroleum" in subsection (7), for "the Petroleum (Production) Act 1934" there shall be substituted "Part I of the Petroleum Act 1998".

THE TRADE UNION AND LABOUR RELATIONS (CONSOLIDATION) ACT 1992 (C. 52)

34 (1) Section 287 of the Trade Union and Labour Relations (Consolidation) Act 1992 (offshore employment) shall be amended as follows.
(2) For subsection (1) there shall be substituted—
"(1) In this Act "offshore employment" means employment for the purposes of—
(a) any activities in the territorial sea adjacent to the United Kingdom, and
(b) any such activities as are mentioned in section 11(2) of the Petroleum Act 1998 in waters within subsection (8)(b) or (c) of that section.".
(3) Subsection (5) shall be omitted.

THE OFFSHORE, AND PIPELINES, SAFETY (NORTHERN IRELAND) ORDER 1992 (S.I. 1992/1728 (N.I. 17))

35 In Article 3 of the [S.I. 1978/1039 (N.I. 9).] Offshore, and Pipelines, Safety (Northern Ireland) Order 1992 (application of Part II of the Health and Safety at Work (Northern Ireland) Order 1978 for offshore purposes)—
(a) in paragraph (3), for sub-paragraph (b) there shall be substituted—
"(b) sections 20 and 25 of the Petroleum Act 1998;", and in sub-paragraph (c) the words from "section" to "requirements and" shall be omitted;
(b) in paragraph (4), for the definitions of "pipe-line" and "pipe-line works" there shall be substituted—
""pipe-line" means, subject to paragraph (4A), a controlled pipeline within the meaning of Part III of the Petroleum Act 1998; and
"pipe-line works" means works of any of the following kinds, namely—
(a) assembling or placing a pipe-line or length of pipe-line;
(b) inspecting, testing, maintaining, adjusting, repairing, altering or renewing a pipe-line or length of pipe-line;
(c) changing the position of or dismantling or removing a pipe-line or length of pipe-line;
(d) opening the bed of the sea for the purposes of works mentioned in paragraphs (a) to (c), tunnelling or boring for those purposes and other works needed for or incidental to those purposes;
(e) works for the purpose of determining whether a place is suitable as part of the site of a proposed pipe-line and the carrying out of surveying operations for the purpose of settling the route of a proposed pipe-line.";
(c) after paragraph (4) there shall be inserted—
"(4A) Subsections (4A) and (4B) of section 1 of the Offshore Safety Act 1992 apply in relation to the definition of "pipe-line" in paragraph (4) as they apply in relation to the definition of "pipe-line" in subsection (4) of that section but as if the reference in subsection (4A) to that section were a reference to this Article."; and
(d) in paragraph (5), sub-paragraph (b) and, in sub-paragraph (c), the words "16(1) or" shall be omitted and at the end of sub-paragraph (c) there shall be inserted— "; or
(d) section 14(2) or 45 of the Petroleum Act 1998,".

THE FINANCE ACT 1993 (C. 34)

36 In section 94A of the Finance Act 1993 (parts of trades: petroleum extraction companies), in subsection (3)(a) for "the Petroleum (Production) Act 1934" there shall be substituted "Part I of the Petroleum Act 1998".

THE PENSION SCHEMES ACT 1993 (C. 48)

37 In section 165 of the Pension Schemes Act 1993 (application of certain provisions to cases with foreign element), in the definition of "continental shelf operations" in subsection (8), for "subsection (6) of section 23 of the Oil and Gas (Enterprise) Act 1982" there shall be substituted "subsection (8) of section 11 of the Petroleum Act 1998".

THE COAL INDUSTRY ACT 1994 (C. 21)

38 (1) The Coal Industry Act 1994 shall be amended as follows.
(2) In section 3 (duties of the Coal Authority with respect to property), in subsection (6) for "section 2 of the Petroleum (Production) Act 1934" there shall be substituted "section 3 of the Petroleum Act 1998".
(3) In section 9 (exploitation rights: oil and gas)—
(a) in subsection (1) for "section 10(2) of the Petroleum (Production) Act 1934" there shall be substituted "section 9(1) of the Petroleum Act 1998";
(b) in subsection (1)(b) for "section 2 of that Act of 1934" there shall be substituted "section 3 of that Act of 1998"; and
(c) in subsection (4) after "section 2 of the Petroleum (Production) Act 1934" there shall be inserted "or section 3 of the Petroleum Act 1998".
(4) In section 57 (public access to information held by the Coal Authority), in subsection (4)(a)(ii) for "section 2 of the Petroleum (Production) Act 1934" there shall be substituted "section 3 of the Petroleum Act 1998".

THE MERCHANT SHIPPING ACT 1995 (C. 21)

39 In section 293 of the Merchant Shipping Act 1995 (functions of Secretary of State in relation to marine pollution), in the definition of "pipeline" in subsection (5), for "the Petroleum and Submarine Pipelines Act 1975" there shall be substituted "the Petroleum Act 1998".

THE EMPLOYMENT RIGHTS ACT 1996 (C. 18)

40 (1) Section 201 of the Employment Rights Act 1996 shall be amended as follows.
(2) For subsection (1) there shall be substituted—
"(1) In this section "offshore employment" means employment for the purposes of—
(a) any activities in the territorial sea adjacent to the United Kingdom, or
(b) any such activities as are mentioned in section 11(2) of the Petroleum Act 1998 in waters within subsection (8)(b) or (c) of that section.".
(3) Subsection (5) shall be omitted.

THE RACE RELATIONS (NORTHERN IRELAND) ORDER 1997 (S.I. 1997/869 (N.I. 6))

41 In Article 69(2) of the Race Relations (Northern Ireland) Order 1997 (power to amend certain provisions of Order)—
(a) in sub-paragraph (a) for "section 23(2) of the Oil and Gas (Enterprise) Act 1982" there shall be substituted "section 11(2) of the Petroleum Act 1998"; and
(b) in sub-paragraph (b) for "section 22(5) of the Oil and Gas (Enterprise) Act 1982" there shall be substituted "section 10(8) of the Petroleum Act 1998".

IMPORTANT LAWS AND REGULATIONS RELATED TO OIL AND GAS EXPLORATION

THE HYDROCARBONS LICENSING DIRECTIVE REGULATIONS 1995

Commencement and citation

1.—(1) These Regulations may be cited as the Hydrocarbons Licensing Directive Regulations and shall come into force on 30th June 1995.

(2) These Regulations do not extend to Northern Ireland.

Interpretation

2. In these Regulations—

"1934 Act Regulations" means any regulations made under section 6 of the Petroleum (Production) Act 1934[3] currently in force;

"applicant" means an entity which has lodged an application for a licence;

"application for a licence" means an application made under 1934 Act Regulations;

"E.C. Treaty" means the Treaty establishing the European Community, signed at Rome on the 25th March 1957;

"entity" means any natural or legal person or any group of such persons;

"licence" means a licence granted following an application for a licence.

Determination of applications

3.—(1) Subject to paragraphs (2) to (4) below, every application for a licence shall be determined on the basis of criteria concerning—

(a) the technical and financial capability of the applicant;

(b) the way in which the applicant proposes to carry out the activities that would be permitted by the licence;

(c) in a case where tenders are invited, the price the applicant is prepared to pay in order to obtain the licence; and

(d) where the applicant holds, or has held a licence of any description under the Petroleum (Production) Act 1934, any lack of efficiency and responsibility displayed by the applicant in operations under that licence,

and the Secretary of State may refuse an application for a licence.

(2) In a case where two or more applications for a licence have equal merit when assessed according to the criteria provided for in paragraph (1) above, other relevant criteria may be applied in order to determine which application should be granted.

(3) Subject to paragraph (4) below, the Secretary of State shall not apply any of the criteria in paragraphs (1) and (2) above in a discriminatory manner.

(4) An application for a licence may be refused on grounds of national security where the applicant is effectively controlled by, or by nationals of, a State other than a member State.

(5) Where an application for a licence is refused, the reasons for the decision shall be notified to the applicant on request.

Scope and application of terms and conditions

4.—(1) No licence shall be granted upon terms and conditions other than such terms and conditions as are justified exclusively for the purpose of—

(a) ensuring the proper performance of the activities permitted by the licence;
(b) providing for the payment of consideration for the grant of the licence;
(c) any of the considerations specified in paragraph (2) below.

(2) The considerations referred to in paragraph (1)(c) above are—

(a) national security;
(b) public safety;
(c) public health;
(d) security of transport;
(e) protection of the environment;
(f) protection of biological resources and of national treasures possessing artistic, historic or archaeological value;
(g) safety of installations and of workers;
(h) planned management of hydrocarbon resources, including in particular the rate at which hydrocarbons are depleted and the optimisation of their recovery;
(i) the need to secure tax revenues.

(3) The terms and conditions provided for in paragraphs (1) and (2) above shall be applied in a non-discriminatory manner.

Advance notice of terms and conditions

5.—(1) Any notice which, in accordance with 1934 Act Regulations—

(a) invites applications for licences; and
(b) is published in the Official Journal

shall set out the criteria to be applied in determining those applications.

(2) In any case where the Secretary of State invites applications for a licence in accordance with 1934 Act Regulations and it is intended that the licence should be granted upon terms or conditions which differ from or are additional to those prescribed in those Regulations for incorporation in licences of the relevant kind, a statement of such terms and conditions shall be made available to any interested person at any time on request.

(3) If any change to the terms and conditions included in the statement provided for in paragraph (1) above is decided upon after the statement is first made available and before the licence to which it relates is granted, the change shall be notified as soon as practicable to every person who has requested the statement.

Duration of the licence

6.—(1) Subject to paragraph (2) below, the Secretary of State shall ensure that—

(a) a licence only grants an entity exclusive rights for the period which is necessary for the proper performance of the activities authorised by the licence; and
(b) the duration of the licence does not exceed the period necessary to carry out the activities authorised by the licence.

(2) The Secretary of State may extend the term of a licence if—

(a) the terms and conditions of the licence permit an extension of the term;

(b) the licensee has performed its obligations in accordance with the terms and conditions of the licence; and
(c) the term of the licence has proved, or is likely to prove, insufficient for the licensee to complete the activities authorised by the licence.

Information
7.—(1) The Secretary of State may only require an entity which has been granted a licence to provide information on its intended or actual sources of procurement of supplies, works or services if that request is made exclusively with a view to the objectives set out in Article 36 of the E.C. Treaty.

(2) The Secretary of State may only request information from an entity which has been granted a licence to monitor the activities of that entity if that monitoring is justified by any of the considerations specified in paragraph (1) and (2) of regulation 4 above.

THE PETROLEUM (CURRENT MODEL CLAUSES) ORDER 1999

Citation and commencement
1. This Order may be cited as the Petroleum (Current Model Clauses) Order 1999 and shall come into force on 15th February 1999.

Interpretation
2. - (1) In this Order -

"the Act" means the Petroleum Act 1998;
"the current model clauses" has the meaning assigned thereto by section 5(1) of the Act.

(2) In Part I of a Schedule to this Order, unless the context otherwise requires -

(a) any reference to a paragraph is a reference to a paragraph of that Part of that Schedule;

(b) any reference to Part II is a reference to Part II of that Schedule.

Current model clauses
3. In relation to a paragraph of Schedule 1 to the Act which is specified in paragraph 1 of Part I of a Schedule to this Order, the current model clauses are those determined in accordance with that Schedule.

SCHEDULE 1

CURRENT MODEL CLAUSES FOR MINING LICENCES DERIVING FROM PARTS 1 AND III OF SCHEDULE 2 TO THE PETROLEUM (PRODUCTION) REGULATIONS 1935 AS THEY HAD EFFECT ON AND AFTER 1ST OCTOBER 1957

PART I

1. This Schedule has effect in relation to paragraph 1 of Schedule 1 to the Act (Parts I and III of Schedule 2 to the Petroleum (Production) Regulations 1935[2] as amended by the Petroleum (Production) (Amendment) Regulations 1954[3] and the Petroleum (Production) (Amendment) Regulations 1957[4]).

2. In relation to the said paragraph 1, the current model clauses are those reproduced in Part

II.

PART II

Interpretation

In these model clauses: -

(1) "The Act of 1934" and "the Act of 1998" mean, respectively, the Petroleum (Production) Act 1934[5] and the Petroleum Act 1998[6].

(2) The "Regulations" mean the Petroleum (Production) Regulations 1935.

(3) "Licensee" means a person to whom a licence under the Act is granted his successors in title and the persons deriving title under him.

(4) "The licensed area" means the area for the time being upon which the Licensee may exercise powers and privileges granted by this licence.

(5) "Petroleum" includes any mineral oil or relative hydrocarbon and natural gas existing in its natural condition in strata, but does not include coal or bituminous shales or other stratified deposits from which oil can be extracted by destructive distillation.

(6) "Crude oil" means oil in its natural state before the same has been refined or otherwise treated but excluding water and foreign substances.

(7) "Natural gas" means gas obtained from boreholes and wells and consisting primarily of hydrocarbons.

(8) "Casinghead petroleum spirit" means any liquid hydrocarbons obtained from natural gas by separation or by any chemical or physical process.

(9) "Ancillary right" means any facility right or privilege other than the rights granted by this licence at any time vested in the Licensee in respect of any part of the licensed area.

(10) "The Minister" means the Secretary of State.

Extension of licensed area

The Licensee may at any time during the term hereby granted or any renewal thereof, but subject nevertheless to the payment of all minimum annual payments and royalties hereby reserved and the performance and observance by the Licensee of all the terms and conditions hereof, apply to the Minister to extend this licence to any lands, the boundaries of which are delineated in manner prescribed by paragraph (5) of regulation 2, adjoining the licensed area:

Provided that the licensed area as thus extended shall comply in all respects with regulation 3.

Right of Licensee to determine Licence

Without prejudice to any obligation or liability imposed by or incurred under the terms and conditions hereof the Licensee may at any time during the term hereby granted or any renewal thereof determine this licence by giving to the Minister not less than eighteen months previous notice in writing to that effect.

Right of Licensee to abandon portions of the licensed area

Without prejudice to any obligation or liability imposed by or incurred under the terms and conditions hereof the Licensee shall be entitled at any time during the term hereby granted or any renewal thereof by giving six months notice in writing to the Minister to surrender the rights granted by this licence in respect of any part or parts of the licensed area:

Provided that -

(a) the part of the licensed area in respect of which the said rights are retained shall comply with the Regulations; and

(b) the part of the licensed area in respect of which the said rights are surrendered shall either be an area in respect of which a licence could be granted in accordance with regulation 3 or be of such shape and size as the Minister may determine.

To the notice hereinbefore referred to shall be attached two copies of the Ordnance Survey Map annexed to the licence upon which shall be delineated the boundaries of the area to be surrendered.

Refund of minimum annual payment on determination or surrender

Upon the determination by the Licensee of the term hereby granted or any renewal thereof, or upon the surrender by him of the rights granted by this licence in respect of any part or parts of the licensed area, the Minister will refund to the Licensee an apportioned part of any minimum annual payment paid by the Licensee in advance in respect of the licensed area or any such part or parts thereof for a period the whole of which has not expired at the date of such determination or surrender.

Avoidance of harmful methods of working

(1) The Licensee shall maintain all apparatus and appliances and all boreholes and wells capable of producing petroleum in good repair and condition and shall execute all operations in or in connection with the licensed area in a proper and workmanlike manner in accordance with methods and practice customarily used in good oilfield practice and without prejudice to the generality of the foregoing provision the Licensee shall take all steps practicable in order -

(a) to control the flow and to prevent the escape or waste of petroleum discovered in or obtained from the licensed area; and

(b) to conserve the licensed area for productive operations; and

(c) to prevent damage to adjoining petroleum bearing strata; and

(d) to prevent the entrance of water through boreholes and wells to petroleum bearing strata; and

(e) to prevent the escape of petroleum into any water-well spring stream river lake reservoir estuary or harbour.

(2) The Licensee shall comply with any instructions from time to time given by the Minister in writing relating to any of the matters set out in sub-clause (1) hereof. If the Licensee objects to any such instruction on the ground that it is unreasonable he may, within 14 days from the date upon which the same was given, refer the matter to arbitration in manner provided by clause .... hereof (the marginal note whereof is "Arbitration").

Provision of storage tanks pipes pipelines or other receptacles

The Licensee shall use methods and practice customarily used in good oilfield practice for confining the petroleum obtained from the licensed area in tanks gasholders pipes pipelines or other receptacles constructed for that purpose. No petroleum shall, save as a temporary measure during an emergency, be placed or kept in an earthen reservoir.

Protection of mines and coal seams

Where any borehole or well drilled within the licensed area shall penetrate any mine or any workable seam of coal the Licensee shall case such borehole or well in such manner as to prevent any water or petroleum in the borehole or well from entering such mine or workable seam of coal.

Disposal of waste oil, salt water and refuse

The Licensee shall drain all waste oil, salt water and refuse from tanks gasholders boreholes and wells into proper receptacles erected and maintained by him for that purpose at a safe distance from such tanks gasholders boreholes and wells and from any buildings or structures whether situate within the licensed area or not and shall dispose of such waste oil salt water and refuse in manner from time to time approved by the Minister. The Licensee shall not use or permit any waste oil, salt water or refuse to flow into or over or to be deposited upon any land, whether situate within the licensed area or not.

Distance of boreholes or wells from boundaries of licensed area

No borehole or well shall except with the consent in writing of the Minister be drilled or made within a distance of 121.92 metres from the boundaries of the licensed area.

Preservation of amenities

The Licensee shall carry out all operations within the licensed area in such a manner as not to interfere unnecessarily with the amenities of the locality in which the licensed area is situate.

Measurement of petroleum obtained from the licensed area

(1) The Licensee shall measure or weigh by a method or methods customarily used in good oilfield practice and from time to time approved by the Minister, all crude oil and natural gas won and saved, other than natural gas used for the purpose of carrying on drilling and production operations and pumping to field storage and refineries, and all casinghead petroleum spirit recovered from the licensed area.

(2) If any measuring or weighing appliance shall at any time be found to be false or unjust the same shall, if the Minister so determines after considering any representations in writing made by the Licensee, be deemed to have existed in that condition during the period of three months prior to the discovery thereof or the period elapsed since the last occasion upon which the same was examined or tested whichever shall be the less and accordingly the royalties payable in respect of such period shall be adjusted.

(3) The Licensee shall not make any alteration in the method or methods of measurement or weighing used by him or any appliances used for that purpose without first informing the Minister and the Minister may in any case require that no alteration shall be made save in the presence of a person authorised by him.

Disposal of crude oil and products thereof

So long as the crude oil or products thereof obtained from the licensed area can be consumed in Great Britain or Northern Ireland, the Licensee shall if so required by the Minister ensure that such crude oil or products thereof shall be sold only for consumption in Great Britain or Northern Ireland.

Licensee to keep records of boreholes

The Licensee shall keep accurate records in a form from time to time approved by the Minister of the drilling, deepening, plugging or abandonment of all boreholes and wells and of any alterations to the casing thereof. A log of all boreholes and wells shall be kept in a form from time to time approved by the Minister containing particulars of the following matters -

(a) the strata and subsoil through which the borehole or well was drilled; and

(b) the casing inserted in any borehole or well and any alteration to such casing; and

(c) any petroleum, water, mines or workable seams of coal encountered; and

(d) such other matters as the Minister may from time to time require.

The Licensee shall deliver copies of the said records and log to the Minister as and when required.

Plans and record

(1) The Licensee shall furnish to the Minister on or before the .... day of each month during the term hereby granted or any renewal thereof a record in a form from time to time approved by the Minister of the progress of his operations in the licensed area. Such record shall contain -

(a) a statement of the depth drilled in each borehole or well; and

(b) a statement of any petroleum, water, mines or workable seams of coal encountered in the course of the said operations; and

(c) a statement of all crude oil produced, and casinghead petroleum spirit recovered; and

(d) a statement of the areas in which any geological work has been carried out.

(2) Within two months after the end of each year comprised in the term hereby granted or any renewal thereof the Licensee shall furnish to the Minister a record in a form from time to time approved by him of the operations conducted in the licensed area during each such year together with a plan upon a scale approved by the Minister showing the situation of all boreholes or wells. The Licensee shall also indicate on the said plan -

(a) all development and other works executed by him in connection with searching boring for and getting petroleum; and

(b) full particulars of any ancillary rights acquired for the exercise of the rights granted by this Licence.

(3) The Licensee shall also keep accurate geological plans, maps and records relating to the licensed area.

(4) The Licensee shall furnish to the Minister such other plans and information as to the progress of operations in the licensed area as he may from time to time require.

(5) The functions of the Minister under sub-clause (4) of this clause shall not only be exerciseable by him but also be concurrently exerciseable by the Chancellor of the Exchequer.

Licensee to keep samples of strata petroleum and water

As far as reasonably practicable the Licensee shall correctly label and preserve for reference for a period of six months characteristic samples of the strata encountered in any borehole or well and samples of any petroleum or water discovered in any borehole or well in the licensed area. The Minister or any person authorised by him shall be entitled to require that representative specimens of any such sample be delivered to the Minister and to retain any specimen so delivered.

Reports to be treated as confidential

All logs records plans maps accounts and information which the Licensee is or may be from time to time required to furnish under the provisions of this licence shall be supplied at the expense of the Licensee and shall (except with the consent in writing of the Licensee which shall not be unreasonably withheld) be treated by the Minister as confidential. The Minister shall nevertheless be entitled at any time to make use of any information received from the Licensee for the purpose of preparing and publishing aggregated returns and general reports on the extent of operations under the Act of 1998.

Ancillary rights

(1) The Licensee shall give notice in writing to the Minister forthwith upon the service or receipt by the Licensee of any notice as to the determination or forfeiture of any ancillary right and shall give at least six months previous notice in writing to the Minister of the date on which the term for which any such right was granted will expire.

(2) The Licensee shall inform the Minister in writing forthwith of the commencement of any action suit proceeding or arbitration either in connection with any ancillary right or arising out of the exercise of the rights and privileges granted by this licence and shall furnish to the Minister such information as to any such action suit proceeding or arbitration as he may from time to time require.

Notice of the site and commencement of boreholes and wells

(1) As soon as the site of any borehole or well has been decided the Licensee shall notify the Minister in writing of the situation thereof and the same shall be described by a certain number in the plans and records which the Licensee is required to keep under the provisions of this licence. The Licensee shall notify the Minister of any change of the number of any such borehole or well which may be made.

(2) No borehole or well shall be commenced and no borehole or well shall be recommenced after work has been discontinued thereat for more than six months unless three clear days notice in writing shall first have been given to the Minister.

Abandonment and plugging of boreholes

(1) The Licensee shall give to the Minister not less than seven days previous notice in writing of his intention to abandon any borehole or well and no cemented string or other permanent form of casing shall be withdrawn from any borehole or well which it is proposed to abandon without the prior consent in writing of the Minister.

(2) Every borehole or well which the Licensee intends to abandon shall, unless the Minister otherwise determines, be so securely plugged

by the Licensee as to shut off all water from all petroleum bearing strata mines or any workable seams of coal.

(3) Before commencing to plug any borehole or well which it is intended to abandon the Licensee shall submit to the Minister for his approval particulars in writing of the method of plugging which it is proposed to adopt.

(4) The Minister may in any case require that no borehole or well shall be plugged or any works be executed for that purpose save in the presence of a person authorised by him.

Local Resident Manager

The Licensee shall before commencing any operations in the licensed area furnish to the Minister the name and address of the manager resident in the locality of the licensed area under whose supervision such operations are to be carried on. Any notice which the Minister or any person authorised by him is in accordance with the terms of this licence required or entitled to serve upon the Licensee shall be sufficiently served if the same shall be delivered or sent by post to such manager at such address.

Advertisements, prospectuses, etc.

(1) No statement shall be made either in any notice advertisement prospectus or other document issued by or to the knowledge of the Licensee or in any other manner claiming or suggesting whether expressly or by implication that Her Majesty or any Government Department or any person or body acting on behalf of Her Majesty has or have formed or expressed any opinion that the licensed area is from its geological formation or otherwise one in which petroleum is likely to be obtainable.

(2) The foregoing provisions of this clause or a statement to the effect thereof shall be included in or indorsed on any prospectus, statement in lieu of prospectus, notice, circular, advertisement, or other invitation issued by, or to the knowledge of, the Licensee offering to the public for subscription or purchase any shares or debentures of a company or intended company.

Indemnity against third party claims

The Licensee shall at all times keep the Minister effectually indemnified against all actions proceedings costs charges claims and demands whatsoever which may be made or brought against the Minister by any third party in relation to or in connection with this licence or any matter or thing done or purported to be done in pursuance thereof.

Security

(1) In this clause -

(a) "deposit" means the sum deposited with the Minister of

Power by the Licensee on the execution of this licence, and

(b) "banker's guarantee" means the banker's guarantee furnished to that Minister by the Licensee on the execution of this licence as an alternative to a deposit,

in accordance with this licence as it had effect when granted and as security for the observance and performance by the Licensee of the terms and conditions of this licence and for the purposes hereinafter mentioned.

SCHEDULE 2

CURRENT MODEL CLAUSES FOR CONTROLLED WATERS OR SEAWARD PRODUCTION LICENCES DERIVING FROM SCHEDULE 2 TO THE PETROLEUM (PRODUCTION) (CONTINENTAL SHELF AND TERRITORIAL SEA) REGULATIONS 1964 OR SCHEDULE 4 TO THE PETROLEUM (PRODUCTION) REGULATIONS 1966 AS THEY FROM TIME TO TIME HAD EFFECT

PART I

1. This Schedule has effect in relation to the following paragraphs of Schedule 1 to the Act, namely -

(a) paragraph 2 of that Schedule (Schedule 2 to the Petroleum (Production) (Continental Shelf and Territorial Sea) Regulations 1964[7]);

(b) paragraph 4 of that Schedule (Schedule 4 to the Petroleum (Production) Regulations 1966[8]);

(c) paragraph 5 of that Schedule (the said Schedule 4 as amended by the Petroleum (Production) (Amendment) Regulations 1971[9]); and

(d) paragraph 6 of that Schedule (Part II of Schedule 2 to the Petroleum and Submarine Pipe-lines Act 1975[10]).

2. Subject to paragraphs 3, 4 and 6, the current model clauses in relation to the said paragraphs 2, 4, 5 and 6 are those reproduced in Part II.

3. - (1) Where the licensed area is in the Scottish area, as defined in article 1(2) of the Civil Jurisdiction (Offshore Activities) Order 1987[11], Part II shall have effect as provided in the two following subparagraphs.

(2) Part II shall have effect in such a case as if for model clause 35 (distress) there were substituted the following clause -

" **Diligence**

35. If and whenever any of the payments mentioned in clause 8(1) of this licence or any part thereof shall be in arrear or unpaid for 28 days next after any of the days whereon the same ought to be paid (whether the same shall have been legally demanded or not) then and so often as the same may happen the Minister may (as an additional remedy and without prejudice to any other rights and remedies to which he would be entitled) do diligence in respect thereof in like manner as a landlord may do diligence in respect of unpaid arrears of rent and such diligence shall be effectual to attach all or any of the stocks of petroleum, engines, machinery, tools, implements and other effects belonging to the Licensee which shall be found on or about any of the Licensee's installations and equipment used or to be used in connection with searching, boring for or getting petroleum in the licensed area, and where in pursuance of such a diligence a sale of such effects as shall have been attached thereby takes place the Minister may out of the proceeds thereof retain and pay all the arrears of the said payments and also the expenses of and incident to such diligence and sale and shall pay the surplus thereof (if any) to the Licensee.".

(3) Part II shall also have effect in such a case as if, in model clause 40 (arbitration) -

(a) for the word "arbitrator", wherever it occurs in paragraphs (2) and (3), there were substituted the word "arbiter", and

(b) for the words "the Lord Chief Justice of England for the time being", in paragraph (2), there were substituted the words "the Lord President of the Court of Session".

4. Where the licensed area is in the Northern Irish area, as defined in article 1(2) of the Civil Jurisdiction (Offshore Activities) Order 1987, Part II shall have effect as if in model clause 40 (arbitration) for the words "the Lord Chief Justice of England", in paragraph (2), there were substituted the words "the Lord Chief Justice of Northern Ireland".

5. In paragraphs 3 and 4, any reference to the licensed area is a reference to the licensed area within the meaning of model clause 1(1) in Part II.

6. Where -

(a) section 1 of the Petroleum Royalties (Relief) Act 1983[12] applies, or

(b) section 1 of the Petroleum Royalties (Relief) and Continental Shelf Act 1989[13] applies,

Part II has effect subject to the provisions of the said Act of 1983 or, as the case may be, the said Act of 1989.

PART II

Interpretation

1. - (1) In the following clauses the following expressions have the meaning hereby respectively assigned to them, that is to say:

"the Act of 1934" means the Petroleum (Production) Act 1934[14];
"the Act of 1964" means the Continental Shelf Act 1964[15];
"the Act of 1998" means the Petroleum Act 1998[16];
"block" means an area comprised in the licence which is delineated on the reference map deposited at the principal office of the Minister's department and to which a reference number was assigned at the date of this licence;
"continuing part" has the meaning assigned thereto by clause 5;
"development scheme" has the meaning assigned thereto by clause 25;
"half year" means the period from 1st January to 30th June in any year and the period from 1st July to 31st December in any year;
"the licensed area" means the area for the time being in which the Licensee may exercise the rights granted by the licence;

"the Licensee" means the person or persons to whom the licence is granted, his personal representatives and any person or persons to whom the rights conferred by the licence may lawfully have been assigned;
"the Minister" means the Secretary of State;
"oil field" has the meaning assigned thereto by clause 25;
"petroleum" includes any mineral oil or relative hydrocarbon and natural gas existing in its natural condition in strata, but does not include coal or bituminous shales or other stratified deposits from which oil can be extracted by destructive distillation;
"section" means a part of a block comprising an area bounded by minute lines of latitude and longitude one minute apart respectively;
"surrendered part" has the meaning assigned thereto by clause 5;
"well" includes borehole.

(2) Any obligations which are to be observed and performed by the Licensee shall at any time at which the Licensee is more than one person be joint and several obligations.

(3) Any clause of this licence which refers to any provision of Part I of the Oil Taxation Act 1975[17] shall, unless a contrary intention appears, be construed as referring to that provision as it has effect for the time being for the purposes of petroleum revenue tax.

Term of licence

3. This licence unless sooner determined under any of the provisions hereof shall be and continue in force for the term of six years next after 19 , but may be further continued as to a part of the area comprised in this licence in manner hereinafter provided.

Right of Licensee to determine licence or surrender part of licensed area

4. Without prejudice to any obligations or liability imposed by or incurred under the terms and conditions hereof the Licensee may, at any time during the said term of six years, by giving to the Minister not less than six months' previous notice in writing to that effect, to expire on the anniversary of the date upon which the said term of six years commenced, determine this licence or surrender any part of the licensed area, being a part which complies with clause 7 hereof.

Option to continue licence as to part of the licensed area

5. - (1) At any time not later than three months before the expiration of the said term of six years the Licensee paying the payments and royalties hereinafter provided and observing and performing the conditions herein contained may give notice in writing to the Minister that he desires the licence to continue as to a part of the licensed area (hereinafter called "the continuing part") in the manner hereinafter provided and to determine as to the residue thereof (hereinafter called "the surrendered part").

(2) Such notice shall describe the surrendered part which together with any area previously surrendered in accordance with clause 4 hereof shall be not less than one half of the number of sections contained in the area originally comprised in this licence.

(3) Such notice shall specify a date (hereinafter called "the surrender date") not later than the expiry of the said term of six years upon which the surrendered part is to be surrendered.

(4) The Licensee may at any time not less than one month before the surrender date give further notice in writing to the Minister varying the part of the licensed area to be surrendered and in the event of such further notice being given the provisions of the previous paragraphs of this clause shall apply *mutatis mutandis* to such notice but so that the surrender date specified in such notice shall be the same as that specified in the first notice.

(5) This licence shall upon the option conferred by this clause being duly exercised and subject to the provisions of this licence continue in respect of the continuing part for a term of forty years next after the surrender date.

Right of the Licensee to determine extended term or surrender part of the licensed area

6. - (1) Without prejudice to any obligation or liability imposed by or incurred under the terms hereof the Licensee may at any time during such term of forty years by giving to the Minister not less than six months' notice in writing to that effect to expire on the anniversary of the date upon which the said term of forty years shall have commenced, determine this licence or surrender any part of the licensed area being a part which complies with clause 7 hereof.

(2) A notice given pursuant to paragraph (1) of this clause may be cancelled by a further notice in writing given to the Minister not less than one month before the expiration of the notice.

Area surrendered

7. - (1) Within a block any area to be surrendered by the Licensee pursuant to any of the last three foregoing clauses and any area accordingly retained by him or, where the surrendered or retained area is comprised of separate parts, each such part shall unless the Minister has otherwise agreed in writing prior to the date at which the appropriate notice is given by the Licensee to the Minister comply with the following requirements -

(a) be bounded by minute lines of latitude extending not less than two minutes of longitude and minute lines of longitude extending not less than two minutes of latitude;

(b) consist of not less than thirty sections;

(c) each separate part of an area surrendered or retained shall be not less than two sections distant from any other part of the same category (surrendered or retained as the case may be); and

(d) the boundaries shall, in the case of those which run due north and south, either coincide with the corresponding boundaries of the block or be not less than two sections distant therefrom and, in the case of those which run due east and west, either coincide with the corresponding boundaries of the block or be not less than two sections distant therefrom.

(2) Upon the date upon which any determination of the licence or any surrender of part of the licensed area in manner provided by the last three foregoing clauses is to take effect the rights granted by the licence shall cease in respect of the licensed area or of the part so surrendered as the case may be, but without prejudice to any obligation or liability imposed upon the Licensee or incurred by him under the terms of the licence prior to that date.

Payment of consideration for licence

8. - (1) The Licensee shall make to the Minister as consideration for the grant of this licence -

(a) payments of royalty in accordance with clauses 9 and 10 of this licence;

(b) deliveries of petroleum in accordance with clause 11 of this licence; and

(c) payments in accordance with Schedule 2 to this licence.

(2) The Licensee shall not by reason of determination of the licence or surrender of any part of the licensed area be entitled to be repaid or allowed any sum payable to the Minister pursuant to

the licence before the date of determination or surrender.

Royalty payments

9. - (1) Subject to paragraph (1A) of this clause the Licensee shall pay to the Minister, in respect of each half year in which this licence is in force (hereafter in this clause and in clauses 9A, 10 and 11A of this licence referred to as a "chargeable period"), a royalty of an amount equal to twelve and a half per cent of the value of the petroleum relating to that period.

(1A) Paragraph (1) of this clause shall not apply to a chargeable period in which the Licensee delivers petroleum to the Minister in pursuance in clause 11 of this licence; but if the petroleum delivered has a value of less than 12½ per cent of the aggregate of -

(a) the value of the petroleum delivered (ignoring any such excess as is mentioned in paragraph (11) of this clause), and

(b) the value of the petroleum relating to that period,

he shall pay to the Minister a royalty of an amount equal to the difference.

(5) For the purposes of this clause and clauses 9A and 10 of this licence the value of the petroleum relating to a chargeable period is, subject to paragraph (6) of this clause, the total of the amounts which, if the words "one-half of" were omitted from paragraph (b) of subsection (4) and paragraph (d) of subsection (5) of section 2 of the Oil Taxation Act 1975[18], would in pursuance of paragraph (a) of the said subsection (4) fall to be taken into account in relation to that period in respect of the persons who by reference to this licence are or are treated as participators for the purposes of those subsections, reduced by -

(a) the total of the market value which would in pursuance of the said paragraph (b) fall to be taken into account as aforesaid; and

(b) a sum ascertained in pursuance of paragraph (7) of this clause in respect of the cost of conveying and treating petroleum.

(6) The value which, in pursuance of paragraph (5) of this clause, is the value of the petroleum relating to a chargeable period shall be increased by -

(a) the amount of the price received or receivable for any petroleum consisting of gas won and saved in the licensed area in that period which is sold to British Gas Trading Ltd. in that period under a contract made before the end of June 1975; and

(b) an amount equal to the value, as determined for the purposes of income tax or the charge of corporation tax on income, of so much of the petroleum won and saved in the licensed area as falls within section 10(1)(b) of the Oil Taxation Act 1975 and was in that period disposed of or relevantly appropriated (within the meaning of Part I of that Act) by the persons mentioned in the said paragraph (5).

(7) The Minister may from time to time, by notice in writing given to the Licensee, determine the mode of ascertaining any sum for the purposes of sub-paragraph (b) of paragraph (5) of this clause but -

(a) the Minister shall not give notice in pursuance of this paragraph unless he has consulted persons appearing to him to be representative of the holders of petroleum production licences about the terms of the notice; and

(b) any dispute between the Minister and the Licensee as to the amount of such a sum shall, in default of agreement before the expiration of fourteen months beginning with the last day of the chargeable period to which the sum relates and subject to sub-paragraph (c) of this paragraph, be determined by the Minister; and

(c) the Licensee may, during the period of 28 days beginning with the day on which he receives from the Minister particulars of a determination in pursuance of sub-paragraph (b) of this paragraph, refer to arbitration in the manner provided by clause 40 of this licence any questions as to whether the determination is in accordance with the relevant notice given to the Licensee in pursuance of this paragraph.

(7A) A notice under paragraph (7) of this clause may, if the Minister thinks fit, provide for the costs in respect of which a sum is ascertained for the purposes of paragraph (5)(b) to include, to such extent as may be specified in the notice -

(a) costs incurred in relation to assets which have ceased to be used in connection with the conveying or treating of petroleum;

(b) costs incurred after the end of the chargeable period to which the sum relates.

(7B) If a notice under paragraph (7) of this clause contains a provision relating to costs incurred after the end of a chargeable period, sub-paragraph (b) of paragraph (7) shall have effect in relation to a dispute concerning such costs as if the chargeable period there referred to were that in which the costs were incurred.

(8) Subject to paragraphs (9) and (10) of this clause, the value of petroleum delivered to the Minister in pursuance of clause 11 of this licence shall be ascertained for the purposes of this clause and clause 9A on such basis (or, where petroleum of more than one kind is delivered, such bases) as the Minister and the Licensee agree.

(9) If the Minister and the Licensee fail to agree on the value of any petroleum delivered to the Minister in pursuance of clause 11 of this licence, it shall be ascertained on such basis as the Minister may specify as fair in a notice in writing given by him to the Licensee.

(10) The Licensee may, during the period of 28 days beginning with the day on which he receives a notice from the Minister under paragraph (9) of this clause, refer to arbitration in the manner provided by clause 40 of this licence any question as to whether the basis of valuation specified in the notice is fair.

(11) In this clause and clauses 9A, 10 and 11A, references to petroleum delivered to the Minister in pursuance of clause 11 include references to any excess over the quantity required to be delivered by a notice served in pursuance of paragraph (1) of that clause.

Payments by the Minister

9A. If in any chargeable period the Licensee delivers to the Minister in pursuance of clause 11 of this licence petroleum having a value greater than 12½ per cent of the aggregate of -

(a) the value of the petroleum delivered (ignoring any such excess as is mentioned in clause 9(11) of this licence), and

(b) the value of the petroleum relating to that period,

the Minister shall pay to the Licensee a sum equal to the difference.

Provisions supplementary to clauses 9 and 9A

10. - (1) The Licensee shall, within two months after the end of each chargeable period, deliver to the Minister, in such form as the Minister may specify, a statement of -

(a) the quantity of petroleum won and saved in the licensed area in that period

(b) the quantity of that petroleum delivered to the Minister in that period in pursuance of clause 11 of this licence;

(c) the amounts of the prices and market values which are required by paragraph 2 of Schedule 2 to the Oil Taxation Act 1975[19] to be stated in the returns made for that period in pursuance of that paragraph in consequence of this licence;

(d) the amount mentioned in clause 9(6)(a) of this licence; and

(e) the amount which the Licensee estimates will be the sum ascertained as respects that period for the purposes of clause 9(5)(b) of this licence (ignoring, in a case where they might otherwise be taken into account in the estimate, any costs incurred after the end of the period).

(2) The Licensee shall, when he delivers a statement to the Minister in pursuance of paragraph (1) of this clause for a chargeable period in respect of which royalty is payable in pursuance of clause 9(1) of this licence, make to the Minister a payment on account of royalty for that period equal to one-eighth of the sum produced by aggregating the amounts which in pursuance of sub-paragraphs (c) and (d) of paragraph (1) of this clause are specified in the statement and reducing the aggregate by the amount so specified in pursuance of sub-paragraph (e) of that paragraph and by the amount which, by virtue of paragraph 2(2)(d)(ii) of Schedule 2 to the said Act of 1975, was specified in the statement delivered to the Minister in pursuance of the said paragraph (1) in respect of the preceding chargeable period; but the Licensee may reduce the amount of the payment by the amount of any deduction from it authorised by paragraph 3(2) of Schedule 2 to this licence.

(3) The Licensee shall, when he delivers a statement to the Minister in pursuance of paragraph (1) of this clause for a chargeable period in respect of which royalty is payable in pursuance of clause 9(1A) of this licence, make to the Minister a payment on account of royalty for that period equal to the amount which would be so payable for that period if the royalty so payable for that period fell to be determined by reference to the amounts specified in the statement and the amount which, by virtue of paragraph 2(2)(d)(ii) of Schedule 2 to the Oil Taxation Act 1975, was specified in the statement delivered to the Minister in pursuance of paragraph (1) of this clause in respect of the preceding chargeable period; but the Licensee may reduce the amount of the payment as mentioned in paragraph (2) of this clause.

(4) The Minister shall make to the Licensee payments equal to the amounts by which in consequence of paragraph (1A) of clause 9 of this licence, deductions which the Licensee was entitled to make in pursuance of paragraph 3(2) of Schedule 2 to this licence fall short of the deductions which the Licensee would have been so entitled to make if royalty were only payable in pursuance of paragraph (1) of that clause and paragraph (1A) of it were omitted and payments by the Minister in pursuance of this paragraph shall be made as soon as the amounts of the relevant deductions have been determined.

(5) The Minister may from time to time, after a statement in respect of any chargeable period

has been delivered to him in pursuance of paragraph (1) of this clause and before he has given to the Licensee a notice in pursuance of paragraph (6) of this clause in respect of that period, give a notice in writing to the Licensee specifying the amount which the Minister estimates is payable by the Licensee in pursuance of clause 9 of this licence in respect of that period; and where the amount specified in the notice is larger or smaller than the total amount already paid by the Licensee in pursuance of this clause in respect of that period, then -

(a) if it is larger the difference shall be paid forthwith by the Licensee to the Minister; and

(b) if it is smaller the difference shall be paid forthwith by the Minister to the Licensee.

(6) When it appears to the Minister that the value of the petroleum relating to any chargeable period has been finally determined for tax purposes he may give to the Licensee a notice in writing specifying the amount which the Minister considers is payable by the Licensee in pursuance of clause 9 of this licence in respect of that period; and where the amount specified in the notice is larger or smaller than the total amount already paid by the Licensee in pursuance of this clause in respect of that period, then, subject to paragraph (8) of this clause -

(a) if it is larger the difference shall be paid forthwith by the Licensee to the Minister; and

(b) if it is smaller the difference shall be paid forthwith by the Minister to the Licensee.

(7) If after the date when the Minister gave notice to the Licensee in pursuance of paragraph (6) of this clause or this paragraph in respect of a chargeable period it appears to the Minister, in consequence of a relevant assessment or determination made after that date which relates directly or indirectly to the value of petroleum by reference to which the amount specified in the notice was determined that another amount ought to have been so specified, he may give notice in writing to the Licensee specifying the other amount; and where he does so, then, subject to paragraph (8) of this clause -

(a) if the other amount is larger than the total amount already paid by the Licensee in pursuance of this clause in respect of that period, the difference shall be paid forthwith by the Licensee to the Minister; and

(b) if it is smaller, the difference shall be paid forthwith by the Minister to the Licensee.

(7A) If, after the date when the Minister gave notice to the Licensee in pursuance of paragraph (6) of this clause or this paragraph in respect of a chargeable period, it appears to the Minister that as a result of costs incurred after the end of the period there is an increase in the sum to be taken into account by virtue of clause 9(5)(b) of this licence, and accordingly a reduction in the amount payable by the Licensee in respect of that period, he may give notice in writing to the Licensee specifying the reduced amount; and where he does so he shall forthwith pay to the Licensee an amount equal to the difference between the reduced amount and the total amount already paid by the Licensee in pursuance of this clause in respect of the period.

(8) A decision made by the Minister for the purposes of paragraph (5), (6), (7) or (7A) of this clause shall not be called in question by the Licensee except that any dispute between the Minister and the Licensee as to whether an amount specified in a notice given in pursuance of the said paragraph (6), (7) or (7A) is payable by virtue of clause 9 of this licence may, during the period of 28 days beginning with the day on which the Licensee receives the notice, be referred to arbitration in the manner provided by clause 40 of this licence; and on a reference to arbitration in pursuance of this paragraph any relevant assessment or determination for the time being in force shall be binding on the Minister and the Licensee so far as the assessment or determination

relates directly or indirectly to the value of petroleum relating to the chargeable period in question.

(9) An amount in respect of interest shall be payable when a notice is given under paragraph (5), (6), (7) or (7A) of this clause, and that amount shall be calculated in such manner as the Minister may specify from time to time in a notice in writing given by him to the Licensee; but -

(a) a notice in pursuance of this paragraph shall provide for amounts by way of interest to be calculated by applying a rate of interest which is for the time being a commercial rate of interest;

(b) any such amount in respect of interest shall be disregarded in calculating for the purposes of paragraph (5), (6), (7) or (7A) of this clause any amount already paid by the Licensee in pursuance of this clause;

(c) where costs of the kind mentioned in clause 9(7A)(b) of this licence are taken into account, they shall not affect the amount of interest payable in respect of any period ending earlier two months after the chargeable period in which they were incurred.

(9A) If a payment is made by the Minister in pursuance of clause 9A of this licence more than two months after the end of the chargeable period to which the payment relates, an amount in respect of interest on the payment from the end of those two months shall also be payable by him to the Licensee.

(9B) Interest under paragraph (9A) of this clause shall be calculated in such manner as the Minister may specify from time to time in a notice in writing given by him to the Licensee (but sub-paragraph (a) of paragraph (9) of this clause shall apply to such a notice as it applies to a notice under paragraph (9)).

(10) In this clause "relevant assessment or determination" means an assessment or determination made by the Commissioners of Inland Revenue for the purposes of petroleum revenue tax, income tax or the charge of corporation tax on income or a determination made in proceedings arising out of such an assessment or determination made by the said Commissioners.

(11) For the purposes of this clause any amount paid by the Licensee or the Minister on account of a prospective liability under paragraph (5), (6), (7) or (7A) of this clause shall be treated as paid in pursuance of that paragraph.

Deliveries of petroleum in place of royalties

11. - (1) If during the term of this licence the Minister serves on the Licensee a notice in writing in accordance with the following provisions of this clause requiring the Licensee to deliver to the Minister part of the petroleum won and saved by the Licensee in the licensed area, the Licensee shall comply with the notice.

(2) Where the Minister proposes to serve a notice on the Licensee in pursuance of paragraph (1) of this clause, he shall before doing so -

(a) give the Licensee a copy of the proposed notice and an opportunity of making representations to the Minister about it, and

(b) consider any representations then made to him by the Licensee about the proposed notice;

and the Minister shall, in deciding upon the terms of the actual notice, have regard to the desirability of not disturbing unduly any arrangements made by the Licensee for transporting and delivering petroleum won and saved from the licensed area.

(3) Subject to paragraph (4) of this clause, a notice served in pursuance of paragraph (1) of this clause -

(a) shall specify the date on which the notice is to come into force and may contain provisions with respect to the time when it shall cease to be in force;

(b) shall specify the quantity of petroleum won and saved in the licensed area during each half year in which the notice is in force which, up to any maximum quantities specified in the notice in pursuance of paragraph (4)(b) of this clause, is to be delivered to the Minister in consequence of the notice;

(c) may relate to all petroleum so won and saved or may be limited to and specify different quantities of such petroleum which is of one or more of the following kinds, namely, crude oil, condensate, natural gas and natural gas liquids, in each case of a quality or composition, or of each quality or composition, determined in the manner specified in the notice;

(d) shall contain provisions with respect to the place or places at which any petroleum or kind of petroleum is to be delivered in pursuance of the notice and may contain provisions with respect to the times at which any quantities of it are to be so delivered.

(4) Such a notice -

(a) shall not specify as the date on which it is to come into force a date before the expiration of the period of six months beginning with the date on which the notice is served on the Licensee but shall, if the Minister serves on the Licensee a further notice in writing stating that it is to cease to be in force at a time specified in the further notice which is not earlier than six months after the date of service of the further notice, cease to be in force at that time;

(b) shall not specify, as the quantity of petroleum won and saved in any half year which is to be delivered in pursuance of the notice or as the quantity of any kind of such petroleum, a quantity greater than 12½ per cent of all the petroleum, or as the case may be of all the petroleum of that kind, which is won and saved by the Licensee in the licensed area in that half year, but may provide that the quantities of the petroleum or of a kind of petroleum so won and saved which are to be so delivered shall not in the aggregate exceed a quantity specified in the notice;

(c) shall not specify, or enable to be specified, as a place at which delivery is to be made in pursuance of the notice a place which is neither a point at sea at which the Licensee normally loads, nor a point on land at which the Licensee normally lands, petroleum of any kind from the licensed area.

---

[12] 1983 c.59; extended by section 2 of the Petroleum Royalties (Relief) and Continental Shelf Act 1989 (c.1) and modified by paragraph 8 of Schedule 3 to the Petroleum Act 1998 (c.17).back

[13] 1989 c.1; modified by paragraph 8 of Schedule 3 to the Petroleum Act 1998

SCHEDULE 3

CURRENT MODEL CLAUSES FOR LANDWARD PRODUCTION LICENCES DERIVING FROM SCHEDULE 3 TO THE PETROLEUM (PRODUCTION) REGULATIONS 1966

PART I

1. This Schedule has effect in relation to paragraph 3 of Schedule 1 to the Act (Schedule 3 to the Petroleum (Production) Regulations 1966[21]).

2. Subject to paragraph 3, the current model clauses in relation to the said paragraph 3 are those reproduced in Part II.

3. Where -

(a) section 1 of the Petroleum Royalties (Relief) Act 1983[22] applies, or

(b) section 1 of the Petroleum Royalties (Relief) and Continental Shelf Act 1989[23] applies,

Part II has effect subject to the provisions of the said Act of 1983 or, as the case may be, the said Act of 1989.

PART II

Interpretation

1. - (1) In the following clauses the following expressions have the meanings hereby respectively assigned to them, that is to say: -

"the Act of 1934" means the Petroleum (Production) Act 1934[24];
"the Act of 1964" means the Continental Shelf Act 1964[25];
"the Act of 1998" means the Petroleum Act 1998[26];
"block" means an area delineated on the reference map deposited at the principal office of the Minister's department;
"continuing part" has the meaning assigned thereto by clause 5 (the marginal note whereof is "Option to continue licence as to part of the licensed area");
"development scheme" has the meaning assigned thereto by clause 25 (the marginal note whereof is "Unit development");
"half year" means the period from 1st January to 30th June in any year and the period from 1st July to 31st December in any year;
"the licensed area" means the area for the time being in which the Licensee may exercise the rights granted by the licence;
"the Licensee" means the person or persons to whom the licence is granted, his personal representatives and any person or persons to whom the rights conferred by the licence may lawfully have been assigned;
"the Minister" means the Secretary of State;
"petroleum" includes any mineral oil or relative hydrocarbon and natural gas existing in its natural condition in strata, but does not include coal or bituminous shales or other stratified deposits from which oil can be extracted by destructive

distillation;
"surrendered part" has the meaning assigned thereto by clause 5 (the marginal note whereof is "Option to continue licence as to part of the licensed area");
"well" includes borehole.

(2) Any obligations which are to be observed and performed by the Licensee shall at any time at which the Licensee is more than one person be joint and several obligations.

(3) Any clause of this licence which refers to any provision of Part I of the Oil Taxation Act 1975[27] shall, unless the contrary intention appears, be construed as referring to that provision as it has effect for the time being for the purposes of petroleum revenue tax.

Term of licence

3. This licence unless sooner determined under any of the provisions hereof shall be and continue in force for the term of six years next after .... 19..., but may be renewed as to a part of the area comprised in this licence in manner hereinafter provided.

Right of Licensee to determine licence or surrender part of licensed area

4. Without prejudice to any obligation or liability imposed by or incurred under the terms and conditions hereof the Licensee may, at any time during the said term of six years, by giving to the Minister not less than six months' previous notice in writing to that effect, determine this licence or surrender any part of the licensed area, being a part which complies with clause 7 hereof (the marginal note whereof is "Areas surrendered").

Option to continue licence as to part of the licensed area

5. - (1) At any time not later than three months before the expiration of the said term of six years the Licensee paying the payments and royalties hereinafter provided and observing and performing the conditions herein contained may give notice in writing to the Minister that he desires the licence to continue as to a part of the licensed area (hereinafter called "the continuing part") in the manner hereinafter provided and to determine as to the residue thereof (hereinafter called "the surrendered part").

(2) Such notice shall describe the surrendered part which shall, together with any area previously surrendered in accordance with clause 4 hereof (the marginal note whereof is "Right of Licensee to determine licence or surrender part of licensed area"), not be less than one half of the area originally comprised in the licence or such smaller part of the area as the Minister may have agreed to in writing prior to the giving of such notice.

(3) Such notice shall specify a date not later than the expiry of the said term of six years upon which the surrendered part is to be surrendered.

(4) This licence shall upon the option conferred by this clause being duly exercised and subject to the provisions of this licence continue in respect of the continuing part for a term of forty years next after the

date specified in the said notice.

Right of Licensee to determine extended term or surrender part of the licensed area

6. Without prejudice to any obligation or liability imposed by or incurred under the terms hereof the Licensee may at any time during such term of forty years by giving the Minister not less than twelve months' notice in writing to that effect, determine this licence or surrender any part of the licensed area, being a part which complies with clause 7 hereof (the marginal note whereof is "Areas surrendered").

Areas surrendered

7. - (1) Any area to be surrendered by the Licensee pursuant to the last three foregoing clauses in any case where, at the date at which the notice is given by the Licensee to the Minister, the licensed area is a block or has been divided into blocks, shall unless the Minister has otherwise agreed in writing prior to the date at which the notice is given by the Licensee to the Minister -

(a) be bounded by lines which unless they are boundaries of the area originally comprised in the licence run either due north and south or due east and west;

(b) not comprise any part of a block being a part having an area of less than twenty square kilometres.

(2) Any area to be surrendered by the Licensee pursuant to the last three foregoing clauses, in any case where the foregoing paragraph does not apply, shall unless the Minister has otherwise agreed in writing prior to the date at which the notice is given by the Licensee to the Minister be -

(a) not less than twenty square kilometres in extent and such that the area remaining subject to this licence after such surrender will be not less than ten square kilometres in extent;

(b) clearly defined and as far as possible compact;

(c) such that any area remaining subject to this licence after such surrender will be clearly defined and as far as possible compact; and

(d) such that the greatest length of any area remaining subject to this licence after such surrender will not exceed three times the average width thereof.

(3) Upon the date upon which any determination of the licence or any surrender of part of the licensed area in manner provided by the last three foregoing clauses is to take effect the rights granted by the licence shall cease in respect of the licensed area or of the part so surrendered as the case may be but without prejudice to any obligation or liability imposed upon the Licensee or incurred by him under the terms of the licence prior to that date.

Payment of consideration for licence

8. - (1) The Licensee shall make to the Minister as consideration for the grant of this licence -

(a) payments of royalty in accordance with clauses 9 and 10 of this licence;

(b) deliveries of petroleum in accordance with clause 11 of this licence; and

(c) payments in accordance with Schedule 2 to this licence.

(2) The Licensee shall not by reason of the determination of this licence or the surrender of any part of the licensed area be entitled to be repaid or allowed any sum payable to the Minister hereunder before the date of the determination or surrender.

Royalty payments

9. - (1) Subject to paragraph (1A) of this clause the Licensee shall pay to the Minister, in respect of each chargeable period, a royalty equal to the sum of the following amounts, namely -

(a) 5 per cent of the value of all relevant units up to the first 100,000 units won and saved in the year which includes that period;

(b) 7½ per cent of the value of all further relevant units up to the next 50,000 units so won and saved;

(c) 10 per cent of the value of all further relevant units up to the next 50,000 units so won and saved; and

(d) 12½ per cent of the value of all further relevant units so won and saved;

and for the purposes of this paragraph "relevant unit" means a unit won and saved in the chargeable period in question and the value of a relevant unit is the amount produced by dividing the value of the petroleum relating to that period by the number of the relevant units.

(1A) Paragraph (1) of this clause shall not apply to a chargeable period in which the Licensee delivers petroleum to the Minister in pursuance of clause 11 of this licence; but if the petroleum delivered has a value of less than the relevant percentage of the aggregate of -

(a) the value of the petroleum delivered (ignoring any such excess as is mentioned in paragraph (7F) of this clause), and

(b) the value of the petroleum relating to that period,

he shall pay to the Minister a royalty of an amount equal to the difference.

(5) For the purposes of this clause and clauses 9A and 10 of this

licence the value of the petroleum relating to a chargeable period is, subject to paragraph (6) of this clause, the total of the amounts which, if the words "one-half of" were omitted from paragraph (b) of subsection (4) and paragraph (d) of subsection (5) of section 2 of the Oil Taxation Act 1975[28], would in pursuance of paragraph (a) of the said subsection (4) fall to be taken into account in relation to that period in respect of the persons who by reference to this licence are or are treated as participators for the purposes of those subsections, reduced by -

(a) the total of the market values which would in pursuance of the said paragraph (b) fall to be taken into account as aforesaid; and

(b) a sum ascertained in pursuance of paragraph (7) of this clause in respect of the cost of conveying and treating petroleum.

(6) The value which, in pursuance of paragraph (5) of this clause, is the value of the petroleum relating to a chargeable period shall be increased by -

(a) the amount of the price received or receivable for any petroleum consisting of gas won and saved in the licensed area in that period which is sold to British Gas Trading Ltd in that period under a contract made before the end of June 1975; and

(b) an amount equal to the value, as determined for the purposes of income tax or the charge of corporation tax on income, of so much of the petroleum won and saved in the licensed area as falls within section 10(1)(b) of the Oil Taxation Act 1975 and was in that period disposed of or relevantly appropriated (within the meaning of Part I of that Act) by the persons mentioned in the said paragraph (5).

(7) The Minister may from time to time, by notice in writing given to the Licensee, determine the mode of ascertaining any sum for the purposes of sub-paragraph (b) of paragraph (5) of this clause; but -

(a) the Minister shall not give a notice in pursuance of this paragraph unless he has consulted persons appearing to him to be representative of the holders of petroleum production licences about the terms of the notice; and

(b) any dispute between the Minister and the Licensee as to the amount of such a sum shall, in default of agreement before the expiration of fourteen months beginning with the last day of the chargeable period to which the sum relates and subject to sub-paragraph (c) of this paragraph, be determined by the Minister; and

(c) the Licensee may, during the period of 28 days beginning with the day on which he receives from the Minister particulars of a determination in pursuance of sub-paragraph (b) of this paragraph, refer to arbitration in the manner provided by clause 38 of this licence any question as to whether the determination is in accordance with the relevant notice given to the Licensee in pursuance of this paragraph.

(7A) A notice under paragraph (7) of this clause may, if the Minister thinks fit, provide for the costs in respect of which a sum is ascertained for the purposes of paragraph (5)(b) to include, to such extent as may be specified in the notice -

(a) costs incurred in relation to assets which have ceased to be used in connection with the conveying or treating of petroleum;

(b) costs incurred after the end of the chargeable period to which the sum relates.

(7B) If a notice under paragraph (7) of this clause contains a provision relating to costs incurred after the end of a chargeable period, sub-paragraph (b) of paragraph (7) shall have effect in relation to a dispute concerning such costs as if the chargeable period there referred to were that in which the costs were incurred.

(7C) Subject to paragraphs (7D) and (7E) of this clause, the value of petroleum delivered to the Minister in pursuance of clause 11 of this licence shall be ascertained for the purposes of this clause and clause 9A on such basis (or, where petroleum of more than one kind is delivered, such bases) as the Minister and the Licensee agree.

(7D) If the Minister and the Licensee fail to agree on the value of any petroleum delivered to the Minister in pursuance of clause 11 of this licence, it shall be ascertained on such basis as the Minister may specify as fair in a notice in writing given by him to the Licensee.

(7E) The Licensee may, during the period of 28 days beginning with the day on which he receives a notice from the Minister under paragraph (7D) of this clause, refer to arbitration in the manner provided by clause 38 of this licence any question as to whether the basis of valuation specified in the notice is fair.

(7F) In this clause and clauses 9A, 10 and 11A, references to petroleum delivered to the Minister in pursuance of clause 11 include references to any excess over the quantity required to be delivered by a notice served in pursuance of paragraph (1) of that clause.

(8) In this clause -

"chargeable period" means a half year in which this licence is in force;
"relevant percentage", in relation to a chargeable period, means the effective rate at which, apart from any notice under clause 11 of this licence, royalty would be payable for that period in pursuance of paragraph (1) of this clause;

"unit" means one metric ton of petroleum won and saved in the licensed area except that in the case of petroleum so won and saved in the form of gas it means a quantity of it equal to 1400 cubic metres of the gas at a temperature of 0 degrees centigrade and a pressure of one kilogramme force per square centimetre; and

"year" means a year consisting of a chargeable period in which such a periodic payment as is mentioned in Schedule 2 to this licence is payable and the following chargeable period.

Payments by the Minister

9A. - (1) If in any chargeable period the Licensee delivers to the Minister in pursuance of clause 11 of this licence petroleum having a value greater than the relevant percentage of the aggregate of -

(a) the value of the petroleum delivered (ignoring any such excess as is mentioned in clause 9(7F) of this licence), and

(b) the value of the petroleum relating to that period,

the Minister shall pay to the Licensee a sum equal to the difference.

(2) In this clause, "chargeable period" and "relevant percentage" have the same meanings as in clause 9 of this licence.

Provisions supplementary to clauses 9 and 9A

10. - (1) The Licensee shall, within two months after the end of each chargeable period, deliver to the Minister, in such form as the Minister may specify, a statement of -

(a) the quantity of petroleum won and saved in the licensed area in that period;

(b) the quantity of that petroleum delivered to the Minister in that period in pursuance of clause 11 of this licence;

(c) the amounts of the prices and market values which are required by paragraph 2 of Schedule 2 to the Oil Taxation Act 1975[29] to be stated in the returns made for that period in pursuance of that paragraph in consequence of this licence;

(d) the amount mentioned in clause 9(6)(a) of this licence; and

(e) the amount which the Licensee estimates will be the sum ascertained as respects that period for the purposes of clause 9(5)(b) of this licence (ignoring, in a case where they might otherwise be taken into account in the estimate, any costs incurred after the end of the period).

(2) The Licensee shall, when he delivers a statement to the Minister in pursuance of paragraph (1) of this clause for a chargeable period in respect of which royalty is payable in pursuance of clause 9(1) of this licence, make to the Minister a payment on account of royalty for that period equal to the relevant percentage of the sum produced by aggregating the amounts which in pursuance of sub-paragraphs (c) and

(d) of paragraph (1) of this clause are specified in the statement and reducing the aggregate by the amount so specified in pursuance of sub-paragraph (e) of that paragraph and by the amount which, by virtue of paragraph 2(2)(d)(ii) of Schedule 2 to the said Act of 1975, was specified in the statement delivered to the Minister in pursuance of the said paragraph (1) in respect of the preceding chargeable period; but the Licensee may reduce the amount of the payment by the amount of any deduction from it authorised by paragraph 2(2) of Schedule 2 to this licence.

(3) The Licensee shall, when he delivers a statement to the Minister in pursuance of paragraph (1) of this clause for a chargeable period in respect of which royalty is payable in pursuance of clause 9(1A) of this licence, make to the Minister a payment on account of royalty for that period equal to the amount which would be so payable for that period if the royalty so payable for that period fell to be determined by reference to the amounts specified in the statement and the amount which, by virtue of paragraph 2(2)(d)(ii) of Schedule 2 to the Oil Taxation Act 1975, was specified in the statement delivered to the Minister in pursuance of paragraph (1) of this clause in respect of the preceding chargeable period; but the Licensee may reduce the amount of the payment as mentioned in paragraph (2) of this clause.

(4) The Minister shall make to the Licensee payments equal to the amounts by which, in consequence of paragraph (1A) of clause 9 of this licence, the deductions which the Licensee was entitled to make in pursuance of paragraph 2(2) of Schedule 2 to this licence fall short of the deductions which the Licensee would have been so entitled to make if royalty were only payable in pursuance of paragraph (1A) of that clause and paragraph (2) of it were omitted; and payments by the Minister in pursuance of this paragraph shall be made as soon as the amounts of the relevant deductions have been determined.

(5) The Minister may from time to time, after a statement in respect of any chargeable period has been delivered to him in pursuance of paragraph (1) of this clause and before he has given to the Licensee a notice in pursuance of paragraph (6) of this clause in respect of that period, give a notice in writing to the Licensee specifying the amount which the Minister estimates is payable by the Licensee in pursuance of clause 9 of this licence in respect of that period; and where the amount specified in the notice is larger or smaller than the total amount already paid by the Licensee in pursuance of this clause in respect of that period, then -

(a) if it is larger the difference shall be paid forthwith by the Licensee to the Minister; and

(b) if it is smaller the difference shall be paid forthwith by the Minister to the Licensee.

(6) When it appears to the Minister that the value of the petroleum relating to any chargeable period has been finally determined for tax purposes, he may give to the Licensee a notice in writing specifying the

amount which the Minister considers is payable by the Licensee in pursuance of that clause in respect of that period; and where the amount specified in the notice is larger or smaller than the total amount already paid by the Licensee in pursuance of clause 9 of this licence in respect of that period, then, subject to paragraph (8) of this clause -

(a) if it is larger the difference shall be paid forthwith by the Licensee to the Minister; and

(b) if it is smaller the difference shall be paid forthwith by the Minister to the Licensee.

(7) If after the date when the Minister gave notice to the Licensee in pursuance of paragraph (6) of this clause or this paragraph in respect of a chargeable period it appears to the Minister, in consequence of a relevant assessment or determination made after that date which relates directly or indirectly to the value of petroleum by reference to which the amount specified in the notice was determined, that another amount ought to have been so specified, he may give notice in writing to the Licensee specifying the other amount; and where he does so, then, subject to paragraph (8) of this clause -

(a) if the other amount is larger than the total amount already paid by the Licensee in pursuance of this clause in respect of that period the difference shall be paid forthwith by the Licensee to the Minister; and

(b) if it is smaller the difference shall be paid forthwith by the Minister to the Licensee.

(7A) If, after the date when the Minister gave notice to the Licensee in pursuance of paragraph (6) of this clause or this paragraph in respect of a chargeable period, it appears to the Minister that as a result of costs incurred after the end of the period there is an increase in the sum to be taken into account by virtue of clause 9(5)(b) of this licence, and accordingly a reduction in the amount payable by the Licensee in respect of that period, he may give notice in writing to the Licensee specifying the reduced amount; and where he does so he shall forthwith pay to the Licensee an amount equal to the difference between the reduced amount and the total amount already paid by the Licensee in pursuance of this clause in respect of the period.

(8) A decision made by the Minister for the purposes of paragraph (5), (6), (7) or (7A) of this clause shall not be called in question by the Licensee except that any dispute between the Minister and the Licensee as to whether an amount specified in a notice given in pursuance of the said paragraph (6), (7) or (7A) is payable by virtue of clause 9 of this licence may, during the period of 28 days beginning with the day on which the Licensee receives the notice, be referred to arbitration in the manner provided by clause 38 of this licence; and on a reference to arbitration in pursuance of this paragraph any relevant assessment or determination for the time being in force shall be binding on the Minister and the Licensee so far as the assessment or

determination relates directly or indirectly to the value of petroleum relating to the chargeable period in question.

(9) An amount in respect of interest shall be payable when a notice is given under paragraph (5), (6), (7) or (7A) of this clause, and that amount shall be calculated in such manner as the Minister may specify from time to time in a notice in writing given by him to the Licensee; but -

(a) a notice in pursuance of this paragraph shall provide for amounts by way of interest to be calculated by applying a rate of interest which is for the time being a commercial rate of interest;

(b) any such amount in respect of interest shall be disregarded in calculating for the purposes of paragraph (5), (6), (7) or (7A) of this clause any amount already paid by the Licensee in pursuance of this clause;

(c) where costs of the kind mentioned in clause 9(7A)(b) of this licence are taken into account, they shall not affect the amount of interest payable in respect of any period ending earlier than two months after the chargeable period in which they were incurred.

(9A) If a payment is made by the Minister in pursuance of clause 9A of this licence more than two months after the end of the chargeable period to which the payment relates, an amount in respect of interest on the payment from the end of those two months shall also be payable by him to the Licensee.

(9B) Interest under paragraph (9A) of this clause shall be calculated in such manner as the Minister may specify from time to time in a notice in writing given by him to the Licensee (but sub-paragraph (a) of paragraph (9) of this clause shall apply to such a notice as it applies to a notice under paragraph (9)).

(10) In this clause -

"chargeable period" and "relevant percentage" have the same meanings as in clause 9 of this licence;
"relevant assessment or determination" means an assessment or determination made by the Commissioners of Inland Revenue for the purposes of petroleum revenue tax, income tax or the charge of corporation tax on income or a determination made in proceedings arising out of such an assessment or determination made by the said Commissioners.

(11) For the purposes of this clause any amount paid by the Licensee or the Minister on account of a prospective liability under paragraph (5), (6), (7) or (7A) of this clause shall be treated as paid in pursuance of that paragraph.

Deliveries of petroleum in place of royalties

11. - (1) If during the term of this licence the Minister serves on the Licensee a notice in writing in accordance with the following provisions of this clause requiring the Licensee to deliver to the Minister part of the petroleum won and saved by the Licensee in the licensed area, the Licensee shall comply with the notice.

(2) Where the Minister proposes to serve a notice on the Licensee in pursuance of paragraph (1) of this clause, he shall before doing so -

(a) give the Licensee a copy of the proposed notice and an opportunity of making representations to the Minister about it; and

(b) consider any representations then made to him by the Licensee about the proposed notice;

and the Minister shall, in deciding upon the terms of the actual notice, have regard to the desirability of not disturbing unduly any arrangements made by the Licensee for transporting and delivering petroleum won and saved from the licensed area.

(3) Subject to paragraph (4) of this clause, a notice served in pursuance of paragraph (1) of this clause -

(a) shall specify the date on which the notice is to come into force and may contain provisions with respect to the time when it shall cease to be in force;

(b) shall specify the quantity of petroleum won and saved in the licensed area during each half year in which the notice is in force which, up to any maximum quantities specified in the notice in pursuance of paragraph (4)(b) of this clause, is to be delivered to the Minister in consequence of the notice;

(c) may relate to all petroleum so won and saved or may be limited to and specify different quantities of such petroleum which is of one or more of the following kinds, namely, crude oil, condensate, natural gas and natural gas liquids, in each case of a quality or composition or of each quality or composition determined in the manner specified in the notice;

(d) shall contain provisions with respect to the place or places at which any petroleum or kind of petroleum is to be delivered in pursuance of the notice and may contain provisions with respect to the times at which any quantities of it are to be so delivered.

(4) Such a notice -

(a) shall not specify as the date on which it is to come into force a date before the expiration of the period of six months beginning with the date on which the notice is served on the

Licensee but shall, if the Minister serves on the Licensee a further notice in writing stating that it is to cease to be in force at a time specified in the further notice which is not earlier than six months after the date of service of the further notice, cease to be in force at that time;

(b) shall not specify, as the quantity of petroleum won and saved in any half year which is to be delivered in pursuance of the notice or as the quantity of any kind of such petroleum, a percentage of all the petroleum or of all that kind of petroleum which is won and saved in the licensed area in that half year exceeding the percentage at which, apart from the notice, royalty for that half year would be payable in respect of the petroleum in pursuance of clause 9(1) of this licence, but may provide that the quantities of petroleum or of a kind of petroleum so won and saved which are to be so delivered shall not in the aggregate exceed a quantity specified in the notice;

(c) shall not specify, or enable to be specified, as a place at which delivery is to be made in pursuance of the notice a place which is not a point at which the Licensee normally delivers petroleum of any kind from the licensed area.

SCHEDULE 4

CURRENT MODEL CLAUSES FOR LANDWARD PRODUCTION LICENCES DERIVING FROM SCHEDULE 4 TO THE PETROLEUM (PRODUCTION) REGULATIONS 1976, AS IT FROM TIME TO TIME HAD EFFECT, OR SCHEDULE 4 TO THE PETROLEUM (PRODUCTION) REGULATIONS 1982

PART I

1. This Schedule has effect in relation to the following paragraphs of Schedule 1 to the Act, namely -

(a) paragraph 7 of that Schedule (Schedule 4 to the Petroleum (Production) Regulations 1976)[32]);

(b) paragraph 8 of that Schedule (the said Schedule 4 as amended by the Oil and Gas (Enterprise) Act 1982[33]), and

(c) paragraph 13 of that Schedule (Schedule 4 to the Petroleum (Production) Regulations 1982[34]).

2. Subject to paragraphs 3 and 4, the current model clauses in relation to the said paragraphs 7, 8 and 13 are those reproduced in Part II.

3. - (1) In relation to paragraph 13 of Schedule 1 to the Act, Part II shall have effect as provided in the two following sub-paragraphs.

(2) Part II shall have effect in such a case as if in model clause 22(1) for the words "as respects that function" there was substituted the words "and the function in question is one to which the approval relates".

(3) Part II shall also have effect in such a case as if in model clause 23 for paragraph (b) and the words following that paragraph there were substituted the following paragraph -

> " (b) with fishing in or conservation of the living resources of any waters in or in the vicinity of the licensed area.".

4. Where section 1 of the Petroleum Royalties (Relief) and Continental Shelf Act 1989[35] applies, Part II has effect subject to the provisions of that Act.

PART II

Interpretation

1. - (1) In the following clauses the following expressions have the meanings hereby respectively assigned to them, that is to say: -

> "the Act of 1934" means the Petroleum (Production) Act 1934[36]
> "the Act of 1964" means the Continental Shelf Act 1964[37];
> "the Act of 1998" means the Petroleum Act 1998[38];
> "block" means an area delineated on the reference map deposited at the principal office of the Minister's department;
> "development scheme" has the meaning assigned thereto by clause 26;
> "half year" means the period from 1st January to 30th June in any year and the period from 1st July to 31st December in any year;
> "initial term" has the meaning assigned thereto by clause 3;
> "the licensed area" means the area for the time being in which the Licensee may exercise the rights granted by this licence;
> "the Licensee" means the person or persons to whom this licence is granted, his personal representatives and any person or persons to whom the rights conferred by this licence may lawfully have been assigned;
> "the Minister" means the Secretary of State for Trade and Industry;
> "petroleum" includes any mineral oil or relative hydrocarbon and natural gas existing in its natural condition in strata, but does not include coal or bituminous shales or other stratified deposits from which oil can be extracted by destructive distillation;
> "well" includes borehole.

(2) Any obligations which are to be observed and performed by the Licensee shall at any time at which the Licensee is more than one person be joint and several obligations.

(3) Any clause of this licence which refers to any provisions of Part I of the Oil Taxation Act 1975[39] shall, unless the contrary intention appears, be construed as referring to that provision as it has effect for the time being for the purposes of petroleum revenue tax.

Term of licence

3. - (1) This licence unless sooner determined under any of the provisions hereof shall be and continue in force for the term of four years next after .... 19... (hereinafter called "the initial term"); but if the terms and conditions hereof are duly performed and observed and in particular, if the work programme described in Schedule 4 to this licence has been duly performed, it may be continued for a further period of twenty years in respect of part of the relevant area in the manner hereinafter provided.

(2) If the Minister sees fit and petroleum is then being got under this licence, it may be further continued for a period of ten years at the expiry of the said period of twenty years.

Extension of term for part of licensed area

4. - (1) The Licensee, if he wishes this licence to continue for a further period of twenty years in respect of a part of the licensed area as provided by clause 3, shall at least three months before the expiry of the initial term give the Minister written notice of continuance and, unless notice has been given under clause 6(1) to surrender at least one half of the original licensed area before such expiry, give written notice of surrender from a date not later than such expiry in respect of an area which satisfied the requirements of clause 6(3) and whose surrender reduces the licensed area to not more than one half its original size.

(2) The Licensee may at any time not less than one month before the surrender date specified in any notice of surrender give further notice in writing to the Minister varying the part of the licensed area to be surrendered and in the event of such further notice being given the provisions of paragraph (1) of this clause shall apply *mutatis mutandis* to such notice but so that the surrender date specified in such notice shall be the same as that specified in the first notice of surrender.

(3) Where notice of continuance is duly given and such area (if any) as may be required to be surrendered by notice under paragraph (1) is duly surrendered, this licence shall, subject to the provisions of clause 3 of this licence, continue in respect of the residual area for a term of twenty years after the expiry of the initial term.

Further extension of term

5. The Licensee, if he wishes the Minister to assent to the further continuance of this licence for a period of ten years following the expiry of the twenty year term, shall apply in writing for such assent during the nineteenth year of that term; and where assent is given, this licence shall, subject to the provisions of clause 3 of this licence, continue in respect of the area to which it then relates for a further period of ten years after the expiry of the said twenty year term.

Right of Licensee to determine licence or surrender part of licensed area

6. - (1) Without prejudice to any obligation or liability imposed by or incurred under the terms and conditions hereof, the Licensee may, at any time, determine this licence or surrender any such part of the licensed area as is mentioned in the following paragraph by giving six months' written notice to that effect to the Minister.

(2) A notice given pursuant to paragraph (1) of this clause may be cancelled by a further notice in writing given to the Minister not less than one month before the expiration of the notice.

(3) Any area to be surrendered in accordance with the preceding provisions of this licence shall, unless the Minister has otherwise agreed in writing prior to the date on which the appropriate notice is given by the Licensee to the Minister, be a clearly defined compact area -

(a) which comprises at least ten square kilometres or one fifth of the subsisting licensed area (whichever is the greater) and has a length not more than three times its average breadth; and

(b) whose surrender leaves as the licensed area one or more clearly defined and reasonably compact areas none of which is less than ten square kilometres or has a length more than three times its average breadth.

Consequences of determination or surrender by Licensee

7. Upon the date on which any determination of this licence by the Licensee or any surrender of a part of the licensed area is to take effect, the rights granted by this licence shall cease or cease in respect of the part so surrendered as the case may be but without prejudice to any obligation or liability imposed upon the Licensee or incurred by him under the terms and conditions of this licence prior to that date.

Payment of consideration for licence

8. - (1) The Licensee shall make to the Minister as consideration for the grant of this licence -

(a) payments of royalty in accordance with clauses 9 and 10 of this licence

(b) deliveries of petroleum in accordance with clause 11 of this licence; and

(c) payments in accordance with Schedule 2 to this licence.

(2) The Licensee shall not by reason of the determination of this licence or the surrender of any part of the licensed area be entitled to be repaid or allowed any sum payable to the Minister hereunder before the date of the determination or surrender.

Royalty payments

9. - (1) Subject to paragraph (1A) of this clause, the Licensee shall pay to the Minister, in respect of each chargeable period, a royalty equal to the sum of the percentages specified in Schedule 3 to this licence of the value of the relevant units won and saved in the year which includes that period and for the purposes of this paragraph "relevant unit" means a unit won and saved in the chargeable period in question and the value of a relevant unit is the amount produced by dividing the value of the petroleum relating to that period by the number of the relevant units.

(1A) Paragraph (1) of this clause shall not apply to a chargeable period in which the Licensee delivers petroleum to the Minister in pursuance of clause 11 of this licence; but if the petroleum delivered has a value of less than the relevant percentage of the aggregate of -

(a) the value of the petroleum delivered (ignoring any such excess as is mentioned in paragraph (6D) of this clause), and

(b) the value of petroleum relating to that period,

he shall pay to the Minister a royalty of an amount equal to the difference.

(5) For the purposes of this clause and clauses 9A and 10 of this licence the value of the petroleum relating to a chargeable period is, subject to paragraph (6) of this clause, the total of the amounts which, if the words "one-half of" were omitted from paragraph (b) of subsection (4) and paragraph (d) of subsection (5) of section 2 of the Oil Taxation Act 1975[40], would in pursuance of paragraph (a) of the said subsection (4) fall to be taken into account in relation to that period in respect of the persons who by reference to this licence are or are treated as participators for the purposes of those subsections, reduced by the total of the market values which would in pursuance of the said paragraph (b) fall to be taken into account as aforesaid.

(6) The value which, in pursuance of paragraph (5) of this clause, is the value of the petroleum relating to a chargeable period shall be increased by an amount equal to the value, as determined for the purposes of income tax or the charge of corporation tax on income, of so much of the petroleum won and saved in the licensed area as falls within section 10(1)(b) of the Oil Taxation Act 1975 and was in that period disposed of or relevantly appropriated (within the meaning of Part I of that Act) by the persons mentioned in the said paragraph (5).

(6A) Subject to paragraphs (6B) and (6C) of this clause, the value of petroleum delivered to the

Minister in pursuance of clause 11 of this licence shall be ascertained for the purposes of this clause and clause 9A on such basis (or, where petroleum of more than one kind is delivered, such bases) as the Minister and the Licensee agree.

(6B) If the Minister and the Licensee fail to agree on the value of any petroleum delivered to the Minister in pursuance of clause 11 of this licence, it shall be ascertained on such basis as the Minister may specify as fair in a notice in writing given by him to the Licensee.

(6C) The Licensee may, during the period of 28 days beginning with the day on which he receives a notice from the Minister under paragraph (6B) of this clause, refer to arbitration in the manner provided by clause 39 of this licence any question as to whether the basis of valuation specified in the notice is fair.

(6D) In this clause and clauses 9A and 10, references to petroleum delivered to the Minister in pursuance of clause 11 include references to any excess over the quantity required to be delivered by a notice served in pursuance of paragraph (1) of that clause.

(7) In this clause -

"chargeable period" means a half year in which this licence is in force;
"relevant percentage", in relation to a chargeable period, means the effective rate at which, apart from any notice under clause 11 of this licence, royalty would be payable for that period in pursuance of paragraph (1) of this clause;
"unit" means one tonne of petroleum won and saved in the licensed area except that in the case of petroleum so won and saved in the form of gas it means a quantity of it equal to 1,115 cubic metres of the gas at a temperature of 15 degrees Celsius and a pressure of 1.0132 bar; and
"year" means a year consisting of a chargeable period in which such a periodic payment as is mentioned in Schedule 2 to this licence is payable and the following chargeable period.

Payments by the Minister

9A - (1) If in any chargeable period the Licensee delivers to the Minister in pursuance of clause 11 of this licence petroleum having a value greater than the relevant percentage of the aggregate of -

(a) the value of the petroleum delivered (ignoring any such excess as is mentioned in clause 9(6D) of this licence), and

(b) the value of the petroleum relating to that period,

the Minister shall pay to the Licensee a sum equal to the difference.

(2) In this clause, "chargeable period" and "relevant percentage" have the same meanings as in clause 9 of this licence.

Provisions supplementary to clauses 9 and 9A

10. - (1) The Licensee shall, within two months after the end of each chargeable period, deliver to the Minister, in such form as the Minister may specify, a statement of -

(a) the quantity of petroleum won and saved in the licensed area in that period;

(b) the quantity of that petroleum delivered to the Minister in that period in pursuance of clause 11 of this licence; and

(c) the amounts of the prices and market values which are required by paragraph 2 of Schedule 2 to the Oil Taxation Act 1975[41] to be stated in the returns made for that period in pursuance of that paragraph in consequence of this licence.

(2) The Licensee shall, when he delivers a statement to the Minister in pursuance of paragraph (1) of this clause for a chargeable period in respect of which royalty is payable in pursuance of clause 9(1) of this licence, make to the Minister a payment on account of royalty for that period equal to the relevant percentage of the sum produced by aggregating the amounts which in pursuance of subparagraph (c) of paragraph (1) of this clause are specified in the statement and reducing the aggregate by the amount which, by virtue of paragraph 2(2)(d)(ii) of Schedule 2 to the said Act of 1975, was specified in the statement delivered to the Minister in pursuance of the said paragraph (1) in respect of the preceding chargeable period.

(3) The Licensee shall, when he delivers a statement to the Minister in pursuance of paragraph (1) of this clause for a chargeable period in respect of which royalty is payable in pursuance of clause 9(1A) of this licence, make to the Minister a payment on account of royalty for that period equal to the amount which would be so payable for that period if the royalty so payable for that period fell to be determined by reference to the amounts specified in the statement and the amount which, by virtue of paragraph 2(2)(d)(ii) of Schedule 2 to the Oil Taxation Act 1975, was specified in the statement delivered to the Minister in pursuance of paragraph (1) of this clause in respect of the preceding chargeable period.

(4) The Minister may from time to time, after a statement in respect of any chargeable period has been delivered to him in pursuance of paragraph (1) of this clause and before he has given to the Licensee a notice in pursuance of paragraph (5) of this clause in respect of that period, give a notice in writing to the Licensee specifying the amount which the Minister estimates is payable by the Licensee in pursuance of clause 9 of this licence in respect of that period; and where the amount specified in the notice is larger or smaller than the total amount already paid by the Licensee in pursuance of this clause in respect of that period, then -

(a) if it is larger the difference shall be paid forthwith by the Licensee to the Minister; and

(b) if it is smaller the difference shall be paid forthwith by the Minister to the Licensee.

(5) When it appears to the Minister that the value of the petroleum relating to any chargeable period has been finally determined for tax purposes, he may give to the Licensee a notice in writing specifying the amount which the Minister considers is payable by the Licensee in pursuance of clause 9 of this licence in respect of that period; and where the amount specified in the notice is larger or smaller than the total amount already paid by the Licensee in pursuance of this clause in respect of that period, then, subject to paragraph (7) of this clause -

(a) if it is larger the difference shall be paid forthwith by the Licensee to the Minister; and

(b) if it is smaller the difference shall be paid forthwith by the Minister to the Licensee.

(6) If after the date when the Minister gave notice to the Licensee in pursuance of paragraph (5) of this clause or this paragraph in respect of a chargeable period it appears to the Minister, in consequence of a relevant assessment or determination made after that date which relates directly or indirectly to the value of petroleum by reference to which the amount specified in the notice was determined, that another amount ought to have been so specified, he may give notice

in writing to the Licensee specifying the other amount; and where he does so then, subject to paragraph (7) of this clause -

(a) if the other amount is larger than the total amount already paid by the Licensee in pursuance of this clause in respect of that period the difference shall be paid forthwith by the Licensee to the Minister; and

(b) if it is smaller the difference shall be paid forthwith by the Minister to the Licensee.

(7) A decision made by the Minister for the purposes of paragraph (4), (5) or (6) of this clause shall not be called in question by the Licensee except that any dispute between the Minister and the Licensee as to whether an amount specified in a notice given in pursuance of the said paragraph (5) or (6) is payable by virtue of clause 9 of this licence may, during the period of 28 days beginning with the day on which the Licensee receives the notice, be referred to arbitration in the manner provided by clause 39 of this licence; and on a reference to arbitration in pursuance of this paragraph any relevant assessment or determination for the time being in force shall be binding on the Minister and the Licensee so far as the assessment or determination relates directly or indirectly to the value of petroleum relating to the chargeable period in question.

(8) When any payment is made by the Licensee or the Minister in pursuance of paragraph (4), (5) or (6) of this clause, an amount in respect of interest on the payment shall also be payable by him to the recipient of the payment and that amount shall be calculated in such manner as the Minister may specify from time to time in a notice in writing given by him to the Licensee; but -

(a) a notice in pursuance of this paragraph shall provide for amounts by way of interest to be calculated by applying a rate of interest which is for the time being a commercial rate of interest; and

(b) any such amount in respect of interest shall be disregarded in calculating for the purposes of the said paragraph (4), (5) or (6) any amount already paid by the Licensee in pursuance of this clause.

(8A) If a payment is made by the Minister in pursuance of clause 9A of this licence more than two months after the end of the chargeable period to which the payment relates, an amount in respect of interest on the payment from the end of those two months shall also be payable by him to the Licensee.

(8B) Interest under paragraph (8A) of this clause shall be calculated in such manner as the Minister may specify from time to time in a notice in writing given by him to the Licensee (but sub-paragraph (a) of paragraph (8) of this clause shall apply to such a notice as it applies to a notice under paragraph (8)).

(9) In this clause -

"chargeable period" and "relevant percentage" have the same meanings as in clause 9 of this licence;
"relevant assessment or determination" means an assessment or determination made by the Commissioners of Inland Revenue for the purposes of petroleum revenue tax, income tax or the charge of corporation tax on income or a determination made in proceedings arising out of such an assessment or determination made by the said Commissioners.

(10) For the purposes of this clause any amount paid by the Licensee or the Minister on account of a prospective liability under paragraph (4), (5) or (6) of this clause shall be treated as

paid in pursuance of that paragraph.

Deliveries of petroleum in place of royalties

11. - (1) If during the term of this licence the Minister serves on the Licensee a notice in writing in accordance with the following provisions of this clause requiring the Licensee to deliver to the Minister part of the petroleum won and saved by the Licensee in the licensed area, the Licensee shall comply with the notice.

(2) Where the Minister proposes to serve a notice on the Licensee in pursuance of paragraph (1) of this clause, he shall before doing so -

(a) give the Licensee a copy of the proposed notice and an opportunity of making representations to the Minister about it; and

(b) consider any representations then made to him by the Licensee about the proposed notice;

and the Minister shall, in deciding upon the terms of the actual notice, have regard to the desirability of not disturbing unduly any arrangements made by the Licensee for transporting and delivering petroleum won and saved from the licensed area.

(3) Subject to paragraph (4) of this clause, a notice served in pursuance of paragraph (1) of this clause -

(a) shall specify the date on which the notice is to come into force and may contain provisions with respect to the time when it shall cease to be in force;

(b) shall specify the quantity of petroleum won and saved in the licensed area during each half year in which the notice is in force which, up to any maximum quantities specified in the notice in pursuance of paragraph (4)(b) of this clause, is to be delivered to the Minister in consequence of the notice;

(c) may relate to all petroleum so won and saved or may be limited to and specify different quantities of such petroleum which is of one or more of the following kinds, namely, crude oil, condensate, natural gas and natural gas liquids, in each case of a quality or composition or of each quality or composition determined in the manner specified in the notice;

(d) shall contain provisions with respect to the place or places at which any petroleum or kind of petroleum is to be delivered in pursuance of the notice and may contain provisions with respect to the times at which any quantities of it are to be so delivered.

(4) Such a notice -

(a) shall not specify as the date on which it is to come into force a date before the expiration of the period of six months beginning with the date on which the notice is served on the Licensee but shall, if the Minister serves on the Licensee a further notice in writing stating that it is to cease to be in force at a time specified in the further notice which is not earlier than six months after the date of service of the further notice, cease to be in force at that time;

(b) shall not specify, as the quantity of petroleum won and saved in any half year which is to be delivered in pursuance of the notice or as the quantity of any kind of such petroleum, a percentage of all the petroleum or of all that kind of petroleum which is won and saved in the licensed area in that half year exceeding the percentage at which, apart from the notice, royalty for that half year would be payable in respect of the petroleum in pursuance of clause 9(1) of this licence, but may provide that the quantities of petroleum or of a kind of petroleum so won and saved which are to be so delivered shall not in the aggregate exceed a quantity specified in the notice;

(c) shall not specify, or enable to be specified, as a place at which delivery is to be made in pursuance of the notice, a place which is not a point at which the Licensee normally delivers petroleum of any kind from the licensed area.

Measurement of petroleum obtained from the licensed area

12. - (1) The Licensee shall measure or weigh by a method or methods customarily used in good oilfield practice and from time to time approved by the Minister all petroleum won and saved from the licensed area.

(1A) If and to the extent that the Minister so directs, the duty imposed by paragraph (1) of this clause shall be discharged separately in relation to petroleum won and saved -

(a) from each part of the licensed area which is an oil field for the purposes of the Oil Taxation Act 1975,

(b) from each part of the licensed area which forms part of such an oil field extending beyond the licensed area, and

(c) from each well producing petroleum from a part of the licensed area which is not within such an oil field.

(1B) If and to the extent that the Minister so directs, the preceding provisions of this clause shall apply as if the duty to measure or weigh petroleum included a duty to ascertain its quality or composition or both; and where a direction under this paragraph is in force, the following provisions of this clause shall have effect as if references to measuring or weighing included references to ascertaining quality or composition.

(2) The Licensee shall not make any alteration in the method or methods of measurement or weighing used by him or any appliances used for that purpose without the consent in writing of the Minister and the Minister may in any case require that no alteration shall be made save in the presence of a person authorised by the Minister.

(3) The Minister may from time to time direct that any weighing or measuring appliance shall be tested or examined in such manner, upon such occasions or at such intervals and by such persons as may be specified by the Minister's direction and the Licensee shall pay to any such person or to the Minister such fees and expenses for test or examination as the Minister may specify.

(4) If any measuring or weighing appliance shall upon any such test or examination as is mentioned in the last foregoing paragraph be found to be false or unjust the same shall if the Minister so determines after considering any representations in writing made by the Licensee be deemed to have existed in that condition during the period since the last occasion upon which the same was tested or examined pursuant to the last foregoing paragraph.

Keeping of accounts

13. - (1) The Licensee shall keep in the United Kingdom full and correct accounts in a form from time to time approved by the Minister of -

(a) the quantity of petroleum in the form of gas won and saved;

(b) the quantity of petroleum in any other form won and saved;

(c) the name and address of any person to whom any petroleum has been supplied by the Licensee, the quantity so supplied, the price or other consideration therefor and the place to which the petroleum was conveyed pursuant to the agreement for such supply; and

(d) such other particulars as the Minister may from time to time direct.

(2) The quantities of petroleum stated in such accounts may exclude any water separated from the petroleum and shall be expressed as volumes in cubic metres measured at, or calculated as if measured at, a temperature of 15 degrees Celsius and a pressure of 1.0132 bar but if the Minister serves notice in writing on the Licensee determining any other manner in which any quantity of petroleum or any quantity of any form of petroleum is to be expressed that quantity shall be so expressed.

(3) Such accounts shall state separately the quantities used for the purposes of carrying on drilling and production operations and pumping to field storage, and quantities not so used, and in the case of petroleum not in the form of gas shall state the specific gravity of the petroleum and, if petroleum of different specific gravities has been won and saved, the respective quantities of petroleum of each specific gravity.

(4) The Licensee shall within two months after the end of each half year in which this licence is in force and within two months after the expiration or determination of this licence deliver to the Minister an abstract in a form from time to time approved by the Minister of the accounts for that half year or for the period prior to such expiration or determination as the case may be.

SCHEDULE 5

CURRENT MODEL CLAUSES FOR SEAWARD PRODUCTION LICENCES DERIVING FROM SCHEDULE 5 TO THE PETROLEUM (PRODUCTION) REGULATIONS 1976 AS IT FROM TIME TO TIME HAD EFFECT

PART I

1. This Schedule has effect in relation to the following paragraphs of Schedule 1 to the Act, namely -

(a) paragraph 9 of that Schedule (Schedule 5 to the Petroleum (Production) Regulations 1976[46]);

(b) paragraph 10 of that Schedule (the said Schedule 5 as amended by the Petroleum (Production) (Amendment) Regulations 1978[47]);

(c) paragraph 11 of that Schedule (the said Schedule 5 as amended as aforesaid and further amended by the Petroleum (Production) (Amendment) Regulations 1980[48]), and

(d) paragraph 12 of that Schedule (the said Schedule 5 as amended as aforesaid and further amended by the Oil and Gas (Enterprise) Act 1982[49]).

2. Subject to paragraphs 3, 4, 6, 7 and 8, the current model clauses in relation to the said paragraphs 9 to 12 are those reproduced in Part II.

3. - (1) Where the licensed area is in Scotland or the Scottish area, as defined in article 1(2) of the Civil Jurisdiction (Offshore Activities) Order 1987[50], Part II shall have effect as provided in the two following sub-paragraphs.

(2) Part II shall have effect in such a case as if for model clause 36 (distress) there were substituted the following clause -

" **Diligence**

36. If and whenever any of the payments mentioned in clause 8(1) of this licence or any part thereof shall be in arrear or unpaid for 28 days next after any of the days whereon the same ought to be paid (whether the same shall have been legally demanded or not) then and so often as the same may happen the Minister may (as an additional remedy and without prejudice to any other rights and remedies to which he would be entitled) do diligence in respect thereof in like manner as a landlord may do diligence in respect of unpaid arrears of rent and such diligence shall be effectual to attach all or any of the stocks of petroleum, engines, machinery, tools, implements and other effects belonging to the Licensee which shall be found on or about any of the Licensee's installations and equipment used or to be used in connection with searching, boring for or getting petroleum in the licensed area, and where in pursuance of such a diligence a sale of such effects as shall have been attached thereby takes place the Minister may out of the proceeds thereof retain and pay all the arrears of the said payments and also the expenses of and incident to such diligence and sale and shall pay the surplus thereof (if any) to the Licensee.".

(3) Part II shall also have effect in such a case as if, in model clause 41 (arbitration) -

(a) for the word "arbitrator", wherever it occurs in paragraphs (2) and (3), there were substituted the word "arbiter", and

(b) for the words "the Lord Chief Justice of England for the time being", in paragraph (2), there were substituted the words "the Lord President of the Court of Session".

4. Where the licensed area is in both a designated area, within the meaning of the Continental Shelf Act 1964[51], and the Northern Irish area, as defined in article 1(2) of the Civil Jurisdiction (Offshore Activities) Order 1987, Part II shall have effect as if in model clause 41 (arbitration) for the words "the Lord Chief Justice of England", in paragraph (2), there were substituted the words "the Lord Chief Justice of Northern Ireland".

5. In paragraphs 3 and 4, any reference to the licensed area is a reference to the licensed area within the meaning of model clause 1(1) in Part II.

6. - (1) In relation to paragraph 10, 11 or 12 of Schedule 1 to the Act, Part II shall have effect as provided in the following sub-paragraph.

(2) Part II shall have effect in such a case as if in model clause 22(1) for the words "as respects that function" there were substituted the words "and the function in question is one to which the approval relates".

7. - (1) In relation to paragraph 11 or 12 of Schedule 1 to the Act, Part II shall also have effect as provided in the five following sub-paragraphs.

(2) Part II shall have effect in such a case as if in model clause 3 -

(a) in paragraph (1) -

(i) for the word "four" there were substituted the word "six",

(ii) the words "Part I of" were omitted; and

(iii) for the word "three" there were substituted the word "thirty"; and

(b) paragraph (2) were omitted.

(3) Part II shall also have effect in such a case as if for model clauses 4 and 5 there were substituted the following clause -

" **Option to continue licence as to part of the licensed area**

4. - (1) At any time not later than three months before the expiration of the initial term the Licensee paying the payments and royalties hereinafter provided and observing and performing the terms and conditions herein contained may give notice in writing to the Minister that he desires the licence to continue as to a part of the licensed area (hereinafter called "the continuing part") in the manner hereinafter provided and to determine as to the residue thereof (hereinafter called "the surrendered part").

(2) Such notice shall -

(a) describe the surrendered part which shall be an area which shall together with any area previously surrendered in accordance with clause 6 hereof -

(i) if the area originally comprised in this licence consisted of sixty or more sections, be not less than half the number of such sections; or

(ii) if the area originally comprised in this licence consisted of more than thirty but less than sixty sections, be such a number of sections as will leave a continuing part consisting of thirty sections;

provided that if the area originally comprised in this licence consisted of not more than thirty sections the Licensee shall not be obliged to surrender any part of the licensed area and provided that any area surrendered in accordance with this clause shall comply with clause 7 hereof; and

(b) specify a date (hereinafter called "the surrender date") not later than the expiry of the initial term upon which the surrendered part is to be surrendered.

(3) The Licensee may at any time not less than one month before the surrender date give further notice in writing to the Minister varying the part of the licensed area to be surrendered and in the event of such further notice being given the provisions of the previous paragraphs of this clause shall apply *mutatis mutandis* to such notice but so that the surrender date specified in such notice shall be the same as that specified in the first

notice.

(4) This licence shall upon the option conferred by this clause being duly exercised but subject to the provisions of clause 3 of this licence continue in respect of the continuing part for a term of thirty years next after the surrender date.",

and the definitions of "second term" and "third term" in model clause 1(1) were omitted.

(4) Part II shall also have effect in such a case as if for model clause 7 there were substituted the following clause -

" **Areas Surrendered**

7. - (1) Within a block any area surrendered by the Licensee pursuant to either clause 4 or clause 6 of this licence and any area accordingly retained by him or, where the surrendered or retained area comprises separate parts, each part of each area shall, unless the Minister has otherwise agreed in writing before the date at which the appropriate notice is given by the Licensee to the Minister, -

(a) be bounded by minute lines of latitude extending not less than two minutes of longitude and minute lines of longitude extending not less than two minutes of latitude;

(b) subject to clause 4(2)(a) hereof, consist of not less than thirty sections; and

(c) have boundaries which, whether they run north and south or east and west, either coincide with the corresponding boundaries of the block or are not less than two sections distant from those boundaries;

and where the surrendered or retained area comprises separate parts, each part of that area shall be not less than two sections distant from any other part of that area.

(2) Upon the date upon which any determination of this licence or any surrender of part of the licensed area in manner provided by either clause 4 or clause 6 of this licence is to take effect the rights granted by this licence shall cease in respect of the licensed area or of the part so surrendered as the case may be but without prejudice to any obligation or liability imposed upon the Licensee or incurred by him under the terms of this licence prior to that date.".

(5) Part II shall also have effect in such a case as if in model clause 9(6) for the words "section 10(1)(b)" there were substituted the words "section 10(1)".

(6) Part II shall also have effect in such a case as if for model clause 14 there were substituted the following clause -

" **Working obligations**

14. - (1) The Licensee shall before the expiry of the initial term of this licence carry out such scheme of prospecting including any geological survey by any physical or chemical means and such programme of test drilling (hereinafter collectively referred to as a "work programme") as may be set out in Schedule 4 to this licence.

(2) If at any time the Minister serves a notice in writing on the Licensee requiring him to submit to the Minister, before a date specified in the notice, an appropriate programme for exploring for petroleum in the licensed area during a period so specified, the Licensee

shall comply with the notice; and for the purposes of this paragraph an appropriate programme is one which any person who, if he -

(a) were entitled to exploit the rights granted by this licence; and

(b) had the competence and resources needed to exploit those rights to the best commercial advantage; and

(c) were seeking to exploit those rights to the best commercial advantage,

could reasonably be expected to carry out during the period specified in the notice, and that period must be within the term of this licence.

(3) If a programme is submitted to the Minister in consequence of a notice served by him in pursuance of paragraph (2) of this clause, then -

(a) he shall not be entitled to revoke this licence on the ground that the programme does not satisfy the requirements of that paragraph (hereafter in this clause referred to as "the relevant requirements"); but

(b) if he is of opinion that the programme does not satisfy the relevant requirements he may serve a notice in writing on the Licensee stating his opinion and the reasons for it.

(4) Where notice in respect of a programme is served on the Licensee in pursuance of paragraph (3) of this clause he shall either -

(a) within 28 days beginning with the date of service of the notice refer to arbitration, in the manner provided by clause 41 of this licence, the question of whether the programme satisfies the relevant requirements; or

(b) within a reasonable period beginning with that date submit to the Minister a further programme which satisfies the relevant requirements;

and where it is determined in consequence of any reference to arbitration in pursuance of sub-paragraph (a) of this paragraph that the programme in question does not satisfy the relevant requirements the Licensee shall submit to the Minister, as soon as possible after the date of the determination, a further programme which satisfies the relevant requirements.

(5) The Licensee shall carry out any programme submitted by him in pursuance of this clause as to which either -

(a) the Minister serves notice in writing on the Licensee stating that the Minister approves the programme; or

(b) it is determined in consequence of any reference to arbitration in pursuance of this licence that the programme satisfies the relevant requirements;

and any programme approved by the Minister in pursuance of this paragraph shall be deemed for the purposes of this licence to satisfy the relevant requirements.

(6) Where, in consequence of any breach or non-observance by the Licensee of any provision of paragraph (2), (4) or (5) of this clause, the Minister has power by virtue of paragraph (1) of clause 40 of this licence to revoke this licence, he may if he thinks fit exercise that power in relation to such part only of the licensed area as he may specify; and where he does so the rights granted by this licence shall cease in respect of the specified part of that area without prejudice to any obligation or liability imposed upon the Licensee or incurred by him under the terms of this licence.

(7) Where the Licensee has a duty by virtue of this clause to carry out a programme during a part of the term of this licence, the Minister may serve notice in pursuance of paragraph (2) of this clause in respect of another part of that term.".

8. Where -

(a) section 1 of the Petroleum Royalties (Relief) Act 1983[52] applies, or

(b) section 1 of the Petroleum Royalties (Relief) and Continental Shelf Act 1989[53] applies

Part II has effect subject to the provisions of the said Act of 1983 or, as the case may be, the said Act of 1989.

PART II

Interpretation

1. - (1) In the following clauses, the following expressions have the meanings hereby respectively assigned to them, that is to say: -

"the Act of 1934" means the Petroleum (Production) Act 1934[54];
"the Act of 1964" means the Continental Shelf Act 1964[55];
"the Act of 1998" means the Petroleum Act 1998[56];
"appropriate percentage" has the meaning assigned thereto by clause 9;
"block" means an area comprised in this licence which is delineated on the reference map deposited at the principal office of the Minister's department and to which a reference number was assigned at the date of this licence;
"chargeable period" has the meaning assigned thereto by clause 9;
"development scheme" has the meaning assigned thereto by clause 26;
"half year" means the period from 1st January to 30th June in any year and the period from 1st July to 31st December in any year;
"initial term" has the meaning assigned thereto by clause 3;
"the licensed area" means the area for the time being in which the Licensee may exercise the rights granted by this licence;
"the Licensee" means the person or persons to whom this licence is granted, his personal representatives and any person or persons to whom the rights conferred by this licence may lawfully have been assigned;
"the Minister" means the Secretary of State for Trade and Industry;
"oil field" has the meaning assigned thereto by clause 26;
"petroleum" includes any mineral oil or relative hydrocarbon and natural gas existing in its natural condition in strata but does not include coal or bituminous shales or other stratified deposits from which oil can be extracted by destructive distillation;
"second term" has the meaning assigned thereto by clause 4;
"section" means a part of a block comprising an area bounded by minute lines of latitude and longitude one minute apart respectively;
"third term" has the meaning assigned thereto by clause 5;

"well" includes borehole.

(2) Any obligations which are to be observed and performed by the Licensee shall at any time at which the Licensee is more than one person be joint and several obligations.

(3) Any clause of this licence which refers to any provision of Part I of the Oil Taxation Act 1975[57] shall, unless the contrary intention appears, be construed as referring to that provision as it has effect for the time being for the purposes of petroleum revenue tax.

Term of licence

3. - (1) This licence unless sooner determined under any of the provisions hereof shall be and continue in force for the term of four years next after .... (hereinafter called "the initial term"); but if the terms and conditions hereof are duly performed and observed and, in particular, if the work programme described in Part I of Schedule 4 to this licence has been duly performed it may be continued for a further term of three years as hereinafter provided.

(2) If the terms and conditions of this licence are duly performed and observed and, in particular, if the work programme described in Part II of Schedule 4 to this licence has been duly performed, this licence may be continued for a further term of thirty years in respect of part of the licensed area as hereinafter provided.

Option to continue licence

4. - (1) At any time not later than three months before the expiration of the initial term the Licensee paying the payments and royalties hereinafter provided and observing and performing the terms and conditions herein contained may give notice in writing to the Minister that he desires the licence to continue on the expiration of the initial term in respect of the area to which it then relates.

(2) This licence shall upon the option conferred by this clause being duly exercised and subject to the provisions of clause 3 of this licence continue for a term of three years next after the expiration of the initial term (hereinafter called "the second term") in respect of the area to which it then relates.

Option to continue licence further as to part of licensed area

5. - (1) At any time not later than three months before the expiration of the second term the Licensee paying the payments and royalties hereinafter provided and observing and performing the terms and conditions herein contained may give notice in writing to the Minister that he desires the licence to continue as to a part of the licensed area (hereinafter called "the continuing part") in the manner hereinafter provided and to determine as to the residue thereof (hereinafter called "the surrendered part").

(2) Such notice shall -

(a) describe the surrendered part which shall be a part which complies with clause 7 hereof and shall together with any area previously surrendered in accordance with clause 6 hereof be not less than two-thirds of the number of sections contained in the area originally comprised in this licence; and

(b) specify a date (hereinafter called "the surrender date") not later than the expiry of the second term upon which the surrendered part is to be surrendered.

(3) The Licensee may at any time not less than one month before the surrender date give further notice in writing to the Minister varying the part of the licensed area to be surrendered and

in the event of such further notice being given the provisions of the previous paragraphs of this clause shall apply *mutatis mutandis* to such notice but so that the surrender date specified in such notice shall be the same as that specified in the first notice.

(4) This Licence shall upon the option conferred by this clause being duly exercised and subject to the provisions of clause 3 of this licence continue in respect of the continuing part for a term of thirty years next after the second surrender date (hereinafter called "the third term").

Right of licensee to determine licence or surrender part of licensed area

6. - (1) Without prejudice to any obligation or liability imposed by or incurred under the terms hereof the Licensee may at any time by giving to the Minister not less than six months' notice in writing to that effect to expire on an anniversary of the date of commencement of the initial term, determine this licence or surrender any part of the licensed area being a part which complies with clause 7 hereof.

(2) A notice given pursuant to paragraph (1) of this cause may be cancelled by a further notice in writing given to the Minister not less than one month before the expiration of the notice.

Areas surrendered

7. - (1) Within a block any area to be surrendered by the Licensee pursuant to any of the last three foregoing clauses and any area accordingly retained by him or, where the surrendered or retained area is comprised of separate parts, each such part shall unless the Minister has otherwise agreed in writing prior to the date at which the appropriate notice is given by the Licensee to the Minister comply with the following requirements -

(a) be bounded by minute lines of latitude extending not less than two minutes of longitude and minute lines of longitude extending not less than two minutes of latitude;

(b) consist of not less than thirty sections;

(c) each separate part of an area surrendered or retained shall be not less than two sections distant from any other part of the same category (surrendered or retained as the case may be); and

(d) the boundaries shall, in the case of those which run due north and south, either coincide with the corresponding boundaries of the block or be not less than two sections distant therefrom and, in the case of those which run due east and west, either coincide with the corresponding boundaries of the block or be not less than two sections distant therefrom.

(2) Upon the date upon which any determination of this licence or any surrender of part of the licensed area in manner provided by the last three foregoing clauses is to take effect the rights granted by this licence shall cease in respect of the licensed area or of the part so surrendered as the case may be but without prejudice to any obligation or liability imposed upon the Licensee or incurred by him under the terms of this licence prior to that date.

Payment of consideration for licence

8. - (1) The Licensee shall make to the Minister as consideration for the grant of this licence -

(a) payments of royalty in accordance with clauses 9 and 10 of this licence;

(b) deliveries of petroleum in accordance with clause 11 of this licence; and

(c) payments in accordance with Schedule 2 to this licence.

(2) The Licensee shall not by reason of determination of the licence or surrender of any part of the licensed area be entitled to be repaid or allowed any sum payable to the Minister pursuant to this licence before the date of determination or surrender.

Royalty payments

9. - (1) Subject to paragraph (1A) of this clause the Licensee shall pay to the Minister, in respect of each half year in which this licence is in force (hereafter in this clause and in clauses 9A and 10 of this licence referred to as a "chargeable period"), a royalty of an amount equal to the percentage specified in Schedule 3 to this licence (hereinafter referred to as "the appropriate percentage") of the value of the petroleum relating to that period.

(1A) Paragraph (1) of this clause shall not apply to a chargeable period in which the Licensee delivers petroleum to the Minister in pursuance of clause 11 of this licence; but if the petroleum delivered has a value of less than the appropriate percentage of the aggregate of -

(a) the value of the petroleum delivered (ignoring any such excess as is mentioned in paragraph (10) of this clause), and

(b) the value of the petroleum relating to that period,

he shall pay to the Minister a royalty of an amount equal to the difference.

(5) For the purposes of this clause and clauses 9A and 10 of this licence the value of the petroleum relating to a chargeable period is, subject to paragraph (6) of this clause, the total of the amounts which, if the words "one-half of" were omitted from paragraph (b) of subsection (4) and paragraph (d) of subsection (5) of section 2 of the Oil Taxation Act 1975[58] would in pursuance of paragraph (a) of the said subsection (4) fall to be taken into account in relation to that period in respect of the persons who by reference to this licence are or are treated as participators for the purposes of those subsections, reduced by the total of the market values which would in pursuance of the said paragraph (b) fall to be taken into account as aforesaid.

(6) The value which, in pursuance of paragraph (5) of this clause, is the value of the petroleum relating to a chargeable period shall be increased by an amount equal to the value, as determined for the purposes of income tax or the charge of corporation tax on income, of so much of the petroleum won and saved in the licensed area as falls within section 10(1)(b) of the Oil Taxation Act 1975 and was in that period disposed of or relevantly appropriated (within the meaning of Part I of that Act) by the persons mentioned in the said paragraph (5).

(7) Subject to paragraphs (8) and (9) of this clause, the value of petroleum delivered to the Minister in pursuance of clause 11 of this licence shall be ascertained for the purposes of this clause and clause 9A on such basis (or, where petroleum of more than one kind is delivered, such bases) as the Minister and the Licensee agree.

(8) If the Minister and the Licensee fail to agree on the value of any petroleum delivered to the Minister in pursuance of clause 11 of this licence, it shall be ascertained on such basis as the Minister may specify as fair in a notice in writing given by him to the Licensee.

(9) The Licensee may, during the period of 28 days beginning with the day on which he receives a notice from the Minister under paragraph (8) of this clause, refer to arbitration in the manner provided by clause 41 of this licence any question as to whether the basis of valuation

specified in the notice is fair.

(10) In this clause and clauses 9A and 10, references to petroleum delivered to the Minister in pursuance of clause 11 include references to any excess over the quantity required to be delivered by a notice served in pursuance of paragraph (1) of that clause.

Payments by the Minister

9A. If in any chargeable period the Licensee delivers to the Minister in pursuance of clause 11 of this licence petroleum having a value greater than the appropriate percentage of the aggregate of -

(a) the value of the petroleum delivered (ignoring any such excess as is mentioned in clause 9(10) of this licence), and

(b) the value of the petroleum relating to that period,

the Minister shall pay to the Licensee a sum equal to the difference.

Provisions supplementary to clauses 9 and 9A

10. - (1) The Licensee shall, within two months after the end of each chargeable period, deliver to the Minister, in such form as the Minister may specify, a statement of -

(a) the quantity of petroleum won and saved in the licensed area in that period;

(b) the quantity of that petroleum delivered to the Minister in that period in pursuance of clause 11 of this licence; and

(c) the amounts of the prices and market values which are required by paragraph 2 of Schedule 2 to the Oil Taxation Act 1975[59] to be stated in the returns made for that period in pursuance of that paragraph in consequence of this licence.

(2) The Licensee shall, when he delivers a statement to the Minister in pursuance of paragraph (1) of this clause for a chargeable period in respect of which royalty is payable in pursuance of clause 9(1) of this licence, make to the Minister a payment on account of royalty for that period equal to the appropriate percentage of the sum produced by aggregating the amounts which in pursuance of sub-paragraph (c) of paragraph (1) of this clause are specified in the statement and reducing the aggregate by the amount which, by virtue of paragraph 2(2)(d)(ii) of Schedule 2 to the Oil Taxation Act 1975, was specified in the statement delivered to the Minister in pursuance of the said paragraph (1) in respect of the preceding chargeable period.

(3) The Licensee shall, when he delivers a statement to the Minister in pursuance of paragraph (1) of this clause for a chargeable period in respect of which royalty is payable in pursuance of clause 9(1A) of this licence, make to the Minister a payment on account of royalty for that period equal to the amount which would be so payable for that period if the royalty so payable for that period fell to be determined by reference to the amounts specified in the statement and the amount which, by virtue of paragraph 2(2)(d)(ii) of Schedule 2 to the Oil Taxation Act 1975, was specified in the statement delivered to the Minister in pursuance of paragraph (1) of this clause in respect of the preceding chargeable period.

(4) The Minister may from time to time, after a statement in respect of any chargeable period has been delivered to him in pursuance of paragraph (1) of this clause and before he has given to the Licensee a notice in pursuance of paragraph (5) of this clause in respect of that period, give a notice in writing to the Licensee specifying the amount which the Minister estimates is payable by

the Licensee in pursuance of clause 9 of this licence in respect of that period and where the amount specified in the notice is larger or smaller than the total amount already paid by the Licensee in pursuance of this clause in respect of that period, then -

(a) if it is larger the difference shall be paid forthwith by the Licensee to the Minister; and

(b) if it is smaller the difference shall be paid forthwith by the Minister to the Licensee.

(5) When it appears to the Minister that the value of the petroleum relating to any chargeable period has been finally determined for tax purposes, he may give to the Licensee a notice in writing specifying the amount which the Minister considers is payable by the Licensee in pursuance of clause 9 of this licence in respect of that period; and where the amount specified in the notice is larger or smaller than the total amount already paid by the Licensee in pursuance of this clause in respect of that period, then, subject to paragraph (7) of this clause -

(a) if it is larger the difference shall be paid forthwith by the Licensee to the Minister; and

(b) if it is smaller the difference shall be paid forthwith by the Minister to the Licensee.

(6) If after the date when the Minister gave notice to the Licensee in pursuance of paragraph (5) of this clause or this paragraph in respect of a chargeable period it appears to the Minister, in consequence of a relevant assessment or determination made after that date which relates directly or indirectly to the value of petroleum by reference to which the amount specified in the notice was determined, that another amount ought to have been so specified, he may give notice in writing to the Licensee specifying the other amount; and where he does so, then, subject to paragraph (7) of this clause -

(a) if the other amount is larger than the total amount already paid by the Licensee in pursuance of this clause in respect of that period the difference shall be paid forthwith by the Licensee to the Minister; and

(b) if it is smaller the difference shall be paid forthwith by the Minister to the Licensee.

(7) A decision made by the Minister for the purposes of paragraph (4), (5) or (6) of this clause shall not be called in question by the Licensee except that any dispute between the Minister and the Licensee as to whether an amount specified in a notice given in pursuance of the said paragraph (5) or (6) is payable by virtue of clause 9 of this licence may, during the period of 28 days beginning with the day on which the Licensee receives the notice, be referred to arbitration in the manner provided by clause 41 of this licence; and on a reference to arbitration in pursuance of this paragraph any relevant assessment or determination for the time being in force shall be binding on the Minister and the Licensee so far as the assessment or determination relates directly or indirectly to the value of petroleum relating to the chargeable period in question.

(8) When any payment is made by the Licensee or the Minister in pursuance of paragraph (4), (5) or (6) of this clause, an amount in respect of interest on the payment shall also be payable by him to the recipient of the payment and that amount shall be calculated in such manner as the Minister may specify from time to time in a notice in writing given by him to the Licensee; but -

(a) a notice in pursuance of this paragraph shall provide for amounts by way of interest to be calculated by applying a rate of interest which is for the time being a commercial rate of interest; and

(b) any such amount in respect of interest shall be disregarded in calculating for the purposes of the said paragraph (4), (5) or (6) any amount already paid by the Licensee in pursuance of this clause.

(8A) If a payment is made by the Minister in pursuance of clause 9A of this licence more than two months after the end of the chargeable period to which the payment relates, an amount in respect of interest on the payment from the end of those two months shall also be payable by him to the Licensee.

(8B) Interest under paragraph (8A) of this clause shall be calculated in such manner as the Minister may specify from time to time in a notice in writing given by him to the Licensee (but sub-paragraph (a) of paragraph (8) of this clause shall apply to such a notice as it applies to a notice under paragraph (8)).

(9) In this clause "relevant assessment or determination" means an assessment or determination made by the Commissioners of Inland Revenue for the purposes of petroleum revenue tax, income tax or the charge of corporation tax on income or a determination made in proceedings arising out of such an assessment or determination made by the said Commissioners.

(10) For the purposes of this clause any amount paid by the Licensee or the Minister on account of a prospective liability under paragraph (4), (5) or (6) of this clause shall be treated as paid in pursuance of that paragraph.

CURRENT MODEL CLAUSES FOR SEAWARD PRODUCTION LICENCES DERIVING FROM SCHEDULE 5 TO THE PETROLEUM (PRODUCTION) REGULATIONS 1982 AS IT FROM TIME TO TIME HAD EFFECT

PART I

1. This Schedule has effect in relation to the following paragraphs of Schedule 1 to the Act, namely -

(a) paragraph 14 of that Schedule (Schedule 5 to the Petroleum (Production) Regulations 1982)[61]); and

(b) paragraph 15 of that Schedule (the said Schedule 5 as amended by the Petroleum Act 1987[62]).

2. Subject to paragraphs 3, 4 and 6, the current model clauses in relation to the said paragraphs 14 and 15 are those reproduced in Part II.

3. - (1) Where the licensed area is in Scotland or the Scottish area as defined in article 1(2) of the Civil Jurisdiction (Offshore Activities) Order 1987[63], Part II shall have effect as provided in the two following sub-paragraphs.

(2) Part II shall have effect in such a case as if for model clause 35 (distress) there were substituted the following clause -

" **Diligence**

35. If and whenever any of the payments mentioned in clause 7(1) of this licence or any part thereof shall be in arrear or unpaid for 28 days next after any of the days whereon the same ought to be paid (whether the same shall have been legally demanded or not) then and so often as the same may happen the Minister may (as an additional remedy and without prejudice to any other rights and remedies to which he would be entitled) do diligence in respect thereof in like manner as a landlord may do diligence in respect of unpaid arrears of rent and such diligence shall be effectual to attach all or any of the stocks of petroleum, engines, machinery, tools, implements and other effects belonging to the Licensee which shall be found on or about any of the Licensee's installations and equipment used or to be used in connection with searching, boring for or getting petroleum in the licensed area, and where in pursuance of such a diligence a sale of such effects as shall have been attached thereby takes place the Minister may out of the proceeds thereof retain and pay all the arrears of the said payments and also the expenses of and incident to such diligence and sale and shall pay the surplus thereof (if any) to the Licensee.".

(3) Part II shall also have effect in such a case as if, in model clause 40 (arbitration) -

(a) for the word "arbitrator", wherever it occurs in paragraphs (2) and (3), there were substituted the word "arbiter", and

(b) for the words "the Lord Chief Justice of England for the time being", in paragraph (2), there were substituted the words "the Lord President of the Court of Session".

4. Where the licensed area is in both a designated area, within the meaning of the Continental Shelf Act 1964[64], and the Northern Irish area, as defined in article 1(2) of the Civil Jurisdiction (Offshore Activities) Order 1987, Part II shall have effect as if in model clause 40 (arbitration) for the words "the Lord Chief Justice of England", in paragraph (2), there were substituted the words "the Lord Chief Justice of Northern Ireland".

5. In paragraphs 3 and 4, any reference to the licensed area is a reference to the licensed area within the meaning of model clause 1(1) in Part II.

6. Where -

(a) section 1 of the Petroleum Royalties (Relief) Act 1983[65] applies, or

(b) section 1 of the Petroleum Royalties (Relief) and Continental Shelf Act 1989[66] applies,

Part II has effect subject to the provisions of the said Act of 1983 or, as the case may be, the said Act of 1989.

PART II

Interpretation

1. - (1) In the following clauses the following expressions have the meanings hereby respectively assigned to them, that is to say -

"the Act of 1934" means the Petroleum (Production) Act 1934[67];
"the Act of 1964" means the Continental Shelf Act 1964[68];
"the Act of 1998" means the Petroleum Act 1998[69];
"appropriate percentage" has the meaning assigned thereto by clause 8;
"block" means an area comprised in this licence which is delineated on the reference map deposited at the principal office of the Minister's department and to which a reference number was assigned at the date of this licence;
"chargeable period" has the meaning assigned thereto by clause 8;

"development scheme" has the meaning assigned thereto by clause 25;
"half year" means the period from 1st January to 30th June in any year and the period from 1st July to 31st December in any year;
"initial term" has the meaning assigned thereto by clause 3;
"the licensed area" means the area for the time being in which the Licensee may exercise the rights granted by this licence;
"the Licensee" means the person or persons to whom this licence is granted, his personal representatives and any person or persons to whom the rights conferred by this licence may lawfully have been assigned;
"the Minister" means the Secretary of State for Trade and Industry;
"oil field" has the meaning assigned thereto by clause 25;
"petroleum" includes any mineral oil or relative hydrocarbon and natural gas existing in its natural condition in strata but does not include coal or bituminous shales or other stratified deposits from which oil can be extracted by destructive distillation;
"section" means a part of a block comprising an area bounded by minute lines of latitude and longitude one minute apart respectively;
"well" includes borehole.

(2) Any obligations which are to be observed and performed by the Licensee shall at any time at which the Licensee is more than one person be joint and several obligations.

(3) Any clause of this licence which refers to any provision of Part I of the Oil Taxation Act 1975[70] shall, unless the contrary intention appears, be construed as referring to that provision as it has effect for the time being for the purposes of petroleum revenue tax.

Term of licence

3. This licence unless sooner determined under any of the provisions hereof shall be and continue in force for the term of six years next after .... 19... (hereinafter called "the initial term"); but if the terms and conditions hereof are duly performed and observed and, in particular, if the work programme described in Schedule 4 to this licence has been duly performed, it may be continued for a further term of thirty years as hereinafter provided.

Option to continue licence as to part of the licensed area

4. - (1) At any time not later than three months before the expiration of the initial term the Licensee paying the payments and royalties hereinafter provided and observing and performing the terms and conditions herein contained may give notice in writing to the Minister that he desires the licence to continue as to a part of the licensed area (hereinafter called "the continuing part") in the manner hereinafter provided and to determine as to the residue thereof (hereinafter called "the surrendered part").

(2) Such notice shall -

(a) describe the surrendered part which shall be an area which shall together with any area previously surrendered in accordance with clause 5 hereof -

(i) if the area originally comprised in this licence consisted of sixty or more sections, be not less than half the number of such sections; or

(ii) if the area originally comprised in this licence consisted of more than thirty but less than sixty sections, be such a number of sections as will leave a continuing part consisting of thirty sections;

provided that if the area originally comprised in this licence consisted of not more than thirty sections the Licensee shall not be obliged to surrender any part of the licensed area and provided that any area surrendered in accordance with this clause shall comply with clause 6 hereof; and

(b) specify a date (hereinafter called "the surrender date") not later than the expiry of the initial term upon which the surrendered part is to be surrendered.

(3) The Licensee may at any time not less than one month before the surrender date give further notice in writing to the Minister varying the part of the licensed area to be surrendered and in the event of such further notice being given the provisions of the previous paragraphs of this clause shall apply *mutatis mutandis* to such notice but so that the surrender date specified in such notice shall be the same as that specified in the first notice.

(4) This licence shall upon the option conferred by this clause being duly exercised but subject to the provisions of clause 3 of this licence continue in respect of the continuing part for a term of thirty years next after the surrender date.

Right of Licensee to determine licence or surrender part of licensed area

5. - (1) Without prejudice to any obligation or liability imposed by or incurred under the terms hereof, the Licensee may at any time, by giving to the Minister not less than six months' notice in writing to that effect to expire on an anniversary of the date of commencement of the initial term, determine this licence or surrender any part of the licensed area being a part which complies with clause 6 hereof.

(2) A notice given pursuant to paragraph (1) of this clause may be cancelled by a further notice in writing given to the Minister not less than one month before the expiration of the notice.

Areas surrendered

6. - (1) Within a block any area surrendered by the Licensee pursuant to either clause 4 or clause 5 of this licence and any area accordingly retained by him or, where the surrendered or retained area comprises separate parts, each part of each area shall, unless the Minister has otherwise agreed in writing before the date at which the appropriate notice is given by the Licensee to the Minister -

(a) be bounded by minute lines of latitude extending not less than two minutes of longitude and minute lines of longitude extending not less than two minutes of latitude;

(b) subject to clause 4(2)(a) hereof, consist of not less than thirty sections; and

(c) have boundaries which, whether they run north and south or east and west, either coincide with the corresponding boundaries of the block or are not less than two sections distant from those boundaries;

and where the surrendered or retained area comprises separate parts, each part of that area shall be not less than two sections distant from any other part of that area.

(2) Upon the date upon which any determination of this licence or any surrender of part of the licensed area in manner provided by either clause 4 or clause 5 of this licence is to take effect the rights granted by this licence shall cease in respect of the licensed area or of the part so surrendered as the case may be but without prejudice to any obligation or liability imposed upon the Licensee or incurred by him under the terms of this licence prior to that date.

Payment of consideration for licence

7. - (1) The Licensee shall make to the Minister as consideration for the grant of this licence -

(a) payments of royalty in accordance with clauses 8 and 9 of this licence;

(b) deliveries of petroleum in accordance with clause 10 of this licence; and

(c) payments in accordance with Schedule 2 to this licence.

(2) The Licensee shall not by reason of the determination of the licence or the surrender of any part of the licensed area be entitled to be repaid or allowed any sum payable to the Minister pursuant to this licence before the date of the determination or surrender.

Royalty payments

8. - (1) Subject to paragraph (1A) of this clause the Licensee shall pay to the Minister, in respect of each half year in which this licence is in force (hereafter in this clause and in clauses 8A and 9 of this licence referred to as a "chargeable period"), a royalty of an amount equal to the percentage specified in Schedule 3 to this licence (hereinafter referred to as "the appropriate percentage") of the value of the petroleum relating to that period.

(1A) Paragraph (1) of this clause shall not apply to a chargeable period in which the Licensee delivers petroleum to the Minister in pursuance of clause 10 of this licence; but if the petroleum delivered has a value of less than the appropriate percentage of the aggregate of -

(a) the value of the petroleum delivered (ignoring any such excess as is mentioned in paragraph (10) of this clause), and

(b) the value of the petroleum relating to that period,

he shall pay to the Minister a royalty of an amount equal to the difference.

(5) For the purposes of this clause and clauses 8A and 9 of this licence the value of the petroleum relating to a chargeable period is, subject to paragraph (6) of this clause, the total of the amounts which, if the words "one-half of" were omitted from paragraph (b) of subsection (4) and paragraph (d) of subsection (5) of section 2 of the Oil Taxation Act 1975[71], would in pursuance of paragraph (a) of the said subsection (4) fall to be taken into account in relation to that period in respect of the persons who by reference to this licence are or are treated as participators for the purposes of those subsections, reduced by the total of the market values which would in pursuance of the said paragraph (b) fall to be taken into account as aforesaid.

(6) The value which, in pursuance of paragraph (5) of this clause, is the value of the petroleum relating to a chargeable period shall be increased by an amount equal to the value, as determined for the purposes of income tax or the charge of corporation tax on income, of so much of the petroleum won and saved in the licensed area as falls within section 10(1)(b) of the Oil Taxation Act 1975 and was in that period disposed of or relevantly appropriated (within the meaning of Part I of that Act) by the persons mentioned in the said paragraph (5).

(7) Subject to paragraphs (8) and (9) of this clause, the value of petroleum delivered to the Minister in pursuance of clause 10 of this licence shall be ascertained for the purposes of this clause and clause 8A on such basis (or, where petroleum of more than one kind is delivered, such bases) as the Minister and the Licensee agree.

(8) If the Minister and the Licensee fail to agree on the value of any petroleum delivered to the Minister in pursuance of clause 10 of this licence, it shall be ascertained on such basis as the Minister may specify as fair in a notice in writing given by him to the Licensee.

(9) The Licensee may, during the period of 28 days beginning with the day on which he receives a notice from the Minister under paragraph (8) of this clause, refer to arbitration in the manner provided by clause 40 of this licence any question as to whether the basis of valuation specified in the notice is fair.

(10) In this clause and clauses 8A and 9, references to petroleum delivered to the Minister in pursuance of clause 10 include references to any excess over the quantity required to be delivered by a notice served in pursuance of paragraph (1) of that clause.

Payments by the Minister

8A If in any chargeable period the Licensee delivers to the Minister in pursuance of clause 10 of this licence petroleum having a value greater than the appropriate percentage of the aggregate of -

(a) the value of the petroleum delivered (ignoring any such excess as is mentioned in clause 8(10) of this licence), and

(b) the value of the petroleum relating to that period,

the Minister shall pay to the Licensee a sum equal to the difference.

Provisions supplementary to clauses 8 and 8A

9. - (1) The Licensee shall, within two months after the end of each chargeable period, deliver to the Minister, in such form as the Minister may specify, a statement of -

(a) the quantity of petroleum won and saved in the licensed area in that period;

(b) the quantity of that petroleum delivered to the Minister in that period in pursuance of clause 10 of this licence; and

(c) the amounts of the prices and market values which are required by paragraph 2 of Schedule 2 to the Oil Taxation Act 1975[72] to be stated in the returns made for that period in pursuance of that paragraph in consequence of this licence.

(2) The Licensee shall, when he delivers a statement to the Minister in pursuance of paragraph (1) of this clause for a chargeable period in respect of which royalty is payable in pursuance of clause 8(1) of this licence, make to the Minister a payment on account of royalty for that period equal to the appropriate percentage of the sum produced by aggregating the amounts which in pursuance of subparagraph (c) of paragraph (1) of this clause are specified in the statement and reducing the aggregate by the amount which, by virtue of paragraph 2(2)(d)(ii) of Schedule 2 to the said Act of 1975, was specified in the statement delivered to the Minister in pursuance of the said paragraph (1) in respect of the preceding chargeable period.

(3) The Licensee shall, when he delivers a statement to the Minister in pursuance of paragraph (1) of this clause for a chargeable period in respect of which royalty is payable in pursuance of clause 8(1A) of this licence, make to the Minister a payment on account of royalty for that period equal to the amount which would be so payable for that period if the royalty so payable for that period fell to be determined by reference to the amounts specified in the statement and the amount which, by virtue of paragraph 2(2)(d)(ii) of Schedule 2 to the Oil Taxation Act 1975, was

specified in the statement delivered to the Minister in pursuance of paragraph (1) of this clause in respect of the preceding chargeable period.

(4) The Minister may from time to time, after a statement in respect of any chargeable period has been delivered to him in pursuance of paragraph (1) of this clause and before he has given to the Licensee a notice in pursuance of paragraph (5) of this clause in respect of that period, give a notice in writing to the Licensee specifying the amount which the Minister estimates is payable by the Licensee in pursuance of clause 8 of this licence in respect of that period; and where the amount specified in the notice is larger or smaller than the total amount already paid by the Licensee in pursuance of this clause in respect of that period, then -

(a) if it is larger the difference shall be paid forthwith by the Licensee to the Minister; and

(b) if it is smaller the difference shall be paid forthwith by the Minister to the Licensee.

(5) When it appears to the Minister that the value of the petroleum relating to any chargeable period has been finally determined for tax purposes, he may give to the Licensee a notice in writing specifying the amount which the Minister considers is payable by the Licensee in pursuance of clause 8 of this licence in respect of that period; and where the amount specified in the notice is larger or smaller than the total amount already paid by the Licensee in pursuance of this clause in respect of that period, then, subject to paragraph (7) of this clause -

(a) if it is larger the difference shall be paid forthwith by the Licensee to the Minister; and

(b) if it is smaller the difference shall be paid forthwith by the Minister to the Licensee.

(6) If after the date when the Minister gave notice to the Licensee in pursuance of paragraph (5) of this clause or this paragraph in respect of a chargeable period it appears to the Minister, in consequence of a relevant assessment or determination made after that date which relates directly or indirectly to the value of petroleum by reference to which the amount specified in the notice was determined, that another amount ought to have been so specified, he may give notice in writing to the Licensee specifying the other amount; and where he does so then, subject to paragraph (7) of this clause -

(a) if the other amount is larger than the total amount already paid by the Licensee in pursuance of this clause in respect of that period the difference shall be paid forthwith by the Licensee to the Minister; and

(b) if it is smaller the difference shall be paid forthwith by the Minister to the Licensee.

(7) A decision made by the Minister for the purposes of paragraph (4), (5) or (6) of this clause shall not be called in question by the Licensee except that any dispute between the Minister and the Licensee as to whether an amount specified in a notice given in pursuance of the said paragraph (5) or (6) is payable by virtue of clause 8 of this licence may, during the period of 28 days beginning with the day on which the Licensee receives the notice, be referred to arbitration in the manner provided by clause 40 of this licence; and on a reference to arbitration in pursuance of this paragraph any relevant assessment or determination for the time being in force shall be binding on the Minister and the Licensee so far as the assessment or determination relates directly or indirectly to the value of petroleum relating to the chargeable period in question.

(8) When any payment is made by the Licensee or the Minister in pursuance of paragraph (4), (5) or (6) of this clause, an amount in respect of interest on the payment shall also be payable by

him to the recipient of the payment and that amount shall be calculated in such manner as the Minister may specify from time to time in a notice in writing given by him to the Licensee; but -

(a) a notice in pursuance of this paragraph shall provide for amounts by way of interest to be calculated by applying a rate of interest which is for the time being a commercial rate of interest; and

(b) any such amount in respect of interest shall be disregarded in calculating for the purposes of the said paragraph (4), (5) or (6) any amount already paid by the Licensee in pursuance of this clause.

(8A) If a payment is made by the Minister in pursuance of clause 8A of this licence more than two months after the end of the chargeable period to which the payment relates, an amount in respect of interest on the payment from the end of those two months shall also be payable by him to the Licensee.

(8B) Interest under paragraph (8A) of this clause shall be calculated in such manner as the Minister may specify from time to time in a notice in writing given by him to the Licensee (but sub-paragraph (a) of paragraph (8) of this clause shall apply to such a notice as it applies to a notice under paragraph (8)).

(9) In this clause "relevant assessment or determination" means an assessment or determination made by the Commissioners of Inland Revenue for the purposes of petroleum revenue tax, income tax or the charge of corporation tax on income or a determination made in proceedings arising out of such an assessment or determination made by the said Commissioners.

(10) For the purposes of this clause any amount paid by the Licensee or the Minister on account of a prospective liability under paragraph (4), (5) or (6) of this clause shall be treated as paid in pursuance of that paragraph.

Deliveries of petroleum in place of royalties

10. - (1) If during the term of this licence the Minister serves on the Licensee a notice in writing in accordance with the following provisions of this clause requiring the Licensee to deliver to the Minister part of the petroleum won and saved by the Licensee in the licensed area, the Licensee shall comply with the notice.

(2) Where the Minister proposes to serve a notice on the Licensee in pursuance of paragraph (1) of this clause, he shall before doing so -

(a) give the Licensee a copy of the proposed notice and an opportunity of making representations to the Minister about it; and

(b) consider any representations then made to him by the Licensee about the proposed notice;

and the Minister shall, in deciding upon the terms of the actual notice, have regard to the desirability of not disturbing unduly any arrangements made by the Licensee for transporting and delivering petroleum won and saved from the licensed area.

(3) Subject to paragraph (4) of this clause, a notice served in pursuance of paragraph (1) of this clause -

(a) shall specify the date on which the notice is to come into force and may contain provisions with respect to the time when it shall cease to be in force;

(b) shall specify the quantity of petroleum won and saved in the licensed area during each half year in which the notice is in force which, up to any maximum quantities specified in the notice in pursuance of paragraph (4)(b) of this clause, is to be delivered to the Minister in consequence of the notice;

(c) may relate to all petroleum so won and saved or may be limited to and specify different quantities of such petroleum which is of one or more of the following kinds, namely, crude oil, condensate, natural gas and natural gas liquids, in each case of a quality or composition or of each quality or composition determined in the manner specified in the notice;

(d) shall contain provisions with respect to the place or places at which any petroleum or kind of petroleum is to be delivered in pursuance of the notice and may contain provisions with respect to the times at which any quantities of it are to be so delivered.

(4) Such a notice -

(a) shall not specify as the date on which it is to come into force a date before the expiration of the period of six months beginning with the date on which the notice is served on the Licensee but shall, if the Minister serves on the Licensee a further notice in writing stating that it is to cease to be in force at a time specified in the further notice which is not earlier than six months after the date of service of the further notice, cease to be in force at that time;

(b) shall not specify, as the quantity of petroleum won and saved in any half year which is to be delivered in pursuance of the notice or as the quantity of any kind of such petroleum, a quantity greater than the appropriate percentage of all the petroleum, or as the case may be of all the petroleum of that kind, which is won and saved by the Licensee in the licensed area in that half year, but may provide that the quantities of the petroleum or of a kind of petroleum so won and saved which are to be so delivered shall not in the aggregate exceed a quantity specified in the notice;

(c) shall not specify, or enable to be specified, as a place at which delivery is to be made in pursuance of the notice a place which is neither a point at sea at which the Licensee normally loads, nor a point on land at which the Licensee normally lands, petroleum of any kind from the licensed area.

Measurement of petroleum obtained from the licensed area

11. - (1) The Licensee shall measure or weigh by a method or methods customarily used in good oilfield practice and from time to time approved by the Minister all petroleum won and saved from the licensed area.

(1A) If and to the extent that the Minister so directs, the duty imposed by paragraph (1) of this clause shall be discharged separately in relation to petroleum won and saved -

(a) from each part of the licensed area which is an oil field for the purposes of the Oil Taxation Act 1975,

(b) from each part of the licensed area which forms part of such an oil field extending beyond the licensed area, and

(c) from each well producing petroleum from a part of the licensed area which is not within such an oil field.

(1B) If and to the extent that the Minister so directs, the preceding provisions of this clause shall apply as if the duty to measure or weigh petroleum included a duty to ascertain its quality or composition or both; and where a direction under this paragraph is in force, the following provisions of this clause shall have effect as if references to measuring or weighing included references to ascertaining quality or composition.

(2) The Licensee shall not make any alteration in the method or methods of measurement or weighing used by him or any appliances used for that purpose without the consent in writing of the Minister and the Minister may in any case require that no alteration shall be made save in the presence of a person authorised by the Minister.

(3) The Minister may from time to time direct that any weighing or measuring appliance shall be tested or examined in such manner, upon such occasions or at such intervals and by such persons as may be specified by the Minister's direction and the Licensee shall pay to any such person or to the Minister such fees and expenses for test or examination as the Minister may specify.

(4) If any measuring or weighing appliance shall upon any such test or examination as is mentioned in the last foregoing paragraph be found to be false or unjust the same shall if the Minister so determines after considering any representations in writing made by the Licensee be deemed to have existed in that condition during the period since the last occasion upon which the same was tested or examined pursuant to the last foregoing paragraph.

Keeping of accounts

12. - (1) The Licensee shall keep in the United Kingdom full and correct accounts in a form from time to time approved by the Minister of -

(a) the quantity of petroleum in the form of gas won and saved;

(b) the quantity of petroleum in any other form won and saved;

(c) the name and address of any person to whom any petroleum has been supplied by the Licensee, the quantity so supplied, the price or other consideration therefor and the place to which the petroleum was conveyed pursuant to the agreement for such supply; and

(d) such other particulars as the Minister may from time to time direct.

(2) The quantities of petroleum stated in such accounts may exclude any water separated from the petroleum and shall be expressed as volumes in cubic metres measured at, or calculated as if measured at, a temperature of 15 degrees Celsius and a pressure of 1.0132 bar but if the Minister serves notice in writing on the Licensee determining any other manner in which any quantity of petroleum or any quantity of any form of petroleum is to be expressed that quantity shall be so expressed.

(3) Such accounts shall state separately the quantities used for the purposes of carrying on drilling and production operations and pumping to field storage, and quantities not so used, and in the case of petroleum not in the form of gas shall state the specific gravity of the petroleum and, if petroleum of different specific gravities has been won and saved, the respective quantities of

petroleum of each specific gravity.

(4) The Licensee shall within two months after the end of each half year in which this licence is in force and within two months after the expiration or determination of this licence deliver to the Minister an abstract in a form from time to time approved by the Minister of the accounts for that half year or for the period prior to such expiration or determination as the case may be.

Notes:

[59] Paragraph 2 was amended by section 62 of, and part X of Schedule 16 to, the Finance Act 1987 (c.16), section 187 of the Finance Act 1993 (c.34) and section 236 of, and Schedule 23 to, the Finance Act 1994 (c.9).

SCHEDULE 7

CURRENT MODEL CLAUSES FOR METHANE DRAINAGE LICENCES DERIV ING FROM SCHEDULE 8 TO THE PETROLEUM (PRODUCTION) REGULATIONS 1982

PART I

1. This Schedule has effect in relation to paragraph 16 of Schedule 1 to the Act (Schedule 8 to the Petroleum (Production) Regulations 1982[74]).

2. The current model clauses in relation to the said paragraph 16 are those reproduced in Part II.

PART II

Interpretation

1. - (1) In the following clauses the following expressions have the meanings hereby respectively assigned to them, that is to say: -

"the licensed area" means the area in which the Licensee may exercise the rights granted by this licence;
"the Licensee" means the person or persons to whom this licence is granted, his personal representatives and any person or persons to whom the rights conferred by this licence may lawfully have been assigned;
"mine" has the same meaning as in the Mines and Quarries Act 1954[75];
"the Minister" means the Secretary of State for Trade and Industry.

(2) Any obligations which are to be observed and performed by the Licensee shall at any time at which the Licensee is more than one person be joint and several obligations.

Term of licence

3. This licence unless sooner determined under any of the provisions hereof shall be and continue in force for the term of twenty-five years after .... 19....

Right of Licensee to determine licence

4. Without prejudice to any obligation or liability imposed by or incurred under the terms and conditions hereof the Licensee may at any time during the term hereby granted determine this licence by giving to the Minister not less than one month's previous notice in writing to that effect.

Payment of consideration for licence

5. - (1) The Licensee shall pay to the Minister during the term of this licence the consideration for the grant of this licence specified in the Schedule to this licence at the times and in the manner so specified.

(2) The Licensee shall not by reason of the determination of this licence be entitled to be repaid or allowed any part of any sum payable to the Minister pursuant to this licence.

Records

6. The Licensee shall keep and furnish to the Minister such records relating to the operations conducted in the licensed area under this licence, the result thereof and the disposal of any natural gas won and saved as the Minister may from time to time determine.

Power to inspect accounts, etc.

7. Any person authorised by the Minister may at all reasonable times enter into and upon any land for the time being possessed or occupied by the Licensee in the licensed area and inspect and make abstracts or copies of any records or accounts which the Licensee is required to keep or make in accordance with the provisions of this licence.

Records to be treated as confidential

8. All records, accounts and information which the Licensee is or may be from time to time required to furnish under the provisions of this licence shall be supplied at the expense of the Licensee and shall not (except with the consent in writing of the Licensee which shall not be unreasonably withheld) be disclosed to any person not in the service or employment of the Crown. The Minister shall nevertheless be entitled at any time to make use of any information received from the Licensee for the purpose of preparing and publishing such returns and reports as may be required of the Minister by law.

Notice of commencement and termination of operations

9. As soon as the Licensee has decided to get natural gas at any place he shall notify the Minister in writing of the situation thereof stating -

(a) the name of the mine for the safety of which the operations are to be undertaken;

(b) whether such mine is a disused mine or not.

The Licensee shall also give to the Minister notice in writing of the termination of any such operations within one month of the date of termination.

Indemnity against third party claims

10. The Licensee shall at all times keep the Minister effectually indemnified against all actions, proceedings, costs, charges, claims and demands whatsoever which may be made or brought against the Minister by any third party in relation to or in connection with this licence or any matter or thing done or purported to be done in pursuance thereof.

Agreement not to assign

11. The Licensee shall not without the consent of the Minister in writing assign or part with any of the rights granted by this licence in relation to the whole or any part of the licensed area or grant any sub-licence in respect of any of such rights.

Power of revocation

12. If there shall be any breach or non-observance by the Licensee of any of the terms and conditions herein contained the Minister may revoke this licence and thereupon the same and all the rights hereby granted shall cease and determine but subject nevertheless and without prejudice to any obligation or liability imposed by or incurred under the terms and conditions hereof.

Arbitration

13. - (1) If at any time any dispute, difference or question shall arise between the Minister and the Licensee as to any matter arising under or by virtue of this licence or as to their respective rights and liabilities in respect thereof then the same shall, except where it is expressly provided by this licence that the matter or thing to which the same relates is to be determined or consented to by the Minister, be referred to arbitration as provided by the following paragraph.

(2) The arbitration referred to in the foregoing paragraph shall be by a single arbitrator who, in default of agreement between the Minister and the Licensee as to his appointment, shall be appointed by the Lord Chief Justice of England for the time being.

SCHEDULE 8

CURRENT MODEL CLAUSES FOR LANDWARD DEVELOPMENT LICENCES DERIVING FROM SCHEDULE 5 TO THE PETROLEUM (PRODUCTION) (LANDWARD AREAS) REGULATIONS 1984 AS AMENDED BY THE PETROLEUM ACT 1987

PART I

1. This Schedule has effect in relation to paragraph 17 of Schedule 1 to the Act (Schedule 5 to the Petroleum (Production) (Landward Areas) Regulations 1984[76] as amended by the Petroleum Act 1987[77]).

2. Subject to paragraph 3, the current model clauses in relation to the said paragraph 17 are those reproduced in Part II.

3. Where section 1 of the Petroleum Royalties (Relief) and Continental Shelf Act 1989[78] applies, Part II has effect subject to the provisions of that Act.

PART II

Interpretation

1. - (1) In the following clauses the following expressions have the meanings hereby respectively assigned to them, that is to say -

"the Act of 1934" means the Petroleum (Production) Act 1934[79];
"the Act of 1964" means the Continental Shelf Act 1964[80];
"the Act of 1998" means the Petroleum Act 1998[81];
"block" means an area delineated on the reference map deposited at the principal office of the Minister's department;
"development scheme" has the meaning assigned thereto by clause 24;
"half year" means the period from 1st January to 30th June in any year and the period from 1st July to 31st December in any year;

"the licensed area" means the area for the time being in which the Licensee may exercise the rights granted by this licence;
"the Licensee" means the person or persons to whom this licence is granted, his personal representatives and any person or persons to whom the rights conferred by this licence may lawfully have been assigned;
"the Minister" means the Secretary of State for Trade and Industry;
"petroleum" includes any mineral oil or relative hydrocarbon and natural gas existing in its natural condition in strata, but does not include coal or bituminous shales or other stratified deposits from which oil can be extracted by destructive distillation;
"well" includes borehole.

(2) Any obligations which are to be observed and performed by the Licensee shall at any time at which the Licensee is more than one person be joint and several obligations.

(3) Any clause of this licence which refers to any provision of Part I of the Oil Taxation Act 1975[82] shall, unless the contrary intention appears, be construed as referring to that provision as it has effect for the time being for the purposes of petroleum revenue tax.

Term of licence
3. This licence unless sooner determined under any of the provisions hereof shall be and continue in force for the term of twenty years next after .... 19..., but if the terms and conditions hereof are duly performed and observed it may be continued for a further period or periods under clause 4.

Extension or further extension of term
4. The Minister, on application being made to him in writing prior to the final year of the term or any extension thereof, may grant an extension or further extension of this licence. If granted, the extension or further extension shall be for such period as the Minister may determine.

Right of Licensee to determine licence or surrender part of licensed area
5. - (1) Without prejudice to any obligation or liability imposed by or incurred under the terms and conditions hereof, the Licensee may, at any time, determine this licence or surrender any such part of the licensed area as is mentioned in paragraph (3) of this clause by giving six months' written notice to that effect to the Minister.

(2) A notice given pursuant to paragraph (1) of this clause may be cancelled by a further notice in writing given to the Minister not less than one month before the expiration of the notice.

(3) Any area to be surrendered in accordance with paragraph (1) of this clause shall be a clearly defined area whose surrender will leave a retained area -

(a) which comprises at least 20 square kilometres;

(b) the boundaries of which run north, south, east and west; and

(c) the shortest boundary of which extends for at least 2 kilometres;

Provided that if the licensed area is contiguous to an area which is comprised in a licence granted under -

(i) the Act of 1934, or

(ii) Part I of the Act of 1998,

the boundaries of which do not coincide with the grid marked on the reference map deposited at the principal office of the Minister's department or is bounded by a line drawn in accordance with the provisions of Schedule 1 to the Petroleum (Production) (Landward Areas) Regulations 1984 the Minister may agree in writing prior to the date the appropriate notice is given by the Licensee to accept a surrender of part of the licensed area which does not comply with the requirements of this paragraph.

Consequences of determination or surrender by Licensee

6. Upon the date on which any determination of this licence by the Licensee or any surrender of a part of the licensed area is to take effect, the rights granted by this licence shall cease or cease in respect of the part so surrendered as the case may be but without prejudice to any obligation or liability imposed upon the Licensee or incurred by him under the terms and conditions of this licence prior to that date.

Payment of consideration for licence

7. - (1) The Licensee shall make to the Minister as consideration for the grant of this licence -

(a) payments of royalty in accordance with clauses 8 and 9 of this licence;

(b) deliveries of petroleum in accordance with clause 10 of this licence; and

(c) payments in accordance with Schedule 2 to this licence.

(2) The Licensee shall not by reason of the determination of this licence or the surrender of any part of the licensed area be entitled to be repaid or allowed any sum payable to the Minister hereunder before the date of the determination or surrender.

Royalty payments

8. - (1) Subject to paragraph (1A) of this clause the Licensee shall pay to the Minister, in respect of each chargeable period, a royalty equal to the sum of the percentages specified in Schedule 3 to this licence of the value of the relevant units won and saved in the year which includes that period, and for the purposes of this paragraph "relevant unit" means a unit won and saved in the chargeable period in question and the value of a relevant unit is the amount produced by dividing the value of the petroleum relating to that period by the number of the relevant units.

(1A) Paragraph (1) of this clause shall not apply to a chargeable period in which the Licensee delivers petroleum to the Minister in pursuance of clause 10 of this licence; but if the petroleum delivered has a value of less than the relevant percentage of the aggregate of -

(a) the value of the petroleum delivered (ignoring any such excess as is mentioned in paragraph (6D) of this clause), and

(b) the value of the petroleum relating to that period,

he shall pay to the Minister a royalty of an amount equal to the difference.

(5) For the purposes of this clause and clauses 8A and 9 of this licence the value of the petroleum relating to a chargeable period is, subject to paragraph (6) of this clause, the total of the amounts which, if the words "one-half of" were omitted from paragraph (b) of subsection (4) and paragraph (d) of subsection (5) of section 2 of the Oil Taxation Act 1975[83], would in pursuance of paragraph (a) of the said subsection (4) fall to be taken into account in relation to that period in respect of the persons who by reference to this licence are or are treated as

participators for the purposes of those subsections, reduced by the total of the market values which would in pursuance of the said paragraph (b) fall to be taken into account as aforesaid.

(6) The value which, in pursuance of paragraph (5) of this clause, is the value of the petroleum relating to a chargeable period shall be increased by an amount equal to the value, as determined for the purposes of income tax or the charge of corporation tax on income, of so much of the petroleum won and saved in the licensed area as falls within section 10(1) of the Oil Taxation Act 1975 and was in that period disposed of or relevantly appropriated (within the meaning of Part I of that Act) by the persons mentioned in the said paragraph (5).

(6A) Subject to paragraphs (6B) and (6C) of this clause, the value of petroleum delivered to the Minister in pursuance of clause 10 of this licence shall be ascertained for the purposes of this clause and clause 8A on such basis (or, where petroleum of more than one kind is delivered, such bases) as the Minister and the Licensee agree.

(6B) If the Minister and the Licensee fail to agree on the value of any petroleum delivered to the Minister in pursuance of clause 10 of this licence, it shall be ascertained on such basis as the Minister may specify as fair in a notice in writing given by him to the Licensee.

(6C) The Licensee may, during the period of 28 days beginning with the day on which he receives a notice from the Minister under paragraph (6B) of this clause, refer to arbitration in the manner provided by clause 37 of this licence any question as to whether the basis of valuation specified in the notice is fair.

(6D) In this clause and clauses 8A and 9, references to petroleum delivered to the Minister in pursuance of clause 10 include references to any excess over the quantity required to be delivered by a notice served in pursuance of paragraph (1) of that clause.

(7) In this clause -

"chargeable period" means a half year in which this licence is in force;
"relevant percentage", in relation to a chargeable period, means the effective rate at which, apart from any notice under clause 11 of this licence, royalty would be payable for that period in pursuance of paragraph (1) of this clause;
"unit" means one tonne of petroleum won and saved in the licensed area except that in the case of petroleum so won and saved in the form of gas it means a quantity of it equal to 1,115 cubic metres of the gas at a temperature of 15 degrees Celsius and a pressure of 1.0132 bar; and
"year" means a year consisting of a chargeable period in which such a periodic payment as is mentioned in Schedule 2 to this licence is payable and the following chargeable period.

Payments by the Minister

8A. - (1) If in any chargeable period the Licensee delivers to the Minister in pursuance of clause 10 of this licence petroleum having a value greater than the relevant percentage of the aggregate of -

(a) the value of the petroleum delivered (ignoring any such excess as is mentioned in clause 8(6D) of this licence), and

(b) the value of the petroleum relating to that period,

the Minister shall pay to the Licensee a sum equal to the difference.

(2) In this clause, "chargeable period" and "relevant percentage" have the same meanings as in clause 8 of this licence.

Provisions supplementary to clauses 8 and 8A

9. - (1) The Licensee shall, within two months after the end of each chargeable period, deliver to the Minister, in such form as the Minister may specify, a statement of -

(a) the quantity of petroleum won and saved in the licensed area in that period;

(b) the quantity of that petroleum delivered to the Minister in that period in pursuance of clause 10 of this licence; and

(c) the amounts of the prices and market values which are required by paragraph 2 of Schedule 2 to the Oil Taxation Act 1975[84] to be stated in the returns made for that period in pursuance of that paragraph in consequence of this licence.

(2) The Licensee shall, when he delivers a statement to the Minister in pursuance of paragraph (1) of this clause for a chargeable period in respect of which royalty is payable in pursuance of clause 8(1) of this licence, make to the Minister a payment on account of royalty for that period equal to the relevant percentage of the sum produced by aggregating the amounts which in pursuance of sub-paragraph (c) of paragraph (1) of this clause are specified in the statement and reducing the aggregate by the amount which, by virtue of paragraph 2(2)(d)(ii) of Schedule 2 to the Oil Taxation Act 1975, was specified in the statement delivered to the Minister in pursuance of the said paragraph (1) in respect of the preceding chargeable period.

(3) The Licensee shall, when he delivers a statement to the Minister in pursuance of paragraph (1) of this clause for a chargeable period in respect of which royalty is payable in pursuance of clause 8(1A) of this licence, make to the Minister a payment on account of royalty for that period equal to the amount which would be so payable for that period if the royalty so payable for that period fell to be determined by reference to the amounts specified in the statement and the amount which, by virtue of paragraph 2(2)(d)(ii) of Schedule 2 to the Oil Taxation Act 1975, was specified in the statement to be delivered to the Minister in pursuance of paragraph (1) of this clause in respect of the preceding chargeable period.

(4) The Minister may from time to time, after a statement in respect of any chargeable period has been delivered to him in pursuance of paragraph (1) of this clause and before he has given to the Licensee a notice in pursuance of paragraph (5) of this clause in respect of that period, give a notice in writing to the Licensee specifying the amount which the Minister estimates is payable by the Licensee in pursuance of clause 8 of this licence in respect of that period; and where the amount specified in the notice is larger or smaller than the total amount already paid by the Licensee in pursuance of this clause in respect of that period, then -

(a) if it is larger the difference shall be paid forthwith by the Licensee to the Minister; and

(b) if it is smaller the difference shall be paid forthwith by the Minister to the Licensee.

(5) When it appears to the Minister that the value of the petroleum relating to any chargeable period has been finally determined for tax purposes, he may give to the Licensee a notice in writing specifying the amount which the Minister considers is payable by the Licensee in pursuance of clause 8 of this licence in respect of that period; and where the amount specified in

the notice is larger or smaller than the total amount already paid by the Licensee in pursuance of this clause in respect of that period, then subject to paragraph (7) of this clause -

(a) if it is larger the difference shall be paid forthwith by the Licensee to the Minister; and

(b) if it is smaller the difference shall be paid forthwith by the Minister to the Licensee.

(6) If after the date when the Minister gave notice to the Licensee in pursuance of paragraph (5) of this clause or this paragraph in respect of a chargeable period it appears to the Minister, in consequence of a relevant assessment or determination made after that date which relates directly or indirectly to the value of petroleum by reference to which the amount specified in the notice was determined, that another amount ought to have been specified, he may give notice in writing to the Licensee specifying the other amount; and where he does so, then, subject to paragraph (7) of this clause -

(a) if the other amount is larger than the total amount already paid by the Licensee in pursuance of this clause in respect of that period the difference shall be paid forthwith by the Licensee to the Minister; and

(b) if it is smaller the difference shall be paid forthwith by the Minister to the Licensee.

(7) A decision made by the Minister for the purposes of paragraph (4), (5) or (6) of this clause shall not be called in question by the Licensee except that any dispute between the Minister and the Licensee as to whether an amount specified in a notice given in pursuance of the said paragraph (5) or (6) is payable by virtue of clause 8 of this licence may, during the period of 28 days beginning with the day on which the Licensee receives the notice, be referred to arbitration in the manner provided by clause 37 of this licence; and on a reference to arbitration in pursuance of this paragraph any relevant assessment or determination for the time being in force shall be binding on the Minister and the Licensee so far as the assessment or determination relates directly or indirectly to the value of petroleum relating to the chargeable period in question.

(8) When any payment is made by the Licensee or the Minister in pursuance of paragraph (4), (5) or (6) of this clause, an amount in respect of interest on the payment shall also be payable by him to the recipient of the payment and that amount shall be calculated in such manner as the Minister may specify from time to time in a notice in writing given by him to the Licensee; but -

(a) a notice in pursuance of this paragraph shall provide for amounts by way of interest to be calculated by applying a rate of interest which is for the time being a commercial rate of interest; and

(b) any such amount in respect of interest shall be disregarded in calculating for the purposes of the said paragraph (4), (5) or (6) any amount already paid by the Licensee in pursuance of this clause.

(8A) If a payment is made by the Minister in pursuance of clause 8A of this licence more than two months after the end of the chargeable period to which the payment relates, an amount in respect of interest on the payment from the end of those two months shall also be payable by him to the Licensee.

(8B) Interest under paragraph (8A) of this clause shall be calculated in such manner as the Minister may specify from time to time in a notice in writing given by him to the Licensee (but sub-paragraph (a) of paragraph (8) of this clause shall apply to such a notice as it applies to a notice under paragraph (8)).

(9) In this clause -

"chargeable period" and "relevant percentage" have the same meanings as in clause 8 of this licence;
"relevant assessment or determination" means an assessment or determination made by the Commissioners of Inland Revenue for the purposes of petroleum revenue tax, income tax or the charge of corporation tax on income or a determination made in proceedings arising out of such an assessment or determination made by the said Commissioners.

(10) For the purposes of this clause, any amount paid by the Licensee or the Minister on account of a prospective liability under paragraph (4), (5) or (6) of this clause shall be treated as paid in pursuance of that paragraph.

Deliveries of petroleum in place of royalties

10. - (1) If during the term of this licence the Minister serves on the Licensee a notice in writing in accordance with the following provisions of this clause requiring the Licensee to deliver to the Minister part of the petroleum won and saved by the Licensee in the licensed area, the Licensee shall comply with the notice.

(2) Where the Minister proposes to serve a notice on the Licensee in pursuance of paragraph (1) of this clause, he shall before doing so -

(a) give the Licensee a copy of the proposed notice and an opportunity of making representations to the Minister about it; and

(b) consider any representations then made to him by the Licensee about the proposed notice;

and the Minister shall, in deciding upon the terms of the actual notice, have regard to the desirability of not disturbing unduly any arrangements made by the Licensee for transporting and delivering petroleum won and saved from the licensed area.

(3) Subject to paragraph (4) of this clause, a notice served in pursuance of paragraph (1) of this clause -

(a) shall specify the date on which the notice is to come into force and may contain provisions with respect to the time when it shall cease to be in force;

(b) shall specify the quantity of petroleum won and saved in the licensed area during each half year in which the notice is in force which, up to any maximum quantities specified in the notice in pursuance of paragraph (4)(b) of this clause, is to be delivered to the Minister in consequence of the notice;

(c) may relate to all petroleum so won and saved or may be limited to and specify different quantities of such petroleum which is of one or more of the following kinds, namely, crude oil, condensate, natural gas and natural gas liquids, in each case of a quality or composition or of each quality or composition determined in the manner specified in the notice;

(d) shall contain provisions with respect to the place or places at which any petroleum or kind of petroleum is to be delivered in pursuance of the notice and may contain provisions with respect to the times at which any quantities of it are to be so delivered.

(4) Such a notice -

(a) shall not specify as the date on which it is to come into force a date before the expiration of the period of six months beginning with the date on which the notice is served on the Licensee but shall, if the Minister serves on the Licensee a further notice in writing stating that it is to cease to be in force at a time specified in the further notice which is not earlier than six months after the date of service of the further notice, cease to be in force at that time;

(b) shall not specify, as the quantity of petroleum won and saved in any half year which is to be delivered in pursuance of the notice or as the quantity of any kind of such petroleum, a percentage of all the petroleum or of all that kind of petroleum which is won and saved in the licensed area in that half year exceeding the percentage at which, apart from the notice, royalty for that half year would be payable in respect of the petroleum in pursuance of clause 8(1) of this licence, but may provide that the quantities of petroleum or of a kind of petroleum so won and saved which are to be so delivered shall not in the aggregate exceed a quantity specified in the notice;

(c) shall not specify, or enable to be specified, as a place at which delivery is to be made in pursuance of the notice a place which is not a point at which the Licensee normally delivers petroleum of any kind from the licensed area.

Measurement of petroleum obtained from the licensed area

11. - (1) The Licensee shall measure or weigh by a method or methods customarily used in good oilfield practice and from time to time approved by the Minister all petroleum won and saved from the licensed area.

(1A) If and to the extent that the Minister so directs, the duty imposed by paragraph (1) of this clause shall be discharged separately in relation to petroleum won and saved -

(a) from each part of the licensed area which is an oil field for the purposes of the Oil Taxation Act 1975,

(b) from each part of the licensed area which forms part of such an oil field extending beyond the licensed area, and

(c) from each well producing petroleum from a part of the licensed area which is not within such an oil field.

(1B) If and to the extent that the Minister so directs, the preceding provisions of this clause shall apply as if the duty to measure or weigh petroleum included a duty to ascertain its quality or composition or both; and where a direction under this paragraph is in force, the following provisions of this clause shall have effect as if references to measuring or weighing included references to ascertaining quality or composition.

(2) The Licensee shall not make any alteration in the method or methods of measurement or weighing used by him or any appliances used for that purpose without the consent in writing of the Minister and the Minister may in any case require that no alteration shall be made save in the presence of a person authorised by the Minister.

(3) The Minister may from time to time direct that any weighing or measuring appliance shall be tested or examined in such manner, upon such occasions or at such intervals and by such persons as may be specified by the Minister's direction and the Licensee shall pay to any such

person or to the Minister such fees and expenses for the test or examination as the Minister may specify.

(4) If any measuring or weighing appliance shall upon any such test or examination as is mentioned in the last foregoing paragraph be found to be inaccurate to a material degree the same shall, if the Minister so determines after considering any representations in writing made by the Licensee, be deemed to have existed in that condition during the period since the last occasion upon which the same was tested or examined pursuant to the last foregoing paragraph.

Keeping of accounts

12. - (1) The Licensee shall keep in the United Kingdom full and correct accounts in a form from time to time approved by the Minister of -

(a) the quantity of petroleum in the form of gas won and saved;

(b) the quantity of petroleum in any other form won and saved;

(c) the name and address of any person to whom any petroleum has been supplied by the Licensee, the quantity so supplied, the price or other consideration therefor and the place to which the petroleum was conveyed pursuant to the agreement for such supply; and

(d) such other particulars as the Minister may from time to time direct.

(2) The quantities of petroleum stated in such accounts may exclude any water separated from the petroleum and shall be expressed as volumes in cubic metres measured at, or calculated as if measured at, a temperature of 15 degrees Celsius and a pressure of 1.0132 bar but if the Minister serves notice in writing on the Licensee determining any other manner in which any quantity of petroleum or any quantity of any form of petroleum is to be expressed that quantity shall be so expressed.

(3) Such accounts shall state separately the quantities used for the purposes of carrying on drilling and production operations and pumping to field storage, and quantities not so used, and in the case of petroleum not in the form of gas shall state the specific gravity of the petroleum and, if petroleum of different specific gravities has been won and saved, the respective quantities of petroleum of each specific gravity.

(4) The Licensee shall within two months after the end of each half year in which this licence is in force and within two months after the expiration or determination of this licence deliver to the Minister an abstract in a form from time to time approved by the Minister of the accounts for that half year or for the period prior to such expiration or determination as the case may be.

Development and production programmes

13. - (1) The Licensee shall not -

(a) erect or carry out any relevant works, either in the licensed area or elsewhere, for the purpose of getting petroleum from that area or for the purposes of conveying to a place on land petroleum got from that area; or

(b) get petroleum from that area otherwise than in the course of searching for petroleum or drilling wells, except with the consent in writing of the Minister or in accordance with any programme approved by the Minister or served on the Licensee in pursuance of the following provisions of this clause.

(2) The Licensee shall prepare and submit to the Minister, in such form and by such time and in respect of such period during the term of this licence as the Minister may direct, a programme specifying -

(a) the relevant works which the Licensee proposes to erect or carry out during that period for either of the purposes mentioned in paragraph (1)(a) of this clause;

(b) the proposed locations of the works, the purposes for which it is proposed to use the works and the times at which it is proposed to begin and to complete the erection or carrying out of the works;

(c) the maximum and minimum quantities of petroleum in the form of gas and the maximum and minimum quantities of petroleum in other forms which, in each calendar year during the period aforesaid or in such other periods during that period as the Minister may specify, the Licensee proposes to get as mentioned in paragraph (1)(b) of this clause.

(3) If the Minister directs the Licensee -

(a) to prepare different programmes in pursuance of paragraph (2) of this clause in respect of petroleum from such different parts of the licensed area as are specified in the direction; or

(b) where a programme approved or served in pursuance of this clause relates to a particular period during the term of this licence, to prepare a programme or programmes in pursuance of paragraph (2) of this clause in respect of a further period or further periods during that term,

the Licensee shall comply with the direction.

(4) It shall be the duty of the Minister expeditiously to consider any programme submitted to him in pursuance of paragraph (2) of this clause and when he has done so to give notice in writing to the Licensee stating -

(a) that the Minister approves the programme; or

(b) that the Minister approves the programme subject to the condition that such of the relevant works as are specified in the notice shall not be used before the expiration of the period so specified in relation to the works or shall not be used without the consent in writing of the Minister; or

(c) that the Minister rejects the programme on one or both of the following grounds, namely -

(i) that the carrying out of any proposals included in the programme in pursuance of paragraph (2) of this clause would be contrary to good oilfield practice;

(ii) that the proposals included in the programme in pursuance of sub-paragraph (c) of the said paragraph (2) are, in the opinion of the Minister, not in the national interest;

and a notice in pursuance of sub-paragraph (b) of this paragraph may contain different conditions in respect of different works.

(5) Where the Minister gives notice of rejection of a programme in pursuance of sub-paragraph (c) of paragraph (4) of this clause, then -

(a) if the grounds of the rejection consist of or include the ground mentioned in paragraph (i) of that sub-paragraph he shall include in the notice a statement of the matters in consequence of which he rejected the programme on that ground; and

(b) if the grounds of the rejection consist of or include the ground mentioned in paragraph (ii) of that sub-paragraph he shall include in the notice a statement of the rates at which he considers that, in the national interest, petroleum should be got from the area to which the programme relates; and

(c) the Licensee shall prepare and submit to the Minister, before the time specified in that behalf in the notice -

(i) where the notice contains such a statement as is mentioned in sub-paragraph (a) above, modifications of the programme which ensure that the carrying out of the programme with those modifications would not be contrary to good oilfield practice;

(ii) where the notice contains such a statement as is mentioned in sub-paragraph (b) above, modifications of the programme which ensure the getting of petroleum from the area there mentioned at the rates specified in the statement and which (except so far as may be necessary in order to get petroleum at those rates) are not such that the carrying out of the programme with those modifications would be contrary to good oilfield practice;

but the Licensee shall not be required by virtue of paragraph (i) of this sub-paragraph to submit modifications if the carrying out of the programme without modifications would not be contrary to good oilfield practice.

(6) If the Minister gives notice in writing to the Licensee that the Minister approves the modifications of a programme which have been submitted to him in pursuance of sub-paragraph (c) of paragraph (5) of this clause, the programme with those modifications shall be deemed to be approved by the Minister, but if the Licensee fails to perform the duty imposed on him by that sub-paragraph the Minister may, if he thinks fit, instead of revoking this licence in consequence of the failure, serve on the Licensee such a programme as the Minister considers that the Licensee should have submitted to him in respect of the area and period to which the rejected programme related.

(7) Where the Minister proposes to approve a programme subject to a condition in pursuance of paragraph (4)(b) of this clause or to reject a programme in pursuance of paragraph (4)(c) of this clause or to serve a programme on the Licensee in pursuance of paragraph (6) of this clause he shall before doing so -

(a) give the Licensee particulars of the proposal and an opportunity of making representations to the Minister about the technical and financial factors which the Licensee considers are relevant in connection with the proposal; and

(b) consider any such representations then made to him by the Licensee;

and the Minister shall not approve a programme subject to such a condition unless he is satisfied that the condition is required in the national interest.

(8) The Licensee shall carry out any programme approved by the Minister or served on the Licensee in pursuance of this clause or, if such a programme is varied in pursuance of clause 14 of this licence, the programme as so varied, except so far as the Licensee is authorised in writing by the Minister to do otherwise or is required to do otherwise by such a condition as is mentioned in paragraph (4)(b) of this clause; but if it is necessary to carry out certain works in order to comply with provisions included in a programme by virtue of paragraph (5)(c) of this clause or provisions of a programme served on the Licensee in pursuance of paragraph (6) of this clause or provisions of a programme as varied in pursuance of clause 14 of this licence, then, notwithstanding anything in the programme as to the time when those provisions are to be complied with, the Licensee shall not be treated as having failed to comply with those provisions before the expiration of the period reasonably required for carrying out the works.

(9) In this clause "relevant works" means any structures and any other works whatsoever which are intended by the Licensee to be permanent and are neither designed to be moved from place to place without major dismantling nor intended by the Licensee to be used only for searching for petroleum.

Provisions supplementary to clause 13

14. - (1) A consent or approval given by the Minister in pursuance of clause 13(1) of this licence may be given subject to such conditions as are specified in the document signifying the consent or approval and may in particular, without prejudice to the generality of the preceding provisions of this paragraph, be limited to a period so specified.

(2) Where -

(a) the Minister approves a programme in pursuance of clause 13(1) or gives a notice in respect of a programme in pursuance of paragraph (4)(a) or (b) or paragraph (6) of clause 13 of this licence or serves a programme in pursuance of the said paragraph (6); or

(b) it is determined by arbitration that the Licensee is not required by virtue of paragraph (i) of clause 13(5)(c) of this licence to submit modifications of a programme in respect of which notice of rejection containing such a statement as is mentioned in the said paragraph (i) was given by the Minister in pursuance of clause 13(4)(c) of this licence,

the Minister may give to the Licensee, with the approval or notice given or the programme served as mentioned in sub-paragraph (a) of this paragraph or, in a case falling within sub-paragraph (b) of this paragraph, within the period of three months beginning with the date of the arbitrator's or arbiter's determination, a notice (hereafter in this clause referred to as a "limitation notice") authorising the Minister, by a further notice given to the Licensee from time to time after the expiration of the period specified in that behalf in the limitation notice, to provide that the programme to which the limitation notice relates shall have effect while the further notice is in force with the substitution for any quantity of petroleum or any period specified in the programme in pursuance of clause 13(2)(c) of this licence of a different quantity of petroleum or a different period specified in the further notice.

(3) A quantity or period specified in such a further notice as that to be substituted for a quantity or period which is specified in the programme in question shall be within the limits specified in the limitation notice as those applicable to that quantity or period specified in the programme; and those limits shall be such as to secure that the expenditure to be incurred by the Licensee in

complying with the further notice, in a case where an effect of the notice is to increase the quantity of petroleum which the Licensee is required to get from the licensed area in any period, is less than the cost of drilling a new well in the licensed area at the time when the further notice is given.

(4) Where the Minister proposes to give a limitation notice or any such further notice as aforesaid he shall before doing so -

(a) give the Licensee particulars of the proposal and an opportunity of making representations to the Minister about the technical and financial factors which the Licensee considers are relevant in connection with the proposal; and

(b) consider any such representations then made to him by the Licensee;

and the Minister shall not give such a further notice of which an effect is to increase the quantity of petroleum which the Licensee is required to get from the licensed area during any period unless the Minister is satisfied that the notice is required by reason of a national emergency and shall not give any other such further notice as aforesaid, unless he is satisfied that the notice is required in the national interest.

(5) A limitation notice or such a further notice as aforesaid may -

(a) specify any quantity or period by reference to such factors as the Minister thinks fit; and

(b) in the case of such a further notice, contain provisions as to -

(i) the date when the notice is to come into force,

(ii) the date when the notice is to cease to be in force,

and specify different dates in pursuance of this sub-paragraph for different provisions of the notice;

and the Minister may revoke such a further notice at a particular time by serving on the Licensee a notice in writing stating that the further notice is revoked at that time.

(6) Any question arising under clause 13 of this licence or this clause as to what is, or is required, in the national interest or as to what is, or is required by reason of, a national emergency shall be determined by the Minister.

(7) The Licensee shall ensure that any conditions to which an approval is subject in pursuance of clause 13(4)(b) of this licence or a consent or approval is subject in pursuance of paragraph (1) of this clause are complied with.

(8) If in respect of part of the licensed area -

(a) a consent or approval has been given in pursuance of paragraph (1) of clause 13 of this licence; or

(b) the Licensee has submitted to the Minister, in accordance with a direction given by virtue of paragraph (3)(a) of that clause, a programme in pursuance of paragraph (2) of that clause -

(i) as respects which the Minister has served notice in pursuance of paragraph (4)(a) or (b) or paragraph (6) of that clause, or

(ii) in consequence of which the Minister has served a programme on the Licensee in pursuance of the said paragraph (6), or

(iii) in respect of which it has been determined by arbitration that the Licensee is not required by virtue of paragraph (5)(c)(i) of that clause to submit modifications,

paragraph (1) of clause 36 of this licence shall not authorise the Minister to revoke this licence in relation to that part of the licensed area in consequence of any breach or non-observance, while the consent is in force or during the period to which the programme relates, of any provision of the said clause 13 in connection with a different part of the licensed area.

(9) Where in consequence of any breach or non-observance by the Licensee or any provision of clause 13 of this licence the Minister has power by virtue of paragraph (1) of clause 36 of this licence to revoke this licence, or in consequence of paragraph (8) of this clause, to revoke it in respect of part only of the licensed area, he may if he thinks fit -

(a) in a case where he has power to revoke this licence, exercise the power in relation to such part only of the licensed area as he may specify; and

(b) in a case where by virtue of the said paragraph (8) he has power to revoke it in respect of part only of the licensed area, exercise the power in relation to such portion only of that part as he may specify;

and where in consequence of the said paragraph (8) or by virtue of the preceding provisions of this paragraph the Minister revokes this licence in respect of a part or portion of the licensed area, the rights granted by this licence shall cease in respect of that part or portion without prejudice to any obligation or liability imposed upon the Licensee or incurred by him under the terms of this licence.

Commencement and abandonment and plugging of wells

15. - (1) The Licensee shall not commence, or after abandoning in the manner hereinafter provided shall not recommence, the drilling of any well without the consent in writing of the Minister.

(2) The Licensee shall not abandon any well without the consent in writing of the Minister.

(3) The Licensee shall ensure compliance with any conditions subject to which any consent under either of the foregoing paragraphs is given.

(4) If any such condition under paragraph (1) of this clause relates to the position, depth or direction of the well, or to any casing of the well, or if any condition under either paragraph (1) or paragraph (2) of this clause relates to any plugging or sealing of the well, the Minister may from time to time direct that the well and all records relating thereto shall be examined in such manner, upon such occasions or at such intervals and by such persons as may be specified by the Minister's direction and the Licensee shall pay to any such person or to the Minister such fees and expenses for such examination as the Minister may specify.

(5) The plugging of any well shall be done in accordance with a specification approved by the Minister applicable to that well or to wells generally or to a class of wells to which that well

belongs and shall be carried out in an efficient and workmanlike manner.

(6) Any well drilled by the Licensee pursuant to this licence, which at the expiry or determination of the Licensee's rights in respect of the area or part thereof in which that well is drilled has not with the consent of the Minister been abandoned, shall be left in good order and fit for further working together with all casings and any well head fixtures the removal whereof would cause damage to such well, or, if the Minister so directs in the manner provided by paragraph (8) of this clause, be plugged and sealed in accordance with the Minister's direction.

(7) All casings and fixtures left in position pursuant to the last foregoing paragraph shall be the property of the Minister.

(8) In any case to which paragraph (6) of this clause applies, a direction by the Minister may be given by notice in writing to the Licensee not less than one month before the Licensee's rights in respect of the area or part thereof in which the well is situate expire or determine, specifying the manner in which the well is to be plugged and sealed and the time within which such work is to be done.

(9) An application for the consent of the Minister to the drilling of a well at any place above the low water line shall be accompanied by evidence that the planning authority for the relevant place has been consulted about the drilling and that any planning permission required by the Town and Country Planning Act 1990 for the drilling of that well has been granted.

Distance of wells from boundaries of licensed area

16. No well shall except with the consent in writing of the Minister be drilled or made so that any part thereof is less than one hundred and twenty-five metres from any of the boundaries of the licensed area.

Control of development wells

17. - (1) The Licensee shall not suspend work on the drilling of a development well, or having suspended it in accordance with this paragraph shall not begin it again, except with the consent in writing of the Minister and in accordance with the conditions, if any, subject to which the consent is given.

(2) When work on the drilling of a development well is suspended in accordance with paragraph (1) of this clause, the Licensee shall forthwith furnish the Minister with such information relating to the well as the Minister may specify.

(3) The Licensee -

(a) shall not do any completion work in respect of a well in the licensed area except in accordance with a programme of completion work approved by the Minister in respect of the well;

(b) shall furnish to the Minister, in accordance with the provisions of such a programme, particulars of any completion work done by him in respect of a well in the licensed area; and

(c) shall not remove or alter any casing or equipment installed by way of completion work in respect of a well except with the consent in writing of the Minister and in accordance with the conditions, if any, subject to which the consent is given.

(4) In this clause -

"completion work", in relation to a well, means work, by way of the installation of a casing or equipment or otherwise after the well has been drilled, for the purpose of bringing the well into use as a development well; and
"development well" means a well which the Licensee uses or intends to use in connection with the getting of petroleum in the licensed area, other than a well which for the time being he uses or intends to use only for searching for petroleum.

Provision of storage tanks, pipes, pipelines or other receptacles
18. The Licensee shall use methods and practice customarily used in good oilfield practice for confining the petroleum obtained from the licensed area in tanks, gasholders, pipes, pipelines or other receptacles constructed for that purpose.

Avoidance of harmful methods of working
19. - (1) The Licensee shall maintain all apparatus and appliances and all wells in the licensed area which have not been abandoned and plugged as provided by clause 15 of this licence in good repair and condition and shall execute all operations in or in connection with the licensed area in a proper and workmanlike manner in accordance with methods and practice customarily used in good oilfield practice. Without prejudice to the generality of the foregoing provision the Licensee shall take all steps practicable in order -

(a) to control the flow and to prevent the escape or waste of petroleum discovered in or obtained from the licensed area;

(b) to conserve the licensed area for productive operations;

(c) to prevent damage to adjoining petroleum bearing strata;

(d) to prevent the entrance of water through wells to petroleum bearing strata except for the purposes of secondary recovery; and

(e) to prevent the escape of petroleum into any waters or water-bearing strata in or in the vicinity of the licensed area.

(2) The Licensee shall comply with any instructions from time to time given by the Minister in writing relating to any of the matters set out in the foregoing paragraph. If the Licensee objects to any such instruction on the ground that it is unreasonable he may, within fourteen days from the date upon which the same was given, refer the matter to arbitration in the manner provided by clause 37 of this licence.

(3) Notwithstanding anything in the preceding provisions of this clause, the Licensee shall not -

(a) flare any gas from the licensed area; or

(b) use gas for the purpose of creating or increasing the pressure by means of which petroleum is obtained from that area,

except with the consent in writing of the Minister and in accordance with the conditions, if any, of the consent.

(4) An application for consent in pursuance of paragraph (3) of this clause must be made in writing to the Minister and must specify the date on which the Licensee proposes to begin the flaring or use in question; and subject to paragraph (5) of this clause that date must not be before the expiration of the period of 12 months beginning with the date when the Minister receives the

application.

(5) If the Minister gives notice in writing to the Licensee stating that, in consequence of plans made by the Licensee which the Minister considers are reasonable, the Minister will entertain an application for consent in pursuance of paragraph (3) of this clause which specifies a date after the expiration of a period mentioned in the notice which is shorter than the period mentioned in paragraph (4) of this clause, an application made in consequence of the notice may specify, as the date on which the applicant proposes to begin the flaring or use in question, a date after the expiration of that shorter period.

(6) Before deciding to withhold consent or to grant it subject to conditions in pursuance of paragraph (3) of this clause, the Minister shall give the Licensee an opportunity of making representations in writing to the Minister about the technical and financial factors which the Licensee considers are relevant in connection with the case and shall consider any such representations then made to him by the Licensee.

(7) Consent in pursuance of paragraph (3) of this clause shall not be required for any flaring which, in consequence of an event which the Licensee did not foresee in time to deal with it otherwise than by flaring, is necessary in order -

(a) to remove or reduce the risk of injury to persons in the vicinity of the well in question; or

(b) to maintain a flow of petroleum from that or any other well;

but when the Licensee does any flaring which is necessary as aforesaid he shall forthwith inform the Minister that he has done it and shall, in the case of flaring to maintain a flow of petroleum, stop the flaring upon being directed by the Minister to stop it.

(8) The Licensee shall give notice to the Minister of any event causing escape or waste of petroleum, damage to petroleum bearing strata or entrance of water through wells to petroleum bearing strata except for the purposes of secondary recovery forthwith after the occurrence of that event and shall, forthwith after the occurrence of any event causing escape of petroleum into the sea, give notice of the event to the Chief Inspector of Her Majesty's Coastguard.

(9) The Licensee shall comply with any reasonable instructions from time to time given by the Minister with a view to ensuring that funds are available to discharge any liability attributable to the release or escape of petroleum in the course of activities connected with the exercise of rights granted by this licence; but where the Minister proposes to give such instructions he shall before giving them -

(a) give the Licensee particulars of the proposal and an opportunity of making representations to the Minister about the proposal; and

(b) consider any representations then made to him by the Licensee about the proposal.

Appointment of operators

20. - (1) The Licensee shall ensure that another person (including, in the case where the Licensee is two or more persons, any of those persons) does not exercise any function of organising or supervising all or any of the operations of searching or boring for or getting petroleum in pursuance of this licence unless that other person is a person approved in writing by the Minister and the function in question is one to which that approval relates.

(2) The Minister shall not refuse to give his approval of a person in pursuance of paragraph (1) of this clause if that person is competent to exercise the function in question; but where an approved person is no longer competent to exercise that function the Minister may, by notice in writing given to the Licensee, revoke his approval.

Fishing and navigation

21. The Licensee shall not carry out any operations authorised by this licence in or about the licensed area in such manner as to interfere unjustifiably -

(a) with navigation in any navigable waters; or

(b) with fishing in or conservation of the living resources of any waters in or in the vicinity of the licensed area.

Training

23. - (1) The Minister may from time to time give to the Licensee instructions in writing as to the training of persons employed or to be employed, whether by the Licensee or by any other person, in any activity which is related to the exercise of the rights granted by this licence and the Licensee shall ensure that any instructions so given are complied with.

(2) The Licensee shall furnish the Minister with such information relating to the training of persons referred to in paragraph (1) of this clause as the Minister may from time to time request.

Unit development

24. - (1) If at any time in which this licence is in force the Minister shall be satisfied that the strata in the licensed area or any part thereof form part of a single geological petroleum structure or petroleum field (hereinafter referred to as "an oil field") other parts whereof are formed by strata in areas in respect of which other licences granted in pursuance of -

(a) the Act of 1934, or

(b) that Act as applied by the Act of 1964, or

(c) Part I of the Act of 1998,

are then in force and the Minister shall consider that it is in the national interest in order to secure the maximum ultimate recovery of petroleum and in order to avoid unnecessary competitive drilling that the oil field should be worked and developed as a unit in co-operation by all persons including the Licensee whose licences extend to or include any part thereof the following provisions of this clause shall apply.

(2) Upon being so required by notice in writing by the Minister the Licensee shall co-operate with such other persons, being persons holding licences under -

(a) the Act of 1934, or

(b) that Act as applied by the Act of 1964, or

(c) Part I of the Act of 1998,

in respect of any part or parts of the oil field (hereinafter referred to as "the other Licensees") as may be specified in the said notice in the preparation of a scheme (hereinafter referred to as "a development scheme") for the working and development of the oil field as a unit by the Licensee and the other Licensees in co-operation, and shall, jointly with the other Licensees, submit such scheme for the approval of the Minister.

(3) The said notice shall also contain or refer to a description of the area or areas in respect of which the Minister requires a development scheme to be submitted and shall state the period within which such scheme is to be submitted for approval by the Minister.

(4) If a development scheme shall not be submitted to the Minister within the period so stated or if a development scheme so submitted shall not be approved by the Minister, the Minister may himself prepare a development scheme which shall be fair and equitable to the Licensee and all other Licensees, and the Licensee shall perform and observe all the terms and conditions thereof.

(5) If the Licensee shall object to any such development scheme prepared by the Minister he may within 28 days from the date on which notice in writing of the said scheme shall have been given to him by the Minister refer the matter to arbitration in the manner provided by clause 37 hereof.

Licensee to keep records

25. - (1) The Licensee shall keep accurate records in a form from time to time approved by the Minister of the drilling, deepening, plugging or abandonment of all wells and of any alterations in the casing thereof. Such records shall contain particulars of the following matters -

(a) the site of, number and name (if any) assigned to every well;

(b) the subsoil and strata through which the well was drilled;

(c) the casing inserted in any well and any alteration to such casing;

(d) any petroleum, water, mines or workable seams of coal encountered; and

(e) such other matters as the Minister may from time to time direct.

(2) The Licensee shall keep in the United Kingdom accurate geological plans and maps relating to the licensed area and such other records in relation thereto as may be necessary to preserve all information which the Licensee has about the geology of the licensed area.

(3) The Licensee shall deliver copies of the said records, plans and maps referred to in the two foregoing paragraphs to the Minister as and when required.

Returns

26. - (1) The Licensee shall furnish to the Minister 3 months from the date of this licence and at intervals of 3 months thereafter during the period in which this licence is in force a return in a form from time to time approved by the Minister of the progress of his operations in the licensed area. Such return shall contain -

(a) a statement of all geological work, including surveys and tests, which has been carried out, and the areas in which and the persons by whom the work has been carried out and the results thereof;

(b) the number and name (if any) assigned to each well and, in the case of any well the drilling of which was begun or the number of which has been changed during such period of 3 months, the site thereof;

(c) a statement of the depth drilled in each well;

(d) a statement of any petroleum, water, mines or workable seams of coal or other minerals encountered in the course of the said operations; and

(e) a statement of all petroleum won and saved.

(2) Within 2 months after the end of each calendar year in which this licence is in force and within 2 months after the expiration or determination of this licence or any renewal thereof the Licensee shall furnish to the Minister an annual return in a form from time to time approved by the Minister of the operations conducted in the licensed area during that year or the period prior to such expiration or determination as the case may be together with a plan upon a scale approved by the Minister showing the situation of all wells. The Licensee shall also indicate on the said plan all development and other works executed by him in connection with searching, boring for or getting petroleum.

(3) The Licensee shall furnish the Minister with such information as the Minister may from time to time request about any aspect of the activities of the Licensee which are attributable directly or indirectly to the grant of this licence, except that the Licensee shall not by virtue of this paragraph be required to furnish information in respect of his activities in connection with any crude oil after he has appropriated it for refining by him.

(4) The functions of the Minister under paragraph (3) of this clause shall not only be exercisable by him but also be concurrently exercisable by the Chancellor of the Exchequer.

Licensee to keep samples

27. - (1) As far as reasonably practicable the Licensee shall correctly label and preserve for reference for a period of five years samples of the strata encountered in any well (including, where the site of such well is on land covered by water, the surface of such land) and samples of any petroleum or water discovered in any well in the licensed area.

(2) The Licensee shall not dispose of any sample after the expiry of the said period of five years unless -

(a) he has at least six months before the date of the disposal given notice in writing to the Minister of his intention to dispose of the sample; and

(b) the Minister or any person authorised by him has not within the said period of six months informed the Licensee in writing that he wishes the sample to be delivered to him.

(3) The Minister or any person authorised by him shall be entitled at any time -

(a) to inform the Licensee in writing that he wishes part of any sample preserved by the Licensee to be delivered to him; or

(b) to inspect and analyse any sample preserved by the Licensee.

(4) The Licensee shall forthwith comply with any request for the delivery of the whole or any part of any sample which is made in accordance with the preceding provisions of this clause.

Reports to be treated as confidential

28. All records, returns, plans, maps, samples, accounts and information (in this clause referred to as "the specified data") which the Licensee is or may be from time to time required to furnish under the provisions of this licence shall be supplied at the expense of the Licensee and shall not (except with the consent in writing of the Licensee which shall not be unreasonably withheld) be disclosed at any time to any person not in the service or employment of the Crown:

Provided that -

(i) the Minister shall be entitled at any time to make use of any of the specified data for the purpose of preparing and publishing such returns and reports as may be required of the Minister by law;

(ii) the Minister shall be entitled at any time to furnish any of the specified data to the Natural Environment Research Council and to any other body of a like nature as may from time to time be carrying on activities of a substantially similar kind to the geological activities at present carried on by the said Council;

(iii) the Minister, the said Council and any such other body shall be entitled at any time to prepare and publish reports and surveys of a general nature using information derived from any of the specified data;

(iv) the Minister, the said Council and any such other body shall be entitled to publish any of the specified data of a geological, scientific or technical kind after the expiration of the period of five years beginning with the date when the Minister received the data or after the expiration of such longer period as the Minister may determine after considering any representations made to him by the Licensee about the publication of data in pursuance of this sub-paragraph.

Inspection of records, etc.

29. The Licensee shall -

(a) permit any person in the service or employment of the Crown who is appointed by the Minister for the purpose to inspect, and to take copies of and make notes from, all books, papers, maps and other records of any kind kept by the Licensee in pursuance of this licence or in connection with activities about which the Minister is entitled to obtain information in pursuance of clauses 23(2) and 26(3) of this licence; and

(b) furnish that person at reasonable times with such information and provide him at reasonable times with such reasonable assistance as he may request in connection with or arising out of an inspection in pursuance of this clause.

Rights of access

30. Any person or persons authorised by the Minister shall be entitled at all reasonable times to enter into and upon any land for the time being possessed or occupied by the Licensee in the licensed area or to enter into and upon any of the Licensee's installations or equipment used or to be used in connection with searching, boring for or getting petroleum in the licensed area for the purposes hereinafter mentioned -

(a) to examine the installations, wells, plant, appliances and works made or executed by the Licensee in pursuance of this licence and the state of repair and condition thereof; and

(b) to execute any works or to provide and install any equipment which the Minister may be entitled to execute or provide and install in accordance with the provisions hereof.

Power to execute works

31. If the Licensee shall at any time fail to perform the obligations arising under the terms and conditions of any of clauses 11, 15, 18 or 19 of this licence the Minister shall be entitled, after giving to the Licensee reasonable notice in writing of his intention to do so, to execute any works and to provide and install any equipment which in the opinion of the Minister may be necessary to secure the performance of the said obligations or any of them and to recover the costs and expenses of so doing from the Licensee.

Right of distress

32. If and whenever any of the payments mentioned in clause 7(1) of this licence or any part thereof shall be in arrear or unpaid for 28 days next after any of the days whereon the same ought to have been paid (whether the same shall have been legally demanded or not) then and so often as the same may happen the Minister may (as an additional remedy and without prejudice to the power of distress and any other rights and remedies to which he would be entitled) enter into and upon any land which shall for the time being be possessed or occupied by the Licensee for the purposes of this licence or the exercise of any of the rights thereby granted or into and upon any of the Licensee's installations and equipment used or to be used in connection with searching, boring for or getting petroleum in the licensed area and may seize and distrain and sell, as a landlord may do for rent in arrear, all or any of the stocks of petroleum, engines, machinery, tools, implements, chattels and effects belonging to the Licensee which shall be found in or upon or about the land, installations and equipment so entered upon, and out of the moneys arising from the sale of such distress may retain and pay all the arrears of the said payments and also the costs and expenses of and incidental to any such distress and sale rendering the surplus (if any) to the Licensee.

Indemnity against third party claims

33. The Licensee shall at all times keep the Minister effectually indemnified against all actions, proceedings, costs, charges, claims and demands whatsoever which may be made or brought against the Minister by any third party in relation to or in connection with this licence or any matter or thing done or purported to be done in pursuance thereof.

Advertisements, prospectuses, etc.

34. No statement shall be made either in any notice, advertisement, prospectus or other document issued by or to the knowledge of the Licensee or in any other manner claiming or suggesting whether expressly or by implication that Her Majesty or any Government Department or any person or body acting on behalf of Her Majesty has or have formed or expressed an opinion that the licensed area is from its geological formation or otherwise one in which petroleum is likely to be obtainable.

Restrictions on assignments, etc.

35. - (1) The Licensee shall not, except with the consent in writing of the Minister and in accordance with the conditions (if any) of the consent, do anything whatsoever whereby, under the law (including the rules of equity) of any part of the United Kingdom or of any other place, any right granted by this licence or derived from a right so granted becomes exercisable by or for the benefit of or in accordance with the directions of another person.

(2) The Licensee shall not enter into any agreement providing for a person other than the Licensee to become entitled to, or to any proceeds of sale of, any petroleum which, at the time when the agreement is made, has not been but may be won and saved from the licensed area unless the terms of the agreement have been approved in writing by the Minister either unconditionally or subject to conditions; but the preceding provisions of this paragraph do not apply to -

(a) an agreement for the sale of such petroleum under which the price is payable after the petroleum is won and saved; and

(b) an agreement insofar as it provides that, after any petroleum has been won and saved from the licensed area, it shall be exchanged for other petroleum.

(3) The Licensee shall not, without the consent of the Minister, dispose of any petroleum won and saved in the licensed area or any proceeds of sale of such petroleum in such a manner that the disposal does, to the knowledge of the Licensee or without his knowing it, fulfil or enable another person to fulfil obligations which a person who controls the Licensee, or a person who is controlled by a person who controls the Licensee, is required to fulfil by an agreement which, if the person required to fulfil the obligations were the Licensee, would be an agreement of which the terms require approval by virtue of paragraph (2) of this clause; and subsections (2) and (4) to (6) of section 416 of the Income and Corporation Taxes Act 1988[85] shall apply, for the purpose of determining whether for the purposes of this paragraph a person has control of another person, with the following modifications, namely -

(a) for the words "the greater part" wherever they occur in the said subsection (2) there shall be substituted the words "one-third or more"; and

(b) in the said subsection (6), for the word "may" there shall be substituted the word "shall", the words from "and such attributions" onwards shall be omitted and in the other provisions of that subsection any reference to an associate of a person shall be construed as including only a relative of his (as defined by section 417(4) of that Act), a partner of his and a trustee of a settlement (as defined by section 681(4) of that Act) of which he is a beneficiary.

(4) Where the Licensee is two or more persons, then without prejudice to the preceding provisions of this clause, none of those persons shall enter into an agreement with respect to the entitlement of any of them to -

(a) the benefit of any right granted by this licence;

(b) any petroleum won and saved from the licensed area; or

(c) any proceeds of sale of such petro<

unless the terms of the agreement have been approved in writing by the Minister; but the preceding provisions of this paragraph do not apply to an agreement for the sale of such petroleum under which the price is payable after the petroleum is won and saved and an agreement insofar as it provides that, after any petroleum has been won and saved from the licensed area, it shall be exchanged for other petroleum.

Power of revocation

36. - (1) If any of the events specified in the following paragraph shall occur then and in any such case the Minister may revoke this licence and thereupon the same and all the rights hereby granted shall cease and determine but subject nevertheless and without prejudice to any obligation or liability incurred by the Licensee or imposed upon him by or under the terms and conditions hereof.

(2) The events referred to in the foregoing paragraph are -

(a) any payments mentioned in clause 7(1) of this licence or any part thereof being in arrear or unpaid for two months next after any of the days whereon the same ought to have been paid;

(b) any breach or non-observance by the Licensee of any of the terms and conditions of this licence;

(c) the bankruptcy of the Licensee;

(d) the making by the Licensee of any arrangement or composition with his creditors;

(e) if the Licensee is a company, the appointment of a receiver or any liquidation whether compulsory or voluntary;

(f) any breach or non-observance by the Licensee of the terms and conditions of a development scheme;

(g) the Licensee's ceasing in the case of a company to have its central management and control in the United Kingdom;

(h) any breach of a condition subject to which the Minister gave his approval in pursuance of clause 35(2) of this licence;

(i) any breach of clause 35(4) of this licence;

and where two or more persons are the Licensee any reference to the Licensee in sub-paragraphs (c) to (g) of this paragraph is a reference to any of those persons.

(3) The Minister may revoke this licence, with the like consequences as are mentioned in paragraph (1) of this clause, if -

(a) the Licensee is a company; and

(b) there is a change in the control of the Licensee; and

(c) the Minister serves a notice in writing on the Licensee stating that the Minister proposes to revoke this licence in pursuance of this paragraph unless such a further change in the control of the Licensee as is specified in the notice takes place within the period of three months beginning with the date of service of the notice; and

(d) that further change does not take place within that period.

(4) There is a change in the control of the Licensee for the purposes of paragraph (3)(b) of this clause whenever a person has control of the Licensee who did not have control of the Licensee when this licence was granted; and subsections (2) and (4) to (6) of section 416 of the Income and Corporation Taxes Act 1988 shall apply for the purpose of determining whether for the purposes of this paragraph a person has or had control of the Licensee, with the modifications specified in clause 35(3) of this licence.

(5) Where two or more persons are the Licensee and any of them is a company, paragraphs (3) and (4) of this clause shall have effect as if -

(a) sub-paragraph (a) of paragraph (3) were omitted;

(b) in sub-paragraph (b) of that paragraph, after the word "of" there were inserted the words "any company included among the persons who together constitute"; and

(c) for the word "Licensee" in any other provision of those paragraphs, there were substituted the word "company".

Arbitration

37. - (1) If at any time any dispute, difference or question shall arise between the Minister and the Licensee as to any matter arising under or by virtue of this licence or as to their respective rights and liabilities in respect thereof then the same shall, except where it is expressly provided by this licence that the matter or thing to which the same relates is to be determined, decided, directed, approved or consented to by the Minister, be referred to arbitration as provided by the following paragraph.

(2) The arbitration referred to in the foregoing paragraph shall be by a single arbitrator who, in default of agreement between the Minister and the Licensee and, in the case of arbitration in relation to a development scheme, other Licensees affected by the scheme, as to his appointment, shall be appointed by the Lord Chief Justice of England.

(3) In the case of any such arbitration which relates to a development scheme the Licensee shall, unless the arbitrator otherwise determines, perform and observe the terms and conditions of the development scheme pending the decision of the arbitrator.

SCHEDULE 9

CURRENT MODEL CLAUSES FOR SEAWARD PRODUCTION LICENCES DERIVING FROM SCHEDULE 4 TO THE PETROLEUM (PRODUCTION) (SEAWARD AREAS) REGULATIONS 1988 AS IT FROM TIME TO TIME HAD EFFECT BEFORE 16TH DECEMBER 1996

PART I

1. This Schedule has effect in relation to the following paragraphs of Schedule 1 to the Act, namely -

(a) paragraph 18 (Schedule 4 to the Petroleum (Production) (Seaward Areas) Regulations 1988[86]);

(b) paragraph 19 (the said Schedule 4 as amended by the Offshore Safety Act 1992)[87]), and

(c) paragraph 20 (the said Schedule 4 as amended as aforesaid and further amended by the Petroleum (Production) (Seaward Areas) (Amendment) Regulations 1995[88]).

2. Subject to paragraphs 3, 4, 6 and 7, the current model clauses in relation to the said paragraphs 18, 19 and 20 are those reproduced in Part II.

3. - (1) Where the licensed area is in the Scottish area, as defined in article 1(2) of the Civil Jurisdiction (Offshore Activities) Order 1987[89], Part II shall have effect as provided in the two following sub-paragraphs.

(2) Part II shall have effect in such a case as if for model clause 38 (distress) there were substituted the following clause -

" **Diligence**

38. If and whenever any of the payments mentioned in clause 9(1) of this licence or any part thereof shall be in arrear or unpaid for 28 days next after any of the days whereon the same ought to be paid (whether the same shall have been legally demanded or not) then and so often as the same may happen the Minister may (as an additional remedy and without prejudice to any other rights and remedies to which he would be entitled) do diligence in respect thereof in like manner as a landlord may do diligence in respect of unpaid arrears of rent and such diligence shall be effectual to attach all or any of the stocks of petroleum, engines, machinery, tools, implements and other effects belonging to the Licensee which shall be found on or about any of the Licensee's installations and equipment used or to be used in connection with searching, boring for or getting petroleum in the licensed area, and where in pursuance of such a diligence a sale of such effects as shall have been attached thereby takes place the Minister may out of the proceeds thereof retain and pay all the arrears of the said payments and also the expenses of and incident to such diligence and sale and shall pay the surplus thereof (if any) to the Licensee.".

(3) Part II shall also have effect in such a case as if, in model clause 43 (arbitration) -

(a) for the word "arbitrator", wherever it occurs in paragraphs (2) and (3), there were substituted the word "arbiter", and

(b) for the words "the Lord Chief Justice of England for the time being", in paragraph (2), there were substituted the words "the Lord President of the Court of Session".

4. Where the licensed area is in the Northern Irish area, as defined in article 1(2) of the Civil Jurisdiction (Offshore Activities) Order 1987, Part II shall have effect as if in model clause 43 (arbitration) for the words "the Lord Chief Justice of England", in paragraph (2), there were substituted the words "the Lord Chief Justice of Northern Ireland".

5. In paragraphs 3 and 4, any reference to the licensed area is a reference to the licensed area within the meaning of model clause 1(1) in Part II.

6. - (1) In relation to paragraph 20 of Schedule 1 to the Act, Part II shall have effect as provided in the following nine sub-paragraphs.

(2) Part II shall have effect in such a case as if in model clause 9(1) -

(a) at the end of sub-paragraph (a) there were inserted the word "and"; and

(b) sub-paragraph (b) were omitted.

(3) Part II shall also have effect in such a case as if in model clause 10 -

(a) in paragraph (1) -

(i) the words "Subject to paragraph (2) of this clause" were omitted, and

(ii) for the words "clauses 11 and 12" there were substituted the words "clause 12";

(b) paragraph (2) were omitted;

(c) in paragraph (3), for the words "clauses 11 and 12" there were substituted the words "clause 12"; and

(d) paragraphs (5) to (8) were omitted.

(4) Part II shall also have effect in such a case as if model clause 11 were omitted.

(5) Part II shall also have effect in such a case as if in model clause 12(1) -

(a) at the end of sub-paragraph (a) there were inserted the word "and"; and

(b) sub-paragraph (b) were omitted.

(6) Part II shall also have effect in such a case as if model clauses 13 and 30 were omitted.

(7) Part II shall also have effect in such a case as if for model clause 31(3) there were substituted the following paragraph -

" (3) The Licensee shall deliver copies of the said records, plans and maps referred to in the two foregoing paragraphs to the Minister when requested to do so either -

(a) within any time limit specified in the request; or

(b) if there is no time limit specified, within four weeks of the request.".

(8) Part II shall also have effect in such a case as if at the end of model clause 32 there were added the following paragraph -

" (4) The Licensee shall comply with any request for information made in accordance with paragraph (3) above either -

(a) within any time limit specified in the request; or

(b) if there is no time limit specified, within four weeks of the request.".

(9) Part II shall also have effect in such a case as if for proviso (iv) to model clause 34 there were substituted the following proviso -

" (iv) the Minister, the said Council and any other such body shall be entitled to publish any of the specified data of a geological, scientific or technical kind either -

(a) after the expiration of the period of five years beginning with the date when the data was due to be supplied to the Minister in accordance with clause 31 or 32 of this licence, or if earlier, the date when the Minister received that data; or

(b) after the expiration of such longer period as the Minister may determine after considering any representations made to him by the Licensee about the publication of data in pursuance of this sub-paragraph.".

(10) Part II shall also have effect in such a case as if for model clause 42(2)(g) there were substituted the following sub-paragraph -

" (g) if the Licensee is a company, the Licensee's ceasing to direct and control either -

(i) its operations under the licence; or

(ii) any commercial activities in connection with those operations from a fixed place within the United Kingdom;".

7. Where

(a) section 1 of the Petroleum Royalties (Relief Act) 1983[90] applies, or

(b) section 1 of the Petroleum Royalties (Relief) and Continental Shelf Act 1989[91] applies,

Part II has effect subject to the provisions of the said Act of 1983, or, as the case may be, the said Act of 1989.

PART II

Interpretation

1. - (1) In the following clauses, the following expressions have the meanings hereby respectively assigned to them, that is to say: -

"the Act of 1934" means the Petroleum (Production) Act 1934[92];
"the Act of 1964" means the Continental Shelf Act 1964[93];
"the Act of 1998" means the Petroleum Act 1998[94];
"appropriate percentage" has the meaning assigned thereto by clause 10;
"block" means an area comprised in this licence which is delineated on the reference map deposited at the principal office of the Minister's department and to which a reference number was assigned at the date of this licence;
"chargeable period" has the meaning assigned thereto by clause 10;
"development scheme" has the meaning assigned thereto by clause 28;
"half year" means the period from 1st January to 30th June in any year and the period from 1st July to 31st December in any year;
"initial term" has the meaning assigned thereto by clause 3 and "second term" has the meaning assigned thereto by clause 4(4);
"the licensed area" means the area for the time being in which the Licensee may exercise the rights granted by this licence;
"the Licensee" means the person or persons to whom this licence is granted, his personal representatives and any person or persons to whom the rights conferred by this licence may lawfully have been assigned;
"the Minister" means the Secretary of State for Trade and Industry;
"oil field" has the meaning assigned thereto by clause 28;
"petroleum" includes any mineral oil or relative hydrocarbon and natural gas existing in its natural condition in strata but does not include coal or bituminous shales or other stratified deposits from which oil can be extracted by destructive distillation;

"section" means a part of a block comprising an area bounded by minute lines of latitude and longitude one minute apart respectively;
"well" includes borehole.

(2) Any obligations which are to be observed and performed by the Licensee shall at any time at which the Licensee is more than one person be joint and several obligations.

Term of licence

3. This licence unless sooner determined under any of the provisions hereof shall be and continue in force for the term of six years next after 19 , (hereinafter called "the initial term"); but if the terms and conditions of this licence are duly performed and observed and, in particular, if the work programme described in Schedule 4 to this licence has been duly performed, it may be continued for a further term of twelve years as provided by clause 4 of this licence and, if the terms and conditions of this licence continue to be duly performed and observed, thereafter as provided by clause 5 (and subject to the provisions of clause 6) of this licence for a further maximum period of eighteen years.

Option to continue licence as to part of the licensed area

4. - (1) At any time not later than three months before the expiration of the initial term the Licensee paying the payments and royalties hereinafter provided and observing and performing the terms and conditions herein contained may give notice in writing to the Minister that he desires the licence to continue as to a part of the licensed area (hereinafter called "the continuing part") in the manner hereinafter provided and to determine as to the residue thereof (hereinafter called "the surrendered part").

(2) Such notice shall -

(a) describe the surrendered part which shall be an area which shall together with any area previously surrendered in accordance with clause 7 thereof -

(i) if the area originally comprised in this licence consisted of sixty or more sections, be not less than half the number of such sections; or

(ii) if the area originally comprised in this licence consisted of more than thirty but less than sixty sections, be such a number of sections as will leave a continuing part consisting of thirty sections;

provided that if the area originally comprised in this licence consisted of not more than thirty sections the Licensee shall not be obliged to surrender any part of the licensed area and provided that any area surrendered in accordance with this clause shall comply with clause 8 hereof; and

(b) specify a date (hereinafter called "the surrender date") not later than the expiry of the initial term upon which the surrendered part is to be surrendered.

(3) The Licensee may at any time not less than one month before the surrender date give further notice in writing to the Minister varying the part of the licensed area to be surrendered and in the event of such further notice being given the provisions of the previous paragraphs of this clause shall apply *mutatis mutandis* to such notice but so that the surrender date specified in such notice shall be the same as that specified in the first notice.

(4) This licence shall upon the option conferred by this clause being duly exercised but subject to the provisions of clause 3 of this licence continue in respect of the continuing part for a term of

twelve years next after the surrender date ("the second term").

Continuance of licence after the second term

5. - (1) At any time not later than three months before the expiry of the second term the Licensee paying the payments and royalties hereinafter provided and observing and performing the terms and conditions herein contained may give notice in writing to the Minister that he desires this licence to continue in force thereafter.

(2) If such notice is given this licence shall continue in force after the expiry of the second term as provided by the following paragraphs of this clause in the event that before that date -

(a) the Minister has given a consent in pursuance of clause 17(1) of this licence and such consent is still in force at that date, or

(b) the Minister has in pursuance of clause 17(4) of this licence approved a programme submitted to him in pursuance of clause 17(2) and such approval is still in force at that date, or

(c) the Minister has served a programme on the Licensee in pursuance of clause 17(6) of this licence and such programme is still in force at that date, or

(d) the Minister has in his discretion so directed in writing.

(3) Where the Minister has given a direction extending the second term of this licence in pursuance of paragraph (2)(d) of this clause he may in his discretion, on notice in writing being given to him by the Licensee not later than three months before the expiry of such extension or any further extension that he desires the licence to continue in force thereafter, give a further direction that this licence shall so continue in force.

(4) Where this licence continues in force by virtue of paragraph (2)(a), (b) or (c) of this clause it shall, subject to the provisions of clause 3 of this licence, so continue in force for a further period of eighteen years after the expiry of the second term.

(5) Where this licence continues in force by virtue of a direction given in pursuance of paragraph (2)(d) or further direction given in pursuance of paragraph (3) of this clause it shall, subject to the provisions of clause 3 hereof, continue in force for such further period after the expiry of the second term as the Minister may prescribe provided that in any event the period for which this licence continues in force after the expiry of the second term by virtue of any such directions shall not in aggregate exceed eighteen years.

(6) A direction given by the Minister in pursuance of paragraph (2)(d) of this clause or further direction given by the Minister in pursuance of paragraph (3) of this clause may be given subject to such conditions as he may specify and (without prejudice to the generality of the foregoing) such conditions may, subject to the provisions of paragraph (5) of this clause, include conditions as to the duration of the extension or further extension (as the case may be) of the second term.

Power further to extend term of licence

6. Where this licence has continued in force by virtue of clause 5 of this licence for a total period of eighteen years after the expiry of the second term, the Minister, on application being made to him in writing not later than three months before the expiry of such period, may in his discretion agree with the Licensee that this licence shall continue in force thereafter for such further period as the Minister and the Licensee may agree and subject to such modification of the terms and conditions of this licence (which modification may include making provision for any further extension of the term of this licence) as the Minister and the Licensee may then agree is appropriate.

Right of licensee to determine licence or surrender part of licensed area

7. - (1) Without prejudice to any obligation or liability imposed by or incurred under the terms hereof the Licensee may at any time by giving to the Minister not less than six months' notice in writing to that effect to expire on an anniversary of the date of commencement of the initial term, determine this licence or surrender any part of the licensed area being a part which complies with clause 8 hereof.

(2) A notice given pursuant to paragraph (1) of this clause may be cancelled by a further notice in writing given to the Minister not less than one month before the expiration of the notice.

Areas surrendered

8. - (1) Within a block any area surrendered by the Licensee pursuant to either clause 4 or clause 7 of this licence and any area accordingly retained by him or, where the surrendered or retained area comprises separate parts, each part of each area shall, unless the Minister has otherwise agreed in writing before the date at which the appropriate notice is given by the Licensee to the Minister -

(a) be bounded by minute lines of latitude extending not less than two minutes of longitude and minute lines of longitude extending not less than two minutes of latitude;

(b) subject to clause 4(2)(a) hereof, consist of not less than thirty sections; and

(c) have boundaries which, whether they run north and south or east and west, either coincide with the corresponding boundaries of the block or are not less than two sections distant from those boundaries;

and where the surrendered or retained area comprises separate parts, each part of that area shall be not less than two sections distant from any other part of that area.

(2) Upon the date on which any determination of this licence or any surrender of part of the licensed area in manner provided by any of clauses 4, 5 and 7 of this licence is to take effect the rights granted by this licence shall cease in respect of the licensed area or of the part so surrendered as the case may be but without prejudice to any obligation or liability imposed upon the Licensee or incurred by him under the terms of this licence prior to that date.

Payment of consideration for licence

9. - (1) The Licensee shall make to the Minister as consideration for the grant of this licence -

(a) payments of royalty in accordance with clauses 10 to 12 of this licence;

(b) deliveries of petroleum in accordance with clause 13 of this licence; and

(c) payments in accordance with Schedule 2 to this licence.

(2) The Licensee shall not by reason of determination of the licence or surrender of any part of the licensed area be entitled to be repaid or allowed any sum payable to the Minister pursuant to this licence before the date of determination or surrender.

Royalty payments

10. - (1) Subject to paragraph (2) of this clause the Licensee shall pay to the Minister, in respect of each half year in which this licence is in force (hereafter in this clause and in clauses 11 and 12 of this licence referred to as a "chargeable period"), a royalty of an amount equal to the percentage specified in Schedule 3 to this licence (hereinafter referred to as "the appropriate percentage") of the value of the petroleum relating to that period.

(2) Paragraph (1) of this clause shall not apply to a chargeable period in which the Licensee delivers petroleum to the Minister in pursuance of clause 13 of this licence; but if the petroleum delivered has a value of less than the appropriate percentage of the aggregate of -

(a) the value of the petroleum delivered (ignoring any such excess as is mentioned in paragraph (8) of this clause), and

(b) the value of the petroleum relating to that period,

he shall pay to the Minister a royalty of an amount equal to the difference.

(3) For the purposes of this clause and clauses 11 and 12 of this licence the value of the petroleum relating to a chargeable period is, subject to paragraph (4) of this clause, the total of the amounts which, if the words "one-half of" were omitted from paragraph (b) of subsection (4) and paragraph (d) of subsection (5) of section 2 of the Oil Taxation Act 1975[95], would in pursuance of paragraph (a) of the said subsection (4) fall to be taken into account in relation to that period in respect of the persons who by reference to this licence are or are treated as participators for the purposes of those subsections, reduced by the total of the market values which would in pursuance of the said paragraph (b) fall to be taken into account as aforesaid.

(4) The value which, in pursuance of paragraph (3) of this clause, is the value of the petroleum relating to a chargeable period shall be increased by an amount equal to the value as determined for the purposes of income tax or the charge of corporation tax on income, of so much of the petroleum won and saved in the licensed area as falls within section 10(1) of the Oil Taxation Act 1975 and was in that period disposed of or relevantly appropriated (within the meaning of Part I of that Act) by the persons mentioned in the said paragraph (3).

(5) Subject to paragraphs (6) and (7) of this clause, the value of petroleum delivered to the Minister in pursuance of clause 13 of this licence shall be ascertained for the purposes of this clause and clause 11 on such basis (or, where petroleum of more than one kind is delivered, such bases) as the Minister and the Licensee agree.

(6) If the Minister and the Licensee fail to agree on the value of any petroleum delivered to the Minister in pursuance of clause 13 of this licence, it shall be ascertained on such basis as the Minister may specify as fair in a notice in writing given by him to the Licensee.

(7) The Licensee may, during the period of 28 days beginning with the day on which he receives a notice from the Minister under paragraph (6) of this clause, refer to arbitration in the manner provided by clause 43 of this licence any question as to whether the basis of valuation specified in the notice is fair.

(8) In this clause and clauses 11 and 12, references to petroleum delivered to the Minister in pursuance of clause 13 include references to any excess over the quantity required to be delivered by a notice served in pursuance of paragraph (1) of that clause.

Payments by the Minister

11. If in any chargeable period the Licensee delivers to the Minister in pursuance of clause 13 of this licence petroleum having a value greater than the appropriate percentage of the aggregate of -

(a) the value of the petroleum delivered (ignoring any such excess as is mentioned in clause 10(8) of this licence), and

(b) the value of the petroleum relating to that period,

the Minister shall pay to the Licensee a sum equal to the difference.

Provisions supplementary to clauses 10 and 11

12. - (1) The Licensee shall, within two months after the end of each chargeable period, deliver to the Minister, in such form as the Minister may specify, a statement of -

(a) the quantity of petroleum won and saved in the licensed area in that period;

(b) the quantity of that petroleum delivered to the Minister in that period in pursuance of clause 13 of this licence; and

(c) the amounts of the prices and market values which are required by paragraph 2 of Schedule 2 to the Oil Taxation Act 1975[96] to be stated in the returns made for that period in pursuance of that paragraph in consequence of this licence.

(2) The Licensee shall, when he delivers a statement to the Minister in pursuance of paragraph (1) of this clause for a chargeable period in respect of which royalty is payable in pursuance of clause 10(1) of this licence, make to the Minister a payment on account of royalty for that period equal to the appropriate percentage of the sum produced by aggregating the amounts which in pursuance of sub-paragraph (c) of paragraph (1) of this clause are specified in the statement and reducing the aggregate by the amount which, by virtue of paragraph 2(2)(d)(ii) of Schedule 2 to the Oil Taxation Act 1975, was specified in the statement delivered to the Minister in pursuance of the said paragraph (1) in respect of the preceding chargeable period.

(3) The Licensee shall, when he delivers a statement to the Minister in pursuance of paragraph (1) of this clause for a chargeable period in respect of which royalty is payable in pursuance of clause 10(2) of this licence, make to the Minister a payment on account of royalty for that period equal to the amount which would be so payable for that period if the royalty so payable for that period fell to be determined by reference to the amounts specified in the statement and the amount which, by virtue of paragraph 2(2)(d)(ii) of Schedule 2 to the Oil Taxation Act 1975, was specified in the statement delivered to the Minister in pursuance of paragraph (1) of this clause in respect of the preceding chargeable period.

(4) The Minister may from time to time, after a statement in respect of any chargeable period has been delivered to him in pursuance of paragraph (1) of this clause and before he has given to the Licensee a notice in pursuance of paragraph (5) of this clause in respect of that period, give a notice in writing to the Licensee specifying the amount which the Minister estimates is payable by the Licensee in pursuance of clause 10 of this licence in respect of that period, and where the amount specified in the notice is larger or smaller than the total amount already paid by the Licensee in pursuance of this clause in respect of that period, then -

(a) if it is larger the difference shall be paid forthwith by the Licensee to the Minister; and

(b) if it is smaller the difference shall be paid forthwith by the Minister to the Licensee.

(5) When it appears to the Minister that the value of the petroleum relating to any chargeable period has been finally determined for tax purposes, he may give to the Licensee a notice in writing specifying the amount which the Minister considers is payable by the Licensee in pursuance of clause 10 of this licence in respect of that period; and where the amount specified in the notice is larger or smaller than the total amount already paid by the Licensee in pursuance of this clause in respect of that period, then, subject to paragraph (7) of this clause -

(a) if it is larger the difference shall be paid forthwith by the Licensee to the Minister; and

(b) if it is smaller the difference shall be paid forthwith by the Minister to the Licensee.

(6) If after the date when the Minister gave notice to the Licensee in pursuance of paragraph (5) of this clause or this paragraph in respect of a chargeable period it appears to the Minister, in consequence of a relevant assessment or determination made after that date which relates directly or indirectly to the value of petroleum by reference to which the amount specified in the notice was determined, that another amount ought to have been so specified, he may give notice in writing to the Licensee specifying the other amount; and where he does so, then subject to paragraph (7) of this clause -

(a) if the other amount is larger than the total amount already paid by the Licensee in pursuance of this clause in respect of that period the difference shall be paid forthwith by the Licensee to the Minister; and

(b) if it is smaller the difference shall be paid forthwith by the Minister to the Licensee.

(7) A decision made by the Minister for the purposes of paragraph (4), (5) or (6) of this clause shall not be called in question by the Licensee except that any dispute between the Minister and the Licensee as to whether an amount specified in a notice given in pursuance of the said paragraph (5) or (6) is payable by virtue of clause 10 of this licence may during the period of 28 days beginning with the day on which the Licensee receives the notice be referred to arbitration in the manner provided by clause 43 of this licence; and on a reference to arbitration in pursuance of this paragraph any relevant assessment or determination for the time being in force shall be binding on the Minister and the Licensee so far as the assessment or determination relates directly or indirectly to the value of petroleum relating to the chargeable period in question.

(8) When any payment is made by the Licensee or the Minister in pursuance of paragraph (4), (5), or (6) of this clause, an amount in respect of interest on the payment shall also be payable by him to the recipient of the payment and that amount shall be calculated in such manner as the Minister may specify from time to time in a notice in writing given by him to the Licensee; but -

(a) a notice in pursuance of this paragraph shall provide for amounts by way of interest to be calculated by applying a rate of interest which is for the time being a commercial rate of interest; and

(b) any such amount in respect of interest shall be disregarded in calculating for the purposes of the said paragraph (4), (5) or (6) any amount already paid by the Licensee in pursuance of this clause.

(9) If a payment is made by the Minister in pursuance of clause 11 of this licence more than two months after the end of the chargeable period to which the payment relates, an amount in respect of interest on the payment from the end of those two months shall also be payable by him to the Licensee.

(10) Interest under paragraph (9) of this clause shall be calculated in such manner as the Minister may specify from time to time in a notice in writing given by him to the Licensee (but sub-paragraph (a) of paragraph (8) of this clause shall apply to such a notice as it applies to a notice under paragraph (8)).

(11) In this clause "relevant assessment or determination" means an assessment or determination made by the Commissioners of Inland Revenue for the purposes of petroleum revenue tax, income tax or the charge of corporation tax on income or a determination made in proceedings arising out of such an assessment or determination made by the said Commissioners.

(12) For the purposes of this clause any amount paid by the Licensee or the Minister on account of a prospective liability under paragraph (4), (5) or (6) of this clause shall be treated as paid in pursuance of that paragraph.

Notes:

[84] Paragraph 2 was amended by section 62 of, and Part X of Schedule 16 to, the Finance Act 1987 (c.16), section 187 of the Finance Act 1993 (c.34) and section 236 of, and Schedule 23 to, the Finance Act 1994 (c.9

Deliveries of petroleum in place of royalties

13. - (1) If during the term of this licence the Minister serves on the Licensee a notice in writing in accordance with the following provisions of this clause requiring the Licensee to deliver to the Minister part of the petroleum won and saved by the Licensee in the licensed area, the Licensee shall comply with the notice.

(2) Where the Minister proposes to serve a notice on the Licensee in pursuance of paragraph (1) of this clause, he shall before doing so -

(a) give the Licensee a copy of the proposed notice and an opportunity of making representations to the Minister about it; and

(b) consider any representation then made to him by the Licensee about the proposed notice;

and the Minister shall, in deciding upon the terms of the actual notice, have regard to the desirability of not disturbing unduly any arrangements made by the Licensee for transporting and delivering petroleum won and saved from the licensed area.

(3) Subject to paragraph (4) of this clause, a notice served in pursuance of paragraph (1) of this clause -

(a) shall specify the date on which the notice is to come into force and may contain provisions with respect to the time when it shall cease to be in force;

(b) shall specify the quantity of petroleum won and saved in the licensed area during each half year in which the notice is in force which, up to any maximum quantities specified in the notice in pursuance of paragraph (4)(b) of this clause, is to be delivered to the Minister in consequence of the notice;

(c) may relate to all petroleum so won and saved or may be limited to and specify different quantities of such petroleum which is of one or more of the following kinds, namely, crude oil, condensate, natural gas and natural gas liquids, in each case of a quality or composition or of each quality or composition determined in the manner specified in the notice;

(d) shall contain provisions with respect to the place or places at which any petroleum or kind of petroleum is to be delivered in pursuance of the notice and may contain provisions with respect to the times at which any quantities of it are to be so delivered.

(4) Such a notice -

(a) shall not specify as the date on which it is to come into force a date before the expiration of the period of six months beginning with the date on which the notice is served on the Licensee but shall, if the Minister serves on the Licensee a further notice in writing stating that it is to cease to be in force at a time specified in the further notice which is not earlier than six months after the date of service of the further notice, cease to be in force at that time;

(b) shall not specify, as the quantity of petroleum won and saved in any half year which is to be delivered in pursuance of the notice or as the quantity of any kind of such petroleum, a quantity greater than the appropriate percentage of all the petroleum, or as the case may be of all the petroleum of that kind, which is won and saved by the Licensee in the licensed area in that half year, but may provide that the quantities of the petroleum or of a kind of petroleum so won and saved which are to be so delivered shall not in the aggregate exceed a quantity specified in the notice;

(c) shall not specify, or enable to be specified, as a place at which delivery is to be made in pursuance of the notice a place which is neither a point at sea at which the Licensee normally loads, nor a point on land at which the Licensee normally lands, petroleum of any kind from that area.

Measurement of petroleum obtained from the licensed area

14. - (1) The Licensee shall measure or weigh by a method or methods customarily used in good oilfield practice and from time to time approved by the Minister all petroleum won and saved from the licensed area.

(2) If and to the extent that the Minister so directs, the duty imposed by paragraph (1) of this clause shall be discharged separately in relation to petroleum won and saved -

(a) from each part of the licensed area which is an oil field for the purposes of the Oil Taxation Act 1975,

(b) from each part of the licensed area which forms part of such an oil field extending beyond the licensed area, and

(c) from each well producing petroleum from a part of the licensed area which is not within such an oil field.

(3) If and to the extent that the Minister so directs, the preceding provisions of this clause shall apply as if the duty to measure or weigh petroleum included a duty to ascertain its quality or composition or both; and where a direction under this paragraph is in force, the following provisions of this clause shall have effect as if references to measuring or weighing included

references to ascertaining quality or composition.

(4) The Licensee shall not make any alteration in the method or methods of measuring or weighing used by him or any appliances used for that purpose without the consent in writing of the Minister and the Minister may in any case require that no alteration shall be made save in the presence of a person authorised by the Minister.

(5) The Minister may from time to time direct that any weighing or measuring appliance shall be tested or examined in such manner, upon such occasions or at such intervals and by such persons as may be specified by the Minister's direction and the Licensee shall pay to any such person or to the Minister such fees and expenses for test or examination as the Minister may specify.

(6) If any measuring or weighing appliance shall upon any such test or examination as is mentioned in the last foregoing paragraph be found to be false or unjust the same shall if the Minister so determines after considering any representations in writing made by the Licensee be deemed to have existed in that condition during the period since the last occasion upon which the same was tested or examined pursuant to the last foregoing paragraph.

Keeping of accounts

15. - (1) The Licensee shall keep in the United Kingdom full and correct accounts in a form from time to time approved by the Minister of -

(a) the quantity of petroleum in the form of gas won and saved;

(b) the quantity of petroleum in any other form won and saved;

(c) the name and address of any person to whom any petroleum has been supplied by the Licensee, the quantity so supplied, the price or other consideration therefor and the place to which the petroleum was conveyed pursuant to the agreement for such supply; and

(d) such other particulars as the Minister may from time to time direct.

(2) The quantities of petroleum stated in such accounts may exclude any water separated from the petroleum and shall be expressed as volumes in cubic metres measured at, or calculated as if measured at, a temperature of 15 degrees Celsius and a pressure of 1.0132 bar but if the Minister serves notice in writing on the Licensee determining any other manner in which any quantity of petroleum or any quantity of any form of petroleum is to be expressed that quantity shall be so expressed.

(3) Such accounts shall state separately the quantities used for the purposes of carrying on drilling and production operations and pumping to field storage, and quantities not so used, and in the case of petroleum not in the form of gas shall state the specific gravity of the petroleum and, if petroleum of different specific gravities has been won and saved, the respective quantities of petroleum of each specific gravity.

(4) The Licensee shall within two months after the end of each half year in which this licence is in force and within two months after the expiration or determination of this licence deliver to the Minister an abstract in a form from time to time approved by the Minister of the accounts for that half year or for the period prior to such expiration or determination as the case may be.

Working obligations

16. - (1) The Licensee shall before the expiry of the initial term of this licence carry out such scheme of prospecting including any geological survey by any physical or chemical means and such programme of test drilling (hereinafter collectively referred to as a "work programme") as may be set out in Schedule 4 to this licence.

(2) If at any time the Minister serves a notice in writing on the Licensee requiring him to submit to the Minister, before a date specified in the notice, an appropriate programme for exploring for petroleum in the licensed area during a period so specified, the Licensee shall comply with the notice; and for the purposes of this paragraph an appropriate programme is one which any person who, if he -

(a) were entitled to exploit the rights granted by this licence; and

(b) had the competence and resources needed to exploit those rights to the best commercial advantage; and

(c) were seeking to exploit those rights to the best commercial advantage,

could reasonably be expected to carry out during the period specified in the notice, and that period must be within the term of this licence.

(3) If a programme is submitted to the Minister in consequence of a notice served by him in pursuance of paragraph (2) of this clause, then -

(a) he shall not be entitled to revoke this licence on the ground that the programme does not satisfy the requirements of that paragraph (hereafter in this clause referred to as "the relevant requirements"); but

(b) if he is of opinion that the programme does not satisfy the relevant requirements he may serve a notice in writing on the Licensee stating his opinion and the reasons for it.

(4) Where notice in respect of a programme is served on the Licensee in pursuance of paragraph (3) of this clause he shall either -

(a) within 28 days beginning with the date of service of the notice refer to arbitration, in the manner provided by clause 43 of this licence, the question of whether the programme satisfies the relevant requirements; or

(b) within a reasonable period beginning with that date submit to the Minister a further programme which satisfies the relevant requirements;

and where it is determined in consequence of any reference to arbitration in pursuance of sub-paragraph (a) of this paragraph that the programme in question does not satisfy the relevant requirements the Licensee shall submit to the Minister, as soon as possible after the date of the determination, a further programme which satisfies the relevant requirements.

(5) The Licensee shall carry out any programme submitted by him in pursuance of this clause as to which either -

(a) the Minister serves notice in writing on the Licensee stating that the Minister approves the programme; or

(b) it is determined in consequence of any reference to arbitration in pursuance of this licence that the programme satisfies the relevant requirements;

and any programme approved by the Minister in pursuance of this paragraph shall be deemed for the purposes of this licence to satisfy the relevant requirements.

(6) Where, in consequence of any breach or non-observance by the Licensee of any provision of paragraph (2), (4) or (5) of this clause, the Minister has power by virtue of paragraph (1) of clause 42 of this licence to revoke this licence, he may if he thinks fit exercise that power in relation to such part only of the licensed area as he may specify; and where he does so the rights granted by this licence shall cease in respect of the specified part of that area without prejudice to any obligation or liability imposed upon the Licensee or incurred by him under the terms of this licence.

(7) Where the Licensee has a duty by virtue of this clause to carry out a programme during a part of the term of this licence, the Minister may serve notice in pursuance of paragraph (2) of this clause in respect of another part of that term.

Development and production programmes

17. - (1) The Licensee shall not -

(a) erect or carry out any relevant works, either in the licensed area or elsewhere, for the purpose of getting petroleum from that area or for the purpose of conveying to a place on land petroleum got from that area; or

(b) get petroleum from that area otherwise than in the course of searching for petroleum or drilling wells,

except with the consent in writing of the Minister or in accordance with a programme which the Minister has approved or served on the Licensee in pursuance of the following provisions of this clause.

(2) The Licensee shall prepare and submit to the Minister, in such form and by such time and in respect of such period during the term of this licence as the Minister may direct, a programme specifying -

(a) the relevant works which the Licensee proposes to erect or carry out during that period for either of the purposes mentioned in paragraph (1)(a) of this clause;

(b) the proposed locations of the works, the purposes for which it is proposed to use the works and the times at which it is proposed to begin and to complete the erection or carrying out of the works;

(c) the maximum and minimum quantities of petroleum in the form of gas and the maximum and minimum quantities of petroleum in other forms, which, in each calendar year during the period aforesaid or in such other periods during that period as the Minister may specify, the Licensee proposes to get as mentioned in paragraph (1)(b) of this clause.

(3) If the Minister directs the Licensee -

(a) to prepare different programmes in pursuance of paragraph (2) of this clause in respect of petroleum from such different parts of the licensed area as are specified in the direction; or

(b) where a programme approved or served in pursuance of this clause relates to a particular period during the term of this licence, to prepare a programme or programmes in pursuance of paragraph (2) of this clause in respect of a further period or further periods during that term,

the Licensee shall comply with the direction.

(4) It shall be the duty of the Minister expeditiously to consider any programme submitted to him in pursuance of paragraph (2) of this clause and when he has done so to give notice in writing to the Licensee stating -

(a) that the Minister approves the programme; or

(b) that the Minister approves the programme subject to the condition that such of the relevant works as are specified in the notice shall not be used before the expiration of the period so specified in relation to the works or shall not be used without the consent in writing of the Minister; or

(c) that the Minister rejects the programme on one or both of the following grounds, namely -

(i) that the carrying out of any proposals included in the programme in pursuance of paragraph (2) of this clause would be contrary to good oilfield practice;

(ii) that the proposals included in the programme in pursuance of sub-paragraph (c) of the said paragraph (2) are, in the opinion of the Minister, not in the national interest;

and in a notice in pursuance of sub-paragraph (b) of this paragraph may contain different conditions in respect of different works.

(5) Where the Minister gives notice of rejection of a programme in pursuance of sub-paragraph (c) of paragraph (4) of this clause, then -

(a) if the grounds of the rejection consist of or include the ground mentioned in paragraph (i) of that sub-paragraph he shall include in the notice a statement of the matters in consequence of which he rejected the programme on that ground; and

(b) if the grounds of the rejection consist of or include the ground mentioned in paragraph (ii) of that sub-paragraph he shall include in the notice a statement of the rates at which he considers that, in the national interest, petroleum should be got from the area to which the programme relates; and

(c) the Licensee shall prepare and submit to the Minister, before the time specified in that behalf in the notice -

(i) where the notice contains such a statement as is mentioned in sub-paragraph (a) above, modifications of the programme which ensure that the carrying out of the programme with those modifications would not be contrary to good oilfield practice;

(ii) where the notice contains such a statement as is mentioned in sub-paragraph (b) above, modifications of the programme which ensure the getting of petroleum from the area there mentioned at the rates specified in the statement and which (except so far as may be necessary in order to get petroleum at those rates) are not such that the carrying out of the programme with those modifications would be contrary to good oilfield practice;

but the Licensee shall not be required by virtue of paragraph (i) of this sub-paragraph to submit modifications if the carrying out of the programme without modifications would not be contrary to good oilfield practice.

(6) If the Minister gives notice in writing to the Licensee that the Minister approves the modifications of a programme which have been submitted to him in pursuance of sub-paragraph (c) of paragraph (5) of this clause, the programme with those modifications shall be deemed to be approved by the Minister; but if the Licensee fails to perform the duty imposed on him by that sub-paragraph the Minister may if he thinks fit, instead of revoking this licence in consequence of the failure, serve on the Licensee such a programme as the Minister considers that the Licensee should have submitted to him in respect of the area and period to which the rejected programme related.

(7) Where the Minister proposes to approve a programme subject to a condition in pursuance of paragraph (4)(b) of this clause or to reject a programme in pursuance of paragraph (4)(c) of this clause or to serve a programme on the Licensee in pursuance of paragraph (6) of this clause he shall before doing so -

(a) give the Licensee particulars of the proposal and an opportunity of making representations to the Minister about the technical and financial factors which the Licensee considers are relevant in connection with the proposal; and

(b) consider any such representations then made to him by the Licensee;

and the Minister shall not approve a programme subject to such a condition unless he is satisfied that the condition is required in the national interest.

(8) The Licensee shall carry out any programme approved or served on him by the Minister in pursuance of this clause or, if such a programme is varied in pursuance of clause 18 of this licence, the programme as so varied except so far as the Licensee is authorised in writing by the Minister to do otherwise or is required to do otherwise by such a condition as is mentioned in paragraph (4)(b) of this clause; but if it is necessary to carry out certain works in order to comply with provisions included in a programme by virtue of paragraph (5)(c) of this clause or provisions of a programme served on the Licensee in pursuance of paragraph (6) of this clause or provisions of a programme as varied in pursuance of clause 18 of this licence, then, notwithstanding anything in the programme as to the time when those provisions are to be complied with, the Licensee shall not be treated as having failed to comply with those provisions before the expiration of the period reasonably required for carrying out the works.

(9) In this clause "relevant works" means any structures and any other works whatsoever which are intended by the Licensee to be permanent and are neither designed to be moved from place to place without major dismantling nor intended by the Licensee to be used only for searching for petroleum.

Provisions supplementary to clause 17

18. - (1) A consent given by the Minister in pursuance of clause 17(1) of this licence may be given subject to such conditions as are specified in the document signifying the consent and may in particular, without prejudice to the generality of the preceding provisions of this paragraph, be limited to a period so specified.

(2) Where -

(a) the Minister gives notice in respect of a programme in pursuance of paragraph (4)(a) or (b) or paragraph (6) of clause 17 of this licence or serves a programme in pursuance of the said paragraph (6); or

(b) it is determined by arbitration that the Licensee is not required by virtue of paragraph (i) of clause 17(5)(c) of this licence to submit modifications of a programme in respect of which notice of rejection containing such a statement as is mentioned in the said paragraph (i) was given by the Minister in pursuance of clause 17(4)(c) of this licence,

the Minister may give to the Licensee, with the notice given or the programme served as mentioned in sub-paragraph (a) of this paragraph or, in a case falling within sub-paragraph (b) of this paragraph, within the period of three months beginning with the date of the arbitrator's or arbiter's determination, a notice (hereafter in this clause referred to as a "limitation notice") authorising the Minister, by a further notice given to the Licensee from time to time after the expiration of the period specified in that behalf in the limitation notice, to provide that the programme to which the limitation notice relates shall have effect while the further notice is in force with the substitution for any quantity of petroleum or any period specified in the programme in pursuance of clause 17(2)(c) of this licence of a different quantity of petroleum or a different period specified in the further notice.

(3) A quantity or period specified in such a further notice as that to be substituted for a quantity or period which is specified in the programme in question shall be within the limits specified in the limitation notice as those applicable to that quantity or period specified in the programme; and those limits shall be such as to secure that the expenditure to be incurred by the Licensee in complying with the further notice, in a case where an effect of the notice is to increase the quantity of petroleum which the Licensee is required to get from the licensed area in any period, is less than the cost of drilling a new well in the licensed area at the time when the further notice is given.

(4) Where the Minister proposes to give a limitation notice or any such further notice as aforesaid he shall before doing so -

(a) give the Licensee particulars of the proposal and an opportunity of making representations to the Minister about the technical and financial factors which the Licensee considers are relevant in connection with the proposal; and

(b) consider any such representations then made to him by the Licensee;

and the Minister shall not give such a further notice of which an effect is to increase the quantity of petroleum which the Licensee is required to get from the licensed area during any period unless the Minister is satisfied that the notice is required by reason of a national emergency and shall not give any other such further notice as aforesaid unless he is satisfied that the notice is required in the national interest.

(5) A limitation notice or such a further notice as aforesaid may -

(a) specify any quantity or period by reference to such factors as the Minister thinks fit; and

(b) in the case of such a further notice, contain provisions as to -

(i) the date when the notice is to come into force,

(ii) the date when the notice is to cease to be in force, and specify different dates in pursuance of this sub-paragraph for different provisions of the notice;

and the Minister may revoke such a further notice at a particular time by serving on the Licensee a notice in writing stating that the further notice is revoked at that time.

(6) Any question arising under clause 17 of this licence or this clause as to what is, is not or is required in the national interest or as to what is, or is required by reason of, a national emergency shall be determined by the Minister.

(7) The Licensee shall ensure that any conditions to which an approval is subject in pursuance of clause 17(4)(b) of this licence or a consent is subject in pursuance of paragraph (1) of this clause are complied with.

(8) If in respect of part of the licensed area -

(a) a consent has been given in pursuance of paragraph (1) of clause 17 of this licence; or

(b) the Licensee has submitted to the Minister, in accordance with a direction given by virtue of paragraph (3)(a) of that clause, a programme in pursuance of paragraph (2) of that clause -

(i) as respects which the Minister has served notice in pursuance of paragraph (4)(a) or (b) or paragraph (6) of that clause, or

(ii) in consequence of which the Minister has served a programme on the Licensee in pursuance of the said paragraph (6), or

(iii) in respect of which it has been determined by arbitration that the Licensee is not required by virtue of paragraph (5)(c)(i) of that clause to submit modifications,

paragraph (1) of clause 42 of this licence shall not authorise the Minister to revoke this licence in relation to that part of the licensed area in consequence of any breach or non-observance, while the consent is in force or during the period to which the programme relates, of any provision of the said clause 17 in connection with a different part of the licensed area.

(9) Where in consequence of any breach or non-observance by the Licensee of any provision of clause 17 of this licence the Minister has power by virtue of paragraph (1) of clause 42 of this licence to revoke this licence or, in consequence of paragraph (8) of this clause, to revoke it in respect of part only of the licensed area, he may if he thinks fit -

(a) in a case where he has power to revoke this licence, exercise the power in relation to such part only of the licensed area as he may specify; and

(b) in a case where by virtue of the said paragraph (8) he has power to revoke it in respect of part only of the licensed area, exercise the power in relation to such portion only of that part as he may specify;

and where in consequence of the said paragraph (8) or by virtue of the preceding provisions of this paragraph the Minister revokes this licence in respect of a part or portion of the licensed area, the rights granted by this licence shall cease in respect of that part or portion without prejudice to any obligation or liability imposed upon the Licensee or incurred by him under the terms of this licence.

Commencement and abandonment and plugging of wells

19. - (1) The Licensee shall not commence or, after abandoning in manner hereinafter provided shall not recommence, the drilling of any well without the consent in writing of the Minister.

(2) The Licensee shall not abandon any well without the consent in writing of the Minister.

(3) The Licensee shall ensure compliance with any conditions subject to which any consent under either of the foregoing paragraphs is given.

(4) If any such condition under paragraph (1) of this clause relates to the position, depth or direction of the well, or to any casing of the well or if any condition under either paragraph (1) or paragraph (2) of this clause relates to any plugging or sealing of the well, the Minister may from time to time direct that the well and all records relating thereto shall be examined in such manner upon such occasions or at such intervals and by such person as may be specified by the Minister's direction and the Licensee shall pay to any such person or to the Minister such fees and expenses for such examination as the Minister may specify.

(5) The plugging of any well shall be done in accordance with a specification approved by the Minister applicable to that well or to wells generally or to a class of wells to which that well belongs and shall be carried out in an efficient and workmanlike manner.

(6) Any well drilled by the Licensee pursuant to this licence, which, at the expiry or determination of the Licensee's rights in respect of the area or part thereof in which that well is drilled, has not with the consent of the Minister been abandoned, shall be left in good order and fit for further working together with all casings and any well head fixtures the removal whereof would cause damage to such well or if the Minister so directs in manner provided by paragraph (8) of this clause be plugged and sealed in accordance with the Minister's direction.

(7) All casings and fixtures left in position pursuant to the last foregoing paragraph shall be the property of the Minister.

(8) In any case to which paragraph (6) of this clause applies, a direction by the Minister may be given by notice in writing to the Licensee not less than one month before the Licensee's rights in respect of the area or part thereof in which the well is situate expire or determine specifying the manner in which the well is to be plugged and sealed and the time within which such work is to be done.

Distance of wells from boundaries of licensed area

20. No well shall except with the consent in writing of the Minister be drilled or made so that any part thereof is less than one hundred and twenty-five metres from any of the boundaries of the licensed area.

Control of development wells

21. - (1) The Licensee shall not suspend work on the drilling of a development well, or having suspended it in accordance with this paragraph shall not begin it again, except with the consent in writing of the Minister and in accordance with the conditions, if any, subject to which the consent is given.

(2) When work on the drilling of a development well is suspended in accordance with paragraph (1) of this clause, the Licensee shall forthwith furnish the Minister with such information relating to the well as the Minister may specify.

(3) The Licensee -

(a) shall not do any completion work in respect of a well in the licensed area except in accordance with a programme of completion work approved by the Minister in respect of the well;

(b) shall furnish to the Minister, in accordance with the provisions of such a programme, particulars of any completion work done by him in respect of a well in the licensed area; and

(c) shall not remove or alter any casing or equipment installed by way of completion work in respect of a well except with the consent in writing of the Minister and in accordance with the conditions, if any, subject to which the consent is given.

(4) In this clause -

"completion work", in relation to a well, means work, by way of the installation of a casing or equipment or otherwise after the well has been drilled, for the purpose of bringing the well into use as a development well; and
"development well" means a well which the Licensee uses or intends to use in connection with the getting of petroleum in the licensed area, other than a well which for the time being he uses or intends to use only for searching for petroleum.

Provision of storage tanks, pipes, pipe-lines or other receptacles

22. The Licensee shall use methods and practice customarily used in good oilfield practice for confining the petroleum obtained from the licensed area in tanks, gasholders, pipes, pipe-lines or other receptacles constructed for that purpose.

Avoidance of harmful methods of working

23. - (1) The Licensee shall maintain all apparatus and appliances and all wells in the licensed area which have not been abandoned and plugged as provided by clause 19 of this licence in good repair and condition and shall execute all operations in or in connection with the licensed area in a proper and workmanlike manner in accordance with methods and practice customarily used in good oilfield practice and without prejudice to the generality of the foregoing provision the Licensee shall take all steps practicable in order -

(a) to control the flow and to prevent the escape or waste of petroleum discovered in or obtained from the licensed area;

(b) to conserve the licensed area for productive operations;

(c) to prevent damage to adjoining petroleum bearing strata;

(d) to prevent the entrance of water through wells to petroleum bearing strata except for the purposes of secondary recovery; and

(e) to prevent the escape of petroleum into any waters in or in the vicinity of the licensed area.

(2) The Licensee shall comply with any instructions from time to time given by the Minister in writing relating to any of the matters set out in the foregoing paragraph. If the Licensee objects to any such instruction on the ground that it is unreasonable he may, within fourteen days from the date upon which the same was given, refer the matter to arbitration in manner provided by clause 43 of this licence.

(3) Notwithstanding anything in the preceding provisions of this clause, the Licensee shall not -

(a) flare any gas from the licensed area; or

(b) use gas for the purpose of creating or increasing the pressure by means of which petroleum is obtained from that area,

except with the consent in writing of the Minister and in accordance with the condition, if any, of the consent.

(4) An application for consent in pursuance of paragraph (3) of this clause must be made in writing to the Minister and must specify the date on which the Licensee proposes to begin the flaring or use in question; and subject to paragraph (5) of this clause that date must not be before the expiration of the period of two years beginning with the date when the Minister receives the application.

(5) If the Minister gives notice in writing to the Licensee stating that, in consequence of plans made by the Licensee which the Minister considers are reasonable, the Minister will entertain an application for consent in pursuance of paragraph (3) of this clause which specifies a date after the expiration of a period mentioned in the notice which is shorter than the period mentioned in paragraph (4) of this clause, an application made in consequence of the notice may specify, as the date on which the applicant proposes to begin the flaring or use in question, a date after the expiration of that shorter period.

(6) Before deciding to withhold consent or to grant it subject to conditions in pursuance of paragraph (3) of this clause, the Minister shall give the Licensee an opportunity of making representations in writing to the Minister about the technical and financial factors which the Licensee considers are relevant in connection with the case and shall consider any such representations then made to him by the Licensee.

(7) Consent in pursuance of paragraph (3) of this clause shall not be required for any flaring which, in consequence of an event which the Licensee did not foresee in time to deal with it otherwise than by flaring, is necessary in order -

(a) to remove or reduce the risk of injury to persons in the vicinity of the well in question; or

(b) to maintain a flow of petroleum from that or any other well;

but when the Licensee does any flaring which is necessary as aforesaid he shall forthwith inform the Minister that he has done it and shall, in the case of flaring to maintain a flow of petroleum, stop the flaring upon being directed by the Minister to stop it.

(8) The Licensee shall give notice to the Minister of any event causing escape or waste of petroleum, damage to petroleum bearing strata or entrance of water through wells to petroleum bearing strata except for the purposes of secondary recovery forthwith after the occurrence of that event and shall, forthwith after the occurrence of any event causing escape of petroleum into the sea, give notice of the event to the Chief Inspector of Her Majesty's Coastguard.

(9) The Licensee shall comply with any reasonable instructions from time to time given by the Minister with a view to ensuring that funds are available to discharge any liability for damage attributable to the release or escape of petroleum in the course of activities connected with the exercise of rights granted by this licence; but where the Minister proposes to give such instructions he shall before giving them -

(a) give the Licensee particulars of the proposal and an opportunity of making representations to the Minister about the proposal; and

(b) consider any representations then made to him by the Licensee about the proposal.

Appointment of operators

24. - (1) The Licensee shall ensure that another person (including, in the case where the Licensee is two or more persons, any of those persons) does not exercise any function of organising or supervising all or any of the operations of searching or boring for or getting petroleum in pursuance of this licence unless that other person is a person approved in writing by the Minister and the function in question is one to which that approval relates.

(2) The Minister shall not refuse to give his approval of a person in pursuance of paragraph (1) of this clause if that person is competent to exercise the function in question; but where an approved person is no longer competent to exercise that function the Minister may, by notice in writing given to the Licensee, revoke his approval.

Fishing and navigation

25. The Licensee shall not carry out any operations authorised by this licence in or about the licensed area in such manner as to interfere unjustifiably with navigation or fishing in the waters of the licensed area or with the conservation of the living resources of the sea.

OFFSHORE PETROLEUM DEVELOPMENT (SCOTLAND) ACT 1975

An Act to provide for the acquisition by the Secretary of State of land in Scotland for purposes relating to exploration for and exploitation of offshore petroleum; to enable the Secretary of State to carry out works and facilitate operations for those purposes; to regulate such operations in certain sea areas; to provide for the reinstatement of land used for those purposes; and for purposes connected with those matters.

[13th March 1975]

ACQUISITION OF LAND FOR PURPOSES OF OFFSHORE PETROLEUM DEVELOPMENT

1 ACQUISITION OF LAND FOR PURPOSES CONNECTED WITH OFFSHORE PETROLEUM

(1)The Secretary of State may acquire by agreement or compulsorily any land in Scotland for any purpose relating to exploration for or exploitation of offshore petroleum [F1or the storage of gas in or under the sea bed or the recovery of gas so stored].
(2)The purposes mentioned in subsection (1) above include in particular the provision or use of—
(a)sites or facilities for the construction or assembly of platforms or other installations for use in or under the sea in connection with the exploration for or exploitation of such petroleum [F2or the storage of gas in or under the sea bed or the recovery of gas so stored];
(b)pipe-lines or associated apparatus or works for conveying such petroleum from places under the sea where it is extracted [F3or conveying gas to or from the places in or under the sea bed where it is stored or to be stored];
(c)shore terminals for the reception of such petroleum and for its storage or onward despatch [F4or for the reception of gas and for its storage or onward despatch to or from the places in or under the sea bed where it is stored or to be stored and any treatment incidental thereto]; and
(d)means of access, housing, sources of material or other services or facilities required for the development or use of land for any purpose referred to in this subsection, or for meeting the needs of persons employed or to be employed in connection with any such purpose.
(3)The purposes for which land may be acquired under this Act shall not include the refining of crude petroleum, except so far as is necessary for its onward despatch.
(4)Except in the case of a purchase of land under subsection (5) below, the M1Acquisition of Land (Authorisation Procedure) (Scotland) Act 1947 shall apply to a compulsory purchase of land by the Secretary of State under this section as it applies to a compulsory purchase of land by a Minister in a case falling within section 1(1) of that Act.
(5)If it appears to the Secretary of State that any land should be acquired under this Act for a purpose mentioned in subsection (2) above as a matter of urgency, he may, instead of being authorised to purchase the land by a compulsory purchase order under the said Act of 1947, be authorised to purchase it by an order made by him under this subsection.
An order made under this subsection is in this Act referred to as an "expedited acquisition order".
(6)A statutory instrument containing an expedited acquisition order shall not be made unless a draft of it has been laid before, and approved by resolution of, each House of Parliament.
(7)Any such statutory instrument on the expiry of 28 days from the laying of the draft thereof in a House of Parliament shall, whether or not it has been referred to a Committee of that House as aftermentioned, proceed in that House as if its provisions would, apart from this Act, require to be enacted by a public Bill which cannot be referred to a Committee under Standing Orders of that House relating to private Bills.
(8)Schedule 1 to this Act shall have effect as respects the making and revocation of expedited acquisition orders; and any such order shall have effect as provided in Schedule 2 to this Act.
(9)An expedited acquisition order shall not be made in respect of any land unless the Secretary of State is satisfied that the land is required for a purpose—
(a)which is in accordance with planning permission in force at the making of the order, granted on an application made under [F5Part III of the Town and Country Planning (Scotland) Act 1997] or under any enactment replaced by that Part; or
(b)which is in accordance with such permission in force as aforesaid, granted by a general development order under [F5section 30] of that Act or under any enactment replaced by that section; or
(c)which does not involve development for the purposes of that Act.

ANNOTATIONS:

Amendments (Textual)

F1Words inserted by Oil and Gas (Enterprise) Act 1982 (c. 23, SIF 86), s. 26(1)(*a*)
F2Words inserted by Oil and Gas (Enterprise) Act 1982 (c. 23, SIF 86), s. 26(1)(*b*)
F3Words inserted by Oil and Gas (Enterprise) Act 1982 (c. 23, SIF 86), s. 26(1)(*c*)

F4Words inserted by Oil and Gas (Enterprise) Act 1982 (c. 23, SIF 86), s. 26(1)(*d*)
F5Words in s. 1(9)(a)(b) substituted (27.5.1997) by 1997 c. 11, ss. 4, 6(2), Sch. 2 para. 24(1)

2 EXTINCTION OF RIGHTS AFFECTING LAND

(1)[F1Section 194 of the Town and Country Planning (Scotland) Act 1997] (extinction of rights over land compulsorily acquired under [F1Part VIII] of that Act) shall apply—
(a)upon the completion by the Secretary of State of a compulsory acquisition of land under this Act by means of a compulsory purchase order;
(b)upon his taking possession of land under this Act by means of an expedited acquisition order, as that section applies upon the completion by an acquiring authority of a compulsory acquisition of land under [F1Part VIII] of that Act.
(2)The provisions of [F1the Town and Country Planning (Scotland) Act 1997] mentioned in subsection (3) below shall apply in relation to—
(a)any land of which possession has been taken under this Act and any other land, being Crown land, which is used or is intended to be used for any purpose referred to in section 1(1) of this Act; and
(b)any relevant operations on that land either by or on behalf of the Secretary of State or any other person,
as they apply in relation to the land, operations and works referred to respectively in those provisions; and accordingly, for the purposes of such application, references in [F1section 196 of the said Act of 1997] to a planning authority shall be construed as references to the Secretary of State.
(3)The provisions referred to in subsection (2) above are—
(a)[F1section 196 of the said Act of 1997] (power to override servitudes and other rights);
(b)[F1section 197] of that Act (provisions as to churches and burial grounds); and
(c)[F1section 198] of that Act (use and development of land for open spaces).
(4)The Secretary of State may by order direct that [F1 sections 224 and 227 of the said Act of 1997] (extinction of rights of way, and rights as to apparatus, of statutory undertakers) and [F1sections 232(2) and 233] of that Act so far as applicable for the purposes [F1of sections 224 and 227], shall apply, with such modifications as appear to him to be necessary, in relation to any such land as is mentioned in subsection (2)(*a*) above, as they apply in relation to land referred to in [F1the said section 224] which has been acquired by a Minister.
(5)The Secretary of State may by order extinguish any public rights of way or other public rights which in his opinion are hindering or would hinder any relevant operations carried on or proposed to be carried on, on any such land as is mentioned in subsection (2)(*a*) above, by or on behalf of the Secretary of State or any other person.
(6)An order under subsection (5) above shall, if the Secretary of State is satisfied that it should do so, provide for the creation of an alternative right of way for use as a replacement for any right of way which is extinguished by the order.
(7)In this section references to particular provisions of the said Act of 1972 shall be construed as including references to those provisions as applied in relation to the National Coal Board by regulations made under section 259 of that Act.

ANNOTATIONS:

Amendments (Textual)

F1Words in s. 2(1)(2)(3)(a)(b)(c)(4) substituted (27.5.1997) by 1997 c. 11, ss. 4, 6(2), Sch. 2 para. 24(2)(a)(b)(c)(d)

DESIGNATED SEA AREAS

3 DESIGNATED SEA AREAS

(1)If it appears to the Secretary of State that it is desirable, for the purpose of facilitating or controlling the execution of relevant operations in any part of the sea surrounding Scotland and which is within United Kingdom waters, that any of the provisions of sections 4 to 7 of this Act should apply in relation to that area, he may, after consulting such local authorities and such organisations representing the interests of fishermen as appear to him to be concerned, by an order made under this subsection, declare that part of the sea to be a designated sea area. An order made under this subsection is in this Act referred to as a "sea designation order".
(2)A statutory instrument containing an order made under this section shall be subject to annulment in pursuance of a resolution of either House of Parliament.
(3)Schedule 3 to this Act shall have effect as respects the making and revocation of sea designation orders.

ANNOTATIONS:

Modifications etc. (not altering text)

C1S. 3: power to transfer certain functions conferred (1.7.1999) by S.I. 1999/1750, arts. 1(1), 4, Sch. 3

4 LICENCES IN RELATION TO OPERATIONS IN DESIGNATED SEA AREAS

(1)No relevant operations shall be executed in a designated sea area unless the person responsible for the operations is authorised to execute them by a licence granted by the Secretary of State under this section.
(2)Subject to subsection (3) below, no other works shall be executed in a designated sea area unless the person responsible for the works is authorised to execute them by such a licence as aforesaid.

(3)Where a designated sea area includes any part of the area of a harbour authority, that authority shall remain entitled to grant any licence or permission for the execution of works in the designated sea area which they could have granted but for the passing of this Act, except to the extent that the said works are, in the opinion of the Secretary of State, relevant operations, and (except as aforesaid) in such a case no licence under this section shall be required; and the authority shall (except as aforesaid) remain entitled without such a licence to execute any works which they could have executed but for the passing of this Act.
(4)The Secretary of State, before granting a licence under this section for any relevant operations within the area of a harbour authority, shall consult with that authority.
(5)A harbour authority, before executing works or granting any licence or permission for executing works in any part of their area which is within a designated sea area, shall, to such extent as the Secretary of State may direct, consult with him.
(6)For the purposes of this section and sections 5 to 7 of this Act, the execution of operations or other works by the Secretary of State in terms of this Act shall be deemed to be licensed under this section, and any reference to a licence shall be construed accordingly; and the reference in subsection (4) above to granting a licence under this section for any relevant operations shall include a reference to executing such operations.

5 TERMS AND EFFECT, ETC. OF LICENCES UNDER S. 4

(1)A licence under section 4 of this Act may be granted subject to conditions relating to the conduct of the operations or works subject thereto; and the said conditions may include conditions in respect of any relevant operations (whether or not within the designated sea area to which the licence relates) which are related to the operations or works which are the subject of the licence.

(2)A licence granted in respect of relevant operations in terms of section 4(1) of this Act shall supersede any inconsistent provision in any local enactment or in any byelaw or licence made or granted (whether before or after the granting of the licence first mentioned) by a local authority, harbour authority or other public authority; . . . F1
(3)Subject to subsection (4) below, a licence granted in respect of relevant operations in terms of section 4(1) of this Act shall have the effect that no action shall lie in respect of any interference with any public or private rights of navigation or fishery or other public or private rights in the sea or sea bed in the designated sea area to which the licence relates, arising from operations carried on in accordance with the licence.
(4)Where a private right is interfered with under the authority of subsection (3) above, the person to whom the licence has been granted shall be liable to pay compensation for any resulting loss or damage suffered by the person entitled to the right; and any question of disputed compensation under this subsection shall be referred to and determined by the Lands Tribunal for Scotland.
(5)Any person responsible for operations or works requiring a licence under section 4 of this Act who executes such operations or works without such a licence, and any holder of such a licence who contravenes a condition imposed under subsection (1) above, shall be guilty of an offence, and shall be liable—
(a)on conviction on indictment, to a fine;
(b)on summary conviction, to a fine not exceeding £5,000;
and if the contravention consists in failing to execute any operations or works the Secretary of State may execute them and recover the cost of doing so from the person in default.
(6)The Secretary of State may charge, for the issue of a licence under section 4 of this Act, such fee as he may with the approval of the Treasury determine.
(7)A licence granted under section 4 of this Act may at any time be varied or revoked by the Secretary of State.

ANNOTATIONS:

Amendments (Textual)

F1Words repealed by Ports (Finance) Act 1985 (c. 30, SIF 58), s. 6(2), Sch.

6 REGULATIONS FOR PROTECTION AND CONTROL OF OPERATIONS IN DESIGNATED SEA AREAS

(1)The Secretary of State may make regulations with respect to designated sea areas, and such regulations may include provisions with respect to—
(a)the regulation and protection of relevant operations and other works executed in a designated sea area in accordance with a licence granted under section 4 of this Act;
(b)the prohibition or restriction of entry into or into any part of any such area, and the control and protection of navigation there;
(c)the organisation or control of pilotage in any such area;
(d)the protection of fishing in any such area;
(e)the safety of persons in any such area;
(f)the prevention of pollution and nuisance in any such area;
(g)the levying by the Secretary of State of charges on vessels, platforms and other installations located in or entering or leaving any such area;
(h)enabling the Secretary of State to regulate, for the purposes of this subsection, the activities of any persons and the movement of any vehicles or vessels in any such area;
and such regulations may apply to one or more designated sea areas and may make different provision in respect of different designated sea areas or parts thereof.
(2)Before making, varying or revoking regulations under this section, the Secretary of State shall consult any harbour authority . . . F1 whose area includes any part of a designated sea area to which the regulations relate.

(3)Regulations made under this section shall supersede any inconsistent provision in any local enactment or in any byelaw or licence made or granted (whether before or after the making of the regulations) by a local authority, harbour authority or other public authority.
(4)Any person who contravenes any regulation made under this section shall be guilty of an offence, and shall be liable—
(a)on conviction on indictment, to a fine;
(b)on summary conviction, to a fine not exceeding £5,000.

ANNOTATIONS:

Amendments (Textual)

F1Words repealed by Pilotage Act 1987 (c. 21, SIF 111), s. 32(4)(5), Sch. 2 para. 3, Sch. 3

7 EXECUTION AND ENFORCEMENT OF REGULATIONS, ETC. IN DESIGNATED SEA AREAS

(1)The power of the Secretary of State to enforce the conditions of licences granted under section 4 of this Act and to execute and enforce regulations made under section 6 of this Act may be exercised by him or his officers or servants, or may by order be delegated by him, in relation to any designated sea area, to any harbour authority or local authority designated by him.
(2)The power of the Secretary of State referred to in subsection (1) above shall include power, for the purposes of execution and enforcement as aforesaid, to operate any vehicle or vessel within designated sea areas, and to acquire the same for such purposes.
(3)For the purpose of executing or enforcing regulations made under section 6 of this Act, any officer or servant of the Secretary of State or of a harbour authority or local authority to whom the powers of the Secretary of State have been delegated under subsection (1) above may, if authorised to execute or enforce the said regulations,
(a)at any reasonable time board or enter any vessel, platform or other installation located in a designated sea area;
(b)if the person in charge of the said vessel, platform or other installation cannot be found or if he neglects or refuses to do anything reasonably required for the purpose of execution or enforcement of the said regulations, himself (at the expense of the owner) do anything reasonably required for that purpose, including the removal of any vessel.
(4)An order in terms of subsection (1) above may confer, upon the authority to whom the powers are delegated, jurisdiction to exercise those powers within any part of the designated sea area which is outside the area of the authority, but before making an order which confers jurisdiction as aforesaid to exercise powers in an area which includes any part of the area of a harbour authority, the Secretary of State shall consult with the said harbour authority.
(5)The Secretary of State may defray or contribute towards any expenses incurred by any authority in the exercise of the powers delegated to them under subsection (1) above.
(6)Proceedings against any person for an offence under section 5 or 6 of this Act may be taken, and the offence may for all incidental purposes be treated as having been committed, at any place in the United Kingdom where he is for the time being.

REINSTATEMENT OF LAND

8 REINSTATEMENT OF LAND HELD UNDER ACT

(1)If it appears to the Secretary of State that any land of which possession has been taken under this Act is no longer needed for the purposes of this Act, he shall, subject to subsection (2) below, reinstate it, or secure its reinstatement, to the condition in which it was before such possession was taken so far as in his opinion, after consulting such local authorities and such other bodies as appear to him to be concerned, is reasonably practicable.
(2)Subsection (1) above shall not apply where the Secretary of State is satisfied, after consulting as aforesaid, that the land—

(a)should be used for a purpose other than that for which it was formerly used as aforesaid; or
(b)should not for any other reason be reinstated as aforesaid;
and in a case within paragraph (*a*) above the Secretary of State may, if he thinks fit, carry out, or contribute to the cost of, works for making the land suitable for use for the proposed purpose.

9 Arrangements to ensure reinstatement of other land developed for purposes connected with offshore petroleum

(1)Where a planning authority grant planning permission for any development of land for the purpose of any relevant operation, not being land of which possession has been taken under this Act, and where the permission is granted subject to a condition requiring the carrying out of any works required for the reinstatement of land, the authority may require that, before the commencement of such development, arrangements satisfactory to them should be made for the purpose of ensuring that money is set aside or otherwise made available or guaranteed, under the control of the authority or otherwise, for payment of the cost of such reinstatement; and any such requirement shall have effect as if it were a further condition of the grant of planning permission, and shall be enforceable accordingly.
(2)No requirement under subsection (1) above may be imposed except with the approval of the Secretary of State.
(3)The Secretary of State may—
(a)direct the planning authority to impose a requirement under subsection (1) above in the case of any development to which that subsection applies;
(b)impose such a requirement in the case of any such development in respect of which the application for planning permission has been referred to him under [F1section 46 of the Town and Country Planning (Scotland) Act 1997], and in such a case the said subsection (1) shall apply with the substitution for references to the planning authority of references to the Secretary of State.
(4)The Secretary of State may give directions with regard to the exercise of the power conferred by this section and to the terms of arrangements thereunder, and such directions may either be given generally or may relate to a particular application or to applications of a class specified in the direction, and may make different provision in respect of different cases.

Annotations:

Amendments (Textual)

F1Words in s. 9(3)(b) substituted (27.5.1997) by 1997 c. 11, ss. 4, 6(2), Sch. 2 para. 24(3)

Miscellaneous and general

10 Execution of works and disposal of land held under Act

(1)The Secretary of State may, with the approval of the Treasury, carry out—
(a)on land of which possession has been taken under this Act; and
(b)on other land, by agreement with the persons interested therein,
works for any purpose for which land may be acquired under this Act and (in any designated sea area) works for facilitating the execution of relevant operations, and may, with the like approval, defray or contribute towards the cost of such works.
(2)The Secretary of State may dispose of the whole of his interest in any land, of which possession has been taken under this Act, to any body or person in order to enable them to provide any such housing, services or facilities as are required in terms of paragraph (*d*) of section 1(2) of this Act; but, save as aforesaid, the Secretary of State shall not dispose of the whole of his interest in any such land unless it appears to him—
(a)that the land is no longer needed for any purpose for which land may be acquired under this Act; and
(b)either that such steps have been taken as appear to him to be required for the purpose of reinstating the land in terms of subsection (1) of section 8 of this Act, or that, in terms of subsection (2) of that section, the said subsection (1) does not apply in relation to the land.
(3)[F1Scottish Enterprise, Highlands and Islands Enterprise] or any local authority may act as agent for the Secretary of State in the carrying out of any works under this section or under section 8 of this Act, and may provide other services for the Secretary of State in relation to his functions under this Act.

(4)The Secretary of State may defray or contribute towards any expenses incurred by [F2Scottish Enterprise, Highlands and Islands Enterprise] or by a local authority in relation to any functions performed by [F3it or]them under subsection (3) above.

ANNOTATIONS:

Amendments (Textual)

F1Words substituted by Enterprise and New Towns (Scotland) Act 1990 (c. 35, SIF 64), s. 38(1), Sch. 4 para. 5(a)
F2Words substituted by Enterprise and New Towns (Scotland) Act 1990 (c. 35, SIF 64), s. 38(1), Sch. 4 para. 5(b)
F3Words inserted by Enterprise and New Towns (Scotland) Act 1990 (c. 35, SIF 64), s. 38(1), Sch. 4 para. 5(b)

11 Loans and guarantees by Secretary of State for facilitating relevant operations

(1)The Secretary of State may, with the approval of the Treasury, make loans to any person for the purpose of enabling him or assisting him to make arrangements for the execution of relevant operations.
(2)The Secretary of State may, with the approval of the Treasury, guarantee the payment by any person of any sum payable by that person in respect of principal or interest under arrangements (whether by way of loan or otherwise) entered into by that person for the purpose of the execution of relevant operations.
(3)Any loan made under this section, and any sums issued in fulfilment of a guarantee given under this section, shall be paid out of money provided by Parliament, and shall be made or issued on such terms as to recovery by the Secretary of State of principal and interest and otherwise as the Secretary of State may with the approval of the Treasury determine.

12 Supplementary provisions as to acquisition and appropriation of land

(1)The power of the Secretary of State to acquire land compulsorily under this Act shall include power to acquire a servitude or other right over land by the creation of a new right.
(2)For the purpose of the acquisition of land by agreement by the Secretary of State under this Act, the Lands Clauses Acts (except the provisions relating to the acquisition of land otherwise than by agreement and the provisions relating to access to the special Act, and except sections 120 to 125 of the M1Lands Clauses Consolidation (Scotland) Act 1845) and section 6 and sections 70 to 78 of the M2Railways Clauses Consolidation (Scotland) Act 1845 as originally enacted and not as amended for certain purposes by section 15 of the M3Mines (Working Facilities and Support) Act 1923, shall be incorporated with section 1 of this Act, and in construing those Acts for the purposes of that section, that section shall be deemed to be the special Act and the Secretary of State to be the promoter of the undertaking or company, as the case may require.
(3)Where the Secretary of State holds land for a purpose other than a purpose for which land may be acquired under this Act, he may appropriate it for the latter purpose; and any reference in this Act to land of which possession has been taken under this Act includes a reference to land appropriated by him under this subsection.
(4)For the avoidance of doubt it is hereby declared that the power to purchase land by an expedited acquisition order is exercisable notwithstanding any enactment providing that the land is or may be declared to be inalienable.

13 Compensation for adjoining owners and exclusion of actions for nuisance

(1)Subject to subsection (2) below, the Secretary of State may by order direct that the provisions of Parts I and II of the M1Land Compensation (Scotland) Act 1973 (compensation for depreciation caused by, and mitigation of injurious effect of public works) shall apply, with such modifications as appear to him to be necessary, in relation to any relevant operations carried on or proposed to be carried on by or on behalf of the Secretary of State or any other person, as those provisions apply in relation to the use of public works.
(2)No action for nuisance shall lie in respect of operations in relation to which the provisions mentioned in subsection (1) above apply by virtue of an order under that subsection.

ANNOTATIONS:

Marginal Citations

M11973 c. 56.

14 POWER TO REQUIRE INFORMATION AS TO INTERESTS IN LAND

(1)For the purpose of enabling the Secretary of State to make any order or serve any notice which he is authorised or required by this Act to make or serve, he may require the occupier of any land and any person who either directly or indirectly receives rent in respect of any land to state in writing the nature of his interest therein and the name and address of any other person known to him as having an interest therein, whether as superior, owner, heritable creditor, lessee or otherwise.
(2)Any person who, having been required in pursuance of this section to give any information, fails to give that information shall be guilty of an offence and liable on summary conviction to a fine not exceeding [F1level 3 on the standard scale].
(3)Any person who, having been so required to give any information, knowingly makes any mis-statement in respect thereof shall be guilty of an offence and liable on summary conviction to a fine not exceeding £400 or on conviction on indictment to imprisonment for a term not exceeding two years or to a fine or both.

ANNOTATIONS:

Amendments (Textual)

F1Words substituted by virtue of Criminal Procedure (Scotland) Act 1975 (c. 21, SIF 39:1), ss. 289F, 289G

15 RIGHTS OF ENTRY

(1)Any person duly authorised in writing by the Secretary of State may, at any reasonable time, enter any land for the purpose of surveying it in connection with the exercise of the Secretary of State's powers under this Act to acquire land or for the purpose of affixing any notice which under this Act is required to be affixed thereon.
(2)[F1Sections 269(6) and 270 of the Town and Country Planning (Scotland) Act 1997], (ancillary provisions about rights of entry) shall apply in relation to this section as they apply in relation to [F1section 269].

ANNOTATIONS:

Amendments (Textual)

F1Words in s. 15(2) substituted (27.5.1997) by 1997 c. 11, ss. 4, 6(2), Sch. 2 para. 24(4)

16 APPLICATION TO CROWN LAND

(1)The power to acquire land under this Act may be exercised in relation to any private interest in Crown land.
(2)If the Secretary of State considers it expedient for the purpose of enabling him to acquire any private interest that may subsequently be shown to exist in any land, he may make a compulsory purchase order or expedited acquisition order in terms of this Act in respect of that land notwithstanding that there is or may be no interest in the land other than a Crown interest.
(3)An order made in respect of any land by virtue of subsection (2) above shall not affect any Crown interest in the land but—
(a)any general vesting declaration executed by the Secretary of State under [F1Schedule 15 to the Town and Country Planning (Scotland) Act 1997] in respect of the land shall have effect in relation to any private interest therein (whether or not ascertained when the declaration is executed);
(b)the Secretary of State shall be liable to pay, in respect of any such private interest in relation to which the declaration has effect, the like compensation and the like interest on the compensation agreed or awarded as he would have been required to pay if he had, at the time mentioned in subsection (4) below, taken possession under paragraph 3 of Schedule 2 to the M1Acquisition of Land (Authorisation Procedure) (Scotland) Act 1947.
(4)The time referred to in subsection (3)(*b*) above is, in the case of a declaration executed by virtue of a compulsory purchase order, the time when the interest vested in the Secretary of State by virtue of the declaration or entry was taken, whichever is the earlier, and, in the case of a declaration executed by virtue

of an expedited acquisition order, the time when the land vested in the Secretary of State or entry was taken, whichever is the earlier.
(5)Without prejudice to subsection (3) above, none of the provisions of this Act relating to Crown land shall be construed as prejudicing any Crown interest therein.
(6)In this section "private interest" means any interest other than a Crown interest.

ANNOTATIONS:

Amendments (Textual)

F1Words in s. 16(3)(a) substituted (27.5.1997) by 1997 c. 11, ss. 4, 6(2), Sch. 2 para. 24(5)

Marginal Citations

M11947 c. 42.

17 Financial provisions

(1)There shall be defrayed out of moneys provided by Parliament—
(a)any expenses incurred by the Secretary of State under this Act;
(b)any increase attributable to this Act in the sums payable out of money so provided under any other Act; and any sums received by the Secretary of State by virtue of this Act shall be paid into the Consolidated Fund.
(2)The aggregate of—
(a)expenditure of the Secretary of State under section 10 of this Act, plus
(b)loans by the Secretary of State under section 11 of this Act, plus
(c)liabilities of the Secretary of State under any guarantees given by him under the said section 11 (exclusive of any liability in respect of interest on a principal sum so guaranteed)
less any sums received by the Secretary of State—
(i)in respect of the recovery of expenditure incurred by him under the said section 10, and
(ii)by way of repayment of loans under the said section 11, and
(iii)by way of repayment of principal sums paid to meet guarantees under the said section 11,
shall not at any time exceed £40 million.

18 Savings

Nothing in this Act shall affect—
(a)the powers of the Crown Estate Commissioners;
(b)the powers of the Commissioners of Northern Lighthouses;
[F1(c)the M1Pilotage Act 1987;]
(d)Part II of the M2Coast Protection Act 1949 (safety of navigation);
(e)the M3Land Powers (Defence) Act 1958;
(f)the M4Pipe-lines Act 1962;
(g)the M5Mineral Workings (Offshore Installations) Act 1971;
(h). F2
(i)the M6Health and Safety at Work etc. Act 1974;
[F3(j)Part II of the Food and Environment Protection Act 1985,]
but this section shall not enable any person to execute any relevant operations requiring a licence under section 4 of this Act without obtaining such a licence.

ANNOTATIONS:

Amendments (Textual)

F1S. 18 para.(*c*) substituted by Pilotage Act 1987 (c. 21, SIF 111), s. 32(4)(5), Sch. 2 para. 1(3)(b)
F2S. 18 para.(*h*) repealed by Food and Environment Protection Act 1985 (c. 48, SIF 111), s. 15(5)(*a*)
F3S. 18 para.(*j*) added by Food and Environment Protection Act 1985 (c. 48, SIF 111), s. 15(5)(*b*)

Marginal Citations

M11987 c. 21.
M21949 c. 74.
M31958 c. 30.

M41962 c. 58.
M51971 c. 61.
M61974 c. 37.

19 Orders, etc

(1)The power to make any order or regulation under this Act shall be exercisable by statutory instrument.
(2)The power to make any order or direction under this Act includes power to vary or revoke a previous order or direction.
(3)Any order, regulation or direction made under this Act may contain such incidental, consequential and supplemental provisions as appear to the Secretary of State to be necessary or proper for giving full effect thereto.

20 Short title, interpretation and extent

(1)This Act may be cited as the Offshore Petroleum Development (Scotland) Act 1975.
(2)In this Act—

- "Crown land" means land in which there is a Crown interest;
- "Crown interest" means an estate or interest belonging to Her Majesty in right of the Crown or belonging to a government department or held in trust for Her Majesty for the purposes of a government department, and includes any estate or interest held in right of the Prince and Steward of Scotland;
- "designated sea area" has the meaning conferred by section 3(1) of this Act;
- "expedited acquisition order" means an order made under section 1(5) of this Act;
- "harbour authority" has the same meaning as in the M1Harbours Act 1964;
- [F1"installation"includes any floating structure or device maintained on a station by whatever means;]
- "land" includes the fore-shore and other land covered with water and (except where the context otherwise requires) any estate or interest in or right over land, and any other heritable estate;
- "local authority" means (before 16th May 1975) a county council or town council and (thereafter) any local authority within the meaning of the M2Local Government (Scotland) Act 1973;
- "offshore petroleum" means petroleum situated under any part of the sea bed;
- "petroleum" has the same meaning as in [F2 Part I of the Petroleum Act 1998];
- "relevant operations" means operations for any purpose for which land may be acquired under this Act, and operations for or in connection with the offshore construction, assembly and testing of platforms and other installations for use in or under the sea in connection with exploration for or exploitation of offshore petroleum [F3or the storage of gas in or under the sea bed or the recovery of gas so stored];
- . . . F4
- "the sea" includes any area submerged at mean high water springs, and also includes, so far as the tide flows at mean high water springs, an estuary or an arm of the sea and the waters of any channel, creek, bay or river;
- "the sea bed" includes its subsoil;
- "sea designation order" means an order made under section 3(1) of this Act; and
- "United Kingdom waters" means any part of the sea within the seaward limits of United Kingdom territorial waters.

(3)Except where the context otherwise requires, this Act shall apply in relation to any estate or interest in or right over the sea bed as it applies in relation to land, and the M3Acquisition of Land (Authorisation Procedure) (Scotland) Act 1947 and the compulsory purchase enactments specified in paragraph 1(2) of Schedule 2 to this Act shall apply accordingly.
(4)Except where the context otherwise requires, references in this Act to any enactment are references to that enactment as amended or extended by any other enactment.
(5)This Act (except section 7(6)) shall extend to Scotland only.

ANNOTATIONS:

Amendments (Textual)

F1Definition inserted by Oil and Gas (Enterprise) Act 1982 (c. 23, SIF 86), s. 26(2)(*a*)
F2S. 20(2): words in definition of "petroleum" substituted (15.2.1999) by 1998 c. 17, s. 50, Sch. 4 para. 6 (with Sch. 3 para. 5(1)); S.I. 1999/161, art. 2(1)
F3Words inserted by Oil and Gas (Enterprise) Act 1982 (c.23, SIF 86), s. 26(2)(*b*)
F4Definition repealed by Scottish Development Agency Act 1975 (c. 69), Sch. 5

Section 1.

SCHEDULE 1 MAKING AND REVOCATION OF EXPEDITED ACQUISITION ORDERS

1(1)Before making an expedited acquisition order the Secretary of State shall—
(a)serve on every owner, lessee and occupier of any of the land to be specified in the order; and
(b)publish in two successive weeks in one or more newspapers circulating in the locality in which that land is situated, in the London and Edinburgh Gazettes and, if any of the land is situated below the level of mean high water springs, in Lloyd's List,
a notice complying with this paragraph.
(2)Except where the order relates only to land below the level of mean high water springs, the Secretary of State shall also before making the order affix to a conspicuous object or objects on the land a notice or notices complying with this paragraph.
(3)Every notice under this paragraph shall—
(a)state that the Secretary of State is considering making the order;
(b)describe the land to which it relates; and
(c)state that representations in writing with respect to the proposed order may be made to the Secretary of State at a specified address and within a specified period, not ending earlier than 21 days from the date on which the notice is first published.
2(1)If any representations with respect to the proposed order are duly made the Secretary of State shall consider those representations; but the Secretary of State shall not be obliged to cause any inquiry to be held or afford to any person an opportunity of being heard.
(2)After considering any such representations, the Secretary of State may make the order either without modification or subject to such modifications as he thinks fit.
(3)If the order is made, the Secretary of State shall—
(a)serve a notice to that effect together with a copy of the order on every owner, lessee and occupier of any of the land which is the subject of the order; and
(b)publish and affix notices to that effect in the manner required by paragraphs 1(1)(*b*) and (2) above;
4If the Secretary of State decides not to make the order, he shall serve notices to that effect on the persons, and publish and affix such notices in the manner referred to respectively in paragraphs (*a*) and (*b*) of paragraph 3 above.
5(1)Subject to the provisions of this paragraph, the Secretary of State may by statutory instrument revoke the order and, if he does so, he shall serve notices to that effect on the persons, and publish and affix such notices in the manner referred to respectively in paragraphs (*a*) and (*b*) of paragraph 3 above.
(2)No order shall be revoked after possession is taken of the land under Schedule 2 to this Act.
6Section 5(3) of the M1Acquisition of Land (Authorisation Procedure) (Scotland) Act 1947 and paragraph 19 of Schedule 1 to that Act shall apply to the service of notices under this Schedule.

ANNOTATIONS:

Marginal Citations

M11947 c. 42.
7A certificate by the Secretary of State that all or any of the requirements of paragraphs 1 and 3 above have been complied with in respect of the order, and have been complied with before a specified date shall be conclusive evidence of those facts in any legal proceedings whether brought before or after the completion of the compulsory acquisition of the land specified in the order.
Section 1.

SCHEDULE 2EFFECT OF EXPEDITED ACQUISITION ORDERS

APPLICATION OF COMPULSORY PURCHASE ENACTMENTS

1(1)As from the date on which the order comes into operation the compulsory purchase enactments shall have effect—
(a)as if the Secretary of State had been authorised to acquire the land specified in the order by a compulsory purchase order coming into operation on that date; and
(b)as if the compulsory purchase of the land authorised by the order were a compulsory purchase to which the provisions of Schedule 1 to the M1Acquisition of Land (Authorisation Procedure) (Scotland) Act 1947 apply;
and references in the compulsory purchase enactments to a compulsory purchase order shall be construed accordingly.
(2)In sub-paragraph (1) above "the compulsory purchase enactments" means the Lands Clauses Acts and section 6 and sections 70 to 78 of the M2Railways Clauses Consolidation (Scotland) Act 1845, the M3Land Compensation (Scotland) Act 1963, [F1section 195 of the Town and Country Planning (Scotland) Act 1997 and Schedule 15] to that Act, and Parts III and IV of the M4Land Compensation (Scotland) Act 1973.
(3)In their application by virtue of this paragraph, sections 34(3)(*a*) and 36(6)(*a*) of the said Act of 1973 (material date for entitlement to disturbance payment or rehousing in case of compulsory acquisition under compulsory purchase order) shall have effect as if the references to the time of first publication of the notices there mentioned were references to the time of first publication of the notice required by paragraph 1(1)(*b*) of Schedule 1 to this Act.
(4)In their application to the purchase of land authorised by the order, sections 49 and 50 of the said Act of 1973 (notice to treat in respect of part of agricultural land) shall have effect as if the person mentioned in subsection (1) of section 49 included a person having an interest no greater than as tenant for a year or from year to year and as if subsection (3)(*a*) of that section were omitted.
(5)Paragraph 6 of Schedule 2 to the said Act of 1947 (which provides for the incorporation of certain provisions relating to minerals) shall have effect in relation to the order as if it were a compulsory purchase order made in accordance with the provisions of Schedule 1 to that Act.

ANNOTATIONS:

Amendments (Textual)

F1Words in Sch. 2 para. 1(2) substituted (27.5.1997) by 1997 c. 11, ss. 4, 6(2), Sch. 2 para. 24(6)(a)

Marginal Citations

M11947 c. 42.
M21845 c. 33.
M31963 c. 51.
M41973 c. 56.

POWER TO TAKE POSSESSION

2(1)The Secretary of State shall be entitled to enter on and take possession of the land specified in the order at any time after the expiration of the period of 14 days beginning with the date on which the order comes into operation.
(2)Sub-paragraph (1) above has effect notwithstanding sections 83 and 114 of the M1Lands Clauses Consolidation (Scotland) Act 1845 (compensation to be paid before entry) and paragraph 3 of Schedule 2 to the said Act of 1947 (notice before entry), but where the Secretary of State takes possession of land by virtue of this paragraph he shall be liable to pay the like compensation and the like interest on the compensation agreed or awarded, as he would have been required to pay if he had taken possession of the land under the said paragraph 3.
(3)Where the Secretary of State is authorised under this paragraph to enter on and take possession of land, and the owner or occupier of any of that land, or any other person, refuses to give up possession of it, then a copy of the order shall be sufficient warrant for the ejection of the person refusing to give up or hindering possession; and in such a case section 89 of the said Act of 1845 (proceedings in case of refusal to deliver possession of lands) shall not apply.

ANNOTATIONS:

Marginal Citations

M11845 c. 19.

DUTY TO ACQUIRE THE LAND IF POSSESSION IS TAKEN

3(1)As soon as may be after taking possession of any land under paragraph 2 above the Secretary of State shall either—
(a)serve notices to treat in respect of that land in accordance with section 17 of the said Act of 1845, or
(b)execute a general vesting declaration in respect of that land under [F1Schedule 15 to the Town and Country Planning (Scotland) Act 1997].
(2)Sub-paragraph (1)(*a*) above requires the service of a notice to treat on a person having an interest in the land no greater than as tenant for a year or from year to year as well as on persons having greater interests; and the power conferred by section 39 of the M1Land Compensation (Scotland) Act 1963 to withdraw a notice to treat shall not be exercisable in respect of any notice to treat served by the Secretary of State in respect of land specified in the order.
(3)The power to execute a general vesting declaration in respect of the land specified in the order shall not be exercisable by the Secretary of State until he has taken possession of the land; but the foregoing provision shall not apply where the land was included in the order by virtue of section 15(2) of this Act.

ANNOTATIONS:

Amendments (Textual)

F1Words in Sch. 2 para. 3(1)(b) substituted (27.5.1997) by 1997 c. 11, ss. 4, 6(2), Sch. 2 para. 24(6)(b)

Marginal Citations

M11963 c. 51.
4(1)In their application to a general vesting declaration executed by the Secretary of State in respect of land specified in the order, the provisions of [F1 Schedule 15 to the Town and Country Planning (Scotland) Act 1997] shall have effect with the following modifications.
(2)The following provisions of that Schedule shall be omitted—
(a)in paragraph 1(1) the words following "specified in the declaration";
(b)in paragraph 6 the words following "could have served such a notice";
(c)in paragraph 7 the words "together with the right to enter upon and take possession of it";
(d)in paragraph 18 the words following "paragraphs 6 to 8 above";
(e)paragraphs 2, 3, 5, 8, 14, 21, 22(*a*), 24, 26, 29, 30 and 38;
but the omission of paragraph 26 is without prejudice to the making by the Tribunal of any such determination as is mentioned in that paragraph.
(3)In paragraph 4 of that Schedule for the words following "shall serve" there shall be substituted the words "on every owner, lessee and occupier of any land specified in the declaration a notice specifying the land, stating the effect of the declaration, referring to the rights of objection to severance exercisable in respect of the declaration and inviting claims for compensation."
(4)For any reference in Part II of that Schedule to paragraphs 6 to 8, there shall be substituted a reference to paragraphs 6 and 7.
(5)For paragraph 20(2) of that Schedule there shall be substituted—
"(2)A notice of objection to severance served by any person shall not have effect if it is served more than twenty-eight days after the date on which he first had knowledge of the execution of the general vesting declaration."
(6)In paragraph 23 of that Schedule for the words "sub-paragraph (*a*)" there shall be substituted the words "sub-paragraph (*b*)".

ANNOTATIONS:

Amendments (Textual)

F1Words in Sch. 2 para. 4(1) substituted (27.5.1997) by 1997 c. 11, ss. 4, 6(2), Sch. 2 para. 24(6)(c)

SCHEDULE 3 MAKING AND REVOCATION OF SEA DESIGNATION ORDERS

1Before making a sea designation order the Secretary of State shall publish in two successive weeks in one or more local newspapers circulating in the localities near to the designated area and in such other newspapers as he thinks appropriate, in the London and Edinburgh Gazettes and in Lloyd's List a notice—
(a)stating that the Secretary of State is considering making the order;
(b)describing the parts of the sea to which it relates; and
(c)stating that representations in writing with respect to the proposed order may be made to the Secretary of State at a specified address and within a specified period, not ending earlier than 21 days from the date on which the notice is first published.
2(1)If any representations with respect to the proposed order are duly made the Secretary of State shall consider those representations; but the Secretary of State shall not be obliged to cause any inquiry to be held or afford to any person an opportunity of being heard.
(2)After considering any such representations, the Secretary of State may make the order either without modification or subject to such modifications as he thinks fit.
3If the Secretary of State decides to make the order he shall publish a notice to that effect in the manner required by paragraph 1 above.
4If the Secretary of State decides not to make the order he shall publish a notice to that effect in the manner required by paragraph 1 above.
5(1)The Secretary of State may by statutory instrument revoke the order and, if he does so, he shall publish a notice to that effect in the manner required by paragraph 1 above.
(2)The revocation of the order shall not affect any licence or regulation previously granted or made under section 4 or 6 of this Act in relation to the area to which the order relates.

SCHEDULE 3 MAKING AND REVOCATION OF SEA DESIGNATION ORDERS

1Before making a sea designation order the Secretary of State shall publish in two successive weeks in one or more local newspapers circulating in the localities near to the designated area and in such other newspapers as he thinks appropriate, in the London and Edinburgh Gazettes and in Lloyd's List a notice—
(a)stating that the Secretary of State is considering making the order;
(b)describing the parts of the sea to which it relates; and
(c)stating that representations in writing with respect to the proposed order may be made to the Secretary of State at a specified address and within a specified period, not ending earlier than 21 days from the date on which the notice is first published.
2(1)If any representations with respect to the proposed order are duly made the Secretary of State shall consider those representations; but the Secretary of State shall not be obliged to cause any inquiry to be held or afford to any person an opportunity of being heard.
(2)After considering any such representations, the Secretary of State may make the order either without modification or subject to such modifications as he thinks fit.
3If the Secretary of State decides to make the order he shall publish a notice to that effect in the manner required by paragraph 1 above.
4If the Secretary of State decides not to make the order he shall publish a notice to that effect in the manner required by paragraph 1 above.
5(1)The Secretary of State may by statutory instrument revoke the order and, if he does so, he shall publish a notice to that effect in the manner required by paragraph 1 above.
(2)The revocation of the order shall not affect any licence or regulation previously granted or made under section 4 or 6 of this Act in relation to the area to which the order relates.

THE CONTINENTAL SHELF ACT 1964

An Act to make provision as to the exploration and exploitation of the continental shelf; to enable effect to be given to certain provisions of the Convention on the High Seas done in Geneva on 29th April 1958; and for matters connected with those purposes.

[15th April 1964]

Commencement Information

I1Act wholly in force at Royal Assent.

1 EXPLORATION AND EXPLOITATION OF CONTINENTAL SHELF

(1)Any rights exercisable by the United Kingdom outside territorial waters with respect to the sea bed and subsoil and their natural resources, except so far as they are exercisable in relation to coal, are hereby vested in Her Majesty.

(6)The general duty of [F5the Secretary of State] of securing the effective and co-ordinated development of such resources in Great Britain as are mentioned in section 1(1) of the M1Ministry of Fuel and Power Act 1945 shall extend to any such resources outside Great Britain with respect to which the said rights are exercisable.

(7)Her Majesty may from time to time by Order in Council designate any area as an area within which the rights mentioned in subsection (1) of this section are exercisable, and any area so designated is in this Act referred to as a designated area [F6; and the power to make Orders under this subsection shall include power to revoke Orders for the purpose of consolidating them.]

(8)In this section "coal" has the same meaning as in the M2Coal Industry Nationalisation Act 1946 F7. . ..

Amendments (Textual)

F1S. 1(2) repealed (31.10.1994) by 1994 c. 21, s. 67, Sch. 11 Pt. II (with ss. 40(7), 66); S.I. 1994/2553, art. 2

F2S. 1(3) repealed (15.2.1999) by 1998 c. 17, ss. 50, 51, Sch. 4 para. 2(2), Sch. 5 Pt. I (with Sch. 3 para. 5(1)); S.I. 1999/161, art. 2(1)

F3S. 1(4) repealed (E.W.S.)(30.11.1993) by Offshore Safety Act 1992 (c. 15), ss. 3(1)(a), 7(2), Sch. 2; S.I. 1993/2406, art. 2

F4S. 2(5) repealed by Petroleum Act 1987 (c. 12, SIF 86), ss. 20, 30, Sch. 3

F5Words substituted by virtue of S.I. 1969/1498, arts. 2(1), 5(6) and 1970/1537, arts. 2(2), 7(4).

F6Words inserted by Oil and Gas (Enterprise) Act 1982 (c. 23, SIF 86), s. 37, Sch. 3 para. 1

F7Words in s. 1(8) repealed (15.2.1999) by 1998 c. 17, ss. 50, 51, Sch. 4 para. 2(2), Sch. 5 Pt. I (with Sch. 3 para. 5(1)); S.I. 1999/161, art. 2(1)

Amendments (Textual)

F1S. 2 repealed and superseded by Oil and Gas (Enterprise) Act 1982 (c. 23, SIF 86), s. 21(11), Sch. 4

Amendments (Textual)

F1S. 3 repealed and superseded by Oil and Gas (Enterprise) Act 1982 (c. 23, SIF 86), s. 22(8), Sch. 4

4 SAFETY OF NAVIGATION

(1)Part II of the M1Coast Protection Act 1949 (which requires the consent of [F1the Board of Trade] to the carrying out of certain works on the sea shore if obstruction or danger to navigation is likely to result) except section 34(1)(*b*) (which restricts the deposit of materials) shall apply in relation to any part of the sea bed in a designated area as it applies in relation to the sea shore; and section 46 of that Act (local inquiries) shall extend to any matter arising under this section.

(2)Any person guilty of an offence under the said Part II as applied by this section shall be liable, on summary conviction to a fine not exceeding one hundred pounds, and on conviction on indictment to a fine.

Amendments (Textual)

F1Words substituted by virtue of S.I. 1965/145, arts 2, 3(2), Sch. 1

Marginal Citations

M11949 c. 74.

Amendments (Textual)

F1S. 5 repealed by Prevention of Oil Pollution Act 1971 (c. 60), Sch.

6 WIRELESS TELEGRAPHY

An Order in Council under [F1section 11 of the Petroleum Act] may make provision for treating for the purposes of the M1Wireless Telegraphy Act 1949 [F2and the Wireless Telegraphy Act 1998 and any regulations made under either of those Acts] any installation in [F3waters to which that section applies and] with respect to which provision is made under that section and any waters within five hundred metres of such an installation as if they were situated in such part of the United Kingdom as may be specified in the Order.

Amendments (Textual)

F1Words in s. 6 substituted (15.2.1999) by 1998 c. 17, s. 50, Sch. 4 para. 2(3) (with Sch. 3 para. 5(1)); S.I. 1999/161, art. 2(1)
F2Words in s. 6 substituted (18.6.1998) by 1998 c. 6, ss. 7, 10(2), Sch. 1 para. 3
F3Words substituted by Telecommunications Act 1984 (c. 12, SIF 96), s. 107(2)

7 RADIOACTIVE SUBSTANCES

An Order in Council under [F1section 11 of the Petroleum Act 1998] may make provision for treating for the purposes of the [F2Radioactive Substances Act 1993] and any orders and regulations made thereunder any installation in an area or part with respect to which provision is made under that section and any waters within five hundred metres of such an installation as if they were situated in such part of the United Kingdom as may be specified in the Order, and for modifying the provisions of that Act in their application to such an installation or waters.

Amendments (Textual)

F1Words in s. 7 substituted (15.2.1999) by 1998 c. 17, s. 50, Sch. 4 para. 2(3); S.I. 1999/161, art. 2(1) (with Sch. 3 para. 5(1))
F2Words in s. 7 substituted (27.8.1993) by 1993 c. 12, ss. 49(1), 51(2), Sch. 4 para. 1

8 SUBMARINE CABLES AND PIPE-LINES

(1)Section 3 (punishment for damaging cables) of the M1Submarine Telegraph Act 1885 and Article IV and paragraph 1 of Article VII (liability to pay compensation for damage to cables and for loss of gear sacrificed to avoid such damage) of the Convention set out in the Schedule to that Act (which by virtue of section 2 thereof has the force of law) shall apply in relation to all submarine cables under the high seas (and not only to those to which that Convention applies) and to pipe-lines under the high seas; and the said section 3 shall be construed as referring to telephonic as well as telegraphic communication, and, in relation to high-voltage power cables and to pipe-lines, as if the words from "in such manner" to the end of subsection (1) were omitted.
[F1(1A)It is hereby declared that the reference in subsection (1) of this section to pipe-lines under the high seas includes pipe-lines under the territorial sea adjacent to the United Kingdom.]
(2). F2

Amendments (Textual)

F1S. 8(1A) inserted (15.2.1999) by 1998 c. 17, s. 50, Sch. 4 para, 2(4) (with Sch. 3 para. 5(1)); S.I. 1999/161, art. 2(1)
F2S. 8(2) repealed by Statute Law (Repeals) Act 1974 (c. 22), Sch. Pt XI

Modifications etc. (not altering text)

C1S. 8(1) explained by Petroleum and Submarine Pipe-lines Act 1975 (c. 74), s. 45(1)

ANNOTATIONS:

Amendments (Textual)

F1S. 9 repealed by Energy Act 1976 (c. 76), s. 22, Sch. 4 Pt. I

Amendments (Textual)

F1S. 10 repealed by Statute Law Revision (Consequential Repeals) Act 1965 (c. 55)

11 PROSECUTION OF OFFENCES, ETC

(1)Proceedings for any offence [F1under another Act as applied by or under this Act] may be taken, and the offence may for all incidental purposes be treated as having been committed, in any place in the United Kingdom.

(2)Where a body corporate is guilty of such an offence and the offence is proved to have been committed with the consent or connivance of, or to be attributable to any neglect on the part of, any director, manager, secretary or other similar officer of the body corporate or any person who was purporting to act in any such capacity he, as well as the body corporate, shall be guilty of the offence and shall be liable to be proceeded against and punished accordingly.
In this subsection, "director" in relation to a body corporate established for the purpose of carrying on under national ownership any industry or part of an industry or undertaking, being a body corporate whose affairs are managed by its members, means a member of that body corporate.

Amendments (Textual)

F1Words substituted by Oil and Gas (Enterprise) Act 1982 (c. 23, SIF 96), s. 37, Sch. 3 para. 3
F2S. 11(3) repealed by Oil and Gas (Enterprise) Act 1982 (c. 23, SIF 86), s. 37, Sch. 4

In this Act "installation" includes any floating structure or device maintained on a station by whatever means.]

THE PETROLEUM ROYALTIES (RELIEF) AND CONTINENTAL SHELF ACT 1989 (C. 1)

An Act to confer on holders of certain petroleum licences an exemption from royalties (including royalties in kind) in respect of petroleum from certain onshore and offshore fields and to confer power to amend the Continental Shelf (Designation of Additional Areas) Order 1974 to give effect to an Agreement made between Her Majesty's Government in the United Kingdom and the Government of the Republic of Ireland relating to their respective rights in relation to the continental shelf.

[7th February 1989]

Be it enacted by the Queen's most Excellent Majesty, by and with the advice and consent of the Lords Spiritual and Temporal, and Commons, in this present Parliament assembled, and by the authority of the same, as follows:—

PETROLEUM ROYALTIES RELIEF

1 ROYALTY EXEMPTION FOR PETROLEUM FROM CERTAIN SOUTHERN BASIN AND LANDWARD AREAS

(1) Petroleum won and saved from any relevant Southern Basin or onshore field or relevant onshore area shall be disregarded in determining whether any and, if so, what—
(a) payments of royalty; and
(b) deliveries of petroleum,
are to be made in relation to chargeable periods ending after 30th June 1988 as consideration for the grant of a licence to which this section applies.
(2) This section applies to any licence granted under section 2 of the [1934 c. 36.] Petroleum (Production) Act 1934 which incorporates all or any of—
(a) the model clauses listed in Part I of the Schedule to this Act (model clauses for production licences for seaward areas); or
(b) the model clauses listed in Part II of the Schedule to this Act (model clauses for production licences, appraisal licences and development licences for landward areas),
including, in the case of any licence which incorporates all or any of the model clauses set out in Schedule 4 or 5 to the 1984 Regulations or in Schedule 4 to the 1988 Regulations, any licence granted after the passing of this Act.
(3) For the purposes of this section—

(a) "relevant Southern Basin or onshore field" means an oil field (within the meaning of Part I of the [1975 c. 22.] Oil Taxation Act 1975) other than one—
(i) which is a relevant new field for the purposes of section 36 of the [1983 c. 28.] Finance Act 1983 (allowance for fields in seaward areas other than the North Sea Southern Basin having no development consent granted or development programme served or approved before 1st April 1982); or
(ii) for any part of which consent for development was granted to the licensee by the Secretary of State before 1st April 1982; or
(iii) for any part of which a programme of development was served on the licensee or approved by the Secretary of State before that date;
(b) "relevant onshore area" means any onshore area for which a licence has been granted under section 2 of the [1934 c. 36.] Petroleum (Production) Act 1934 which incorporates all or any of the model clauses listed in Part II of the Schedule to this Act other than so much of such a licensed area as is or forms part of an onshore field (within the meaning of the definition in paragraph (a) above disregarding the exclusions);
and "onshore" has the same meaning as "landward" (in the expression "landward areas") in the regulations specified in Part II of the Schedule to this Act and "petroleum" has the same meaning as in the said Act of 1934.
(4) In determining, in accordance with paragraph (a) of subsection (3) above, whether an oil field (in this subsection referred to as "the field in question") is a relevant Southern Basin or onshore field, no account shall be taken of a consent for development granted before 1st April 1982 or a programme of development served on the licensee or approved by the Secretary of State before that date if—
(a) in whole or in part that consent or programme related to another oil field for which a determination under Schedule 1 to the Oil Taxation Act 1975 was made before the determination under that Schedule for the field in question; and
(b) on or after 1st April 1982, a consent for development is or was granted or a programme of development is or was served on the licensee or approved by the Secretary of State and that consent or programme relates, in whole or in part, to the field in question.
(5) In subsections (3) and (4) above "development" means—
(a) the erection or carrying out of permanent works for the purpose of getting oil from the field or area, as the case may be, or for the purpose of conveying oil won from it to a place on land; or
(b) winning oil from the field or area, as the case may be, otherwise than in the course of searching for oil or drilling wells;
and consent for development does not include consent which is limited to the purpose of testing the characteristics of an oil-bearing area and does not relate to the erection or carrying out of permanent works.
(6) In subsection (5) above "permanent works" means any structures or other works whatsoever which are intended by the licensee to be permanent and are neither designed to be moved from place to place without major dismantling nor intended by the licensee to be used only for searching for oil.

2 EXTENSION OF ROYALTY EXEMPTION FOR PETROLEUM FROM CERTAIN NEW OFFSHORE FIELDS

Section 1 of the [1983 c. 59.] Petroleum Royalties (Relief) Act 1983 (royalty exemption for petroleum from certain new offshore fields) shall apply to any licence granted under section 2 of the [1934 c. 36.] Petroleum (Production) Act 1934 which incorporates all or any of the model clauses set out in Schedule 4 to the [S.I.1988/1213.] Petroleum (Production) (Seaward Areas) Regulations 1988 (production licences for seaward areas) as it applies to licences so granted which incorporate all or any of the model clauses specified in subsection (2) of that section, including any licence granted after the passing of this Act.

CONTINENTAL SHELF

3 POWER TO AMEND DESIGNATION ORDER RELATING TO CONTINENTAL SHELF BETWEEN THE UNITED KINGDOM AND THE REPUBLIC OF IRELAND

(1) This section applies in relation to the agreement made between Her Majesty's Government in the United Kingdom and the Government of the Republic of Ireland as to the respective rights of the United Kingdom and the Republic of Ireland in relation to the continental shelf adjacent to the two countries and signed at Dublin on behalf of those Governments on 7th November 1988.
(2) Her Majesty may, by Order in Council, make such provision amending the [S.I.1974/1489.] Continental Shelf (Designation of Additional Areas) Order 1974 made under section 1(7) of the [1964 c. 29.] Continental Shelf Act 1964 (designating an area to the west of Scotland) as appears to Her to be necessary to give effect to the said Agreement.

SCHEDULE LICENCES TO WHICH SECTION 1 APPLIES

PART I MODEL CLAUSES FOR PRODUCTION LICENCES FOR SEAWARD AREAS

The model clauses referred to in section 1(2)(a) are the following—
1 The model clauses set out in Part II of Schedule 2 to the [1975 c. 74.] Petroleum and Submarine Pipe-lines Act 1975.
2 The model clauses set out in Schedule 5 to the [S.I. 1976/1129.] Petroleum (Production) Regulations 1976, as originally made or as amended by the [S.I. 1978/929.] Petroleum (Production) (Amendment) Regulations 1978.
3 The model clauses set out in Schedule 5 to the said Regulations of 1976 as amended by the said Regulations of 1978 and by the [S.I. 1980/721.] Petroleum (Production) (Amendment) Regulations 1980.
4 The model clauses set out in Schedule 5 to the [S.I. 1982/1000.] Petroleum (Production) Regulations 1982 as originally made or as amended by section 18 of and Schedule 2 to the [1987 c. 12.] Petroleum Act 1987.
5 The model clauses set out in Schedule 4 to the [S.I. 1988/1213.] Petroleum (Production) (Seaward Areas) Regulations 1988.

PART II MODEL CLAUSES FOR PRODUCTION, APPRAISAL AND DEVELOPMENT LICENCES FOR LANDWARD AREAS

The model clauses referred to in section 1(2)(b) are the following—
1 The model clauses set out in Part II of Schedule 3 to the Petroleum and Submarine Pipe-lines Act 1975.
2 The model clauses set out in Schedule 4 to the Petroleum (Production) Regulations 1976.
3 The model clauses set out in Schedule 4 to the Petroleum (Production) Regulations 1982.
4 The model clauses set out in Schedule 4 to the [S.I.1984/1832.] Petroleum (Production) (Landward Areas) Regulations 1984 as originally made or as amended by section 18 of and Schedule 2 to the Petroleum Act 1987.
5 The model clauses set out in Schedule 5 to the said Regulations of 1984 as originally made or as amended by section 18 of and Schedule 2 to the Petroleum Act 1987.

SCHEDULE LICENCES TO WHICH SECTION 1 APPLIES

PART I MODEL CLAUSES FOR PRODUCTION LICENCES FOR SEAWARD AREAS

The model clauses referred to in section 1(2)(a) are the following—
1 The model clauses set out in Part II of Schedule 2 to the [1975 c. 74.] Petroleum and Submarine Pipe-lines Act 1975.
2 The model clauses set out in Schedule 5 to the [S.I. 1976/1129.] Petroleum (Production) Regulations 1976, as originally made or as amended by the [S.I. 1978/929.] Petroleum (Production) (Amendment) Regulations 1978.

3 The model clauses set out in Schedule 5 to the said Regulations of 1976 as amended by the said Regulations of 1978 and by the [S.I. 1980/721.] Petroleum (Production) (Amendment) Regulations 1980.
4 The model clauses set out in Schedule 5 to the [S.I. 1982/1000.] Petroleum (Production) Regulations 1982 as originally made or as amended by section 18 of and Schedule 2 to the [1987 c. 12.] Petroleum Act 1987.
5 The model clauses set out in Schedule 4 to the [S.I. 1988/1213.] Petroleum (Production) (Seaward Areas) Regulations 1988.

PART II MODEL CLAUSES FOR PRODUCTION, APPRAISAL AND DEVELOPMENT LICENCES FOR LANDWARD AREAS

The model clauses referred to in section 1(2)(b) are the following—
1 The model clauses set out in Part II of Schedule 3 to the Petroleum and Submarine Pipe-lines Act 1975.
2 The model clauses set out in Schedule 4 to the Petroleum (Production) Regulations 1976.
3 The model clauses set out in Schedule 4 to the Petroleum (Production) Regulations 1982.
4 The model clauses set out in Schedule 4 to the [S.I.1984/1832.] Petroleum (Production) (Landward Areas) Regulations 1984 as originally made or as amended by section 18 of and Schedule 2 to the Petroleum Act 1987.
5 The model clauses set out in Schedule 5 to the said Regulations of 1984 as originally made or as amended by section 18 of and Schedule 2 to the Petroleum Act 1987.

SUPPLEMENTARY

4 SHORT TITLE AND EXTENT

(1) This Act may be cited as the Petroleum Royalties (Relief) and Continental Shelf Act 1989.
(2) Sections 1 and 2 of this Act do not extend to Northern Ireland.

SUPPLEMENTS

UKCS OIL PRODUCTION

OFFSHORE OIL FIELDS

Field Name	1975 - 2002	2003	2004	2005	2006	2007	Sum:
ALBA	34,913,548	4,500,850	3,645,311	3,146,544	2,799,997	2,275,446	51,281,696
ALWYN NORTH	33,288,023	551,385	448,791	432,734	307,459	320,873	35,349,263
ANDREW	16,132,477	1,249,627	864,939	847,026	506,691	610,989	20,211,748
ANGUS	1,870,311	111,787	85,171	62,059	24,695	0	2,154,024
ARBROATH	16,244,123	533,028	588,665	497,449	362,835	341,553	18,567,654
ARDMORE		181,267	403,683	105,560			690,511
ARGYLL	9,876,816						9,876,816
ARKWRIGHT	1,752,752	255,305	202,421	107,211	91,689	163,936	2,573,314
AUK	17,700,986	366,298	308,104	218,893	230,484	128,610	18,953,375
BALMORAL	14,384,255	185,225	94,099	129,135	93,043	83,293	14,969,049
BANFF	3,851,341	665,145	432,182	330,447	263,422	343,758	5,886,295
BEATRICE	20,728,653	269,714	212,425	184,570	106,244	97,928	21,599,533
BEAULY	873,965	212,739	93,748	98,954	56,887	43,906	1,380,200
BEINN	1,889,678	74,911	60,614	32,150	37,271	24,760	2,119,384
BERYL	101,793,431	1,355,911	1,198,046	1,091,918	1,140,743	780,605	107,360,655
BIRCH	3,000,386	8,586	173,280	196,382	187,507	139,130	3,705,271
BITTERN	5,899,901	2,389,635	2,102,956	1,785,330	1,434,692	1,154,250	14,766,763
BLADON	568,873						568,873
BLAIR	25,486						25,486
BLAKE	3,048,000	1,732,530	1,564,839	1,245,269	1,173,252	1,059,920	9,823,810
BLANE						186,778	186,778
BLENHEIM	2,686,804						2,686,804
BRAE CENTRAL	5,928,445	226,683	206,086	379,293	260,996	172,078	7,173,580
BRAE EAST	15,246,663	268,589	208,776	166,421	135,576	92,448	16,118,474
BRAEMAR		45,882	244,708	239,167	196,183	165,855	891,795
BRAE NORTH	16,893,387	250,190	166,477	88,850	111,330	96,781	17,607,015
BRAE SOUTH	32,414,417	142,904	182,589	215,260	239,785	293,585	33,488,539
BRECHIN				140,822	160,695	110,237	411,754
BRENDA					0	493,330	493,330
BRENT	255,786,409	1,122,410	765,637	474,281	395,316	329,340	258,873,392
BRIMMOND	319,290	15,594	8,041	0	0	0	342,925
BRITANNIA	6,372,435	997,628	898,552	761,588	571,699	506,370	10 108,271
BROOM			479,593	1,248,030	919,504	702,465	3,349,591
BRUCE	14,786,996	1,211,516	743,826	637,586	453,734	355,882	18 189,539
BUCHAN	16,352,071	339,899	366,294	337,088	323,179	283,747	18 002,278
BUCKLAND	3,859,680	565,603	373,341	269,151	210,872	136,364	5,415,011

BUZZARD						7,261,893	7,261,893
CALEDONIA		405,687	244,125	115,611	43,468	17,981	826,872
CAPTAIN	15,495,544	2,974,238	3,580,008	2,643,555	2,362,636	2,781,775	29,837,757
CARNOUSTIE				19,892	4,917	3,459	28,269
CHANTER	542,720	1,951	4,207	2,223	39	31,662	582,802
CLAIR			0	690,647	1,298,657	1,525,421	3,514,725
CLAPHAM		0	416,200	367,234	251,746	238,273	1,273,453
CLAYMORE	71,295,683	1,268,189	1,394,066	1,236,716	1,201,459	1,101,314	77,497,427
CLYDE	16,995,823	296,818	287,209	275,701	224,214	163,934	18,243,700
COLUMBA B	649,084						649,084
COLUMBA BD	1,861,817	480,511	558,487	378,225	232,290	186,306	3,697,636
COLUMBA D	1,440,170						1,440,170
COLUMBA E	788,026	73,105	296,140	182,173	93,541	96,351	1,529,335
COOK	2,077,553	544,170	530,942	456,234	385,134	166,431	4,160,464
CORMORANT NORTH	52,332,748	923,197	659,022	668,649	627,676	534,672	55,745,963
CORMORANT SOUTH	26,575,321	394,756	171,234	179,242	348,022	164,228	27,832,803
CRAWFORD	541,342						541,342
CURLEW	4,453,170	211,715	179,107	218,554	243,018	170,634	5,476,197
CYRUS	2,974,992	141,500	118,960	115,227	29,737	55,312	3,435,729
DAUNTLESS	543,089						543,089
DEVERON	2,049,874	18,822	23,787	24,567	13,610	12,369	2,143,030
DON	2,064,003	1,608	0	0	0		2,065,611
DONAN	832,617						832,617
DONAN {MAERSK}						1,590,704	1,590,704
DOUGLAS	7,448,081	645,438	526,065	406,069	343,778	343,849	9,713,280
DOUGLAS WEST		205,239	99,534	92,650	25,536	0	422,958
DRAKE	1,357,599	74,619	46,631	22,648	33,406	10,313	1,545,215
DUART						67,217	67,217
DUNBAR	15,358,092	1,092,937	855,306	618,158	661,143	579,259	19,164,894
DUNCAN	2,267,368						2,267,368
DUNLIN	50,488,593	308,126	181,052	221,272	186,062	298,046	51,683,152
DUNLIN SOUTH WEST	1,204,939	53,766	32,862	49,983	47,564	40,682	1,429,797
DURWARD	906,790						906,790
EGRET	807,802	64,900	282,217	84,211	52,191	24,927	1,316,248
EIDER	14,407,521	170,379	132,941	120,366	121,926	79,508	15,032,640
ELGIN	6,120,348	4,502,177	3,621,552	3,060,531	2,667,565	2,482,239	22,454,412
ELLON	1,309,302	56,999	23,419	36,270	105,844	42,093	1,573,927
EMERALD	2,341,078						2,341,078
ENOCH						237,240	237,240
ERSKINE	3,569,632	816,290	665,167	514,082	358,317	166,245	6,089,733

ESMOND	0						0
EVEREST	2,414,155	244,894	207,228	163,591	116,507	105,084	3,251,460
EWT OFFSHORE	295,427						295,427
FARRAGON				89,704	887,709	625,905	1,603,318
FERGUS	1,434,101	59,983	74,576	48,414	46,269	37,822	1,701,164
FIFE	6,200,752	490,256	294,087	253,049	189,805	112,414	7,540,363
FLEMING	2,167,503	237,159	216,094	159,796	175,620	59,328	3,015,499
FLORA	1,598,627	139,420	124,278	89,203	56,505	33,417	2,041,451
FOINAVEN	22,569,987	4,085,304	3,521,409	2,966,505	2,915,323	2,883,342	38,941,870
FORBES	0						0
FORTIES	331,215,168	2,037,885	2,678,852	3,260,668	2,887,680	2,624,998	344,705,252
FRANKLIN	1,204,470	1,175,373	1,620,756	2,018,917	1,871,598	1,756,785	9,647,899
FULMAR	72,247,289	134,360	100,262	178,580	161,054	89,631	72,911,176
GADWALL				212,188	68,033	2,163	282,384
GALLEY	5,775,124	573,108	456,421	352,022	233,668	103,767	7,494,110
GANNET A	7,750,035	379,695	359,203	372,929	452,796	345,237	9,659,894
GANNET B	652,761	110,329	81,585	94,951	10,479	21,658	971,762
GANNET C	9,740,664	208,410	175,035	145,587	188,564	220,604	10,678,863
GANNET D	3,938,886	339,406	231,386	185,510	300,495	223,660	5,219,343
GANNET E	2,209,102	656,971	487,615	443,418	465,463	323,447	4,586,016
GANNET F	1,587,092	75,492	49,682	32,945	95,366	197,017	2,037,594
GANNET G	1,528,738	188,080	133,786	120,213	130,581	114,466	2,215,863
GLAMIS	2,460,230	13,639	8,812	588	299	9,726	2,493,293
GLENELG					242,082	396,438	638,520
GOLDENEYE			119,768	659,568	574,047	498,169	1,851,552
GOOSANDER					196,722	470,238	666,959
GORDON	0						0
GRANT	926,772	133,480	100,173	125,013	95,657	51,181	1,432,276
GRYPHON	12,426,500	456,281	573,939	944,609	872,319	692,795	15,966,444
GUILLEMOT A	3,205,195	343,985	333,615	294,262	238,108	114,736	4,529,901
GUILLEMOT NW	249,808	194,356	149,567	75,276	70,979	38,750	778,737
GUILLEMOT W	1,278,001	509,006	406,798	130,114	112,316	136,070	2,572,305
HALLEY	175,432	140,745	129,543	0	0	0	445,720
HAMISH	448,133	0	2,942	360	12	0	451,447
HANNAY	148,558	193,907	209,070	205,241	220,772	102,918	1,080,466
HARDING	25,425,223	2,536,200	2,023,853	1,625,906	1,302,822	1.031,644	33,945,648
HAWKINS	17,495	91,193	56,674	27,380	12,400	1.147	206,290
HEATHER {AND EXT}	15,561,303	182,550	116,727	128,941	102,594	76,664	16,168,779
HERON	7,377,282	677,905	326,108	349,301	284,304	207,069	9,221,968
HIGHLANDER	9,896,131	104,573	96,225	120,316	93,857	55,784	10,366,886
HOWE			64,687	456,431	188,377	237,908	947,402

HUDSON	11,554,450	709,475	613,409	473,888	387,383	459,239	14,197,844
HUTTON	26,367,008						26,367,008
HUTTON NORTH WEST	16,638,438	0					16,638,438
INNES	737,308						737,308
IONA	203,348	2,027	423	0	4,573	848	211,219
IVANHOE	9,298,517	185,804	100,482	63,834	63,490	44,638	9,756,764
JADE	507,100	845,054	759,736	701,188	546,350	320,130	3,679,558
JAMES			52,609	154,092	47,002	52,625	306,328
JANICE	4,802,078	574,298	494,910	245,949	327,527	134,007	6,578,770
JOANNE	4,993,199	243,168	152,011	130,993	149,006	178,389	5,846,766
JUDY	3,611,108	809,807	626,847	702,151	993,982	711,187	7,455,083
KEITH	504,724	132,443	105,559	106,036	77,560	70,781	997,103
KESTREL	272,083	326,065	161,367	166,026	91,882	75,108	1,092,532
KINGFISHER	4,800,190	402,710	256,973	269,988	224,897	178,972	6,133,730
KITTIWAKE	9,721,600	112,689	87,568	60,579	72,992	7,620	10,063,048
KYLE	954,585	328,063	192,791	236,069	179,323	193,362	2,084,193
LARCH	836,525	106,170	64,102	41,212	37,981	39,117	1,125,106
LEADON	1,128,591	577,908	425,463	328,824	107,557		2,568,343
LENNOX	7,181,970	1,572,616	1,236,346	904,967	870,774	538,684	12,305,356
LEVEN	823,668	51,861	156,288	80,579	34,715	6,615	1,153,726
LINNHE	98,853						98,853
LOMOND	1,673,065	147,360	150,275	116,865	112,425	79,393	2,279,382
LOYAL	4,133,342	893,095	679,955	491,229	472,213	306,666	6,976,500
LYELL	2,067,201	36,416	117,790	110,631	94,320	149,993	2,576,352
MACCULLOCH	8,220,698	1,408,685	1,318,265	1,091,599	791,485	533,396	13,364,127
MACHAR	7,599,056	433,404	686,353	631,702	877,299	521,482	10,749,295
MACLURE	263,732	475,042	514,033	569,748	526,838	312,042	2,661,436
MADOES	36,411	1,018,352	1,140,173	829,042	499,097	273,833	3,796,908
MAGNUS	98,026,000	1,852,183	1,745,226	1,584,561	1,527,595	1,059,883	105,795,449
MALLARD	1,771,171	156,597	68,539	69,603	292,852	286,151	2,644,913
MARNOCK	2,900,033	308,230	190,161	101,205	96,791	52,964	3,649,384
MAUREEN	29,923,754						29,923,754
MEDWIN	138,462	0	0	7,271	94,425	28,909	269,067
MERGANSER					4,084	164,713	168,797
MERLIN	3,102,252	276,404	96,267	114,902	66,448	83,609	3,739,882
MILLER	43,580,312	408,715	513,745	412,266	251,119	49,834	45,215,991
MIRREN	79,213	430,537	270,092	284,747	300,106	230,403	1,595,098
MOIRA	561,991						561,991
MONAN	919,866	25,973	31,226	7,765	0	204	985,033
MONTROSE	11,500,375	22,284	37,716	60,944	66,273	59,788	11,747,380
MUNGO	9,899,308	1,930,395	1,694,166	1,596,121	1,309,323	944,414	17,373,726
MURCHISON	37,935,674	338,294	266,917	256,098	254,162	230,576	39,281,721
NELSON	44,812,690	3,278,772	2,254,544	1,882,148	1,376,888	1,464,924	55,069,966

NESS	4,330,809	93,548	8,634	4,391	34,706	17,817	4,489,904
NETHAN			13,617	1,058	0	0	14,675
NEVIS	7,143,392	971,143	946,608	839,608	805,103	930,520	11,636,374
NICOL					0	69,303	69,303
NINIAN	151,815,162	1,448,491	1,237,973	1,191,636	1,297,185	1,159,205	158,149,652
ORION	933,443	172,116	149,726	201,086	317,633	240,019	2,014,023
OSPREY	11,566,900	116,089	147,878	171,462	211,491	114,091	12,327,910
OTTER	95,660	1,080,875	1,278,440	888,024	737,739	716,005	4,796,744
PELICAN	7,028,286	344,561	221,493	248,092	254,123	119,993	8,216,548
PENGUIN EAST		659,840	737,660	372,270	464,274	302,439	2,536,483
PENGUIN WEST		91,311	139,546	210,116	105,515	133,887	680,374
PETRONELLA	4,724,372	81,031	72,993	45,008	39,715	28,438	4,991,557
PICT				376,817	485,418	260,029	1,122,264
PIERCE	7,134,905	1,105,237	773,064	1,043,760	649,698	729,349	11,436,013
PIPER	132,935,550	670,053	566,657	551,788	412,902	414,646	135,551,597
PLAYFAIR			41,801	280,725	27,332	46,619	396,477
RENEE	1,061,911	44,690	40,712	25,938	4,869	30	1,178,151
RHUM				2,087	48,253	61,705	112,045
ROB ROY	13,805,502	104,396	105,107	90,853	95,080	51,877	14,252,815
ROSS	2,910,312	330,188	267,495	176,495	149,346	143,701	3,977,536
RUBIE	936,130	161,654	140,902	102,084	41,572	36,000	1,418,342
SALTIRE	11,259,710	166,493	108,526	126,767	136,455	79,978	11,877,929
SAXON						27,339	27,339
SCAPA	14,607,321	377,272	299,560	238,599	109,728	279,627	15,912,107
SCHIEHALLION	20,195,925	5,160,798	4,795,373	3,419,166	3,268,900	2,435,659	39,275,821
SCOTER		0	179,882	242,984	250,066	144,965	817,898
SCOTT	46,353,218	1,264,177	1,126,731	815,185	1,005,270	1,202,455	51,767,036
SEDGWICK	1,582,080						1,582,080
SEYMOUR		99,894	114,140	55,618	56,175	15,527	341,355
SHEARWATER	3,030,424	2,353,041	2,568,011	1,279,581	945,456	547,434	10,723,947
SKENE	335,476	259,327	191,892	112,516	89,586	73,949	1,062,747
SKUA	828,158	289,830	217,034	1,515	3	215	1,336,756
SOUTH MAGNUS	2,252,893	249,410	209,081	153,695	188,262	113,629	3,166,969
STAFFA	533,366						533,366
STATFJORD	73,878,370	612,923	897,018	783,148	600,292	522,984	77,294,735
STIRLING	296,907	24,988	14,997	27,423	30,778	25,810	420,903
STRATHSPEY	5,775,944	419,229	463,652	243,433	383,849	250,785	7,536,892
SYCAMORE		358,492	133,852	20,609	115,784	54,397	683,133
TARTAN	13,834,282	132,585	169,692	137,607	102,052	158,280	14,534,497
TEAL	6,525,099	289,340	222,496	149,912	799	23,916	7,211,561
TEAL SOUTH	777,524	77,320	32,144	0	29,765	1,599	918,351
TELFORD	7,518,221	853,319	628,180	433,755	376,809	281,555	10,091,839

TERN	33,674,648	1,043,219	779,563	600,428	505,568	491,495	37,094,922
THELMA	5,196,660	272,375	283,138	283,199	290,144	261,655	6,587,170
THISTLE	52,572,411	218,862	171,504	141,314	164,237	154,982	53,423,311
TIFFANY	8,515,531	128,850	109,078	121,244	170,129	144,616	9,189,449
TONI	6,368,279	518,896	257,681	217,722	201,935	144,597	7,709,109
TULLICH	253,970	646,265	451,620	353,782	320,004	511,149	2,536,789
TWEEDSMUIR						294,908	294,908
WEST BRAE	5,935,678	882,943	744,021	911,448	697,624	615,188	9,786,901
WOOD						1,120	1,120
Total Crude Oil From Offshore Fields	2,606,420,640	96,867,885	86,905,696	77,180,120	70,072,814	70,250,515	3,007,697,671

ONSHORE OIL FIELDS

Crude Oil Production Tonnes (M3*Reported Density) Per Year (UK Share)

Field Name	1975 - 2002	2003	2004	2005	2006	2007	Sum:
BROCKHAM	1,275	1,516	4,244	5,014	3,711	2,548	18,306
COLD HANWORTH	21,856	19,842	15,498	6,809	7,496	10,047	81,548
CROSBY WARREN	73,139	2,576	1,773	1,876	2,299	2,720	84,383
EAST GLENTWORTH	11,825	1,103	1,892	3,703	2,935	2,389	23,846
EWT ONSHORE	0	583	550				1,133
FARLEYS WOOD	28,892	206	191	42			29,331
FISKERTON AIRFIELD	48,620	0	0	0	0	0	48,620
GOODWORTH	13,248	1,901	1,675	1,567	1,414	1,323	21,127
HERRIARD	30,560	1,677	1,068	713	582	237	34,838
HORNDEAN	197,452	11,060	9,406	8,837	8,129	8,416	243,299
HUMBLY GROVE	688,097	12,680	14,608	15,082	8,808	5,936	745,211
KEDDINGTON	12,392	2,433	2,226	1,499	178	931	19,658
KIRKLINGTON	3,265	542	363	0	0	0	4,170
LIDSEY					0	0	0
LONG CLAWSON	105,012	8,948	9,035	8,968	7,452	7,584	146,999
MINING LICENCES	370,499	37,615	36,589	34,382	29,399	29,896	538,380
NETTLEHAM	186,105	3,646	3,216	2,163	2,141	2,139	199,410
NEWTON ON TRENT	3,253	0	0				3,253
PALMERS WOOD	345,405	10,955	7,486	6,677	4,406	4,079	379,009
REMPSTONE	25,734	736	684	232	600	1,266	29,253
SCAMPTON	3,975	408	131	749	726	899	6,887
SCAMPTON NORTH	188,982	8,910	9,424	8,054	7,361	7,139	229,870
SINGLETON	323,201	19,604	22,129	19,663	24,710	23,541	432,848
STAINTON	21,410	742	588	390	588	764	24,482

STOCKBRIDGE	801,664	35,779	38,136	34,200	41,812	26,489	978,080
STORRINGTON	61,125	20,593	19,593	10,120	11,180	7,828	130,439
WAREHAM	530,672	6,294	9,206	8,492	3,414	0	558,078
WELTON	1,995,714	58,339	53,925	54,490	45,735	40,566	2,248,770
WEST BECKINGHAM	16,145	966	1,047	901	810	870	20,739
WEST FIRSBY	154,987	4,241	5,757	6,175	5,065	4,235	180,460
WHISBY	24,396	5,154	9,337	7,073			45,959
WYTCH FARM	48,280,370	1,914,525	1,649,392	1,393,987	1,138,777	1,042,167	55,419,219
Total Crude Oil From Land Fields	54,569,266	2,193,575	1,929,168	1,641,856	1,359,729	1,234,010	62,927,604

GAS PRODUCTION

GROSS GAS PRODUCTION TO 2007 IN MILLION CUBIC METRES

	2003	2004	2005	2006	2007	Cumulative to end 2007
Alison	81	51	41	33	44	762
Alison KX	50	48	40	27	28	634
Amethyst East	392	191	351	345	379	14,123
Amethyst West	469	257	223	187	193	5,857
Anglia	225	163	136	99	100	5,301
Ann	98	74	58	110	53	2,715
Apollo	319	392	299	280	353	1,643
Arthur			858	661	539	2,058
Audrey	250	235	192	155	117	19,462
Bains	505	330	201	61	58	1,263
Baird	274	274	220	158	72	3,593
Barque	1,003	654	659	496	519	18,859
Barque South	0	0	0	0	0	16
Bell	389	124	0	152	230	3,515
Bessemer	128	101	38	48	50	5,323
Boulton	713	607	511	370	311	5,389
Boulton H		140	28	7	0	176
Boyle	456	349	240	172	117	1,476
Brigantine A	639	415	252	93	40	2,673
Brigantine B	166	157	138	59	40	1,561
Brigantine C	655	347	173	502	226	2,247
Brigantine D	5	28	0	35	21	90
Brown	0	0	3	32	37	229
Bure	15	2	0	3	4	1,989
Bure West	71	53	25	17	37	737
Caister Bunter	98	56	56	12	27	3,023
Caister Carboniferous	176	118	107	21	86	4,622
Calder		3	0	57	19	79
Callisto	69	53	31	24	38	1,333
Callisto North	40	7	9	5	4	268
Camelot Central & South	52	30	29	3	15	5,998

Camelot North	3	0	0	0	2	906
Carrack	75	1,220	1,098	616	823	3,833
Cavendish					274	274
Chiswick					92	92
CATS (1)	14,972	13,812	11,660	11,125	7,819	135,657
Clipper	409	247	357	268	108	12,026
Corvette	129	471	403	174	39	4,716
Cutter				293	343	636
Dalton	110	121	112	1	0	1,115
Davy	66	157	111	105	152	5,521
Davy East					93	93
Dawn	0	0	0	0	0	488
Delilah	34	0	0	172	68	675
Europa	220	148	115	115	77	1,719
Excalibur	269	224	181	147	123	5,941
FLAGS (2)	7,890	7,528	8,482	7,579	6,659	174,541
Fulmar (3)	0	0	0	0	0	14,654
Galahad	211	175	387	154	111	4,188
Galleon	1,336	1,539	1,227	864	721	16,659
Ganymede	285	229	217	145	111	7,405
Garrow					53	53
Gawain	345	141	114	98	78	6,044
Grove					215	215
Guinevere	96	79	69	42	30	2,616
Hamilton	1,833	1,370	1,174	1,068	864	15,807
Hamilton East	354	216	145	125	75	1,585
Hamilton North	566	428	327	292	248	5,617
Hawksley	610	290	73	0	0	1,462
Helvellyn		255	73	48	38	414
Hewett	593	475	399	343	287	121,032
Horne			246	325	337	908
Hoton	370	271	212	181	191	1,653
Hunter					15	15
Hyde	152	127	112	109	90	3,291
Indefatigable (4)	769	801	562	359	262	132,055
Indefatigable South West (4)	74	62	47	31	17	1,581
Johnston	387	461	327	272	114	5,515
Kelvin					157	157
Ketch	478	317	233	244	411	4,581
Kilmar				252	271	524
Lancelot	414	339	289	230	169	8,011
Leman	3,009	3,178	2,664	2,295	1,492	317,565
Lennox	77	440	730	766	935	2,947
Malory	305	259	219	204	168	3,330
Markham (5)	207	192	342	295	258	7,357
McAdam		514	578	926	465	2,482
Mercury	333	365	243	119	83	2,724
Miller (6)	163	174	144	51	3	16,529
Millom	927	801	606	536	329	5,444
Mimas					172	172

Minerva	577	576	406	317	277	2,153
Minke					133	133
Mordred	26	28	22	24	21	396
Morecambe North	2,594	2,118	1,396	1,215	917	28,911
Morecambe South	7,526	8,055	5,935	2,490	3,827	130 028
Munro			147	354	250	752
Murdoch	627	447	414	443	447	12,114
Murdochk	1,378	1,209	864	636	324	4,411
Neptune	1,301	1,168	922	661	551	9,779
Newsham	34	39	37	28	16	654
North Davy	225	141	71	20	5	974
NUGGETS	1,744	1,678	1,811	1,537	1,422	9,643
Orwell	389	278	214	171	105	8,591
Pickerill	208	142	199	141	102	11,845
Ravenspurn North	317	362	540	435	401	26,649
Ravenspurn South	465	370	409	329	324	15,846
Rose	206	227	165	94		
Rough (7)	0	0	0	0	0	4,812
SAGE (8)	15,707	14,827	13,227	11,910	11,570	170,141
Schooner	485	475	230	337	249	7,768
SEAL (9)	7,391	8,464	7,567	7,096	6,833	46,677
Sean East	36	7	16	7	0	2,230
Sean North & South	601	306	1,794	956	416	11,904
Sinope	0	3	0	0	0	372
Skiff	1,339	924	714	613	480	6,313
Tethys					221	221
St Fergus Frigg (Associated gas) (10)	9,719	7,501	7,474	7,996	7,833	157,107
Thames	53	43	27	43	10	6,808
Thurne					129	129
Trent	195	150	149	208	161	2,873
Tyne North	22	21	16	41	84	971
Tyne South	153	98	108	62	0	2,848
Valiant North	167	137	134	108	107	5,406
Valiant South	238	211	199	169	161	8,584
Valkyrie		210	596	464	227	1,498
Vampire	81	35	0	0	31	1,680
Vanguard	107	113	80	74	73	3,280
Victor	563	503	378	618	616	26,895
Viking B	872	912	708	677	512	83,861
Viscount	12	3	0	0	0	14
Vixen	558	242	234	138	103	3,580
Vulcan	497	423	358	317	271	16,990
Watt		16	0	0	0	16
Waveney	117	95	70	40	42	2 336
Wenlock					38	38
Wensum	0	1	0	0	0	53
West Sole	765	473	574	584	557	54,733
Whittle	397	481	422	308	281	1 889
Windermere (11)	125	87	45	41	37	2 006
Wren			138	283	396	818

Yare	39	9	0	22	15	1,888
Others (12)	4,503	4,513	4,274	4,454	4,646	85,272
Beaufort	0	0	0	0	0	1
Camelot North East	0	0	0	0	0	498
Cleeton	0	0	0	0	0	10,268
Deben	11	6	0	0	0	457
Esmond	0	0	0	0	0	8,866
Forbes	0	0	0	0	0	1,473
Frigg (13)	454	491	0	0	0	74,802
Gordon	0	0	0	0	0	3,994
Tristan	3	0	0	0	0	1,062
Welland North West	0	0	0	0	0	5,378
Welland South	0	0	0	0	0	2,283
Total Offshore	108,025	101,286	93,345	84,204	76,745	2,285,209
Total Onshore (14)	445	285	160	96	111	5,402
Total Production (15)	108,470	101,571	93,505	84,300	76,856	2,290,611
A) Net Production (16)	101,907	94,965	86,415	77,839	70,439	2,156,729
B) Own use and measurement differences (17)	6,564	6,607	7,090	6,461	6,416	133,883

1. Gas delivered to land via the Central Area Transmission System (CATS) from Andrew, Banff, Drake, Egret, Erskine, Everest, Faragon, Fleming, Hawkins, Heron, Jade, James, Janice, Joanne, Judy, Lomond, Machar, Madoes, Marnock, Mirren, Monan, Mungo, Seymour and Skua.
2. Gas delivered to land via the Far-north Liquids and Associated Gas System (FLAGS) from Brent, Clapham, Cormorant North and South, Goldeneye, Kyle, Magnus, Magnus South, Murchison (UK), Pelican, Penguin, Statfjord (UK), Strathspey and Thistle. With effect from 2000 gas previously shown separately as Fulmar is included in the FLAGS figure. Gas used offshore is included in Others (see footnote 12).
3. Gas delivered to land via the Fulmar pipeline from Bittern, Clyde, Cook, Curlew, Fulmar, Gannet A - G, Guillemot A, NW and W, Howe, Kittiwake, Leven, Mallard, Medwin, Nelson, Orion, Pict, Teal and Teal South. See footnote (2) regarding figures from 2000. Gas used offshore is included in Others (see footnote 12).
4. Separate data for Indefatigable South West is only available from October 1995.
5. UK share only. Exported to Netherlands.
6. Gas delivered to Boddam power station by dedicated pipeline.
7. Converted for use as an offshore storage unit from mid-1985.
8. Gas delivered to land via the Scottish Area Gas Evacuation (SAGE) system from Beinn, Beryl, Brae (Central, East, North, South, West), Braemar, Britannia, Caledonia, Enoch (UK), Maclure, Ness, Nevis, Scott, Skene, Thelma, Tiffany, Toni and Tullich.
9. Shearwater - Elgin Area Line (SEAL). Elgin, Franklin, Glenelg, Halley, Scoter, Shearwater.
10. Associated gas delivered to land via the Frigg (FUKA) pipeline from Alwyn North, Bruce, Captain, Dunbar, Ellon, Forvie, Galley, Grant, Ivanhoe, Keith, Piper, Renee, Rob Roy, Ross, Rubie, Tartan and Tweedsmuir.
11. Exported to Netherlands via Markham.
12. Associated gas, mainly methane, produced and used mainly on Northern Basin oil production platforms including those in the CATS, FLAGS (including the Fulmar system) SAGE, St Fergus (Associated gas) and SEAL systems.
13. UK share only.
14. Excluding colliery methane.
15. Gross production, ie includes own use for drilling, production and pumping operations, but excludes gas flared and vented. Will differ from gross production based on terminal receipts because of more accurate measurements at terminals.
16. Sales gas to the National Transmission System and others.
17. Own use, line losses, stock changes, statistical differences and, from 2001, gas used at dry gas terminals.

UK OIL AND GAS RESERVES

UK OIL RESERVES AND ESTIMATED ULTIMATE RECOVERY 2008

Key terms are defined as follows:

Term	Definition
Ultimate recovery	Total recovery from a field, i.e. reserves plus past production.
Reserves	Discovered, remaining reserves which are recoverable and commercial. Can be proven, probable or possible depending on confidence level (as described below).
Potential additional resources	Discovered reserves that are not currently technically or economically producible.
Undiscovered resources	Undiscovered potentially recoverable resources in mapped leads.

Reserves are categorised as being proven probable or possible based on confidence levels, as follows:

Reserves	Description
Proven	Reserves which on the available evidence are virtually certain to be technically and commercially producible, i.e. have a better than 90% chance of being produced.
Probable	Reserves which are not yet proven, but which are estimated to have a better than 50% chance of being technically and commercially producible.
Possible	Reserves which at present cannot be regarded as probable, but which are estimated to have a significant but less than 50% chance of being technically and commercially producible.

Reserves data were collected from each UKCS operator during January to March 2008. Oil reserves include both oil and the liquids obtained from gas fields. Oil reserves are summed in the Oil Table below at different probability levels to give a range of estimates from proven to the maximum level.

The oil reserves presented are in both sanctioned fields (i.e. fields in production or approved fields under development but not yet producing) and other significant discoveries not yet fully appraised. The latter comprise discoveries for which there is an intended field development and a provisional start date. Proven, probable and possible reserves for a large number of individual fields have simply been summed to give the totals shown. There is, thus, a much smaller likelihood that the true figure for total oil reserves is outside the range of estimates than when considering probabilities for an individual field.

Cumulative oil production to the end of 2007 has been added to oil reserves (remaining) to give the estimated ultimate recovery figures.

Reserves and Estimated Ultimate Recovery in the Oil Table are presented in metric units (million tonnes) to facilitate comparison with other energy resources and the inclusion of natural gas liquids. The figures in the table can be converted to "field units" using the approximate conversion factor of 1 tonne of crude oil = 7.5 barrels.

Estimates of UK Oil Reserves and Ultimate Recovery at 31 December 2007[1][2]

[figures in brackets for end 2006]

Oil Reserves units - million tonnes	Proven	Probable	Proven & Probable	Possible	Maximum[3]
Fields in production or under development[4]	452 [479]	233 [221]	685 [700]	297 [370]	982 [1070]
Other significant discoveries not fully appraised	0 [0]	95 [77]	95 [77]	101 [108]	197 [185]
Total Oil Reserves in million tonnes[4]	452 [479]	328 [298]	780 [776]	399 [478]	1179 [1254]
Cumulative Oil Production to end 2007[5]	3243 [3167]				
Estimated Ultimate Recovery in million tonnes	3695 [3645]	328 [298]	4023 [3943]	399 [478]	4422 [4421]

Notes on Oil Table

1. Includes onshore as well as offshore fields. All figures include condensate, gas liquids and liquefied products.
2. All entries are rounded to the nearest one million tonnes.
3. Maximum is the sum of proven, probable and possible reserves.
4. The oil reserves include 11 (70) proven, 12 (53) probable and 9 (57) possible million tonnes in approved fields under development but not yet producing.
5. Cumulative oil production includes 99 (99) million tonnes from decommissioned oil fields.

Note that there are also "Potential additional resources" in fields and drilled prospects for which there are no current plans for development. These are listed in a separate section on the website.

The chart shows how cumulative production and estimated ultimate recovery of oil have both grown over time and also that proven plus probable reserves have tended to decline since 1994 following a period of steady growth. However, the slight flattening of the curve beyond 2000 shows that the rate of reserves decline has lessened since 2000 as the rate of oil production has declined.

REVIEW OF UK OIL RESERVES

The change in UK oil reserves during 2007 arises from a combination of:

- production during the year;
- reserves additions from new field developments including those resulting from recent exploration success;
- reserves revisions in established fields.

Annual oil production was 77 million tonnes in 2007.
There was a net reallocation of 6 million tonnes from Potential Additional Resources and exploration to possible reserves and 6 million tonnes to probable reserves.

From the Oil Table it can be seen that the central estimate of oil reserves remaining based on proven plus probable reserves now stand at 780 million tonnes which is an increase of 4 million tonnes compared to last year. Taking annual oil production of 77 million tonnes into account this leaves a proven plus probable reserves replacement of 81 million tonnes.

Proven oil reserves (remaining) at the end of 2007 stand at 452 million tonnes, which is 27 million tonnes less than at the end of 2006. After accounting for production, there has been a net transfer of 50 million tonnes from probable to proven oil reserves. The main contributing factor to this was the reallocation of probable reserves into the proven category in some producing fields, although development approval during 2007 of several new oil fields including Curlew C, Duart and Saxon - and two new condensate fields - Jura and Starling also contributed.

Probable oil reserves have also increased from 298 to 328 million tonnes. The increase of 30 million tonnes in probable oil reserves reflects a large reallocation of possible reserves to probable reserves in the light of a number of successful appraisal wells during 2007.

Possible oil reserves have decreased by 79 million tonnes. The decrease in possible reserves reflects the reallocation of possible reserves to probable mentioned above, together with some further downward revisions in possible reserves in existing fields and the fact that the progression from Potential Additional Resources and exploration to possible reserves was less than that from possible to probable reserves.

Maximum oil reserves (remaining), combining proven plus probable plus possible reserves figures, have decreased by 75 million tonnes to 1,179 million tonnes.

REVIEW OF UK ESTIMATED ULTIMATE RECOVERY OF OIL

(i.e. Oil Reserves plus Cumulative Production)
Estimated ultimate recovery of oil has increased at all three levels this year. At the proven plus probable level, the estimated ultimate recovery of oil has increased by 80 million tonnes and now stands at 4,023 million tonnes. At the proven level it has increased by 50 million tonnes to 3,695 million tonnes. Maximum estimated ultimate recovery of oil, combining proven plus probable plus possible reserves figures, has increased by 1 million tonnes to 4,422 million tonnes. Cumulative oil production to the end of 2007 stood at 3,243 million tonnes.

UK GAS RESERVES AND ESTIMATED ULTIMATE RECOVERY 2008

Term	Definition
Ultimate recovery	Total recovery from a field, i.e. reserves plus past production.
Reserves	Discovered, remaining reserves which are recoverable and commercial. Can be proven, probable or possible depending on confidence level (as described below).
Potential additional resources	Discovered reserves that are not currently technically or economically producible.
Undiscovered resources	Undiscovered potentially recoverable resources in mapped leads.

Key terms are defined as follows:

Reserves are categorised as being proven probable or possible based on confidence levels, as follows:

Introduction

Reserves data were collected from each UKCS operator during January to March 2008. The gas reserves quoted comprise all the gas reserves expected to be available for sale from dry gas fields, gas condensate fields, oil fields with associated gas and a small amount from coal bed methane projects. Gas reserves are summed in the Gas Table below at different probability levels to give a range of estimates from proven to the maximum level.

The gas reserves presented are in both sanctioned fields (i.e. fields in production or approved fields under development but not yet producing) and other significant discoveries not yet fully appraised. The latter comprise discoveries for which there is an intended field development and a provisional start date. Proven, probable and possible reserves for a large number of individual fields have simply been summed to give the totals shown. There is, thus, a much smaller likelihood that the true figure for total gas reserves is outside the indicated range than when considering probability levels for an individual field.

Cumulative gas production to the end of 2007 has been added to gas reserves (remaining) to give the estimated ultimate recovery figures.

Reserves and Estimated Ultimate Recovery in the Gas Table are presented in units of billion standard cubic metres (bcm). Note that billion means thousand million {10 to the power 9]. The figures in the table can be converted to "field units" using the conversion factor of 1 bcm = 35.31 billion cubic feet (bcf).

Reserves	Description
Proven	Reserves which on the available evidence are virtually certain to be technically and commercially producible, i.e. have a better than 90% chance of being produced.
Probable	Reserves which are not yet proven, but which are estimated to have a better than 50% chance of being technically and commercially producible.
Possible	Reserves which at present cannot be regarded as probable, but which are estimated to have a significant but less than 50% chance of being technically and commercially producible.

Estimates of UK Gas Reserves and Ultimate Recovery at 31st December 2007[1][2]

[figures in brackets are for end 2006]

Gas Reserves units - billion cubic metres (bcm)	Proven	Probable	Proven & Probable	Possible	Maximum[3]
Gas from Dry Gas Fields					
Fields in production or under development					
Southern basin	101 [112]	42 [40]	143 [153]	36 [42]	179 [194]
Other areas	44 [54]	9 [12]	53 [66]	9 [15]	62 [81]
Subtotal	145 [166]	51 [53]	196 [219]	46 [56]	241 [276]
Other significant discoveries not yet fully appraised					
Southern basin	0 [0]	46 [27]	46 [27]	39 [19]	85 [46]
Other areas	0 [0]	3 [4]	3 [4]	2 [2]	5 [6]
Subtotal	0 [0]	49 [31]	49 [31]	41 [20]	90 [52]
Total Dry Gas	145 [166]	101 [84]	245 [250]	86 [77]	332 [327]
Gas From Condensate Fields					
Fields in production or under development	120 [101]	67 [47]	180 [208]	00 [10]	217 [201]
Other significant discoveries not yet fully appraised	0 [0]	83 [83]	83 [83]	69 [79]	152 [161]
Total Condensate Field Gas	129 [161]	140 [130]	269 [291]	129 [124]	398 [415]
Associated Gas from Oil Fields					
Fields in production or under development	69 [85]	46 [45]	114 [130]	55 [56]	169 [186]
Other significant discoveries not yet fully appraised	0 [0]	18 [13]	18 [13]	23 [26]	41 [39]
Total Associated Gas	69 [85]	64 [58]	132 [143]	78 [82]	210 [225]
Total Gas Reserves in bcm [4]	343 [412]	304 [272]	647 [684]	293 [283]	940 [967]
Cumulative dry gas production	**1436 [1404]**				
Cumulative condensate gas & associated gas production	**721 [682]**	**[Note: The cumulative gas production split figures for 2006 have been revised.]**			
Cumulative Gas Production to end 2007[5]	2157 [2086]				
Estimated Ultimate Recovery in bcm	2500 [2499]	304 [272]	2804 [2770]	293 [283]	3097 [3054]

Notes on Gas Table

1. Includes onshore as well as offshore discoveries but excludes flared gas and gas consumed in production operations.
2. All entries are rounded to the nearest one billion cubic metres.
3. Maximum is the sum of proven, probable and possible reserves.
4. The gas reserves include 5 (19) proven, 5 (15) probable and 1 (14) possible billion cubic metres in approved fields under development but not yet producing.
5. Cumulative gas production includes 108 (108) bcm from decommissioned gas fields.

Note that there are also "Potential Additional Resources" in fields and drilled prospects for which there are no current plans for development. These are listed in a separate section on the website.

The chart shows how reserves, cumulative production and estimated ultimate recovery of gas have changed over time. There has been a steady decline in proven plus probable reserves since 1994, associated with a higher rate of production.

Review of UK Gas Reserves

The change in UK gas reserves during 2007 arises from a combination of

- production during the year;
- reserves additions from new field developments including those resulting from recent exploration success;
- reserves revisions in established fields.

Annual gas production was 70 bcm in 2007.

There was a net reallocation of 18 bcm from Potential additional resources and exploration to possible reserves and 15 bcm to probable reserves.

From the Gas Table it can be seen that the central estimate of gas reserves remaining based on proven plus probable reserves now stand at 647 bcm which is a reduction of 37 bcm compared to last year. Taking annual gas production of 70 bcm into account this leaves a proven plus probable reserves replacement of 33 bcm.

Proven gas reserves (remaining) at the end of 2007 now stand at 343 bcm. This decrease of 69 bcm reflects the fact that the technical reallocation of probable reserves to proven reserves did not keep pace with production. However, amongst the gains to proven reserves was the development approval during 2007 of seven offshore dry gas fields - Caravel, Kelvin, Minke [UK], Shamrock, Tristan North West, Victoria and Wissey - and two gas condensate fields - Jura and Starling. The approval of several new oil fields including Curlew C and Saxon has also contributed to proven associated gas reserves.

Probable gas reserves have increased by 32 bcm. This was partly due to the upward revision of probable reserves in a number of fields but also reflects the fact that the reallocation of possible reserves to probable reserves has more than kept pace with that from probable to proven reserves.

Possible gas reserves have also increased by 10 bcm. This increase reflects upward revisions in a number of fields and the fact that the progression from Potential Additional Resources and exploration to possible reserves was greater than that from possible to probable reserves.
At the maximum level, gas reserves (remaining) based on proven plus probable plus possible reserves now stand at 647 bcm which is a reduction of 37 bcm compared to last year.

REVIEW OF UK ESTIMATED ULTIMATE RECOVERY OF GAS

(i.e. Gas Reserves plus Cumulative Production)
Estimated ultimate recovery of gas has increased at all three levels this year. At the proven plus probable level, the estimated ultimate recovery of gas has increased by 34 bcm and now stands at 2804 bcm. At the proven level it has increased by 1 bcm to 2,500 bcm. Maximum estimated ultimate recovery of gas, combining proven plus probable plus possible reserves, has increased by 43 bcm to 3,097 bcm.
Cumulative gas production to the end of 2007 stood at 2,157 bcm.

ESTIMATES OF POTENTIAL ADDITIONAL RESOURCES 2008

Key terms are defined as follows:

Potential additional resources exist in discoveries for which there are no current plans for development and which are not currently technically or commercially producible. These discoveries are not included in the estimates of Reserves which are listed in separate tables on the website. From January to March 2008, each UKCS field and undeveloped discovery was reviewed by DECC with the current operator to establish its reserves and status as at the end of 2007. A total of 678 separate fields or discoveries, both onshore and offshore, were reviewed. The figures shown in the table below take account of all discoveries made up to the end of 2007 which do not or no longer justify inclusion in the Reserves category.

Potential Additional Resources as at end 2007 - [figures in brackets are for end 2006]

Note:

1. Totals are rounded to the nearest one million tonnes and one million barrels of oil or one billion cubic metres and one billion cubic feet of gas. The conversion factors used are 7.5 barrels/tonne for oil and 35.31 bcf/bcm for gas.
2. Central estimates are included in addition to the lower and upper range of Potential additional resources.
3. Billion cubic metres (bcm), billion cubic feet (bcf)

The ranges of Potential additional resources may vary from year to year. As additional data become available, some Potential additional resources are transferred to the Reserves category when possible development is considered. Similarly, reserves may be transferred from Reserves to Potential additional resources if there are no longer plans to develop a discovery.

High levels of activity on undeveloped discoveries have continued. New drilling activity has increased the oil resources estimates held. This is in addition to the discoveries transferred from Potential additional resources to the Reserves category as activity is planned which may lead to development. The upper range estimate for gas has decreased as some transfers to Reserves include discoveries with larger potential upside. Most of the new resources discovered in 2007 are classified in Reserves because they have an intended field development and a provisional start date.

CONTACT DETAILS FOR OPERATORS BEING OFFERED LICENCES IN THE 25TH ROUND

Operator	Contact	Address 1	Address2	Country	EMail
Antrim Resources (N.I.) Limited	Mr Michael Green	Ashbourne House, The Guildway, Old Portsmouth Road	Artington, Guildford Surrey GU3 1LR		m.green@antrimenergy.com
Apache North Sea Ltd	Mr James Crowley	Alba Gate, Stoneywood Park	Dyce, Aberdeen AB21 7DZ		james.crowley@apachecorp.com
ATP Oil & Gas (UK) Limited	Mr John Gill	Victoria House, London Square, Cross Lanes	Guildford, Surrey GU1 1UJ		jgill@atpog.com
BG International (CNS) Limited	Mr Tony Birse	100 Thames Valley Park Drive	Reading RG6 1PT		tony.birse@bg-group.com
Black Sapphire Resources Ltd	Mr Ian Anderson	4 Bear Street, Nayland	Colchester, Essex CO6 4HX		iander1574@aol.com, ian.anderson@bsr-oil.com

Bow Valley Petroleum (UK) Limited	Mr Nick Fairbrother	2 Thames Avenue	Windsor, Berkshire SL4 1QP		nfairbrother@bvenergy.com
BP Exploration Operating Company Ltd	Mr Simon Hendry	1 Wellheads Avenue	Dyce. Aberdeen AB21 7PB		simon.hendry@bp.com
CalEnergy Gas Limited	Mr Rob Youngs	Peer House, Ground Floor	8-14 Verulam Street LONDON WC1X 8LZ		rob.youngs@cegas.co.uk
Canamens Energy North Sea Limited	Mr Morton Heir	7th Floor, Tower House, Southampton Street, Covent Garden	London WC2E 7HA		morton.heir@canamens.com
Carrizo Oil and Gas, Inc.	Mr Gary Uhland	1000 Louisiana Street, Suite 1500	Houston, Texas 77002	USA	Gary.uhland@crzo.net
Centrica Resources Limited	Mr Jeremy Lockett	Millstream, Maidenhead Road	Windsor, Berkshire		jeremy.lockett@centrica.co.uk
Chrysaor Limited	Mr Robert Poddubiuk	1 Maddox Strett	London S1S 2PZ		robert.poddubiuk@chrysaor.co.uk
ConocoPhillips (UK) Ltd	Mr Gus MacLeod	Rubislaw House, Anderson Drive	Aberdeen AB15 6FZ		gus.macleod@conocophillips.com
Conoco (UK) Ltd	Mr Andrew Conway	Rubislaw House, Anderson Drive	Aberdeen AB15 6FZ		andy.Conway@conoco.com
Corsair Petroleum (24th Round) Limited	Mr Simon Gorringe	50 Broadway, St James Park	London SW1H 0RG		simon.gorringe@corsairpetroleum.com
Dana Petroleum (E&P) Limited	Dr Colin Percival	17 Carden Place	Aberdeen AB10 1UR		cpercival@dana-petroleum.com
Deliverit Energy	Mr Igor Morgunov	850, 1015-4th Street SW	Calgary, Alberta	Canada	ivor.morgunov@ch2m.com
DNO UK Limited	Mr Erik Syrdalen Watson	Stranden 1	0113 Oslo	Norway	erik.syrdalen@dno.no
DONG E&P (UK) Ltd	Mr Soren B. Andersen	24-26 Agern Alle	DK-2970 Horsholm	Denmark	sband@dongenergy.dk

E. On Ruhrgas UK E&P Ltd	Mr Mark Stockwell	4th Floor, 4 Millbank	London SW1P 3JA		mark.stockwell@eon-ruhrgas.co.uk
Elixir Petroleum (UK) Limited	Mr James Stockley	8 The Courtyard, Eastern Road	Bracknell Berkshire RG12 2XB		jstockley@elixirpetroleum.com
EnCore Petroleum Ltd	Mr Graham Dore	62-64 Baker Street	London W1U 7DF		graham@encoreoil.co.uk
Endeavour Energy UK Limited	Mr Jim Munns	114 St Martin's Lane	London WC2N 4BE		Jim.Munns@Endeavourcorp.com
EOG Resources UK Limited	Mr Olaf Karlsen	First Floor, Andrews House, College Road	Guildford, Surrey GU1 4QB		Olaf_karlsen@eogresources.com
Excelsior Energy Limited	Mr David A. Winter	1510, 734 - 7th Avenue S.W.	Calgary, Alberta T2P 3P8	Canada	d winter@excelsior-energy.com
Fairfield Cedrus Limited	Mr Jon Gluyas	Ash House, Fairfield Avenue	Staines, Middlesex TW18 4AB		jon.gluyas@fairfield-energy.com
First Oil Expro Limited	Mr Ross Cameron	1 Queens Terrace	Aberdeen AB10 1XL		r.cameron@firstoilexpro.com
Focus Energy	Mr Jeb Tyrie	111 Gallowgate	Aberdeen AB25 1BU		jeb@focusenergy.co.uk
Fox Energy Exploration Ltd	Mr Richard Moore	64 Knightsbridge	London SW1X7JF		rm@foxpetro.com
GDF Britain Ltd	Mr Andy Spencer	60 Grays Inn Road	London WC1X 8LU		andy.spencer@gdfbritain.com
Hannu Exploration Limited	Mr Doug Fenwick	Ground Floor, 1 Bell Court, Leapale Lane	Guildford, Surrey GU1 4LY		doug.fenwick@mpx-limited.com
Holywell Resources Limited	Mr Tim Howell	14 South Audley Street	LONDON W1K 1HN		info@holywellresources.com
Hurricane Exploration plc	Ms Claire Slightam	82, Anstey Road	Alton, Hampshire GU34 1RG		clare.slightam@hex-plc.com
Ithaca Energy (UK) Ltd	Mr Nick Muir	8 Rubislaw Terrace	Aberdeen AB10 1XE		nmuir@ithacaenergy.com
Lundin Heather Ltd	Mr Mike Cooper	Level 5 Consort House, Stell Road	Aberdeen AB11 5QR		mike.cooper@lundinbritain.com
Maersk Oil North Sea	Mr Kevin Flanagan	Maersk House, Crawpeel Road	Altens, Aberdeen		kflanagan@maerskoil.co.uk

UK Limited			AB12 3LG		
Mahona Energy Limited	Mr Scott Pollard	Little Hardings, Harding Lane	North Cheriton, Somerset BA8 0AJ		scott.pollard@mahona.com
Mariner Expro North Sea Limited	Mr Alastair Gordon	40 Springfield Road	Aberdeen AB15 7RR		alastairgordon@marinerexpro.com
MPX North Sea Limited	Mr Doug Fenwick	Ground Floor, 1 Bell Court, Leapale Lane	Guilford, Surrey GU1 4LY		doug.fenwick@mpx-limited.com
Nautical Petroleum Plc	Mr Steve Jenkins	Parnell House, 25 Wilton Road	London SW1V 1YD		s.jenkins@nauticalpetroleum.com
Nexen Petroleum UK Limited	Mr David Chang Kit	Charter Place, Vine Street	Uxbridge, Middlesex UB8 1JG		david_changkit@nexeninc.com
Norfolk Resources UK Limited	Ms Constance Uzwyshyn	28 Beaconsfield Road	St Albans AL1 3RB		constanceu@gmail.com
Oilexco North Sea Limited	Mr Arthur Millholland	3200, 715 - 5th Avenue SW	Calgary, AB T2P 2X6	Canada	amillholland@oilexco.com
Petro-Canada UK Limited	Mr Martin David	1 London Bridge	London SE1 9BG		martin.david@petro-canada.com
REAP UK Limited	Mr Mark Paton	Tyn-y-Coed, Llanrhos	Llandudno, Conwy LL30 1SA		markp@fugro-robertson.com
Revus Energy (E&P) Limited	Mr Ivan Inchenko	83 Baker Street	London W1U 6AG		ivan.inchenko@revus.no
Rocksource UK Limited	Mr Gregor Maxwell	Olav Kyrresgate 22	Bergen N-5014	Norway	gregor.maxwell@rocksource.com
RWE Dea UK SNS Ltd	Mr Adrian Coker	4th Floor, 90 High Holborn	London WC1V 6LJ		adrian.coker@rwedea.com
Sable Energy (UK) LTD	Mr Gerald Fuss	Suite 250, 703 6th Ave S.W.	Calgary, Alberta T2P 0T9	Canada	gfuss@sableenergy.com
Sagex Petroleum UK Ltd	Mr Steinar S. Johansen	Tordenskioldsgate 12	N-0160 Oslo	Norway	johansen@sagex.no
Serica Energy (UK)	Mr Ian Wilson	87-89 Baker Street	LONDON W1U 6RJ		ian.wilson@serica-energy.com

Limited					
Shell UK Ltd	Mr Chris Leigh	Shell UK Exploration and Production, 1 Altens Farm Road	Nigg, Aberdeen AB12 3FY		chris.leigh@shell.com
Silverstone CNS Limited	Mr Steve Horton	9 Albyn Terrace	Aberdeen AB10 1YP		steve.horton@silverstoneenergy.co.uk
Sterling Resources (UK) Limited	Mr Stewart Gibson	Banchory Business Centre, Burn O'Bennie Road	Banchory AB31 5ZU		stewart@sterling-resources.co.uk
Stratic Energy (UK) Limited	Mr Oliver Whitfield	130 Jermyn Street	London SW1Y 4UR		oliver.whitfield@straticenergy.com
Sussex Energy Limited	Mr Nigel Platt	4th Floor Global House, 1 Ashley Avenue	Epsom, Surrey KT18 5AD		nigelplatt@sussexenergy.com
Swift Exploration Ltd	Mr Stefan Stasiuk	27 Linkswood Road	Burnham SL1 8AS		stefan@swiftexploration.com
Talisman Energy (UK) Ltd	Mr Quentin Goodbody	Talisman House, 163 Holburn Street	Aberdeen AB10 7EB		qgoodbody@talisman.co.uk
TGS-NOPEC Geophysical Company (UK) Ltd	Mr Rob Atkinson	TGS, Graylaw House, 21-21A Goldington Road	Bedford MK40 3JY		rob.atkinson@tgsnopec.co.uk
Total E&P UK Limited	Mr Simon Green	Crawpeel Road, Altens Industrial Estate	Aberdeen AB12 3FG		Simon-c.green@total.com
Valiant Exploration Ltd	Mr Justin Morrison	Albion House, Chretsey Road	Woking, Surrey GU21 6BD		jmorrison@valiant-petroleum.com
Venture North Sea Gas Limited	Mr Steve Kemp	Kings Close, 62 Huntley Street	Aberdeen AB10 1RS		skemp@venture-production.com
Venture North Sea Oil Limited	Mr Michael Travis	Kings Close, 62 Huntley Street	Aberdeen AB10 1RS		mtravis@venture-production.com
Veritas Geophysical Limited	Mr Steve Toothill	Crompton Way, Manor Royal Estate	Crawley, West Sussex RH10 9QN		steve.toothill@veritasdgc.com
Volantis Exploration Limited	Mr Andy Mortimer	8 Square Rigger Row, Plantation Wharf	London SW11 3TZ		andy.mortimer@volantisexp.com

Zeus Petroleum Ltd	Mr Michael Rose	c/o Aimwell Energy Ltd, 10 Rosebery Avenue	Harpenden, Herts AL5 2QP		mikerose@aimwellenergy.com

WINNING MARKS BY BLOCK LIST ROUND: 25

Block	AP	Operator	MARKS
2/10a	153 P	Antrim Resources (N.I.) Limited	63
2/15b	153 P	Antrim Resources (N.I.) Limited	65
2/20	13 P	Silverstone CNS Limited	
3/3b	173 T	Ithaca Energy (UK) Ltd	175
3/8d	141 T	Fairfield Cedrus Limited	175
3/11a	48 T	Lundin Heather Ltd	150
3/16	13 P	Silverstone CNS Limited	
3/22	72 T	Nautical Petroleum Plc	
3/23b	162 P	Hannu Exploration Limited	
3/26	72 T	Nautical Petroleum Plc	
8/25b	134 P	Mariner Expro North Sea Limited	74
8/25b	73 T	Canamens Energy North Sea Limited	97
8/30	134 P	Mariner Expro North Sea Limited	63
8/30	20 P	Silverstone CNS Limited	61
9/2c	73 T	Nautical Petroleum Plc	67
9/4a	100 P	Corsair Petroleum (24th Round) Limited	
9/6	73 T	Nautical Petroleum Plc	75
9/7	16 T	Silverstone CNS Limited	112
9/8b	47 T	Lundin Heather Ltd	97
9/9d	175 T	MPX North Sea Limited	95
9/9d	63 T	Lundin Heather Ltd	95
9/10c	30 T	Sagex Petroleum UK Ltd	178
9/12b	16 T	Silverstone CNS Limited	128
9/21	115 T	Valiant Exploration Ltd	108
9/21	193 T	ATP Oil & Gas (UK) Limited	148
9/26	115 T	Valiant Exploration Ltd	74
9/27b	124 P	EnCore Petroleum Ltd	76
9/27b	115 T	Valiant Exploration Ltd	76
13/17	194 T	Fox Energy Exploration Ltd	
13/22b	111 T	Chrysaor Limited	115
13/23a	2 T	Bow Valley Petroleum (UK) Limited	211
13/27e	93 T	Petro-Canada UK Limited	88
13/29c	41 T	EOG Resources UK Limited	101
14/13	10 T	Silverstone CNS Limited	

Block	AP	Operator	MARKS
14/25b	76 T	Petro-Canada UK Limited	95
14/26b	109 T	Zeus Petroleum Ltd	128
14/28c	104 P	Black Sapphire Resources Ltd	64

06 November 2008

Page 1 of 7

Block	AP	Operator	MARKS
14/29c	104 P	Black Sapphire Resources Ltd	63
14/29c	124 P	EnCore Petroleum Ltd	75
14/30b	77 T	Nexen Petroleum UK Limited	103
14/30b	124 P	EnCore Petroleum Ltd	70
15/7	17 T	Silverstone CNS Limited	
15/8	19 T	Silverstone CNS Limited	
15/12a	17 T	Silverstone CNS Limited	
15/18c	19 T	Silverstone CNS Limited	
15/19c	105 P	Sable Energy (UK) LTD	72
15/19c	155 T	Maersk Oil North Sea UK Limited	234
15/20d	105 P	Sable Energy (UK) LTD	58
15/21e	161 T	EnCore Petroleum Ltd	104
15/21e	76 T	Petro-Canada UK Limited	105
15/23e	77 T	Nexen Petroleum UK Limited	121
15/26a	61 T	Oilexco North Sea Limited	146
15/30b	62 T	Oilexco North Sea Limited	160
16/1b	179 P	Excelsior Energy Limited	80
16/2c	179 P	Excelsior Energy Limited	71
16/6b	174 T	Carrizo Oil and Gas, Inc.	115
16/12b	39 T	Dana Petroleum (E&P) Limited	80
16/13b	90 T	Bow Valley Petroleum (UK) Limited	95
19/10b	150 P	Mahona Energy Limited	
19/15	150 P	Mahona Energy Limited	
20/3f	96 T	Nexen Petroleum UK Limited	
20/5b	104 P	Black Sapphire Resources Ltd	74
20/5b	21 T	Silverstone CNS Limited	105
20/7	174 T	Carrizo Oil and Gas, Inc.	88
20/8	95 T	Nexen Petroleum UK Limited	87
20/8	104 P	Black Sapphire Resources Ltd	81
20/9b	104 P	Black Sapphire Resources Ltd	80
20/10	104 P	Black Sapphire Resources Ltd	78
20/15	78 T	Stratic Energy (UK) Limited	79
20/15	85 T	Apache North Sea Ltd	83
20/30	105 P	Sable Energy (UK) LTD	
21/3f	95 T	Nexen Petroleum UK Limited	119
21/6b	110 P	Carrizo Oil and Gas, Inc.	63
21/11b	65 T	Endeavour Energy UK Limited	182

21/11b	85 T	Apache North Sea Ltd	110
21/12b	46 T	Lundin Heather Ltd	121

Block	AP	Operator	MARKS
21/12b	42 T	EOG Resources UK Limited	160
21/13a	46 T	Lundin Heather Ltd	154
21/13a	90 T	Bow Valley Petroleum (UK) Limited	164
21/20c	185 T	Dana Petroleum (E&P) Limited	152
21/20e	185 T	Dana Petroleum (E&P) Limited	93
21/21	81 T	Revus Energy (E&P) Limited	57
21/22	81 T	Revus Energy (E&P) Limited	138
21/24b	54 T	Oilexco North Sea Limited	159
21/24c	154 P	Antrim Resources (N.I.) Limited	
21/26	105 P	Sable Energy (UK) LTD	
21/27b	81 T	Revus Energy (E&P) Limited	164
21/28b	160 T	Antrim Resources (N.I.) Limited	
21/29c	160 T	Antrim Resources (N.I.) Limited	
22/1a	172 T	Venture North Sea Oil Limited	237
22/9b	87 T	Carrizo Oil and Gas, Inc.	
22/19c	172 T	Venture North Sea Oil Limited	201
22/24e	168 T	Talisman Energy (UK) Ltd	183
22/26b	171 T	Talisman Energy (UK) Ltd	104
22/27b	126 P	REAP UK (3) Limited	
22/28b	126 P	REAP UK (3) Limited	
22/29c	157 T	Maersk Oil North Sea UK Limited	160
22/29c	169 T	Talisman Energy (UK) Ltd	166
22/30d	126 P	REAP UK (3) Limited	
23/11b	40 T	EOG Resources UK Limited	
23/26c	187 T	BG International (CNS) Limited	155
23/26c	58 T	Oilexco North Sea Limited	166
26/5	180 P	Deliverit Energy	
26/10	180 P	Deliverit Energy	
27/1	180 P	Deliverit Energy	
29/1c	1 T	Oilexco North Sea Limited	177
29/2e	125 P	REAP UK (2) Limited	
29/2f	125 P	REAP UK (2) Limited	
29/2g	126 P	REAP UK (3) Limited	
29/3b	36 T	Total E&P UK Limited	222
29/4b	23 T	Ithaca Energy (UK) Ltd	81
29/4b	91 T	Shell UK Ltd	70
29/5e	23 T	Ithaca Energy (UK) Ltd	90
29/6a	24 T	First Oil Expro Limited	167
29/7b	57 T	Oilexco North Sea Limited	134
29/8c	125 P	REAP UK (2) Limited	

Block	AP	Operator	MARKS
29/9c	91 T	Shell UK Ltd	70
29/9c	172 T	Venture North Sea Oil Limited	132
29/10b	158 T	Maersk Oil North Sea UK Limited	107
29/23	6 T	Conoco (UK) Ltd	
29/30	6 T	Conoco (UK) Ltd	
30/1f	129 T	GDF Britain Ltd	123
30/7b	183 T	ConocoPhillips (UK) Ltd	128
30/11c	93 T	Petro-Canada UK Limited	
30/12c	145 P	Veritas Geophysical Limited	
30/18b	113 T	Valiant Exploration Ltd	
30/18c	101 P	Sussex Energy Limited	
30/29	142 T	Veritas Geophysical Limited	
35/21	102 P	TGS-NOPEC Geophysical Company (UK) Ltd	
38/4	145 P	Veritas Geophysical Limited	
39/2b	95 T	Nexen Petroleum UK Limited	
42/10	38 T	Sterling Resources (UK) Limited	123
42/15	38 T	Sterling Resources (UK) Limited	129
42/29c	12 T	Silverstone CNS Limited	83
42/30b	176 P	Focus Energy	76
42/30c	12 T	Silverstone CNS Limited	86
43/22b	123 T	Venture North Sea Gas Limited	
43/26b	80 T	E. ON Ruhrgas UK EU Ltd	113
43/27b	80 T	E. ON Ruhrgas UK EU Ltd	110
43/28	122 T	Venture North Sea Gas Limited	
43/29	122 T	Venture North Sea Gas Limited	92
43/30b	164 P	Holywell Resources Limited	78
44/26b	123 T	Venture North Sea Gas Limited	
44/26c	123 T	Venture North Sea Gas Limited	
44/28a	123 T	Venture North Sea Gas Limited	96
44/29c	130 T	GDF Britain Ltd	121
47/4d	39 T	Dana Petroleum (E&P) Limited	101
47/5b	12 T	Silverstone CNS Limited	108
47/5b	39 T	Dana Petroleum (E&P) Limited	109
47/5b	135 T	CalEnergy Gas Limited	84
48/1c	135 T	CalEnergy Gas Limited	115
48/1c	165 T	EnCore Petroleum Ltd	113
48/2b	80 T	E. ON Ruhrgas UK EU Ltd	118
48/3b	80 T	E. ON Ruhrgas UK EU Ltd	102

Block	AP	Operator	MARKS
48/5	149 P	Volantis Exploration Limited	
48/7e	123 T	Venture North Sea Gas Limited	
48/7f	118 T	Centrica Resources Limited	110
48/7f	123 T	Venture North Sea Gas Limited	91
48/10c	71 T	RWE Dea UK SNS Ltd	
48/16a	189 T	Serica Energy (UK) Limited	
49/3	123 T	Venture North Sea Gas Limited	
49/15b	164 P	Holywell Resources Limited	
49/29c	149 P	Volantis Exploration Limited	39
49/29c	15 P	Silverstone CNS Limited	82
49/29c	143 P	Swift Exploration Ltd	67
49/30b	149 P	Volantis Exploration Limited	41
50/26b	149 P	Volantis Exploration Limited	41
53/3e	26 T	First Oil Expro Limited	
53/4c	149 P	Volantis Exploration Limited	
53/4g	26 T	First Oil Expro Limited	
53/5c	166 P	Norfolk Resources UK Limited	56
53/10	166 P	Norfolk Resources UK Limited	54
53/14	144 P	Swift Exploration Ltd	
53/15	144 P	Swift Exploration Ltd	
54/1a	166 P	Norfolk Resources UK Limited	58
54/6	166 P	Norfolk Resources UK Limited	54
110/2d	5 T	Serica Energy (UK) Limited	0
204/18	116 T	Valiant Exploration Ltd	167
204/18	156 T	Maersk Oil North Sea UK Limited	136
205/3	97 T	Nexen Petroleum UK Limited	76
205/4	33 T	Total E&P UK Limited	137
205/4	97 T	Nexen Petroleum UK Limited	112
205/6	52 F	DONG E&P (UK) Ltd	
205/7	52 F	DONG E&P (UK) Ltd	
205/11	52 F	DONG E&P (UK) Ltd	
206/5b	116 T	Valiant Exploration Ltd	
206/11b	163 T	BP Exploration Operating Company Ltd	
206/12b	163 T	BP Exploration Operating Company Ltd	
206/16	163 T	BP Exploration Operating Company Ltd	
206/17	163 T	BP Exploration Operating Company Ltd	
207/1b	116 T	Valiant Exploration Ltd	
208/12	53 T	DONG E&P (UK) Ltd	

Block	AP	Operator	MARKS
208/13b	53 T	DONG E&P (UK) Ltd	
208/17	53 T	DONG E&P (UK) Ltd	
208/18b	53 T	DONG E&P (UK) Ltd	
208/19b	53 T	DONG E&P (UK) Ltd	
208/20b	51 T	DONG E&P (UK) Ltd	93
208/21	45 F	Hurricane Exploration plc	68
208/22	51 T	DONG E&P (UK) Ltd	81
208/23	51 T	DONG E&P (UK) Ltd	104
208/24	51 T	DONG E&P (UK) Ltd	95
208/25	51 T	DONG E&P (UK) Ltd	83
208/27	51 T	DONG E&P (UK) Ltd	91
208/28	51 T	DONG E&P (UK) Ltd	74
209/16	51 T	DONG E&P (UK) Ltd	84
209/17	51 T	DONG E&P (UK) Ltd	87
210/1	182 F	Rocksource UK Limited	
210/2	182 F	Rocksource UK Limited	
210/3	64 F	Lundin Heather Ltd	55
210/4	64 F	Lundin Heather Ltd	56
210/5	64 F	Lundin Heather Ltd	55
210/8	64 F	Lundin Heather Ltd	53
210/9	64 F	Lundin Heather Ltd	58
210/10	64 F	Lundin Heather Ltd	55
210/19b	79 T	Nexen Petroleum UK Limited	101
210/20e	79 T	Nexen Petroleum UK Limited	88
210/23	39 T	Dana Petroleum (E&P) Limited	76
210/24c	79 T	Nexen Petroleum UK Limited	88
210/25b	114 T	Valiant Exploration Ltd	109
210/28	39 T	Dana Petroleum (E&P) Limited	77
210/29b	112 T	Valiant Exploration Ltd	77
210/29b	39 T	Dana Petroleum (E&P) Limited	109
210/30b	112 T	Valiant Exploration Ltd	73
211/6	99 T	Nexen Petroleum UK Limited	72
211/7b	99 T	Nexen Petroleum UK Limited	74
211/8b	99 T	Nexen Petroleum UK Limited	73
211/8b	114 T	Valiant Exploration Ltd	178
211/11b	173 T	Ithaca Energy (UK) Ltd	146
211/12b	94 T	Elixir Petroleum (UK) Limited	89
211/13c	114 T	Valiant Exploration Ltd	89
211/16b	173 T	Ithaca Energy (UK) Ltd	122
211/24c	141 T	Fairfield Cedrus Limited	

Block	AP	Operator	MARKS
211/27d	103 P	DNO UK Limited	
211/27e	141 T	Fairfield Cedrus Limited	
211/28b	114 T	Valiant Exploration Ltd	
213/8	32 F	Sagex Petroleum UK Ltd	
213/12	32 F	Sagex Petroleum UK Ltd	
213/13	32 F	Sagex Petroleum UK Ltd	
213/18	32 F	Sagex Petroleum UK Ltd	
213/24b	99 T	Nexen Petroleum UK Limited	
214/17	35 T	Total E&P UK Limited	
214/21b	35 T	Total E&P UK Limited	
214/22	35 T	Total E&P UK Limited	
219/9	133 F	GDF Britain Ltd	
219/10	131 T	GDF Britain Ltd	
219/13	133 F	GDF Britain Ltd	
219/14	133 F	GDF Britain Ltd	
219/15	131 T	GDF Britain Ltd	
219/18	133 F	GDF Britain Ltd	
219/19	133 F	GDF Britain Ltd	
219/20	131 T	GDF Britain Ltd	
219/29	64 F	Lundin Heather Ltd	53
219/30	64 F	Lundin Heather Ltd	55
220/16	131 T	GDF Britain Ltd	
220/26	64 F	Lundin Heather Ltd	53
220/27	99 T	Nexen Petroleum UK Limited	76

OFFERS OF AWARDS BY OPERATOR 25TH ROUND

Block(s) in offered Licences*	Operator*	Partners	Obligations*		Licence Type
			Firm	Contingent; Drill or Drop (D/D)	
2/10a & 2/15b	Antrim		Obtain 2D; Obtain 3D	D/D	Promote
21/24c	Antrim		Obtain & Reprocess 3D	D/D	Promote
21/28b & 21/29c	Antrim		Obtain & Reprocess 3D; LMR Inversion	1 Contingent Well	Traditional
20/15 (Split) & 21/11b (Split)	Apache		Obtain & Reprocess 3D	D/D	Traditional
9/21 (Split)	ATP	MOST	**1 Firm Well**		Traditional

23/26c (Split)	BG		Shoot LO 3D	D/D	Traditional
14/28c & 14/29c (Split)	Black Sapphire		Obtain 2D; Obtain & Reprocess 3D	D/D	Promote
20/5b (Split) & 20/10	Black Sapphire		Reprocess 3D	D/D	Promote
20/8 (Split) & 20/9b	Black Sapphire		Obtain 2D; Obtain & Reprocess 3D	D/D	Promote
13/23a	Bow Valley	Petro Summit, Reach	**1 Firm Well** Reprocess 3D		Traditional
16/13b	Bow Valley		Obtain LO 2D; Reprocess 3D	D/D	Traditional
21/13a (Split)	Bow Valley		**1 Firm Well**		Traditional
206/11b (Part), 206/12b, 206/16 (Part) & 206/17 (Part)	BP	ConocoPhillips, Chevron, Enterprise, Hess, Britoil	Shoot 3D; Acquire Gravity & Magnetic data	1 Contingent Well	Traditional
47/5b (Split)	CalEnergy	Endeavour, Hunt, Challenger		*To be Confirmed*	Traditional
48/1c (Split)	CalEnergy	Endeavour, Hunt, Challenger		D/D	Traditional
8/25b (Split)	Canamens	Nautical, Celtic	Reprocess 3D	D/D	Traditional
16/6b	Carrizo	MPX	Reprocess 3D	D/D	Traditional
20/7	Carrizo	MPX	Reprocess 3D	D/D	Traditional
21/6b	Carrizo		Obtain 2D; Obtain & Reprocess 3D	D/D	Promote
22/9b	Carrizo	E.ON Ruhrgas, Norwegian Energy	Obtain 3D	D/D	Traditional
48/7f (Split)	Centrica	Sojitz Energy		*To be Confirmed*	Traditional
13/22b	Chrysaor			D/D	Traditional
29/23	Conoco		Shoot 2D	D/D	Traditional
29/30	Conoco			D/D	Traditional
30/7b	ConocoPhillips	BG	Reprocess 3D	D/D	Traditional
9/4a (Part)	Corsair			*To be Confirmed*	Promote

16/12b	Dana		Obtain & Reprocess 3D	D/D	Traditional
21/20c	Dana	Venture		1 Contingent Well	Traditional
21/20e	Dana	Venture		D/D	Traditional
47/4d & 47/5b (Split)	Dana		Obtain & Reprocess 3D	1 Contingent Well	Traditional
210/23 (Part), 210/28 (Part) & 210/29b (Split)	Dana		Obtain 2D; Reprocess 3D	1 Contingent Well	Traditional
26/5, 26/10 & 27/1	Deliverit		Obtain & Reprocess 2D	D/D	Promote
211/27d (Part)	DNO	Elixir, Rocksource		*To be Confirmed*	Promote
205/6, 205/7 & 205/11	DONG	Chevron	Obtain & Reprocess 3D	D/D	Frontier
208/12, 208/13b, 208/17, 208/18b & 208/19b	DONG	Dana, GDF Britain	Shoot 3D	D/D	Traditional
208/20b, 208/22, 208/23, 208/24, 208/25, 208/27, 208/28, 209/16 & 209/17	DONG	Dana, GDF Britain	Shoot 3D	D/D	Traditional
43/26b & 43/27b	E.ON Ruhrgas	Dana		D/D	Traditional
48/2b & 48/3b	E.ON Ruhrgas	Dana	Obtain & Reprocess 3D	D/D	Traditional
211/12b	Elixir		Obtain & Reprocess 3D	D/D	Traditional
14/29c (Split) & 14/30b (Split)	EnCore			D/D	Promote
15/21e (Split)	EnCore	Nautical, Serica	Obtain & Reprocess 3D	D/D	Traditional
9/27b (Split)	EnCore Petroleum		Reprocess 3D	D/D	Promote

48/1c (Split)	EnCore Petroleum	EnCore NNS, NWE Southern Cross, Bharat PetroResourcesTata Petrodyne		D/D	Traditional
21/11b (Split)	Endeavour	Lundin, Revus	**1 Firm Well**		Traditional
13/29c	EOG		Reprocess 3D	D/D	Traditional
21/12b (Split)	EOG		**1 Firm Well**		Traditional
23/11b	EOG		Shoot 3D	D/D	Traditional
16/1b & 16/2c	Excelsior		Reprocess 3D	D/D	Promote
3/8d	Fairfield		**1 Firm Well** Obtain 3D		Traditional
211/24c	Fairfield		Reprocess 3D	D/D	Traditional
211/27e	Fairfield		**1 Firm Well** Reprocess 3D		Traditional
29/6a	First Oil	Sagex	**1 Firm Well** Obtain & Reprocess 3D		Traditional
53/3e & 53/4g	First Oil		Obtain & Reprocess 3D	1 Contingent Well	Traditional
42/30b	Focus			D/D	Promote
13/17	Fox Energy	Aimwell	Obtain 3D	D/D	Traditional
30/1f	GDF Britain	RWE Dea, Centrica, OMV, Endeavour	Reprocess 3D	D/D	Traditional
44/29c	GDF Britain	RWE Dea, Faroe	Reprocess 3D	D/D	Traditional
219/9, 219/13, 219/14, 219/18 & 219/19	GDF Britain		Obtain & Reprocess 2D	D/D	Frontier
219/10, 219/15, 219/20, 220/16	GDF Britain		Obtain & Reprocess 2D	D/D	Traditional
3/23b	Hannu			D/D	Promote
43/30b	Holywell		Obtain & Reprocess 3D	D/D	Promote
49/15b	Holywell		Obtain & Reprocess 3D	D/D	Promote

208/21	Hurricane	Sunshine, Faroe	Obtain 2D; Obtain 3D	D/D	Frontier
3/3b	Ithaca	Revus, MPX	**1 Firm Well** Reprocess 3D		Traditional
29/4b (Split) & 29/5e	Ithaca		Shoot LO 3D; Obtain & Reprocess 3D	D/D	Traditional
211/11b & 211/16b	Ithaca	Revus Energy, MPX	**1 Firm Well** Reprocess 3D		Traditional
3/11a	Lundin		**1 Firm Well** Obtain & Reprocess 3D		Traditional
9/8b	Lundin	Norwegian Energy	Obtain & Reprocess 3D	D/D	Traditional
9/9d (Split)	Lundin	Genesis		*To be Confirmed*	Traditional
21/12b (Split) & 21/13a (Split)	Lundin	Revus, Challenger	**1 Firm Well**		Traditional
210/3, 210/4, 210/5, 210/8, 210/9, 210/10, 219/29, 219/30 & 220/26	Lundin	Genesis	Shoot LO 2D; Shoot 3D; Obtain LO 2D	D/D	Frontier
15/19c (Split)	Maersk		**2 Firm Wells**		Traditional
22/29c (Split)	Maersk	Dana	**1 Firm Well**		Traditional
29/10b	Maersk	Ithaca	Reprocess 3D	D/D	Traditional
204/18 (Split)	Maersk		Acquire CSEM; Reprocess 3D	1 Contingent Well	Traditional
19/10b & 19/15	Mahona		Obtain & Reprocess 2D	D/D	Promote
8/25b (Split) & 8/30 (Split)	Mariner		Obtain & Reprocess 2D; Obtain & Reprocess 3D	D/D	Promote
9/9d (Split)	MPX		Reprocess 3D	D/D	Traditional
3/22	Nautical	Rocksource, Canamens	EM Feasibility	D/D	Traditional
3/26	Nautical	Rocksource, Canamens	EM Feasibility	D/D	Traditional
9/2c	Nautical	Celtic, Canamens		*To be Confirmed*	Traditional

9/6	Nautical	Celtic, Canamens	Shoot HR 2D; Obtain 2D; Obtain & Reprocess 3D	D/D	Traditional
14/30b (Split)	Nexen	Oilexco		1 Contingent Well	Traditional
15/23e	Nexen	Oilexco	Obtain 3D	1 Contingent Well	Traditional
20/3f	Nexen	Bow Valley, Atlantic		D/D	Traditional
20/8 (Split)	Nexen			D/D	Traditional
21/3f	Nexen			1 Contingent Well	Traditional
39/2b	Nexen		Reprocess 3D	D/D	Traditional
205/3, 205/4 (Split)	Nexen	Dana	Obtain & Reprocess 3D	D/D	Traditional
210/19b, 210/20e & 210/24c	Nexen	Apache	Obtain & Reprocess 3D	D/D	Traditional
211/6, 211/7b & 211/8b (Split)	Nexen		Shoot LO 2D; Obtain 2D; Reprocess 2D	D/D	Traditional
213/24b	Nexen		Obtain LO 2D; Obtain 3D	D/D	Traditional
220/27	Nexen		Obtain 3D	D/D	Traditional
53/5c, 53/10 (Part), 54/1a (Part) & 54/6 (Part)	Norfolk Resources		Obtain & Reprocess 2D; Obtain & Reprocess 3D	D/D	Promote
15/26a	Oilexco		**1 Firm Well** Obtain 3D		Traditional
15/30b	Oilexco		**1 Firm Well** Obtain 3D		Traditional
21/24b	Oilexco		**1 Firm Well** Obtain 3D		Traditional
23/26c (Split)	Oilexco		**1 Firm Well** Obtain 3D		Traditional
29/1c	Oilexco	Petro Summit, Reach	**1 Firm Well** Obtain & Reprocess 3D	1 Contingent Well	Traditional
29/7b	Oilexco		**1 Firm Well** Obtain 3D		Traditional
13/27e	Petro-Canada	Silverstone, Norwegian Energy	Obtain & Reprocess 3D	D/D	Traditional

14/25b & 15/21e (Split)	Petro-Canada	Silverstone	Obtain & Reprocess 3D	D/D	Traditional
30/11c	Petro-Canada	Silverstone, Norwegian Energy	Obtain & Reprocess LO 3D	D/D	Traditional
29/2e	REAP (2)		Obtain & Reprocess 3D	D/D	Promote
29/2f	REAP (2)		Obtain & Reprocess 3D	D/D	Promote
29/8c	REAP (2)		Obtain & Reprocess 3D	D/D	Promote
22/27b	REAP (3)		Obtain & Reprocess 3D	D/D	Promote
22/28b	REAP (3)		Obtain & Reprocess 3D	D/D	Promote
22/30d	REAP (3)		Obtain & Reprocess 3D	D/D	Promote
29/2g	REAP (3)		Obtain & Reprocess 3D	D/D	Promote
21/21 & 21/22	Revus		Shoot HR 2D; Reprocess 3D	1 Contingent Well	Traditional
21/27b	Revus		**1 Firm Well** Reprocess 3D		Traditional
210/1 & 210/2	Rocksource		Obtain 2D	D/D	Frontier
48/10c	RWE Dea	Euroil, E.ON Ruhrgas	Reprocess 3D	D/D	Traditional
15/19c (Split) & 15/20d	Sable		Obtain & Reprocess 3D	D/D	Promote
20/30 & 21/26	Sable		Obtain & Reprocess 3D	D/D	Promote
9/10c	Sagex	First Oil	**1 Firm Well** Obtain 2D; Obtain & Reprocess 3D		Traditional
213/8, 213/12, 213/13 & 213/18	Sagex		Obtain 2D; Trial Reprocessing	D/D	Frontier
48/16a (Part)	Serica			*To be Confirmed*	Traditional
110/2d	Serica		Reprocess 3D	1 Contingent Well	Traditional

29/4b (Split) & 29/9c (Split)	Shell	Esso		D/D	Traditional
2/20 & 3/16	Silverstone	Wilderness	Obtain & Reprocess 2D	D/D	Promote
8/30 (Split)	Silverstone	Wilderness	Obtain & Reprocess 2D	D/D	Promote
9/7 & 9/12b	Silverstone	Wilderness	Obtain & Reprocess 3D; Acquire CSEM	1 Contingent Well	Traditional
14/13	Silverstone	Norwegian Energy	Obtain & Reprocess 3D; Acquire CSEM	D/D	Traditional
15/7 & 15/12a	Silverstone	Wilderness	Reprocess 2D; Reprocess 3D; Acquire CSEM	D/D	Traditional
15/8	Silverstone	Wilderness	Obtain & Reprocess 2D; Acquire CSEM	D/D	Traditional
15/18c	Silverstone	Wilderness	Obtain & Reprocess 2D; Reprocess 3D; Acquire CSEM	D/D	Traditional
20/5b (Split)	Silverstone	Norwegian Energy	Obtain & Reprocess 3D	D/D	Traditional
42/29c, 42/30c & 47/5b (Split)	Silverstone	Wilderness	Shoot 3D; Obtain & Reprocess 3D	D/D	Traditional
49/29c (Split)	Silverstone		Obtain & Reprocess 3D	D/D	Promote
42/10 & 42/15	Sterling Resources	Stratic Energy, Petro-Ventures	**1 Firm Well** Shoot 2D; Shoot Pseudo 3D; Reprocess 2D		Traditional
20/15 (Split)	Stratic		Reprocess 3D	D/D	Traditional
30/18c	Sussex			D/D	Promote
49/29c (Split)	Swift	Stelinmatvic	Obtain 3D	D/D	Promote
53/14 (Part) & 53/15 (Part)	Swift			D/D	Promote

22/24e	Talisman		**1 Firm Well** Obtain 3D		Traditional
22/26b	Talisman	Venture	Reprocess 3D	D/D	Traditional
22/29c (Split)	Talisman		**1 Firm Well** Obtain 3D		Traditional
35/21	TGS-NOPEC		Reprocess 2D	D/D	Promote
29/3b	Total	E.ON Ruhrgas	**1 Firm Well** Obtain & Reprocess 3D		Traditional
205/4 (Split)	Total	ENI, DONG, Chevron	Shoot 3D	D/D	Traditional
214/17, 214/21b & 214/22	Total	DONG, ENI	Reprocess 3D	1 Contingent Well	Traditional
9/21 (Split), 9/26 & 9/27b (Split)	Valiant	Silverstone, Century	Obtain & Reprocess 2D; Obtain 3D; EM Feasibility	D/D	Traditional
30/18b	Valiant		**1 Firm Well** Obtain & Reprocess 3D		Traditional
204/18 (Split)	Valiant	Sussex Energy	**1 Firm Well**		Traditional
206/5b & 207/1b	Valiant	Sussex Energy	Shoot 2D	D/D	Traditional
210/25b	Valiant		Reprocess 3D	D/D	Traditional
210/29b (Split) & 210/30b	Valiant		Obtain & Reprocess 3D	D/D	Traditional
211/8b (Split) & 211/13c	Valiant		**1 Firm Well**		Traditional
211/28b	Valiant		**1 Firm Well** Reprocess 3D		Traditional
22/1a	Venture	MPX	**1 Firm Well** Reprocess 3D	1 Contingent Well	Traditional
22/19c	Venture	MPX	**1 Firm Well** Reprocess 3D		Traditional
29/9c (Split)	Venture	MPX	Reprocess 3D	1 Contingent Well	Traditional
43/22b	Venture	Volantis		D/D	Traditional
43/28	Venture	Ithaca, Volantis		D/D	Traditional
43/29	Venture	Ithaca, Volantis		D/D	Traditional
44/26b	Venture	Volantis		D/D	Traditional
44/26c	Venture	Volantis		D/D	Traditional

44/28a	Venture	Volantis		D/D	Traditional
48/7e	Venture	Volantis		D/D	Traditional
48/7f (Split)	Venture	Volantis		D/D	Traditional
49/3	Venture	Volantis		D/D	Traditional
30/12c	Veritas			D/D	Promote
30/29	Veritas			D/D	Traditional
38/4	Veritas			D/D	Promote
48/5	Volantis			D/D	Promote
49/29c (Split) & 49/30b (Split)	Volantis			D/D	Promote
49/30b (Split) & 50/26b	Volantis	SEQ	Obtain 3D	D/D	Promote
53/4c	Volantis			D/D	Promote
14/26b	Zeus	Aimwell	**1 Firm Well**		Traditional

*(Part): Part Blocks are those where a Company has only requested a portion of the available Block

*(Split): Blocks may be split as a way of dealing with the differing prospectivity focus of competing Applications

*Operator: Some further approvals may be required for Operations

*Obligations: Only main Obligations stated

*Obligations: Not stated where the Department is "merging" the offer with a previous Licence

SELECTED UK OIL EXPLORATION COMPANIES

The Association of British Independent Oil Exploration Companies seeks to promote the role played by British independent exploration and production (E&P) companies in maintaining a powerful and effective UK based oil and gas industry.

Contact Jackie Steer: jackie@brindex.co.uk

Independent oil and gas exploration companies are at the heart of the liberalised energy market which provides secure and diverse supplies at competitive prices. The independents will continue to play an important role in shaping a cost effective and imaginative approach to the exploration and development of the UK Continental Shelf and in securing the participation of the banking sector and the capital markets in its ongoing development.

Major oil companies were awarded the great majority of the highly prospective acreage on offer in the first four UK offshore Licensing Rounds. Subsequently, BRINDEX and its members lobbied to create an environment in which an independent oil and gas exploration sector could develop for the benefit of the country. We were successful in persuading successive UK governments of the vital role of the independent and, from the Fifth Round onwards, our success in terms of acreage awards rose dramatically. This resulted in a major deployment of British risk capital and debt finance and the new corporate vehicles for this funding went on to establish many joint-venture partnerships with major companies.

Afren plc.
Kinnaird House
1 Pall Mall
London
SW1Y 5AU

Tel: +44 (0)20 7451 9700
Fax: +44 (0)20 7451 9701
Email: info@afren.com

Afren plc

Bowleven plc
1 North St Andrew Lane
Edinburgh
EH2 1HX

Tel: +44 (0)131 524 5678
Fax: +44 (0)131 524 5690
Email: info@bowleven.co.uk

Bowleven plc

Cairn Energy plc.
50 Lothian Road
Edinburgh
EH3 9BY

Tel: +44 (0)1314 753 000
Fax: +44 (0)1314 753 030
Email: pr@cairn-energy.plc.uk

Cairn Energy plc

Dana Petroleum plc.
17 Carden Place
Aberdeen
AB10 1UR

Tel: +44 (0)1224 652 400
Fax: +44 (0)1224 652 401

Dana Petroleum plc

Fairfield Energy Ltd.
Ash House
Fairfield Avenue
Staines
Middlesex
TW18 4AB

Tel: +44 (0)1224 372 777
Fax: +44 (0)1224 372 633
Email: info@fairfield-energy.com

Fairfield Energy Ltd

Falkland Oil and Gas Limited
32-34 Wigmore Street
London
W1U 2RR

Tel: +44 (0)207 563 1260
Fax: +44 (0)207 486 2330
Email: info@fogl.co.uk

Falkland Oil and Gas Limited

Faroe Petroleum plc.
24 Carden Place
Aberdeen
AB10 1UQ

Tel: +44 (0)1224 652 810
Fax: +44 (0)1224 643 243
Email: info@faroe-petroleum.com

Faroe Petroleum plc

JKX Oil & Gas plc.
6 Cavendish Square
London
W1G 0PD

Tel: +44 (0)20 7323 4464
Fax: +44 (0)20 7323 5258
Email: general@jkx.co.uk

JKX Oil & Gas plc

Melrose Resources plc.
Exchange Tower
19 Canning Street
Edinburgh
EH3 8EG

Tel: + 44 (0)131 221 3360
Fax: + 44 (0)131 221 3361
Email: info@melroseresources.com

Melrose Resources plc

Premier Oil plc.
23 Lower Belgrave Street
London
SW1W 0NR

Tel: + 44 (0)20 7730 1111
Fax: + 44 (0)20 7730 4696
Email: premier@premier-oil.com

Premier Oil plc

Salamander Energy plc.
5th Floor
21 Palmer Street
London
SW1H 0AD

Tel: + 44 (0)20 7222 4553
Fax: + 44 (0)20 7960 1580
Email: info@salamander-energy.com

Salamander Energy plc

Serica Energy plc.
Serica Energy plc
87-89 Baker Street
London
W1U 6RJ

Tel: +44 (0)20 7487 7300
Fax: +44 (0)20 7487 7330
Email: info@serica-energy.com

Serica Energy plc

SOCO International plc.
St James's House, 2nd Floor
23 King Street
London
SW1Y 6QY

Tel: +44 (0)20 7747 2000
Fax: +44 (0)20 7747 2001

SOCO International plc

Stratic Energy (UK) Limited
130 Jermyn Street
London
SW1Y 4UR

Tel: +44 (0)20 7766 7900
Fax: +44 (0)20 7766 7999

Stratic Energy (UK) Limited

Tullow Oil plc.
Tullow Oil UK Limited
3rd Floor Building 11
Chiswick Park
566 Chiswick High Road
London
W4 5YS

Tel: +44 (0)20 8996 1000
Fax: +44 (0)20 8994 5332
Email: information@tullowoil.com

Tullow Oil UK Limited

Valiant Petroleum Ltd.
Albion House
Chertsey Road
Woking
Surrey
GU21 6BD

Tel: +44 (0)1483 755666
Fax: +44(0)1483 776573
Email: contact@valiant-petroleum.com

Valiant Petroleum Ltd

Venture Production plc.
First Floor
Crimon Place Wing
King's Close
62 Huntly Street
Aberdeen
AB10 1RS

Tel: +44 (0)1224 619 000
Fax: +44 (0)1224 658 151
Email: enquiries@vpc.co.uk

Venture Production plc

BRINDEX Officers

Chairman
Tom Cross
Dana Petroleum plc.
17 Carden Place
Aberdeen
AB10 1UR

Tel. +44 (0)1224 652 400

Honorary Secretary
Mark McAllister
Fairfield Energy Ltd.

Honorary Treasurer
Antony Maris
SOCO International plc.

Administrator
Jackie Steer
Brindex
Tel. +44 (0)20 8668 3359
Email: jackie@brindex.co.uk

Sub-Committee Chairman

Taxation
Kathryn Anderson
Cairn Energy plc.

DEPARTMENT OF ENERGY AND CLIMATE CHANGE

HEAD OFFICE ADDRESS

3 Whitehall Place
London
SW1A 2HH
General enquiries: 0300 060 4000 (standard national rate)
Email us: enquiries@decc.gsi.gov.uk

The Department brings together much of the Climate Change Group, previously housed within the Department for Environment, Food and Rural Affairs (Defra), with the Energy Group from the Department for Business, Enterprise and Regulatory Reform (BERR).

MINISTERS

Ed Miliband is Secretary of State for the Department of Energy and Climate Change.
Minister of State - Mike O'Brien MP
Minister of State - Lord Hunt of Kings Heath OBE (jointly with Department for Environment, Food and Rural Affairs); and Deputy Leader of the House of Lords
Parliamentary Under-Secretary of State - Joan Ruddock MP

SENIOR TEAM

Moira Wallace is the Permanent Secretary for the Department.
Mike Anderson is Director General, Climate Change
Willy Rickett is Director General, Energy

Energy Group deals with energy-related matters from production to supply. It is committed to delivering the Government's policy goals of safe, secure and sustainable energy supplies and ultimately a low-carbon economy, through competitive and independently regulated energy markets.

Energy is essential in almost every aspect of our lives and for the success of our economy, but we face two long-term challenges:

- tackling climate change by reducing carbon dioxide emissions both within the UK and abroad; and
- ensuring secure, clean and affordable energy as we become increasingly dependent on imported fuel.

The Government's current energy policy was set out in the Energy White Paper of May 2007, building on previous work including the 2003 Energy White Paper and the Energy Review Report in 2006.
The 2007 White Paper sets out the Government's international and domestic energy strategy to respond to the changing circumstances in global energy markets and to address the long term energy challenges we face. Our strategy can be summarised as follows:

- establish an international framework to tackle climate change;
- reduce emissions progressively, via legally binding carbon targets;
- make further progress towards fully competitive and transparent international markets;
- encourage more energy saving through better information, incentives and regulation;
- provide more support for low-carbon technologies;
- ensure the right conditions for investment.

The Energy community of the BERR website contains detailed information about the work of Energy Group.
The Group is headed by Director General Willy Rickett.

ENERGY CONTACTS

ADVISORY PANEL CONTACTS

- Kanta Varsani, tel: 020 7215 3999
  Energy Strategy and International Unit
  Department of Energy and Climate Change (DECC)
  Bay 277, 1 Victoria Street
  London
  SW1H 0ET

CARBON ABATEMENT TECHNOLOGIES CONTACTS

- Nicholas Aluko, tel: 020 7215 3075
  Cleaner Fossil Fuels Team
  Department of Energy and Climate Change (DECC)
  Bay 221, 1 Victoria Street
  London
  SW1H 0ET

UK CARBON CAPTURE AND STORAGE DEMONSTRATION COMPETITION CONTACTS

- Rachel Crisp, tel: 020 7215 0303

CLIMATE CHANGE CONTACTS

- Barbara Green, tel: 020 7215 5398
  Energy Strategy and International Unit
  Department of Energy and Climate Change (DECC)
  Bay 287, 1 Victoria Street
  London
  SW1H 0ET

COAL CONTACTS

- Clare Harding, tel: 020 7215 6263
  UK Producing Coal Industry, Coal Liabilities Unit
  Department of Energy and Climate Change (DECC)
  Bay 137, 1 Victoria Street
  London
  SW1H 0ET
- David Leitch, tel: 020 7215 5252
  Coal Authority, Coal Pensions, Coal Liabilities Unit

Department of Energy and Climate Change (DECC)
Bay 137, 1 Victoria Street
London
SW1H 0ET

- Jeremy Cousins, tel: 020 7215 6145
  Coal Forum and Bevan Boys Award, Coal Liabilities Unit
  Department of Energy and Climate Change (DECC)
  Bay 137, 1 Victoria Street
  London
  SW1H 0ET
- Coal Health Claims Unit, tel: 020 7215 2869
  Department of Energy and Climate Change (DECC)
  Case tracking at www.coalclaims.com

COMPETITIVENESS CONTACTS

- Stephen Green, tel: 020 7215 6201
  Energy Strategy and International Unit
  Department of Energy and Climate Change (DECC)
  Bay 294, 1 Victoria Street
  London
  SW1H 0ET

DOWNSTREAM GAS & ELECTRICITY CONTACTS

- Andy Stevenson, tel: 020 7215 6254
  Energy Markets Unit
  Department of Energy and Climate Change (DECC)
  Bay 213, 1 Victoria Street
  London
  SW1H 0ET

ELECTRICITY LICENCE EXEMPTIONS CONTACTS

- Chris Chown, tel: 020 7215 2766
  Energy Markets Unit
  Department of Energy and Climate Change (DECC)
  Bay 222, 1 Victoria Street
  London
  SW1H 0ET

ELECTRICITY MARKETS CONTACTS

- Chris Chown, tel: 020 7215 2766
  Energy Markets Unit
  Department of Energy and Climate Change (DECC)
  Bay 222, 1 Victoria Street
  London
  SW1H 0ET

ENERGY BETTER REGULATION CONTACTS

- Energy Better Regulation, tel: 020 7215 2332

'ENERGY CONSUMPTION IN THE UK' PUBLICATION CONTACTS

- Jennifer Knight, tel: 020 7215 6490
  Department of Energy and Climate Change (DECC)
  Bay 297
  1 Victoria Street
  London
  SW1H 0ET

ENERGY EFFICIENCY CONTACTS

- Tom Bastin, tel: 020 7238 5449
  CESPS2 Energy Efficiency
  Department of Energy and Climate Change (DECC)
  Ergon House, Horseferry Road,
  London
  SW1P 2AL

ENERGY & ENVIRONMENT RESEARCH PROGRAMME (EERP) CONTACTS

- Stephen Green, tel: 020 7215 6201
  Energy Strategy and International Unit
  Department of Energy and Climate Change (DECC)
  Bay 294, 1 Victoria Street
  London
  SW1H 0ET

'ENERGY - IT'S IMPACT...' CONTACTS

- Julian Prime, tel: 020 7215 6178
  Department of Energy and Climate Change (DECC)
  Bay 297
  1 Victoria Street
  London
  SW1H 0ET
- Jennifer Knight, tel: 020 7215 6490
  Department of Energy and Climate Change (DECC)
  Bay 297
  1 Victoria Street
  London
  SW1H 0ET

ENERGY MERGERS CONTACTS

- Keith Evans, tel: 020 7215 5694
  Energy Markets Unit
  Department of Energy and Climate Change (DECC)
  Bay 223, 1 Victoria Street
  London
  SW1H 0ET

ENERGY MARKETS OUTLOOK CONTACTS

- Robert Clay, tel: 020 7215 5272
  Market Regulatory Framework Directorate
  Department of Energy and Climate Change (DECC)
  Bay 138, 1 Victoria Street
  London
  SW1H 0ET

ENERGY MARKET STRUCTURES CONTACTS

- Chris Chown, tel: 020 7215 2766
  Energy Markets Unit
  Department of Energy and Climate Change (DECC)
  Bay 222, 1 Victoria Street
  London
  SW1H 0ET

ENERGY PRICES CONTACTS

- Jo Marvin, tel: 020 7215 6935
  Energy Strategy & International Unit
  Department of Energy and Climate Change (DECC)
  Bay 299, 1 Victoria Street
  London
  SW1H 0ET

ENERGY STATISTICS PUBLICATIONS CONTACTS

- Kevin Harris, tel: 020 7215 6049
  Energy Markets Unit
  Department of Energy and Climate Change (DECC)
  Bay 299, 1 Victoria Street
  London
  SW1H 0ET

ENERGY SERVICES CONTACTS

- Geoff Hatherick, tel: 020 7215 5047
  Energy Markets Unit
  Department of Energy and Climate Change (DECC)
  Bay 220, 1 Victoria Street

London
SW1H 0ET

ENERGY WHITE PAPER CONTACTS

- Nicola Robinson, tel: 020 7215 2332
  Energy Strategy and International Unit (ESIU)
  Department of Energy and Climate Change (DECC)
  Bay 277, 1 Victoria Street
  London
  SW1H 0ET

ENVIRONMENTAL TRANSFORMATION FUND CONTACTS

- Farida Isroliwala, tel: 020 7215 3774
  Environmental Transformation Fund (ETF)
  Department of Energy and Climate Change (DECC)
  Bay 215, 1 Victoria Street
  London
  SW1H 0ET
- Jackie Walsh (Defra), tel:
  Environmental Transformation Fund (ETF)
- Ray Eaton, tel: 020 7215 2650
  Renewable Energy and Innovation Unit (REIU)
  Department of Energy and Climate Change (DECC)
  Bay 233, 1 Victoria Street
  London
  SW1H 0ET
- Nicholas Aluko, tel: 020 7215 3075
  Cleaner Fossil Fuels Team
  Department of Energy and Climate Change (DECC)
  Bay 221, 1 Victoria Street
  London
  SW1H 0ET
- Trevor Raggatt, tel: 020 7215 2204
  Marine Renewables Deployment Fund (MRDF)
  Department of Energy and Climate Change (DECC)
  Bay 214, 1 Victoria Street
  London
  SW1H 0ET
- David Hollier, tel: 020 7215 6296
  Bio-energy Capital Grants Scheme
  Department of Energy and Climate Change (DECC)
  Bay 241, 1 Victoria Street
  London
  SW1H 0ET
- Paul Rochester, tel: 020 7215 6389
  Low Carbon Buildings Programme: Phase 1
  Department of Energy and Climate Change (DECC)

Bay 241, 1 Victoria Street
London
SW1H 0ET

- John Moriarty, tel: 020 7215 1969
  Low Carbon Buildings Programme: Phase 2
  Department of Energy and Climate Change (DECC)
  Bay 234, 1 Victoria Street
  London
  SW1H 0ET
- Richard Daniels, tel: 020 7215 0404
  Offshore Wind Capital Grants Scheme
  Department of Energy and Climate Change (DECC)
  Bay 209, 1 Victoria Street
  London
  SW1H 0ET

EU EMISSIONS TRADING SCHEME (EU ETS) CONTACTS

- Martin Bond, tel: 020 7215 0340
  Energy Markets Unit
  Department of Energy and Climate Change (DECC)
  Bay 286, 1 Victoria Street
  London
  SW1H 0ET

FUEL POVERTY CONTACTS

- Damon Wingfield, tel: 020 7215 2720
  Energy Markets Unit (EMU)
  Department of Energy and Climate Change (DECC)
  Bay 208, 1 Victoria Street,
  London,
  SW1H 0ET
- Marina Pappa, tel: 020 7215 1137
  Energy Markets Unit (EMU)
  Department of Energy and Climate Change (DECC)
  Bay 143, 1 Victoria Street,
  London,
  SW1H 0ET

G8 & GLENEAGLES DIALOGUE CONTACTS

- Craig Jones, tel: 020 7215 3563
  Energy Strategy & International Unit (ESIU)
  Department of Energy and Climate Change (DECC)
  Bay 263, 1 Victoria Street
  London
  SW1H 0ET

GAS INFRASTRUCTURE PROJECTS CONTACTS

- John Havard, tel: 020 7215 5546
  Energy Markets Unit
  Department of Energy and Climate Change (DECC)
  Bay 138, 1 Victoria Street
  London
  SW1H 0ET

GAS MARKETS CONTACTS

- John Havard, tel: 020 7215 5546
  Energy Markets Unit
  Department of Energy and Climate Change (DECC)
  Bay 138, 1 Victoria Street
  London
  SW1H 0ET

GENERAL ENERGY STATISTICS CONTACTS

- Clive Sarjantson, tel: 020 7215 2698
  Energy Markets Unit
  Department of Energy and Climate Change (DECC)
  Bay 2101, 1 Victoria Street
  London
  SW1H 0ET

HYDROGEN AND FUEL CELLS CONTACTS

- Ray Eaton, tel: 020 7215 2650
  Renewable Energy and Innovation Unit (REIU)
  Department of Energy and Climate Change (DECC)
  Bay 233, 1 Victoria Street
  London
  SW1H 0ET

IEA CONTACTS

- Alison Zhu, tel: 020 7215 6971
  Energy Strategy and International Unit
  Department of Energy and Climate Change (DECC)
  Bay 261, 1 Victoria Street
  London
  SW1H 0ET

INTER-DEPARTMENTAL ANALYSTS GROUP CONTACTS

- Stephen Green, tel: 020 7215 6201
  Energy Strategy and International Unit
  Department of Energy and Climate Change (DECC)
  Bay 294, 1 Victoria Street

London
SW1H 0ET

INTERNATIONAL OIL MARKETS CONTACTS

- Lynsey Tinios, tel: 020 7215 5450
  Energy Markets Unit
  Department of Energy and Climate Change (DECC)
  Bay 260, 1 Victoria Street
  London
  SW1H 0ET

JWGEE CONTACTS

- Julian Prime, tel: 020 7215 6178
  Department of Energy and Climate Change (DECC)
  Bay 297
  1 Victoria Street
  London
  SW1H 0ET

LIBERALISATION CONTACTS

- Sue Harrison, tel: 020 7215 2778
  Energy Strategy & International Unit
  Department of Energy and Climate Change (DECC)
  Bay 264, 1 Victoria Street
  London
  SW1H 0ET

MICROGENERATION CONTACTS

- Microgeneration, tel: 020 7215 0303

NUCLEAR ENERGY CONTACTS

- Office for Nuclear Development (OND), tel: 020 7215 5000

QUALITY AND CONTINUITY OF UK SUPPLY CONTACTS

- Tim Wickes, tel: 020 7215 2667
  Energy Markets Unit
  Department of Energy and Climate Change (DECC)
  Bay 204, 1 Victoria Street

London
SW1H 0ET

REGULATION OF ENERGY MARKETS CONTACTS

- Chris Chown, tel: 020 7215 2766
  Energy Markets Unit
  Department of Energy and Climate Change (DECC)
  Bay 222, 1 Victoria Street
  London
  SW1H 0ET

REGIONAL ENERGY STATISTICS CONTACTS

- Jennifer Knight, tel: 020 7215 6490
  Department of Energy and Climate Change (DECC)
  Bay 297
  1 Victoria Street
  London
  SW1H 0ET
- Julian Prime, tel: 020 7215 6178
  Department of Energy and Climate Change (DECC)
  Bay 297
  1 Victoria Street
  London
  SW1H 0ET
- Joanna Chan, tel: 020 7215 2703
  Department of Energy and Climate Change (DECC)
  Bay 297
  1 Victoria Street
  London
  SW1H 0ET

RENEWABLES CONTACTS

- Claire Ball, tel: 0207 215 2812
  Energy Industries and Technologies Unit: International programmes
  Department for Business, Enterprise & Regulatory Reform
  Bay 244, 1 Victoria Street
  London
  SW1H 0ET
- Chris Turner, tel: 020 7215 5977
  Energy Development Unit: Press Enquiries
  Department for Business, Enterprise & Regulatory Reform
  Bay 750, 1 Victoria Street
  London
  SW1H 0ET
- Fishing Liaison for Offshore Wind Group, tel: n/a
  Energy Development Unit: Secretary to FLOW
  Department for Business, Enterprise & Regulatory Reform
  Bay 2117, 1 Victoria Street

London
SW1H 0ET

- Fiona Livingston, tel: 01224 254015
  Energy Development Unit: Renewables website/It's Only Natural Campaign
  Department for Business, Enterprise & Regulatory Reform
  Atholl House, 86-88 Guild Street
  Aberdeen
  B11 6AR
- Francis Lajumoke, tel: 0207 215 2660
  Energy Development Unit: Renewables Policy
  Department for Business, Enterprise & Regulatory Reform
  Bay 2106, 1 Victoria Street
  London
  SW1H 0ET
- Georgina Webb, tel: 0870 1906301
  Renewables Advisory Board
  AEA Technology, The Gemini Building
  Fermi Avenue, Harwell International Business Centre
  Didcot
  OX11 0QR
- John Overton, tel: 0207 215 6481
  Energy Development Unit: Grid Issues Under Renewables
  Department for Business, Enterprise & Regulatory Reform
  Bay 2111, 1 Victoria Street
  London
  SW1H 0ET
- John Spurgeon, tel: 0207 215 2134
  Energy Industries and Technologies Unit: Wave and Tidal Energy
  Department for Business, Enterprise & Regulatory Reform
  Bay 238, 1 Victoria Street
  London
  SW1H 0ET
- Martin Marais, tel: 079 7940 6771
  Energy Development Unit: Planning for Renewables
  Department for Business, Enterprise & Regulatory Reform
  Bay 2108, 1 Victoria Street
  London
  SW1H 0ET
- Nicola Barber, tel: 2027 215 2651
  Energy Development Unit: Renewables Obligation
  Department for Business, Enterprise & Regulatory Reform
  Bay 219, 1 Victoria Street
  London
  SW1H 0ET
- Offshore Renewables Energy Environmental Forum, tel: n/a
  Energy Development Unit: Secretariat to OREEF
  Department for Business, Enterprise & Regulatory Reform
  Bay 2117, 1 Victoria Street
  London
  SW1H 0ET
- Patrick Fownes-Walpole, tel: 0207 215 2829
  Energy Development Unit: Hydro
  Department for Business, Enterprise & Regulatory Reform

Bay 2106, 1 Victoria Street
London
SW1H 0ET

- Phillip Baker, tel: 0207 215 2675
  Energy Development Unit: Transmission and Distribution
  Department for Business, Enterprise & Regulatory Reform
  Bay 2111, 1 Victoria Street
  London
  SW1H 0ET
- Renewable Energy Trade Promotion Service , tel: 01664 565083
  Renewables Trade Promotion Service: Trade Promoter
- Research Advisory Group, tel: n/a
  Energy Development Unit: Secretariat to RAG
  Department for Business, Enterprise & Regulatory Reform
  Bay 2117, 1 Victoria Street
  London
  SW1H 0ET
- Richard Brooks, tel: 01224 254094
  Energy Development Unit: Business Development team
  Department for Business, Enterprise & Regulatory Reform
  Atholl House, 86-88 Guild Street
  Aberdeen
  AB11 6AR

SECURITY OF SUPPLY CONTACTS

- Robert Clay, tel: 020 7215 5272
  Market Regulatory Framework Directorate
  Department of Energy and Climate Change (DECC)
  Bay 138, 1 Victoria Street
  London
  SW1H 0ET

SMART METERING CONTACTS

- Phil Nash, tel: 020 7215 5049
  Energy Markets Unit
  Department of Energy and Climate Change (DECC)
  Bay 143, 1 Victoria Street
  London
  SW1H 0ET

THE SOUTHERN CORRIDOR CONTACTS

- Alison Zhu, tel: 020 7215 6971
  Energy Strategy and International Unit
  Department of Energy and Climate Change (DECC)
  Bay 261, 1 Victoria Street

London
SW1H 0ET

TRANSMISSION CHARGES CONTACTS

- Chris Chown, tel: 020 7215 2766
  Energy Markets Unit
  Department of Energy and Climate Change (DECC)
  Bay 222, 1 Victoria Street
  London
  SW1H 0ET

ENERGY PROJECTIONS CONTACTS

- Emissions Projections, tel: 020 7215 6106
  Energy Strategy and International Unit
  Department of Energy and Climate Change (DECC)
  Bay 298, 1 Victoria Street
  London
  SW1H 0ET

WEBSITE PUBLISHER (ENERGY) CONTACTS

- Ian Montague, tel: 020 7215 2709
  Energy Strategy & International Unit
  Department of Energy and Climate Change (DECC)
  Bay 277, 1 Victoria Street,
  London,
  SW1H 0ET

STRATEGIC AND BUSINESS CONTACTS IN UK

1. UK GOVERNMENT AGENCIES

British Overseas Trade Board
Department of Trade & Industry
Kingsgate House
66-74 Victoria Street
London SW1E 6SN
Tel: 44-171-215-5000
Fax: 44-171-215-8000

Invest in Britain Bureau
Department of Trade and Industry
London
Tel: 011-44-171-215-2501
Fax: 011-44-171-215-8451

-Invest in Britain Bureau USA.
Atlanta Tel: (404) 524-8823
Boston Tel: (617) 248-9555
Chicago Tel: (312) 346-1810
Cleveland Tel: (216) 621-7674
Houston Tel: (713) 659-6275
Los Angeles Tel: (310) 477-3322
New York Tel: (212) 745-0495
Seattle Tel: (206) 622-9255
Washington D.C. Tel: (202) 462-1340

Embassy of Great Britain
3100 Massachusetts Avenue
Washington, D.C. 20008, USA
Tel: (202) 462-1340
Fax: (202) 898 4255

Department of Trade and Industry
123 Victoria Street
London SW1H 0NN

Tel:011-44-171-215-5000
Fax:011-44-171-215-6739
- General Inquiries

Consumer Affairs Division 1A
Department of Trade and Industry
10-18 Victoria Street
London SW1H 0NN
Tel: 011-44-171-215-0332
Fax: 011-44-171-215-0315
- Packaging and Labeling Requirements

HM Board of Customs and Excise
Tel: 011-44-171-620-1313
Fax: 011-44-171-865-4944
- Customs and Rules/Regulations for the UK

HM Stationery Office Bookshop
49 Holborn
London WC1V 6HB
Tel: 011-44-171-873-0011
Tel: 011-44-1603-695767
(UK equivalent of the U.S. Government Printing Office)
U.S. Representative: Kraus-Thompson Publishers,
Tel: (914) 762-2200

Central Office of Information
Hercules Road
London SE1 7DU
Tel: 011-44-171-928-2345
Fax: 011-44-171-928-5037

Central Statistical Office
Great George Street
London SW1P 3AQ
Tel: 011-44-171-270-3000

Department of Employment
Caxton House
12 Tothill Street
London SW1H 9NA
Tel: 011-44-171-273-3000
- Work Permits, Consular Matters

Department of the Environment
2 Marsham Street
London SW1P 3EB
Tel: 011-44-171-276-0900 or 276-3000
- Environmental Regulations

Department of Health
Richmond House
79 Whitehall
London SW1
Tel: 011-44-171-210-4850
- Medicinal Licenses and Regulations

Patent and Trademark Office
Concept House
Cardiff Road
Newport NP9 1RH
Tel: 011-44-1645-500505
- UK Patents

Bank of England
Threadneedle Street
London EC2V 8DQ
Tel: 011-44-171-601-4444
- Central Bank

The House of Commons
Houses of Parliament
London SW1A 0AA
Tel: 011-44-171-219-3000

2. UK TRADE ASSOCIATIONS/CHAMBERS OF COMMERCE

The UK's trade associations and chambers of commerce are too numerous to list in a report of this nature. Some notable, multi-sectoral business associations are listed below:

American Chamber of Commerce in the UK
75 Brook Street
London W1Y 2EB, UK
Tel: 011-44-171-493-0381
Fax: 011-44-171-493-2394

Association of British Chambers of Commerce
9 Tufton Street
London SW1P 3QB
Tel: 011-44-171-565-2000
Fax: 011-44-171-565-2049

British American Chamber of Commerce
8 Staple Inn, Holborn
London WC1V 7QH
Tel: 011-44-171-404-6400
Fax: 011-44-171-404-6828

International Chamber of Commerce
14-15 Belgrave Square
London SW1X 8PS
Tel: 011-44-171-823-2811

Fax: 011-44-171-235-5447

British Standards Institution
389 Chiswick High Road
London W4 4AL
Tel: 011-44-181-996-9000
Fax: 011-44-181-996-7400.

Confederation of British Industry
Centre Point
103 New Oxford Street
London WC1A 1DU
Tel: 011-44-171-379-7400
Fax: 011-44-171-240-1578

3. U.S. EMBASSY CONTACTS

American Embassy
24/31 Grosvenor Square
London, WIA 1AE England
Tel: 011-44-171-499-9000
Fax: 011-44-171-491-4022
http://usembassy.org.uk

Address for U.S. mail:
American Embassy (London)
PSC 801
Box 27 (for Economic Section) or
Box 33 (for Commercial Section) or
Box 48 (for Agriculture) or
Box 54 (for Defense)
FPO AE 09498-4033

Economic Minister
Tel: 011-44-171-408-8011
Fax: 011-44-171-409-1637

The Commercial Service
Tel: 011-44-171-408-8019
Fax: 011-44-171-408-8020

The International Marketing Center (IMC)
Tel: 011-44-171-409-2927
Fax: 011-44-171-495-2944
E-Mail: olondon@doc.gov
http://usembassy.org.uk/ukfcs.html

The Office of Agricultural Affairs
Tel: 011-44-171-408-8063
Fax: 011-44-171-409-2019
http://fasuk@fasuk.demon.co.uk

Office of Defense Cooperation (ODC)
Tel: 011-44-171-894-0737
Fax: 011-44-171-514-4634

The European Bank For Reconstruction & Development
Office of the Senior Commercial Officer
Tel: 011-44-171-588-4027/4028
Fax: 011-44-171-588-4026

4. WASHINGTON DC-BASED USG CONTACTS (UK-SPECIFIC)

U.S. Department of Commerce
UK Country Desk Officer Robert McLaughlin
Washington, D.C. 20230
Tel: (202) 482-3748
Fax: (202) 482-2897
http://www.doc.gov

Multilateral Development Bank Office
Janet G. Thomas - Director
Tel: (202) 482 3399
Fax: (202) 273-0927

US&FCS Regional Director (Europe):
Mr. Keith Curtis
Tel: (202) 482-1599
Fax: (202) 482-3159

Bureau of Export Administration
Tel: (202) 482-8547
State Department
UK Desk
Tel: (202) 647-8027
- Political relations

Agriculture Department - food exports
Foreign Agriculture Service
European Area Officer
Tel: (202) 720-2144
Fax: (202) 690-2909

Treasury Department
UK Desk
Tel: (202) 622-0166
- Financial matters

American National Standards Institute
Tel: (212) 642-4900
Fax: (212) 302-1286
- Information on UK standards

National Institute for Standards and Technology (Washington D.C.)
Tel: (301) 975-3058

5. RELEVANT U.S.-BASED MULTIPLIERS

British American Chamber of Commerce
275 Madison Ave.
New York, NY 10016
Tel: (212) 661-4060
Fax: (212) 661-4074

BASIC FOREIGN COMMONWELATH OFFICE TREATIES

The Treaty Section of the FCO's Records and Historical Department keeps records of all multilateral and bilateral treaties to which the UK is a party and provides a treaty enquiry service. Treaty Section also coordinates the UK's responsibilities as depositary for 34 international agreements.

List of current international agreements for which the Government of the United Kingdom is depositary (includes full status lists of parties to the agreements):

- Agreement concerning an International Observer Scheme for Factory Ships engaged in Pelagic Whaling in the Antarctic (not in force)
- Agreement Concerning the European Air Group and Amending Protocol to the Agreement Concerning the European Air Group
- Agreement establishing an International Foot and Mouth Disease Vaccine Bank
- Agreement on CAB International
- Agreement on German External Debts
- Agreement on the Conservation of Bats in Europe
- Agreement On The Rescue Of Astronauts, The Return Of Astronauts And The Return Of Objects Launched Into Outer Space
- Agreement terminating the Commonwealth Telecommunications Organisation Financial Agreement, 1973
- Amendment to the Agreement on the Conservation of Bats in Europe
- Arrangements for the Regulation of Antarctic Pelagic Whaling
- Commonwealth Telecommunications Organisation Financial Agreement, 1983
- Constitution of the United Nations Educational, Scientific and Cultural Organisation
- Convention for the Conservation of Antarctic Seals
- Convention for the Regulation of Meshes of Fishing Nets and the Limits of Fish
- Convention for the Suppression of Unlawful Acts against the Safety of Civil Aviation
- Convention for the Suppression of Unlawful Seizure of Aircraft
- Convention on Civil Liability for Oil Pollution Damage resulting from Exploration for and Exploitation of Seabed Mineral Resources
- Convention on Future Multilateral Co-operation in North-East Atlantic Fisheries (note: the UK is not a signatory)
- Convention on International Liability for Damage caused by Space Objects
- Convention on the Conduct of Fishing Operations in the North Atlantic
- Convention On The Prevention Of Marine Pollution By Dumping Of Wastes And Other Matter
- Convention On The Prohibition Of The Development, Production And Stockpiling Of Bacteriological (Biological) And Toxin Weapons And On Their Destruction
- Fisheries Convention (with Protocol of Provisional Application and two Agreements as to Transitional Rights)
- Framework Agreement between France, Germany, Italy, Spain, Sweden and the UK, concerning Measures to Facilitate the Restructuring and Operation of the European Defence Industry

- International Agreement regarding the Maintenance of Certain Lights in the Red Sea
- International Convention for Permanent Control of Outbreak of the Red Locust
- International Convention relative to the London Preservation of Fauna and Flora in their Natural State
- Modifying the International Convention of 22 February 1949
- North-East Atlantic Fisheries Convention
- Protocol for the Suppression of Unlawful Acts of Violence at Airports serving International Civil Aviation, Supplementary to the Convention for the Suppression of Unlawful Acts against the Safety of Civil Aviation
- Treaty Banning Nuclear Weapon Tests in the Atmosphere, in Outer Space and Under Water
- Treaty on Principles Governing the Activities of States in the Exploration and Use of Outer Space, Including the Moon and Other Celestial Bodies
- Treaty On The Non-Proliferation Of Nuclear Weapons
- Treaty on the Non-Proliferation of Nuclear Weapons (declarations of signatories)
- Treaty On The Prohibition Of The Emplacement Of Nuclear Weapons And Other Weapons Of Mass Destruction On The Sea-Bed And The Ocean Floor And In The Subsoil Thereof

UK OIL & GAS GLOSSARY

Abandon To cease work on a well which is non-productive, to plug off the well with cement plugs and salvage all recoverable equipment Also used in the context of field abandonment. See also decommissioning

Annex B Operator's development plan for an offshore installation. It requires government approval before it can be implemented.

Annulus The space between the drillstring and the well wall, or between casing strings, or between the casing and the production tubing.

Appraisal Well A well drilled as part of an appraisal drilling programme which is carried out to determine the physical extent, reserves and likely production rate of a field.

Associated Gas Natural gas associated with oil accumulations, which may be dissolved in the oil at reservoir conditions or may form a cap of free gas above the oil.

Top of page

Barrel A unit of volume measurement used for petroleum and its products (7.3 barrels = 1 ton: 6.29 barrels = 1 cubic metre).

bbl One barrel of oil; 1 barrel = 35 Imperial gallons (approx.), or 159 litres (approx.); 7.5 barrels = 1 tonne (approx.); 6.29 barrels = 1 cubic metre.

bcf Billion cubic feet; 1 bcf = 0.83 million tonnes of oil equivalent.

bcm Billion cubic metres (1 cubic metre = 35.31 cubic feet).

Block An areal subdivision of the UKCS of 10 minutes of latitude by 12 minutes of longitude measuring approximately 10 x 20 kms, forming part of a quadrant. Each quadrant is divided into a grid five Blocks wide and six deep, and numbered 1 to 30 from NW to SE e.g. Block 9/13 is the 13th block in Quadrant 9.

blow-down Condensate and gas is produced simultaneously from the outset of production.

Blow-out preventers (BOPs) Are high pressure wellhead valves, designed to shut off the uncontrolled flow of hydrocarbons.

Blow-out When well pressure exceeds the ability of the wellhead valves to control it.

	Oil and gas "blow wild" at the surface.
Borehole	The hole as drilled by the drill bit.
	Top of page
Capex	Capital expenditure.
Casing string	The steel tubing that lines a well after it has been drilled. It is formed from sections of steel tube screwed together.
Central estimate	A range of exploration drilling scenarios from which the following activity levels, based on recent historical experience, are adopted as the central estimates.
Christmas tree	The assembly of fittings and valves on the top of the casing which control the production rate of oil.
CNS	Central North Sea.
Commercial field	An oil and/or gas field judged to be capable of producing enough net income to make it worth developing.
Completion	The installation of permanent wellhead equipment for the production of oil and gas.
Condensate	Hydrocarbons which are in the gaseous state under reservoir conditions and which become liquid when temperature or pressure is reduced. A mixture of pentanes and higher hydrocarbons.
Connate water	Salt water occurring with oil and gas in the reservoir.
Coring	Taking rock samples from a well by means of a special tool -- a "core barrel".
Crane barge	A large barge, capable of lifting heavy equipment onto offshore platforms. Also known as a "derrick barge".
Creaming Theory	A statistical technique which recognises that in any exploration province after an initial period in which the largest fields are found, success rates and average field sizes decline as more exploration wells are drilled and knowledge of the area matures.
CRINE	Cost Reduction Initiative for the New Era.
Cubic foot	A standard unit used to measure quantity of gas (at atmospheric pressure); 1 cubic foot = 0.0283 cubic metres.
Cuttings	Rock chippings cut from the formation by the drill bit, and brought to the surface with the mud. Used by geologists to obtain formation data.
	Top of page
Decommissioning	Preferred term (rather than Abandonment) for the re-use, recycling and disposal of redundant oil and gas facilities
Derrick	The tower-like structure that houses most of the drilling controls.
Development phase	The phase in which a proven oil or gas field is brought into production by drilling production (development) wells.
Discovery	An Exploration well which has encountered hydrocarbons.
Drilling rig	A drilling unit that is not permanently fixed to the seabed, e.g. a drillship, a semi-submersible or a jack-up unit. Also means the derrick and its associated machinery.
Dry Gas	Natural gas composed mainly of methane with only minor amounts of ethane, propane and butane and little or no heavier hydrocarbons in the gasoline range.
Dry hole	A well which has proved to contain no hydrocarbons.

Top of page

E&A	Abbreviation for exploration and appraisal.
E&P	Abbreviation for exploration and production.
Enhanced oil recovery	A process whereby oil is recovered other than by the natural pressure in a reservoir.
Exploration drilling	Drilling carried out to determine whether hydrocarbons are present in a particular area or structure.
Exploration phase	The phase of operations which covers the search for oil or gas by carrying out detailed geological and geophysical surveys followed up where appropriate by exploratory drilling.
Exploration well	A well in an unproven area or prospect, may also be known as a "wildcat well".

Top of page

Farm in	When a company acquires an interest in a block by taking over all or part of the financial commitment for drilling an exploration well.
Field	A geographical area under which an oil or gas reservoir lies.
Fishing	Retrieving objects from the borehole, such as a broken drillstring, or tools.
Formation pressure	The pressure at the bottom of a well when it is shut in at the wellhead.
Formation water	Salt water underlying gas and oil in the formation.
Fracturing	A method of breaking down a formation by pumping fluid at very high pressures. The objective is to increase production rates from a reservoir.
FSA	Financial Security Agreement - as used to provide for decommissioning expenditure.

Top of page

G	Gas.
G/C	Gas Condensate.
Gas field	A field containing natural gas but no oil.
Gas injection	The process whereby separated associated gas is pumped back into a reservoir for conservation purposes or to maintain the reservoir pressure.
Gas/oil ratio	The volume of gas at atmospheric pressure produced per unit of oil produced.

Top of page

Hydrocarbon	A compound containing only the elements hydrogen and carbon. May exist as a solid, a liquid or a gas. The term is mainly used in a catch-all sense for oil, gas and condensate.

Top of page

Injection well	A well used for pumping water or gas into the reservoir.
IS	Irish Sea.

Top of page

Jacket	The lower section, or "legs", of an offshore platform.

Top of page

Kick	A well is said to "kick" if the formation pressure exceeds the pressure

	exerted by the mud column.
	Top of page
Lay barge	A barge that is specially equipped to lay submarine pipelines.
Liquefied natural gas (LNG)	Oilfield or naturally occurring gas, chiefly methane, liquefied for transportation.
Liquefied petroleum gas (LPG)	Light hydrocarbon material, gaseous at atmospheric temperature and pressure, held in the liquid state by pressure to facilitate storage, transport and handling. Commercial liquefied gas consists essentially of either propane or butane, or mixtures thereof.
	Top of page
mboe	Million Barrels Oil Equivalent.
Metric tonne	Equivalent to 1000 kilos, 2204.61 lbs; 7.5 barrels.
mmcfd	Millions of cubic feet per day (of gas).
Moonpool	An aperture in the centre of a drillship or semi-submersible drilling rig, through which drilling and diving operations can be conducted.
Mt	Million tonnes.
Mud	A mixture of base substance and additives used to lubricate the drill bit and to counteract the natural pressure of the formation.
	Top of page
Natural gas	Gas, occurring naturally, and often found in association with crude petroleum.
NGLs	Natural gas liquids. Liquid hydrocarbons found in association with natural gas.
NNS	Northern North Sea.
	Top of page
O	Oil.
O&G	Oil and Gas.
Oil	A mixture of liquid hydrocarbons of different molecular weights.
Oil field	A geographic area under which an oil reservoir lies.
Oil in place	An estimated measure of the total amount of oil contained in a reservoir, and, as such, a higher figure than the estimated recoverable reserves of oil.
Operator	The company that has legal authority to drill wells and undertake production of hydrocarbons are found. The Operator is often part of a consortium and acts on behalf of this consortium.
Opex	Operating expenditure.
	Top of page
Payzone	Rock in which oil and gas are found in exploitable quantities.
Permeability	The property of a formation which quantifies the flow of a fluid through the pore spaces and into the wellbore.
Petroleum	A generic name for hydrocarbons, including crude oil, natural gas liquids, natural gas and their products.
Platform	An offshore structure that is permanently fixed to the seabed.
Porosity	The percentage of void in a porous rock compared to the solid formation.

Possible reserves	Those reserves which at present cannot be regarded as 'probable' but are estimated to have a significant but less than 50% chance of being technically and economically producible.
Primary recovery	Recovery of oil or gas from a reservoir purely by using the natural pressure in the reservoir to force the oil or gas out.
Probable reserves	Those reserves which are not yet proven but which are estimated to have a better than 50% chance of being technically and economically producible.
Proven field	An oil and/or gas field whose physical extent and estimated reserves have been determined.
Proven reserves	Those reserves which on the available evidence are virtually certain to be technically and economically producible (i.e. having a better than 90% chance of being produced).
	Top of page
Quadrant	An areal subdivision of the UKCS of 1 degree of longitude by 1 degree of latitude - typically around 6600 sq km. On the UKCS each Quadrant is further subdivided into 30 Blocks.
Recoverable reserves	That proportion of the oil and/gas in a reservoir that can be removed using currently available techniques.
Recovery factor	The ratio of recoverable oil and/or gas reserves to the estimated oil and/or gas in place in the reservoir.
Reservoir	The underground formation where oil and gas has accumulated It consists of a porous rock to hold the oil or gas, and a cap rock that prevents its escape.
Riser (drilling)	A pipe between a seabed BOP and a floating drilling rig.
Riser (production)	The section of pipework that joins a seabed wellhead to the Christmas tree.
Roughneck	Drill crew members who work on the derrick floor, screwing together the sections of drillpipe when running or pulling a drillstring.
Roustabout	Drill crew members who handle the loading and unloading of equipment and assist in general operations around the rig.
Royalty payment	The cash or kind paid to the owner of mineral rights.
	Top of page
Secondary recovery	Recovery of oil or gas from a reservoir by artificially maintaining or enhancing the reservoir pressure by injecting gas, water or other substances into the reservoir rock.
Shutdown	A production hiatus during which the platform ceases to produce while essential maintenance work is undertaken.
Significant Discovery	A BERR definition of a well which flow tested, or would have flowed, at a rate of 1000 barrels of oil a day or 15 million cubic feet of gas a day.
SNS	Southern North Sea.
Spud-in	The operation of drilling the first part of a new well.
Suspended well	A well that has been capped off temporarily.
	Top of page
tcf	Trillion Cubic Feet (of gas).
Toolpusher	Second-in-command of a drilling crew under the drilling superintendent. Responsible for the day-to-day running of the rig and for ensuring that all the necessary equipment is available.

Topsides	The superstructure of a platform.
	Top of page
UKCS	United Kingdom Continental Shelf.
UKOOA	U.K. Offshore Operators Association Limited.
	Top of page
Well log	A record of geological formation penetrated during drilling, including technical details of the operation.
Wildcat well	A well drilled in an unproven area. Also known as a "exploration well". [Ety. The term comes from exploration wells in West Texas in the 1920s. Wildcats were abundant in the locality, and those unlucky enough to be shot were hung from oil derricks.]
WoB	West of Britain.
Workover	Remedial work to the equipment within a well, the well pipework, or relating to attempts to increase the rate of flow.
WoS	West of Shetland Isles.

www.ingramcontent.com/pod-product-compliance
Lightning Source LLC
LaVergne TN
LVHW080028210926
848481LV00011B/3127
9781433078422